**Third Edition**

# Introduction to Private Security

**Third Edition**

# Introduction to Private Security

## Kären M. Hess
Normandale
Community College
Bloomington, Minnesota

## Henry M. Wrobleski
Normandale
Community College
Bloomington, Minnesota

WEST PUBLISHING COMPANY
St. Paul □ New York
Los Angeles □ San Francisco

## PHOTO CREDITS

**Cover** Michael Hayman/Stock Boston; **1** Michael Dwyer/Stock Boston; **5 (top)** Gordon H. Lord/Monkmeyer Press Photo Service; **(bottom)** Henle/Monkmeyer Press Photo Service; **7** Ken Lambert/FPG International; **8** The Bettmann Archive; **10** Historical Pictures Services; **14** Topham/The Image Works, Inc.; **20** Brink's, Inc.; **34** Hap Stewart/Jeroboam; **36** Kent Reno/Jeroboam; **74** Christopher S. Johnson/Stock Boston; **117** Emilio Mercado/Jeroboam; **120** Harry Wilks/Stock Boston; **126** AV-Com Law Enforcement Media, from ''Protect *Your* Business!''; **129** Daniel S. Brody/Stock Boston; **147** ©AP/Wide World Photos; **148 (bottom)** AV-Com Law Enforcement Media, from ''Protect *Your* Business!''; **149 (left)** Irene Bayer/Monkmeyer Press Photo Service; **150** Roswell Angier/Stock Boston; **199** ©Mike Harmon/Picture Group; **205** ©Michael Grecco/Stock Boston; **210** ©1990 David Carmack/Stock Boston; **215** Samuel Thaler/Jeroboam; **235 (left)** Martin Iger/FPG International; **(right)** UPI/Bettmann Newsphotos; **253** ©Gerard Fritz/Jeroboam; **281** ©1989 Ron Grishaber/Photo Edit; **285** Emilio Mercado/Jeroboam; **303** Michael G. Bennett/Imagemakers International Incorporated; **305** Sims Security, Division of Kane; **309** Cheryl A. Traendly/Jeroboam; **313** ©Mario Ruiz/Picture Group; **321** Michael Hayman/Stock Boston; **325** ©AP/Wide World Photos; **347** Carolyn A. McKeone/FPG International; **351** Mark Antman/The Image Works, Inc.; **354** ©Granitsas/The Image Works, Inc.; **376** ©1990 Kathy Willens/AP/Wide World Photos; **381** ©1989 Stock Boston; **384** ©Joe Shom/The Image Works, Inc.; **392** ©Rob Crandall/Picture Group; **393** ©1991 Ed Reinke/AP/Wide World Photos; **398** ©1986 Ed Buryn/Jeroboam; **405** Mimi Forsyth; Monkmeyer Press Photo Service; **409** ©1990 Peter Southwick/Stock Boston

## PRODUCTION CREDITS

Interior Design: David Farr, Imagesmythe
Copyediting: Kathy Pruno
Composition: Carlisle Communications

COPYRIGHT © 1982, 1988 By WEST PUBLISHING COMPANY
COPYRIGHT © 1992    By WEST PUBLISHING COMPANY
50 W. Kellogg Boulevard
P.O. Box 64526
St. Paul, MN 55164-0526

**Library of Congress Cataloging-in-Publication Data**

Hess, Kären M., 1939–
    Introduction to private security / Kären M. Hess, Henry M. Wrobleski — 3rd ed.
        p.  cm.
    Includes bibliographical references and index.
    ISBN 0-314-89380-6
    1. Private security services—United States.  2. Industry-–Security measures.    I. Wrobleski, Henry M., 1992-    II. Title.
HV8291.U6H47    1992
363.2'–89 —dc20

                                                91-29850
                                                CIP∞

# Preface

In our modern, industrial, urban society, private security has become such an important and accepted part of life that an understanding of its development, philosophy, responsibility, and function is imperative for all. A historical and philosophical perspective of private security will help students to better understand the present state of private security, its principles, its legal authority, and its effect on society in general.

*Introduction to Private Security* provides basic information to serve as an overview of the entire field as well as a solid foundation for future courses. The content in each chapter could easily be expanded into an entire book or course, but the basic concepts have been included. This feature alone helps increase the text's usefulness to students and instructors alike.

The text incorporates the major findings and recommendations of the *Report of the Task Force on Private Security* with other current security publications and research, including the Hallcrest Report I and II and the Rand Report.

## ☐ HOW TO USE THIS BOOK

*Introduction to Private Security* is more than a textbook; it is a learning experience requiring your active participation to obtain best results. You will get the most out of this book if you first familiarize yourself with the total scope of private security. Read and think about what is included in the Table of Contents. Then follow these steps as you read each chapter:

1) Read the objectives at the beginning of each chapter:
   DO YOU KNOW
   ➤ What the primary goal of private security is?
     Think about your current knowledge on each question. What preconceptions do you hold?
2) Read the chapter (underlining or taking notes if that is your preferred study style).
   Pay special attention to all information that is boxed:

---

The primary goal of private security is to prevent losses caused by criminal actions and/or disasters.

---

The key concepts of each chapter are highlighted in this manner.

**3)** When you have finished reading the chapter, reread the list of objectives given at the beginning of the chapter to ensure that you are able to give an educated response to each. If you find yourself stumped, find the appropriate material in the chapter and review it.

**4)** Complete the Application at the end of each chapter. These application exercises provide an opportunity to use the concepts in actual or hypothetical cases.

**5)** Finally, read the discussion questions and prepare to contribute to class discussion of these questions.

Good reading and good learning.

# Acknowledgments

We would like to thank the following individuals for their review of the manuscript and their numerous helpful suggestions: William Bopp, Florida Atlanta University; R. B. J. Campbelle, Middle-Tennessee State University; Jerry Dowling, Sam Houston State University; Robert Fischer, Western Illinois University; James Fyke, Illinois Central College; Ernest Kamm, California State University, Los Angeles; Hayes Larkins, Community College of Baltimore; Donald Mayo, Loyola University; Merlyn Moore, Sam Houston State University; Norman Spain, Ohio University; David Steeno, Western Illinois University; Bill Tillett, Eastern Kentucky University; Robert Camp; Janet McClellan, Park College; Susan Hinds; Robert Ives, Rockford College; and Vincent DeCherchio, Bryn Mawr College.

Thank you to the reviewers of the second edition for their insightful suggestions for making this third edition as current and practical as possible: Robert Wyatt Benson, Jacksonville State University; Terry A. Biddle, Cuyahoga Community College; Edmund Grosskopf, Indiana State University; Leo C. Hertoghe, California State University at Sacramento; David MacKenna, University of Texas at Arlington; Michael D. Moberly, Southern Illinois University at Carbondale; Mahesh K. Nalla, Northern Arizona University; Robert L. O'Block, Appalachian State University; and Michael J. Witkowski, University of Detroit.

A special thank you to AIMS Instructional Media Services, Inc., and to AV Com Law Enforcement Media for the numerous photographs provided for use in the text, to the National Crime Prevention Institute for the numerous diagrams provided, and to J&B Innovative Enterprises, Inc., who provided security surveys, charts, and diagrams.

Finally, thank you to our families and colleagues for their support during the development of *Introduction to Private Security*, third edition, to Christine Hess for her indexing and preparation of the Instructor's Guide, and to the fine professional staff at West Publishing Company for their invaluable assistance in preparing the manuscript for publication: Robert Jucha and Diane Colwyn, editors; and Jeff Carpenter and Sandy Gangelhoff, our terrific production editors.

# About the Authors

Kären M. Hess, PhD, has written extensively in the field of law enforcement. She is a member of the English department at Normandale Community College as well as the president of the Institute for Professional Development.

**Kären M. Hess**

Henry M. Wrobleski, LLB, is coordinator of the Law Enforcement Program at Normandale Community College. He is a respected author, lecturer, and consultant with 30 years of experience in law enforcement. He is also Dean of Instruction for the Institute for Professional Development, holds an LLB degree and is a graduate of the FBI Academy.

**Henry M. Wrobleski**

Both are members of the American Society for Industrial Security (ASIS).

# Contents in Brief

# Contents

### Chapter 10    Enhancing Computer Security 251

### Chapter 11    Communicating 273

### Chapter 12    Enhancing Public Relations 301

### Section Three   Security Systems to Prevent Losses 321

### Chapter 13    Industrial Security 323

# Figures

# Tables

# Cases

# Section One

# Private Security: An Overview

The chapters in Section One present an overview of the private security profession, beginning with its history and the methods of protection that have evolved from ancient times to the present (Chapter 1). The various aspects of protection being used in private security, the kinds of personnel and services involved, and whether they are contractual or proprietary is the focus of Chapter 2. The third chapter examines the role of the private security professional, that is, private security as a management function, with the security director being responsible for loss prevention, administration, investigation, and supervision. The basic purpose of private security, loss prevention through risk management, is the focus of Chapter 4. The section concludes with a discussion of the private security/public police interface, the legal authority of private security personnel, and the reality of civil liability in performing security functions (Chapter 5).

It is within this context that the security professionals of the 1990s will operate. The concepts introduced in this section will be of direct relevance in how the basic security responsibilities are performed (Section Two) and what kinds of security systems might be implemented (Section Three).

## □ INTRODUCTION

Since the beginning of recorded time, people have sought *security*—safety, protection, freedom from fear and danger. They have armed themselves, built barriers around their dwellings, and made rules and laws which they have tried to enforce individually, as a group, and through others. Reith (1975, pp. 13–15) outlines four phases in the evolution of the quest for security.

➤ First, individuals or small community groups came together in search of collective security, to ease food finding, or to satisfy other mutually felt individual needs. /

➤ Second, they discovered the need for rules or laws. / Historically people believed that passing "good" laws was sufficient; the ruler's army could enforce them.

➤ Third, they inevitably discovered that some community members would not obey the rules. / Even the best laws man can devise are useless, and rulers and governments are powerless, if the laws are not obeyed.

➤ Fourth, in one form or another, means to compel the observance of _enforcement power_ rules were found and established. /

### DO YOU KNOW

➤ Generally how private security has differed from public law enforcement throughout history?

➤ What security measures were used in ancient times? In the Middle Ages? In eighteenth-century England? In early colonial America?

➤ What security measures were established by the tithing system? The Frankpledge system? The Magna Charta? The Statute of Westminster?

➤ What contributions to private security were made by Henry Fielding, Patrick Colquhoun, Sir Robert Peel, Allan Pinkerton, Washington Perry Brink, and William J. Burns?

➤ What role the railroad police played in the evolution of private security?

➤ What impact the world wars had on the evolution of private security?

➤ Into what status private security has evolved by the 1990s?

Sometimes they worked, but frequently they did not. Consequently, more communities have perished because they could not enforce their laws than have been destroyed by natural disasters or hostile aggression.

Reith's main premise is that past civilizations fell because no police mechanism existed between the army of the ruler and the people. Without such a police mechanism to enforce the laws, the country fell into anarchy. When this occurred, armed troops were called in to restore order, but, as a form of force divorced from the law, they could secure only temporary relief. Thus, the dispatching of troops to restore order became: "as often as not, a pouring of oil on flames" (Reith, 1940, p. 105).

Early civilizations relied on a ruler and his army to govern and protect the people. The people of the Middle Ages tried loosely organized experiments with evolving forms of public law enforcement and isolated instances of private security when public law enforcement was ineffective. Not until the nineteenth century did public law enforcement and private security begin to clearly separate. To that point, the history of private security is intertwined with that of public law enforcement. With

**3**

the acceptance of public police officers, private individuals and organizations began to seek further protection, a means of preventing access to themselves or their property.

Private security evolved from the human desire for additional, individual protection for themselves and their property.

## □ ANCIENT TIMES

Throughout history, people have erected physical barriers for security, and certain individuals, notably rulers, have demanded special security.

In ancient times people relied on physical security measures such as weapons, lake or cliff dwellings, walls, and gates.

The objective then, as it is today, was to prevent others from gaining access to them or their property. Lake dwelling was one popular means of achieving security. Healy (1968) describes some three hundred such lake sites discovered in Switzerland alone, all simple homes, some single units, some entire villages, built with meager tools on sunken pilings. One dwelling on Lake Geneva could house twelve hundred people. Access to these lake dwellings was controlled by drawbridges or boats.

Some prehistoric Americans, surrounded by unfriendly tribes, moved into natural caves high on cliffs. Their security came from "isolating themselves high in the air with ladders that could be pulled up to make their homes impregnable" (Healy, 1968, p. 1).

The most elaborate security system in ancient times was the Great Wall of China, built twenty centuries ago by Emperor Chin to guard China from the Mongols. Requiring fifteen years and half a million workers to build, the Wall was long enough to stretch from New York to Mexico.

Rome also emphasized physical security in the form of broad, straight roads patrolled by legions and bridges controlled by iron gates and guards. Frequently, however, rulers went beyond mere physical controls.

Rulers often appointed individuals to assist them in enforcing the laws, protecting not only the general welfare (public security), but also the safety of the ruler (private security).

These specially appointed individuals who were not part of the military force were the means by which the famous leaders of the massive predatory migrations in Asia and Europe seized authority and leadership.

The Roman Emperor Augustus recognized that the law enforcement machinery of his administration depended solely on the military force of the legions. The legions were a dangerous power in that the emperor was forced to depend on their often unreliable will. To remove this

Cliff dwelling ruins of the ancient Pueblo Indians (A.D. 1275) located in Mesa Verde National Park, Colorado.

The Great Wall of China, 20 to 30 feet high and 15 to 20 feet thick, served as a defense against invaders. It stretched 1,400 miles between Mongolia and China.

power from them and place it on a more sure foundation, he created the Praetorian Guard, a form of bodyguard police, as well as the Urban Cohorts, a form of gendarmerie composed of soldiers with police and military duties, and a large body of Vigiles, who were police-fire fighters (Reith, 1975).

Members of the Praetorian Guard were scattered throughout Rome and probably wore civilian clothes because of the extreme resistance to military control. The Guard was considered an elite group and, consequently, was not asked to function as riot police. This task fell to the Urban Cohort whose specific function was keeping order among the slaves and controlling unruly citizens (Folley, 1980, p. 39). The third group Augustus established, the Vigiles of Rome, was assigned the task of fighting the devastating fires frequently occurring in Rome as part of the general disorder. The Vigiles' assignment was extended beyond fire fighting, however, to also include policing, previously carried out by the Urban Cohort. As noted by Folley (1980, p. 39):

> In this sense, we see the establishment of the first *police-fire integrated service*. Their function was to control fires and to exercise police functions which included the right to arrest thieves and housebreakers as well as to control and suppress riots.

The Praetorian Guard later destroyed its function when it joined the intrigues of the legions, becoming part of the crude, uncontrolled military force that seated and unseated emperors.

## ☐ THE MIDDLE AGES (476–1453)

Early in the Middle Ages **feudalism** held sway, with the lowliest workers (serfs) laboring for a nobleman who answered to the king. The nobleman provided food and security for the serfs who worked the land, and they provided arms for the king and fought in his wars. Castles with moats and drawbridges afforded additional security.

The Anglo-Saxons brought with them to England the acceptance of mutual responsibility for civil and military protection of individuals. Groups of ten families, called **tithings,** banded together for security and to provide collective responsibility for maintaining local law and order. This system was expanded following the Norman Conquest into the **Frankpledge** system under which the king demanded all free Englishmen to swear to maintain the peace.

---

During the Middle Ages the tithing system and the Frankpledge system provided security and collective responsibility for law and order.

---

The first significant change in the feudal system occurred in King John's reign when his lords revolted and forced him to sign the **Magna Charta** (1215). This document established the supremacy of law over arbitrary edict, as well as the lords' individual rights and the responsibilities of the state and its subjects.

---

The Magna Charta, similar to our Bill of Rights, gave Englishmen "due process" of law.

---

The next milestone in the evolution of security and law enforcement was the **Statue of Westminster.** Issued by King Edward in 1285, this

Castles surrounded with moats were common during the Middle Ages.

statute formalized much of England's practice in criminal justice and apprehension. These rules were enforced for many centuries and influenced our common-law elements of arrest. Under the statute, ordinary citizens were greatly involved in criminal justice: ''Not only was it the right of any person to apprehend offenders; there was also a positive duty to drop all work when the hue and cry was raised, and to join immediately in pursuit'' (Hall, 1952, p. 166). The preamble to the statute sets forth its basic objective as being ''to abate the power of felons'' (Critchley, 1967).

---

The Statue of Westminster established three practical measures: (1) the watch and ward, (2) hue and cry, and (3) assize of arms.

---

**The watch and ward** provided town watchmen to patrol the city during the night to supplement the traditional duties of the constable during the day (ward). This was the first distinct difference between town and rural policing. Watchmen, stationed at every gate of the walled town between sunset and sunrise, were given power to arrest strangers during darkness and hand them over to the constable in the morning. All men in the town were placed on a roster for regular service. Those who refused to serve were placed in the stocks.

**The hue and cry** revived the ancient Saxon practice for dealing with those who resisted the watchman's arrest. When resistance occurred, the watchman cried out and all citizens pursued the fugitive and assisted in his capture.

To enforce the hue and cry, the Statue of Westminster also established the **assize of arms,** which required every male between ages fifteen and sixty to keep a weapon in his home as a "harness to keep the peace."

According to Critchley (1967, pp. 6–7): "The Statue of Westminster was the only general public measure of any consequence enacted to regulate the policing of the country between the Norman Conquest in 1066 and the Metropolitan Police Act of 1829."

The Statute of Westminster marked the end of the first police "system" in England, which pivoted around the part-time constable, the ancient principles of personal service to the community, and the power of arrest under common law. Critchley (1967) notes that the preventive aspect of policing was secured by the watch by night and the ward by day, the repressive by the hue and cry, and the punitive by presentment to the constable the next morning.

Merchants of England, however, were often dissatisfied with the protection afforded them. Furthermore, the middle class was rebelling against compulsory watch service, insisting on paying deputies to take their places. Unfortunately, the hired deputies frequently did not protect them, forcing the merchants to take matters into their own hands.

---

Some merchants hired private police to guard their establishments, to investigate crimes against them, and to recover property stolen from them.

---

One futile attempt to establish a military police force occurred in England in 1655 when Cromwell tried to use his highly trained, effi-

Medieval watchmen with cressets and beacon.

cient, victorious army as a police force to prevent and to repress crime. However, he was defeated by lack of cooperation from all classes of people and by the absence of an effective police mechanism between the people and his troops. The watch and ward, although ineffective, remained the primary means of security and law enforcement until the Industrial Revolution.

Early attempts at security and protection reveal two common themes. First was division into geographic sections and the rotation of duties among the citizens. ⌈Second, citizens' dissatisfaction with their duties resulted in the hiring of others to take their place.⌉ (Even up to the American Civil War one could hire another to serve in his place.)

With the passing of feudalism and the rise to power of the state church, the parish* became the unit of local government in rural areas. The parish annually appointed a person to be constable and act as the law officer. This system of maintaining law and order in rural Britain remained from the Middle Ages until the eighteenth century.

## ☐ THE EIGHTEENTH CENTURY

Extensive social and economic changes during the Industrial Revolution brought about the mechanization of production systems and resulted in a change from home or cottage industries to large factories located in cities. One primary reason for the shift from cottage work to factories and shops was an effort to control workers' production and inventory in the textile industry. Too much material was being diverted for personal use.

During this same period, famine struck the rural areas, causing thousands to move from the country into the towns to seek work in the mills and factories. As people left the rural areas for jobs in the cities, the problem of protection from crime gained new impetus. But in this rapidly changing time, little was done to stem the tremendous amount of crime that arose in the cities.

In addition, political extremists often sparked angry mobs, and riots occurred frequently. Because the government had no civil police force to deal with mob violence, it ordered a magistrate to read the "Riot Act" which called in the military to quell the riot.

South (1987, pp. 73–76) describes the "deterioration of formal social control in the late seventeenth and early eighteenth centuries": "As the formal system declined, provision by private self-interest flourished, strongly encouraged by legislation." The former methods of control simply did not work for an industrialized society.

"By the year 1700," says South (p. 76), "disciplined industrial capitalism was already becoming familiar in certain parts of England, with the time sheet, the time keeper, the informers and the fines. For example, the *Law Book of Crowley's Iron Works* represented an entire civil and penal code, running to more than 100,000 words to govern and regulate the refractory labor force."

Rural eighteenth century also used private policing in reaction to increasing rural crime (Critchley, 1967, p. 28):

---

*The area defined by the congregation of a particular church.

Midland Works Foundry, Sheffield, England, around 1863.

The wealthy paid gamekeepers to protect their property and slept with arms near to hand and the middle-class tradesmen formed voluntary protection societies.

During the eighteenth century private citizens carried arms for protection and banded together to hire special police to protect their homes and businesses. The military was used to suppress riots.

Because of prejudices toward those responsible for upholding the law, no serious reform was advocated until the late eighteenth century. The policy was to encourage law-abiding citizens' participation in criminal justice with rewards and to discourage law-breaking citizens with severe punishments. Consequently, a number of self-help organizations sprang up because, as Romilly (1956, p. 12) wrote, "It had become necessary for every man to trust himself for his security."

## Henry Fielding (1707–1754)

In 1748 Henry Fielding, lawyer, novelist, and playwright, became Chief Magistrate of Bow Street in policeless London. Sympathetic to the injustices that abounded in the city, Fielding fought for social and criminal reform and defied the law by discharging prisoners convicted of petty theft. He gave reprimands in place of the death penalty and exercised general leniency (Reith, 1975). He wrote and published books and pamphlets about the poor of London and the causes of crime. In these, he called for an understanding and alleviation of their suffering.

Fielding advocated that all magistrates be paid a salary, making them independent of fees and fines as their source of income. He also suggested that magistrates be given power to inflict light sentences when advisable.

At this time the parish constable was so ineffective that thieves and robbers moved freely in the streets, and no one interfered with looting and rioting. Although riots inevitably brought soldiers, it sometimes was not for two or three days. Law-abiding citizens looked after their own safety: "The rich surrounded themselves with armed servants and were comparatively safe and independent. . . . The less affluent saw to it that their houses were protected as strongly as possible by bars and bolts and heavy doors and shutters, and that blunderbusses and pistols were always close at hand" (Reith, 1975, p. 134).

Fielding conceived the idea that citizens might join forces, go into the streets, trace the perpetrators of crime, and meet the instigators of mob gatherings *before* they assembled a following and caused destruction.

---

Henry Fielding was one of the earliest and most articulate advocates of crime **prevention**.

---

Fielding selected six honest, industrious citizens to form an amateur volunteer force. With his advise and direction, they "swept clean" the Bow Street neighborhood. Many criminals were arrested, and many others fled from the neighborhood.

Henry Fielding was succeeded by his blind half-brother, John, who carried Henry's ideas forward. Critchley (1967, p. 33) notes: "The greatness of the brothers as educators of public opinion lies in the single-minded determination with which, over nearly thirty years, they strove to demonstrate to their contemporaries how serious were the dangers which threatened to engulf the nation."

Several years after Henry Fielding's death, the Bow Street volunteer force turned professional and was known as the **Bow Street Runners,** the first detective agency in England. Unfortunately, the practical results of Fielding's preventive ideas achieved in the Bow Street neighborhood were ignored for thirty years.

## The Defeat of Pitt's Reform Bill

In spite of isolated successes such as those achieved by Henry Fielding, nationwide hostility against a police force existed in England. The general view was: "Once admit a police force into England, and the long-cherished liberties of Englishmen would be swept away in a reign of terror and oppression" (Critchley, 1967, p. 35).

In the summer of 1780 London was subjected to nearly a week of mob violence during the Gordon Riots and had to be rescued by the army. Shocked and angry citizens called for further strengthening of the already savage criminal law, mobilizing the hue and cry, and creating a voluntary association of armed citizens.

In 1785 Prime Minister William Pitt proposed a reform bill to embody all the major proposals of the last thirty years, anticipating Peel's Metropolitan Police Act by nearly half a century. Pitt's Reform Bill provided for establishing a strong police force to act throughout the entire metropolitan area and for a clear separation between law enforcement and the justices. The bill met with widespread hostility by the press, the public, and the justices, and it was consequently defeated.

Pitt was able to affect some positive reform through his Middlesex Justice Bill in 1792, which established seven public offices, each with three salaried magistrates and six paid constables.

### Patrick Colquhoun (1745–1820)

One of the three paid magistrates appointed under Pitt's Middlesex Justice Bill was Patrick Colquhoun. Like Pitt, Colquhoun was vitally interested in social reform and in expanding and adapting the ideas of Henry Fielding to shape his preventive theory into "the new science of preventive police."

In *A Treatise on the Police of the Metropolis* (1796), Colquhoun presented startling statistics supporting the need for a large police force for London. The preface to the sixth edition of his *Treatise* (1800) stated: "Police in this country may be considered as a new science . . . in the prevention and detection of crimes."

Colquhoun also advocated complete separation of police and judicial powers. His treatise was a landmark in presenting statistics on crime and criminals and in using the statistics to draw up wide-ranging plans.

Colquhoun compiled statistics on crime and criminals to support his belief that London be considered as a whole and that it have a large police force to prevent crime. He also established a private security force.

As a result of his treatise, a group of West India planters and merchants approached Colquhoun and asked if he would help them with their problem of thefts from ships at the London docks. Colquhoun produced a plan for river police officers organized for watching and unloading West India ships while in port. The plan, financed and implemented by the planters and merchants, saved them £66,000 during the first eight months (Reith, 1975).

Colquhoun's pleas to extend the plan to all ports and to create police forces in all towns were ignored. The possibility of using police to solve the problems of crime and disorder was abandoned by cabinet ministers while at the same time the intensity of the problem increased.

Toward the end of the eighteenth century it became clear that the institutions of headboroughs, tithingmen, or petty constables, with a chief constable at their head was an inefficient system to police a civilized country, especially its metropolis. The weakness of this system, with its divided authority and inefficient staff, was obvious to many.

### □ NINETEENTH-CENTURY ENGLAND

In the beginning of the nineteenth century, inadequate law enforcement over much of England required a further supplementation of security by private enterprise. Industrial firms that employed large numbers of unruly workers established their own police. The railway companies, in particular, employed a private police force to maintain order. Similar forces were hired by the ironmasters of the Tredegar Works in Monmouthshire and Lancashire. For the most part, however, collective responsibility for repression of disturbances, the employment of special constables, and the formation of the armed associations remained the major forms of law enforcement until the reforms proposed by Sir Robert Peel.

The Bow Street Runners continued in existence, having for nearly a century provided an alternative to the disreputable private thief-takers. But to stay informed about crime, runners frequented the tavern hangouts of thieves. Public outcry plus concern over the corrupting influence of the reward system led to a parliamentary investigation in 1828. Bribery and criminal collusion were discovered and the runners were censured. One critic (Adam, n.d.), Charles Dickens, wrote of the runners:

> We are not by any means devout believers in the old Bow Street Police. To say the truth, we think there was a vast amount of humbug about those worthies. Apart from many of them being men of very indifferent character, and far too much in the habit of consulting with thieves and the like, they never lost a public occasion of jobbing and trading in mystery and making the most of themselves. . . . Although as a preventive police they were utterly inefficient, and as a detective police they were very loose and uncertain in their operations, they remain with some people, a superstition to the present day.

One year after the parliamentary investigation, Robert Peel's new police appeared on the scene.

## Sir Robert Peel (1788—1850)

Public opposition to a police department was still strong when Sir Robert Peel became Home Secretary in 1822, more than thirty years after Pitt's Reform Bill was defeated. Peel, however, was more successful. He devoted his early years as Home Secretary to reforming criminal law. By 1826 he had drawn up a plan for establishing a single police system within a ten-mile radius of London's St. Paul's Cathedral. Ironically, the financial section of London, called the City, was excluded from the plan. In 1827 Sir Robert Peel became a member of a parliamentary committee on criminal matters. This committee's second report, published in 1828, asserted: "The art of crime, if it may be so called, has increased faster than the art of detection."

Based on the committee's report, Peel introduced his "Bill for Improving the Police in and near the Metropolis." Peel, often referred to as the Father of Police Administration, proposed a return to the Anglo-Saxon principle of individual community responsibility for preserving law and order, but also said that London should have a body of civilians appointed and paid by the community to serve as police officers. Parliament agreed and in 1829 organized the Metropolitan Police of London.

---

Robert Peel's Metropolitan Police Act created the London Metropolitan Police, whose principal objective was to be prevention *of crime.*

Sir Robert Peel, father of modern policing (1788-1850).

The First Order of the Metropolitan Police read:

IT SHOULD BE UNDERSTOOD, AT THE OUTSET, THAT THE PRINCIPAL OBJECTIVE TO BE ATTAINED IS THE PREVENTION OF CRIME
To this great end every effort of the police is to be directed. The security of person and property, the preservation of public tranquility, and all other objects of a Police Establishment, will thus be better effected, than by the detection and punishment of the offender, after he has succeeded in committing the crime.

Included in the handbook for the Metropolitan Police were two objectives that again clearly reflect the preventive nature intended:

1) To prevent crime and disorder, as an alternative to their repression by military force and severity of legal punishment.
2) To recognize always that the test of police efficiency is the absence of crime and disorder and not the visible evidence of police action in dealing with them.

But this emphasis on crime prevention did not last. The public police became more and more occupied with investigating crimes and apprehending criminals, and prevention efforts decreased proportionately. Thus, the need for private security as a means to *prevent* crime continued to exist.

## ☐ THE EVOLUTION OF PRIVATE SECURITY IN THE UNITED STATES

The American colonists brought with them the English system of law enforcement and its reliance on collective responsibility.

Constables and night town watchmen were the primary means of security in the United States until the establishment of full-time police forces in the mid-1800s.

Early in the eighteenth century several Societies for the Reformation of Manners appeared, and by the end of the century many moral societies existed, the most prominent of which was the Society for the Suppression of Vice and Encouragement of Religion, founded in 1801. Later in the nineteenth century an "evangelical Police" system developed to watchdog the lower classes with spies and informants and to enforce Puritan propriety.

Out West, the stagecoaches carrying mail, gold, money, and passengers were prey to holdups by road agents. The professionals who went up against these road agents rode shotgun on the stagecoaches. Crime was rampant in the West following the Civil War. It was the era of outlaw gangs such as the James Gang and the Wild Bunch. Stage line companies responded by building their own security forces and hiring detective agencies to track down outlaws. Other industries saw the need to form protective services, especially those industries vulnerable to strikes, such as coal and iron mining.

Violence in the West increased with the discovery of gold in 1848. Cities in the East and South fared little better. Even in Washington, D.C., members attending Congress had to carry arms. Because transporting goods was so fraught with risk, express companies were formed. In 1850 Henry Wells and William Fargo joined to form the American Express, which operated east of the Missouri River. In 1852 Wells Fargo and Company was established to serve the country west of the Missouri. These companies had their own private detectives and shotgun riders. Also extremely vulnerable were the railroads.

### Railroad Police

With the westward expansion in the United States during the 1800s, railroad lines moved into sparsely settled territories that had little or no public law enforcement. Trains were attacked by Indians and roving bands of outlaws who robbed passengers, stole cargos, dynamited tracks, and disrupted communications.

Because of problems of interstate jurisdiction and lack of public police protection, many states passed railway police acts, allowing private railroads to establish proprietary security forces, with full police powers, to protect their goods and passengers.

As noted by Gough (1977, p. 19): "The railroad special agent was a colorful part of the old Wild West. Being able to shoot fast and ride hard were important skills in the late 1800s. In addition to train robbers, there were also station holdup crooks, pickpockets, con men, and bootleggers to contend with. Because of his mission in countering such problems, the railroad special agent of the old West was considered as nearly a duly commissioned law enforcement officer as his modern-day counterpart."

In many parts of the country, the railroad police provided the only protective services until governmental units and law enforcement agencies were established.

As noted by Dewhurst (1955): "A railroad agent who could hold his own in a gun battle with train robbers was considered an asset to the railroad. In this era of the smoking sixshooters, tact and investigative intelligence placed second to the ability to handle physical contact with those who preyed upon the railroad. . . . It was the general custom simply to hand the newly appointed man a badge, a revolver and a club and send him out to work without further instructions as to the laws or how to enforce them, or even how to make an arrest." Nevertheless, the railroad police made a significant contribution to the evolution of private security. In 1921 the Association of American Railroads was formed to help coordinate mutual problems, particularly those associated with security.

## Allan Pinkerton (1819–1884)

Allan Pinkerton was a key figure in the development of the railroad police as well as in the development of contract security forces.

Born in Scotland, he joined the radical Chartist group as a young man and was forced to flee from Scotland or face imprisonment. He and his young wife fled to America, where Pinkerton set up his trade of coopering (making barrels) in Chicago. Soon after, they moved to Dundee, Illinois, where his cooperage became a way station for the underground railroad, a secret network that assisted escaping slaves.

One day Pinkerton accidently found the hideout of a group of counterfeiters and helped the local sheriff capture them. He eventually sold his shop and was appointed deputy sheriff of Cook County. In 1843 he was appointed Chicago's first detective.

Pinkerton resigned his position in 1850 because of economic pressures and took two private clients, the Rock Island and the Illinois Central railroads. The next year he formed the Pinkerton National Detective

Agency. Its slogan was "We Never Sleep," and its logo was an open eye, probably the origin of the term "private eye." His agency concentrated on catching train robbers and setting up security systems for the railroads.

---

Allan Pinkerton was the first law enforcement officer hired to protect railroads. He also established the first and currently the largest private security contract operation in the United States.

---

Very early Pinkerton hired Kate Warner, the first woman in the United States to become a detective (Lavine 1963, p. 33).

Pinkerton's services were important to his clients mainly because public enforcement agencies either were inadequate or lacked jurisdiction. When the Civil War broke out in 1861, President Lincoln called Pinkerton to Washington to discuss establishing a secret service department to "ascertain the social, political, and patriotic relations of the numerous suspected people in and about Washington" (Lavine, 1963, p. 33). Using the name E. J. Allen, Pinkerton did intelligence work for the Union army, work which today would be performed by a governmental agency.

In the 1860s and 1870s the Pinkertons gained national stature by capturing train robbers and bandits. They chased murderous gangs of bank robbers and such notorious criminals as the Dalton Boys, the Hole in the Wall Gang, Jesse James, the Sontags, the Farringtons, and the Renos, much as the FBI hunts wanted criminals today. Gough (1977, p. 17) notes: "Pinkerton encouraged the use of burglarproof safes in all railroad express cars. By using such a heavy safe, any outlaws intending to rob the train had to use a large charge of black powder or dynamite to blow it open. The resulting blast's magnitude usually destroyed the contents of the safe, as well as the roof and sides of the express car. Pinkerton also recommended the employment of express guards heavily armed with high-powered rifles." One reason Pinkertons became so famous was that there was virtually no national enforcement except theirs.

However, during two periods in Pinkerton's history the agency established a poor image. In the last two decades of the nineteenth century and during the Great Depression of the 1930s, the Pinkertons worked as strikebreakers and private guards. One notorious case involved an organization of coal miners called the Mollie Maguires. In the late 1870s a Pinkerton man infiltrated the allegedly terrorist organization and seventeen men (whom many believed innocent) were hanged as a result of his testimony. In 1892, three hundred Pinkerton men suffered a humiliating defeat by sit-in strikers they sought to dislodge at Homestead, Pennsylvania. They were involved in dozens of similar strikebreaking situations in the 1930s. Finally, after a congressional inquiry into the labor-management relations in 1937, Robert A. Pinkerton, then head of the agency, forbade any member of his agency to ever again accept undercover work involving the investigation of a labor union.

Pinkerton's was not the only agency involved in strikebreaking. During the late 1800s, much controversy surrounded the use of private security agencies. For example, the strike on the Erie Railroads in 1877 was broken when Jim Fisk employed a force of approximately one thousand "thugs" and turned them loose on the strikers, "thrashing and maiming them" (Reith, 1975, p. 95). The use of private security agents as strikebreakers led to bitter confrontations between labor and management, often resulting in injuries and setbacks for labor.

Fortunately, Pinkerton's had seen and learned to avoid the dangers inherent in using private security personnel in strikebreaking situations, and the agency continued to thrive. The company became a public corporation in 1965 and changed its name to Pinkerton's Inc. Currently it employs between thirty-six and forty thousand people and concentrates on security in industry and institutions, security for sporting facilities, investigations of industrial thefts, and insurance investigations.

## Other Security Advances

In 1853 August Pope patented one of the first electric burglar alarm systems. The system had electromagnetic contacts mounted on doors and windows and then wired to a battery and bell. He sold his invention to Edwin Holmes who took it to New York City and sold alarms to wealthy homeowners. In 1858 Holmes established the first central burglar alarm service in the country (Green, 1978, p. 12). His operation evolved into Holmes Protection, Inc.

Pope also used electrified metal foil and screens still widely used by many alarm companies. In addition, he built the first central communications center wired to bank and jewelry vaults (Kaye, 1987, p. 243).

By the 1870s and 1880s mansions and businesses were being protected against fire with heat sensors. William Watkins established a company called AFA Protection and was first to use such sensors in a central monitoring station. Other companies followed suit, adding burglar systems to the fire protection systems. The use of alarms and detection devices grew to provide protective services through the use of messengers and telegraph lines. By 1889 the use of such alarms and detection devices in industrial and commercial enterprises was well established. In 1901 Western Union consolidated several of these local alarm companies into American District Telegraph Company (ADT) (Kaye, 1987, p. 243).

In 1858 Washington Perry Brink founded Brink's, Inc., as a freight and package delivery service. He began by shuttling trunks and packages around Chicago in a one-horse dray. At first Brink concentrated on transporting goods for travelers passing through Chicago. Abraham Lincoln used Brink's services when he was in Chicago attending a Republican convention.

Bonded courier and express delivery services flourished partly because provisions in the common law made it risky to use employees or servants as couriers (Hall, 1935, pp. 31–32):

> The common law recognized no criminality in a person who came legally into possession of property and later converted it. Apparently it was thought that the owner should have protected himself by selecting a trustworthy per-

son. Since, presumably, this could readily be done, the owner must have been negligent if he delivered his property to a person who absconded with it.

In 1891, Brinks' carried its first payroll for Western Electric Company. In the early days Brink's tried to be inconspicuous, using standard buggies and wrapping cash in newspapers or overalls. But in 1917, when "Ammunition" Wheed and his gang killed two Brink's men in a holdup, the armored car was born.

---

Washington Perry Brink established armored car and courier services in the United States.

---

Tozer (1960, p. 90) describes how the armored car, "the bankvault on wheels whose invulnerability had been paid for by the blood of good men" came into being.[*]

> Its design began on August 28, 1917, as messenger Barton Allen stepped out of a touring car with $9,100 payroll for Winslow Bros. in Chicago. A bandit drilled him in the stomach. A second thug forced the guard from the car, and a third dropped the driver with a single shot. They fled with the loot. Brink's countered by bolting steel panels to the sides and roof of every car.
>
> But they had more to learn. In March, 1926, Paul Jawarski timed the weekly movement of an armored car from Pittsburgh to the Terminal Coal Co. at Coverdale, Pa. Then he mined two sections of its lonely route with lengths of pipe crammed with explosives. . . .
>
> As the three-ton armored car rumbled over the first mine, they threw a switch. The explosion tossed the car into the air. It landed upside down. The gang smashed through the floor and scrambled off with $104,000.
>
> *Some changes made.* Brink's redesigned its cars again. Out went the wooden floors and frames. In went all-steel frames and steel floors. Frames of today's juggernauts are half-inch cold-rolled steel. Outside panels are 12-gauge, high-carbon steel; inner panels are 18-gauge sheet with a stuffing of fiber-glass between. The result is a car that can be blown open only by an anti-tank weapon.

Today Brink's handles about half the cash that is transported by courier in the United States.

In 1883 jewelers formed the Jewelers Security Alliance for protection against burglary. Advancements in security continued and accelerated in the twentieth century. In 1909 William. J. Burns, a former Secret Service investigator and head of the Bureau of Investigation (forerunner of the FBI), started the William J. Burns' Detective Agency.

---

William J. Burns founded the sole investigating agency for the American Banking Association. It grew to become the second-largest contract guard and investigative service in the United States.

---

[*]Reprinted from *Popular Science* with permission © 1960, Popular Science Publishing Company.

Brink's armored car in 1925.

For all practical purposes, Pinkerton's and Burns' were the only national investigative bodies concerned with nonspecialized crimes in the country until the advent of the FBI in 1924.

## The World Wars and the Depression

Before and during World War I, concern for security intensified in American industry because of fear of sabotage and espionage. Private security forces were used to protect war industries and the docks against destruction by saboteurs. Security services expanded to meet the demands, but tapered off after the war, reaching a low point during the depression.

In 1921, a Burglary Protection Council was formed and held its first meeting, the result of which was establishing Underwriters' Laboratories to establish specifications, testing, and certification of burglar alarm systems and devices.

The period 1930 to 1947 was, according to Weiss (1987, p. 110), "an important period in private policing history, a time during which private industrial policing went from its highest level of activity to a dramatic decline." He noted that in the 1920s the heavy manufacturing industries had the "financial wherewithal to withstand the scattered resistance of strikers" while being supported by states that declared strikes illegitimate. An article in the *New York Times* (January 8, 1928), for example, labeled Henry Ford as "an industrial fascist—the Mussolini of Detroit" (Weiss, 1987, p. 113).

The depression helped to change that. As noted by Weiss (1987, p. 112): "To help deal with the depression crisis, Franklin Roosevelt established the National Recovery Act of 1933, which contained a provision (Section 7A) granting workers the right to organize and bargain collectively, free from employer interference or coercion. A rush to unionization followed." In 1935 the Wagner Act gave "legal force, backed by fines, to labor's right to organize." The result was, as Weiss (1987, p. 113) describes, "the demise of the 'slugging detective' and the ascent of the 'labor relations department.' "

World War II was a significant catalyst in the growth of the private security industry. Before awarding national defense contracts, the federal government required munitions contractors to implement stringent, comprehensive security measures to protect classified materials and defense secrets from sabotage and espionage. The FBI assisted in establishing these security programs. Additionally, the government granted the status of auxiliary military police to more than two hundred thousand plant security guards whose primary duties were protection of war goods and products, supplies, equipment, and personnel. Local law enforcement agencies were responsible for training them.

One of the best kept secrets of World War II was "Ultra," an encoding machine invented by the Germans. Its real name was "Enigma," the Greek word for puzzle. With this machine the British could crack every code the Germans invented. Churchill (BBC/CBN) said of it: "Ultra was my most secret source. It gave me knowledge of the enemy's precise strength and disposition. It told me when and how Hitler and his generals would act. Without it the war in the North African desert, the battles in Normandy, and indeed, the victory in the Middle East, would have been long and arduous, costing heavily in Allied lives."

The British were given the machines by the Poles who, due to lax security, stole several of them from a German factory. The "Ultra" was one of the first complex computers ever invented. It gave the British a precise picture of almost all important events taking place behind the German lines. It was, in reality, an eavesdropping device that shortened the war, saved thousands of lives, and cut down the tremendous costs of a war fought on so many fronts.

According to the British documentary, "Best Kept Secrets," such details as what the British did with the information after it had been decoded, how they extracted even to make sense from Hitler's last scrambled telephone calls, and how Britain fit the information into the total intelligence and made it immediately operational still cannot be told. All this information is secret and will remain so, for to reveal it is an act punishable by life imprisonment.

---

The world wars heightened emphasis on security in the government and made industry increasingly aware of the need for plant security.

---

After World War II, the use of the private security services expanded to encompass all segments of the private sector (*Private Security*, 1976, p. 31). According to Shearing and Stenning (1987, p. 9): "Since World War II the phenomenon of private security has been growing exponentially, and continues to do so."

## Contemporary Private Security

Increases in government regulations and the inability of the public police to respond to every private need promoted the growth of private security. For example, in 1954 George R. Wackenhut and three other former FBI agents formed the Wackenhut Corporation as a private investigative and contract security firm. In only twenty years this firm established itself as the third largest contract guard and investigative agency in the country.

Other businesses began to form their own in-house security services rather than contracting for services from private agencies. However, whether the security personnel were proprietary or contracted, private security provided industry and private businesses with individual protection for persons and homes; guard services for construction sites and business property when they were closed; security services for large shopping centers; advice on internal and external security systems for homes, businesses, and factories; and private investigations.

The *preventive* philosophy underlying the private security field has influenced other areas as well. Notably, it is influencing architecture and building codes, as noted by C. Ray Jeffery in his classic *Crime Prevention Through Environmental Design* (1972): "Criminal behavior can be controlled primarily through the direct alteration of the environment of potential victims. . . . Crime control programs must focus on crime before it occurs, rather than afterward. As criminal opportunity is reduced, so will be the number of criminals."

Perhaps even more significant, the *preventive* aspect of crime is now being stressed by many public law enforcement agencies, as evidenced by the creation of the National Crime Prevention Institute (NCPI), established in 1971 as a division of the University of Louisville's School of Police Administration. This does not mean, however, that the need for private security officers and measures will lessen. Rather, it means that the full importance of preventive measures has become apparent. The public police will probably never have sufficient personnel to meet private needs, and government regulations regarding security will doubtless continue to proliferate.

---

By the 1990s private security has evolved to a multibillion-dollar-a-year business employing more than a million people.

---

From two hundred thousand plant security guards in World War II to over one million private security personnel today, the private security force has experienced tremendous growth. With increased technology and needed protection for sophisticated, delicate machinery, private security employment will increase even more rapidly in the future.

According to the Hallcrest Report, in 1990 private security will employ 1,493,000, an increase of 4 percent. By 2000 it will employ 1,883,000, an increase of 2 percent.

Mangan and Shanahan (1990, p. 18) suggest: "Private security has emerged as a major player in the safeguarding of Americans and their property."

A survey of 420 security directors (1980) supports the contention that use of security personnel and equipment will increase in the 1990s. Well over half the directors responding felt that use of both contract and proprietary private security services would increase, as would the risks threatening business and industry and the use of security equipment to reduce such risks. Very few managers indicated a decrease in use of personnel, threats to be reckoned with, or security equipment. In fact, in only two areas was opinion on future status quite evenly divided: use of polygraph tests and psychological stress evaluation.

The general character of current private security is the focus of Chapter 2.

# SUMMARY

**P**rivate security evolved from the human desire for additional, individual protection and the desire to prevent crimes against one's person or property. In ancient times people relied on physical security such as weapons, lake or cliff dwellings, walls, and gates. In addition, rulers appointed individuals to protect the general safety as well as their own personal safety.

During the Middle Ages the tithing system and the Frankpledge system provided security and collective responsibility for law and order. The Magna Charta, similar to our Bill of Rights, gave Englishmen "due process" of law. Also during this period, King Edward issued the Statute of Westminster to "abate the power of felons" by establishing the watch and ward, which provided town watchmen to patrol the city during the night; reviving the hue and cry, which required all citizens to assist in the capture of anyone resisting arrest; and instituting the assize of arms, which required that every male between the ages of fifteen and sixty have a weapon in his home. Some merchants hired private police to guard their establishments, to investigate crimes against them, and to recover property stolen from them.

During the eighteenth century private citizens carried arms for protection and banded together to hire special police to protect their homes and businesses. The military was used to suppress riots. Midway through the century, Henry Fielding became one of the first and most articulate advocates of crime prevention. Thirty years later Patrick Colquhoun wrote a decisive treatise using statistics on crime and criminals to support his belief that London be considered as a whole and that it have a large police force to *prevent* crime. He also established a private security force for planters and merchants from West India.

The most important development in nineteenth-century England was the introduction of the Metropolitan Police Act by Robert Peel. It passed, creating the London Metropolitan Police, whose principal objective was to be *prevention* of crime.

In colonial America, constables and town watchmen were the primary means of security until the establishment of full-time police forces in the mid-1800s. Because of problems of interstate jurisdiction and lack of public police protection, many states passed railroad police acts, allowing private railroads to establish proprietary security forces, with full police powers, to protect their goods and passengers. In many parts of the country, the railroad police provided the only protective services until governmental units and law enforcement agencies were established.

Allan Pinkerton was the first law enforcement officer hired to protect the railroads. He also established the first and currently the largest private security contract operation in the United States. About the same time, Washington Perry Brink established armored car and courier services in the United States. In the twentieth century, William J. Burns founded the sole investigating agency for the American Banking Association. It grew to become the second-largest contract guard and investigative service in the United States.

The world wars heightened emphasis on security in the government and made industry increasingly aware of the need for plant security. By the 1990s private security has evolved into a multibillion-dollar-a-year business employing more than a million people. The future for private security appears excellent.

## APPLICATION

1) You have been asked to speak to a college class on "The Evolution of Private Security." What facts will you include in your talk? What will you stress most?
2) You have been asked to speak to a class at the local police academy on the historical role of private security as it related to early public law enforcement. What facts would you include? What would you stress most?

## DISCUSSION QUESTIONS

1) What features of ancient security systems may still be found in the 1990s?
2) Until recent times, it was felt a ruler and his army could enforce the laws. Why does Reith feel a "police mechanism" is necessary between the ruler and the army?
3) What relationship exists between the ancient assize of arms and our Constitution's Second Amendment right of the people "to keep and bear arms" for the necessity of a "well-regulated militia"?
4) Throughout history there has been hostility to the establishment of public police. Why were people so opposed to an organization that could have benefited them so greatly?
5) In the absence of public law enforcement, what parallel functions did the Pinkerton Detective Agency and the railroad police perform?

## REFERENCES

Adam, H. L. *The police encyclopedia.* London: Waverly Book Company, n.d. 1:125.
BBC (British Broadcasting Company) and CBN (Canadian Broadcasting Network).
    The importance of industrial espionage. *Best kept secrets.* 1954 television series.
Critchley, T. A. *A history of police in England and Wales,* 2d ed. Montclair, NJ: Patterson

Smith, 1967.

Dewhurst, H. S. *The railroad police*. Springfield, IL: Charles C. Thomas, 1955.

Folley, Vern .L. *American law enforcement*. Boston, MA: Allyn & Bacon, Inc., 1980.

Gough, T. W. Railroad crime: Old west train robbers to modern-day cargo thieves. *FBI law enforcement bulletin*, February 1977, pp. 16–25.

Green, G. and Farber, R. C. *Introduction to security*. Los Angeles: Security World Publishing Company, Inc., 1978.

Hall, J. *Theft, law and society*. Indianapolis, IN: Bobbs-Merrill, 1935.

Hall, J. *Theft, law and society*, 2d ed. Indianapolis, IN: Bobbs-Merrill, 1952.

Healy, R. J. *Design for security*. New York: John Wiley and Sons, 1968.

Jeffery, C. R. *Crime prevention through environmental design*. Beverly Hills, CA: Sage Publications, 1972.

Kaye, Michael S. Residential security in the year 2000. In *Security in the year 2000 and beyond*, by Louis A. Tyska and Lawrence J. Fennelly. Palm Springs, CA: ETC Publications, 1987.

Lavine, S. A. *Allan Pinkerton: America's first private eye*. New York: Dodd, Mead, and Company, 1963.

Mangan, Terence J. and Shanahan, Michael G. Public law enforcement/private security: A new partnership? *FBI law enforcement bulletin*, January 1990, pp. 18–22.

*Private security*. Report of the Task Force on Private Security, National Advisory Committee on Criminal Justice Standards and Goals. Washington, DC: U.S. Government Printing Office, 1976.

Reith, C. *Blind eye of history*. Montclair, NJ: Patterson Smith, 1975.

Reith, C. *Police principles and the problems of war*. London: Oxford University Press, 1940.

Romilly, S. *A history of English criminal law and its administration from 1970*, Vol. 3, *Cross-currents in the movement for the reform of the police*. London: Stevens and Sons, 1956.

Security directors: How much are they earning? *Security world*, December 1980, pp. 19–27.

Shearing, Clifford D. and Stenning, Philip C. Reframing policing. In *Private policing*, by Clifford D. Shearing and Philip C. Stenning, eds. Beverly Hills, CA: Sage Publications, 1987, pp. 9–18.

South, Nigel. Law, profit, and 'private persons': Private and public policing in English history. In *Private policing*, by Clifford D. Shearing and Philip C. Stenning, eds. Beverly Hills, CA: Sage Publications, 1987, pp. 72–107.

Tozer, E. Riding with a million in cash. *Popular science*, March 1960, pp. 3–4, 90–91, 246–247.

Weiss, Robert P. From 'slugging detectives' to 'labor relations,' policing labor at Ford, 1930–1947. In *Private policing*, by Clifford D. Shearing and Philip C. Stenning, eds. Beverly Hills, CA: Sage Publications, 1987, pp. 110–130.-

## Chapter Two

# Modern Private Security: An Overview

## □ INTRODUCTION

Private security has come into its own, as evidenced by the development of college degree programs as well as state and national efforts for registering and licensing. It is a multifaceted industry that has made great advances since the day of the lone watchman or the single guard in a guardhouse. The numerous functions performed by private security personnel and the vast array of security equipment and procedures developed in the past decades offer the potential for more security than ever before.

## □ PRIVATE SECURITY DEFINED

Many definitions of private security have been formulated to characterize the modern security industry. Among the more comprehensive definitions are the following:

➤ Private security includes those self-employed individuals and privately funded business entities and organizations providing security-related services to specific clientele for a fee, for the individual or entity that retains or employs them, or for themselves, in order to protect their persons, private property, or interests from varied hazards (*Private Security*, 1976, p. 4).

➤ The terms private police and private security forces and security personnel . . . include all types of private organizations and individuals providing all types of security-related services, including investigation, guard, patrol, lie detection, alarm, and armored transportation (*Rand Report*, Volume I, p. 3).

➤ Security has been defined as the use of measures designed to safeguard personnel, to prevent unauthorized access to equipment, facilities, materials, and documents, and to safeguard them against espionage, sabotage, theft, and fraud (U.S. Army, FM 1930 *Physical Security*, March 1979, pp. 1–7, 293–98).

**DO YOU KNOW**

➤ What private security is?
➤ What major functions are performed by private security officers?
➤ How proprietary private security differs from contractual private security?
➤ What the major types of private security personnel are?
➤ How private security services might be regulated?
➤ How private investigators/detectives are regulated?
➤ What the requirements for becoming a private investigator are?
➤ What purpose is served by a code of ethics for private security?
➤ What a Certified Protection Professional (CPP) is?
➤ Where private security fits into the overall management plan of a business, industry, or institution?

---

Private security is a profit-oriented industry that provides personnel, equipment, and/or procedures to *prevent* losses caused by human error, emergencies, disasters, or criminal actions.

As the name implies, private security meets the needs of individuals, businesses, institutions, and organizations that require more protection than is afforded by public police officers. The consumer of private security services might be any individual or group of individuals, public or private, large or small. Wealthy individuals may hire a private security patrol for their residences; colleges often hire security patrols; a bank, a shopping center, an office building—almost any conceivable business, organization, or agency—might use private security services.

Consumers of private security services seek protection against many types of natural and human-made risks, with emphasis on the human-made risks of accidents; theft and pilferage; fraud; employee disloyalty and subversion; espionage; sabotage; strikes, riots, and demonstrations; and violent crimes (Paine, 1972, p. 36).

Although the duties assumed by private security personnel may vary greatly, most private security officers spend the majority of their time in nonenforcement, nonpolice functions.

## ☐ PURPOSE AND OBJECTIVES OF PRIVATE SECURITY

The purpose of private security is to protect assets and property and to provide a stable, nonthreatening environment in which employees and visitors of a facility may pursue their work objectives without disruption or harm.

Common objectives of private security include the following:

➤ To fairly and consistently enforce the policies and procedures regarding general security, access and asset control, and employee safety.
➤ To provide a workplace environment that will attract and retain personnel and protect them from exploitation by external pressures.
➤ To prevent the compromise and unauthorized disclosure of the company's assets or technology.
➤ To protect and preserve the company's assets.
➤ To respond to on-site incidents that threaten the well-being of employees or the organization.
➤ To report conditions that constitute a breach of sound security or pose a potential security hazard.

---

The primary function of security personnel is to prevent loss by (1) gathering information, (2) controlling access to and maintaining order on private property, and (3) protecting persons and property against crime and disaster.

---

In addition, private security personnel may provide valuable public relations services. The specific type of security position an individual holds will determine which functions will be of primary concern.

# ■ TYPES OF PRIVATE SECURITY SERVICES

Security objectives may be met through a variety of services. According to the Hallcrest Report II (Cunningham et al., 1990), the most common security services being provided are contract guards, alarm services, private investigators, locksmith services, armored car services, and security consultants. Before looking at specific services, consider how the services might be provided.

The services may be provided by a single individual or by a team of security professionals under the direction of a full-time security manager. They may be the responsibility of individuals on staff, that is, proprietary, or they may be the responsibility of people hired on a contract basis.

# ■ PROPRIETARY VS. CONTRACT PRIVATE SECURITY SERVICES

An important consideration for any security manager is deciding whether loss prevention can be most effectively and efficiently achieved by having one's own security personnel or by hiring an outside agency to supply such personnel.

Proprietary services are *in-house*, directly hired and controlled by the company or organization. In contrast, contract services are *outside* firms or individuals who provide security services for a fee.

The Hallcrest Report II (Cunningham et al., 1990, p. 196) states that: "The proprietary sector continues to be one of the major employers of security personnel, representing more than 25% of all private security employees. In 1990 contract security guards are virtually tied at 35%. Thus, these 2 segments account for almost three-quarters of all employment." The Hallcrest estimates of private security employment for 1990 are summarized in Table 2–1.

The Hallcrest staff predicts that proprietary security will begin to lose ground during the 1990s and that by the year 2000 it will account for only 20 percent of the employment. The staff also predicts that contract services will maintain its 35 percent and that the most employment gains will be made by alarm companies, manufacturers, and services represented in the "other" category.

Hallcrest employment data with the proprietary services omitted is summarized in Table 2–2.

The *manufacturers and distributors* category includes such things as electronic access control systems, safes and vaults, closed-circuit television systems, and communications equipment.

As seen in Table 2–2, well over half of private security personnel work for "guard companies." Table 2–3 summarizes information about the ten largest security guard and patrol companies in the United States.

### Table 2–1 Estimates of private security employment for 1990.

| Segment | Employees in 1990 | Percent of Total |
|---|---|---|
| Armored car | 15,000 | 1.0% |
| Alarm companies | 120,000 | 8.0% |
| Contract guards | 520,000 | 34.8% |
| Private investigators | 70,000 | 4.7% |
| Consultants/engineers | 2,900 | 0.2% |
| Locksmiths | 69,600 | 4.7% |
| Manufacturers and distributors | 88,300 | 5.9% |
| Other | 79,500 | 5.3% |
| Proprietary security | 528,000 | 35.4% |
| TOTAL | 1,493,300 | 100% |

SOURCE: Reprinted from *The Hallcrest Report II: Private Security Trends: 1970 to 2000,* © 1990 Butterworth Heinemann, Stoneham, MA.

## Advantages and Disadvantages of Proprietary and Contract Services

Many companies prefer to have their own security personnel because they are likely to be more loyal, more motivated due to promotion possibilities, more knowledgeable of the specific operation and personnel of the organization, more courteous and better able to recognize VIPs, and more amenable to training and supervision. In addition, having proprietary security personnel is seen as a status symbol among many employers, and there is usually less turnover.

There are also disadvantages to proprietary security services. The most important are cost, lack of flexibility, and administrative burdens. In addition, proprietary security personnel may become *too* familiar with the organization and become ineffective or even corrupt. Also, they may go on strike with the company union members. Because of such reasons, many business executives seek to contract with outside agencies or individuals to receive security services.

Among the most commonly provided contract security services are guard services, private patrol services, and investigative services (such as those provided by Pinkerton's, Wm. J. Burns', Wackenhut, and Walter Kidde) and armored car and courier services (such as those provided by Brink's, Wells Fargo, and Loomis).

One of the most important factors behind the rise in contract services is cost. The Task Force Report (*Private Security,* 1976, p. 245) gives the cost as 20 percent less than in-house, *not counting* administrative savings on such items as insurance, retirement pension, social security, medical care, and vacation and sick days. Supervision, training, and administrative functions are all assumed by the contract service.

Another distinct advantage of contract services is their flexibility; more or fewer personnel are available as needs change, and many contract services can provide a wide variety of services and equipment

**Table 2–2 Number of employees to 2000.**

| Segment | Employees in 1980 | Percent of Total 1980 | Employees in 1990 | Percent of Total 1990 | Average Annual Rate of Growth 1980 to 1990 | Employees in 2000 | Percent of Total 2000 | Average Annual Rate of Growth 1990 to 2000 |
|---|---|---|---|---|---|---|---|---|
| Armored car | 11,500 | 2% | 15,000 | 2% | 3% | 16,500 | 1% | 1% |
| Alarm companies | 55,000 | 10% | 120,000 | 12% | 8% | 250,000 | 17% | 8% |
| Contract guards | 330,000 | 59% | 520,000 | 54% | 5% | 750,000 | 51% | 4% |
| Private investigators | 45,000 | 8% | 70,000 | 7% | 4% | 90,000 | 6% | 2% |
| Consultants/engineers | 1,200 | 0.2% | 2,900 | 0.3% | 9% | 6,200 | 0.4% | 8% |
| Locksmiths | 45,000 | 8% | 69,600 | 7% | 4% | 88,000 | 6% | 2% |
| Manufacturers and distributors | 55,000 | 10% | 88,300 | 9% | 5% | 132,000 | 9% | 4% |
| Other | 13,500 | 2% | 79,500 | 8% | 19% | 140,000 | 10% | 6% |
| TOTAL | 556,200 | | 965,300 | | 6% | 1,472,700 | | 4% |

SOURCE: Reprinted from *The Hallcrest Report II: Private Security Trends: 1970 to 2000*, © 1990 Butterworth Heinemann, Stoneham, MA.

| Table 2–3 Ten largest security guard and patrol companies. | | |
|---|---|---|
| **Company/Head Office** | **Employees** | **1988 Revenues** |
| Pinkerton's, Inc. <br> Van Nuys, California | 55,000 | $ 652,000,000 |
| Burns International Security Services, <br> Paramus, New Jersey *(estimated)* | 30,000 | $ 435,000,000 |
| The Wackenhut Corporation <br> Coral Gables, Florida | 35,000 | $ 400,000,000 |
| Wells Fargo Guard Services <br> Parsippany, New Jersey | 21,500 | $ 250,000,000 |
| American Protective Services <br> Oakland, California | 9,000 | $ 151,000,000 |
| Globe Security <br> Deerfield Beach, Florida | 10,000 | $ 125,000,000 |
| Stanley Smith Security, Inc. <br> San Antonio, Texas | 8,900 | $ 120,000,000 |
| Guardsmark, Inc. <br> Memphis, Tennessee | 8,000 | $ 120,000,000 |
| Allied Security, Inc. <br> Pittsburgh, Pennsylvania *(estimated)* | 6,000 | $ 76,000,000 |
| Advance Security, Inc. <br> Atlanta, Georgia | 6,000 | $ 75,000,000 |
| TOTALS | 189,400 | $2,404,000,000 |

**Notes:** Prepared from questionnaire responses for the *Security Letter Source Book* for revenues through December 31, 1988, except where "estimated" is indicated. Totals may include investigative and consulting services and also some revenues reflect sales of non-guard-related revenues.
SOURCE: Security Letter Source Book 1990–1991.

unavailable to in-house security. In addition, contract security personnel are likely to be more objective, having no special loyalty to the "employer" or contractor.

However, contract services are not necessarily ideal. There is a high turnover in contract guards; they are frequently reassigned; there is less job security and personal satisfaction; and a conflict of loyalties may develop.

The Task Force Report on Private Security summarizes the major advantages and disadvantages of both proprietary and contract security services (*Private Security*, 1976, pp. 245–46):

| **Proprietary** | **Contract** |
|---|---|
| *Advantages* | *Advantages* |
| Loyalty | Selectivity |
| Incentive | Flexibility |
| Knowledge of internal operation | Replacement of absenteeism |
| Tenure (less turnover) | Supervision (at no cost) |
| Control stays in-house | Training (at no cost) |
| Supervision stays in-house | Objectivity |

| | |
|---|---|
| Training geared to specific job | Cost (20% less, not counting administrative costs) |
| Company image improved | Quality |
| Morale | Administration and budgeting taken care of |
| Courtesy to in-house personnel | Little union problems |
| Better law enforcement liaison | Variety of services and equipment |
| Selection controlled | Hiring and screening (at no cost) |
| Better communication; more direct | Better local law enforcement contacts |
| | Sharing expertise and knowledge |
| *Disadvantages* | *Disadvantages* |
| Unions | Turnover (extremely high industrywide) |
| Familiarity with personnel | Divided loyalties |
| Cost | Moonlighting (may be tired and not alert) |
| Inflexibility | Reassignment |
| Administrative burdens | Screening standards (may be inadequate) |
| | Insurance |

Given the numerous advantages and disadvantages of both proprietary and contract services, many organizations elect a combination when economically feasible. Whether proprietary or contract, several types of security officers may be used.

## ☐ TYPES OF PRIVATE SECURITY PERSONNEL

The primary types of private security personnel are guards, patrols, investigators, armed couriers, central alarm respondents, and consultants.

### Private Security Guards

A common and highly visible type of security officer is the private security guard, who is usually in uniform and is sometimes armed. Premises may be guarded twenty-four hours a day, seven days a week; only during the day; only during the night; or only during peak periods, such as when sporting events are being conducted.

Security guards control access to private property, maintain order on the premises, enforce the rules and regulations of the employer, protect against loss from fire or equipment failure, and help to prevent and/or detect criminal acts on private property, which sometimes involves stopping, questioning, and arresting suspects. The amount of crime-related activity varies depending on the particular establishment being guarded.

Security guards are sometimes also responsible for property control, energy conservation, maintaining sign-in logs, opening and closing, escort service, and emergency response and support during medical, fire, or weather emergencies.

Some security guards are responsible for preventing and/or detecting embezzlement, misappropriation or concealment of merchandise, money, bonds, stocks, notes, or other valuable documents. Some security guards protect individuals rather than premises and property. The rising incidence of executive kidnappings and hostage situations has resulted in a dramatic increase in bodyguard service since the mid-1970s. Likewise, escort services increased in demand in the 1980s.

The Hallcrest Report (Cunningham and Taylor, 1985) states that several major corporations are concerned about protecting their chief corporate executives from terrorism or from kidnapping for ransom. This confirms the statement in the Figgie Report (1981) that 40 percent of executives surveyed were concerned about kidnapping, either of themselves or of their families or business associates. Larger companies may carry corporate executive kidnap/ransom insurance policies or may provide armed bodyguards to protect top executives.

## Private Patrol Officers

Patrol has been called the "backbone" of the public police force because it is the primary means of preventing or detecting criminal activity. Private patrol officers perform the same function. Moving from location to location on foot or in a vehicle, they protect the property of specific employers rather than that of the general public. They are, in essence, an extension of public patrol, because many people do not readily differentiate between the vehicles of public police officers and private patrol officers. In other words, the private security patrol officers may prevent criminal activity while en route to an assigned area.

Security officer on duty at discount store in Harlem, NY.

Security patrols are sometimes also responsible for opening and closing facilities, conducting interior and exterior inspections, checking on facilities and equipment, providing escort service, transporting equipment or documents, and responding to alarms.

Some private patrol officers have one employer who is responsible for an establishment with very large premises requiring patrol. Other private patrol officers work for several employers, moving from place to place, sometimes going inside the premises, sometimes not. Some wealthy neighborhoods may employ a private patrol officer to maintain surveillance of the neighborhood and to routinely check homes and property. Likewise, a group of businesspeople or merchants within a neighborhood or within a shopping center may hire a private officer to patrol their establishments. Many communities have established special patrol service agencies.

## Private Investigators

Popular television series have glamorized the vocation of private investigator (P.I.), but in reality, today criminal investigation is only a small part of a private investigator's work.

Private investigators provide services for a fee as independent contractors. It has been estimated that there are five thousand private investigative agencies in the United States, with approximately two hundred thousand employees.

Private investigators' businesses may be structured as individuals doing business as private contractors, as sole proprietorships, as partnerships, or as corporations. In addition, many businesses and industries have their own internal (proprietary) investigators. Both private and proprietary investigators serve similar functions.

Law firms frequently hire private investigators to assist in preparing for civil and criminal trials. Insurance companies use private investigators to investigate such things as arson, life insurance fraud, large theft claims, workers' compensation fraud, automobile accidents, and product liability. Utilities may hire private investigators for a variety of reasons; for example, the telephone company might hire an investigator to look into obscene or threatening telephone calls, pay-phone burglaries, use of illegal telephone equipment, or long-distance billing frauds.

Most investigations conducted by security personnel concentrate on such matters as background checks for employment, insurance, and credit applications; civil litigation matters on assignment from private attorneys; and investigation of insurance or workers' compensation claims. Frequently investigators are brought in to work undercover to detect employee dishonesty, pilferage, or shoplifting.

## Armed Couriers

Most private security courier services use armored cars, vans, or trucks, but they may use airlines and trains as well. The security officers are uniformed and armed to ensure the protection of money, goods, documents, or people as they are transported from one location to another. The public police seldom become involved with armed courier deliveries

Security officers making a payroll delivery.

unless there is a high probability that a crime will be attempted during the delivery.

Brink's, the largest of the armed courier services, has established a credible service record while it carries billions of dollars a day. According to *Business Week* (February 6, 1964, p. 14):

> To its 5,000 employees, Brink's is simply a transportation company whose main service is protection. Says Vice-President E. A. Jones: "Money to us is nothing more than a crate of eggs or groceries. It's really just cartage."
>
> But money moving also is a deadly serious business. One prankster found out the hard way several years ago when he playfully called out to a passing Brink's messenger: "This is a stickup." The guard promptly shot him. . . . The armored car specialist has been called on to move diamonds, Picasso paintings, the original copy of the Gettysburg Address, 15 tons of rare coins, and special materials for World War II's Manhattan Project—the atomic bomb.

In the twenty-five years since that article was written, Brink's has continued providing valuable services to the public.

## Central Alarm Respondents

Some intrusion detection systems simply sound an alarm when an intrusion is detected, thus relying on an employee or a passerby to notify the police. Other alarm systems are connected directly with police headquarters so the police are automatically notified. However, because the false-alarm rate is greater than 95 percent for many currently used systems, some cities have banned direct connection of alarms to police equipment because so much public effort is expended in responding to these private false alarms. Consequently, private central alarm services, dominated by American District Telegraph (ADT), have become a popular, effective alternative.

According to Mosler's Electronic Systems Division, a central station alarm is:

> A system in which the secured area is directly connected to an alarm panel in a centrally located alarm receiving station via a pair of leased telephone wires. Upon receiving an alarm, the company, which is usually a privately owned organization, will dispatch its guards to the location of the secured area and will also notify the police. Alarm installation of this type can only be U.L.* approved when the protected premises are within ten minutes traveling time from the central office (*Private Security,* 1976, p. 3).

Given the extremely high percentage of false alarms, such a system improves relationships with the police, but it also poses considerable hazard to the alarm respondent; an intruder may still be on the premises and may pose a direct threat to anyone answering the alarm. Chapter 6 presents a detailed discussion of the various alternatives available in alarm systems.

## Consultants

As private security expands and becomes professionalized, the need for expertise on security problems also expands. This expansion has given rise to a variety of specialists who provide consultation in areas such as electronic surveillance; protective lighting, fencing, and barricading; alarm systems; access control; key control; and security training. Other individuals have become experts in polygraph examination and psychological stress evaluation (PSE) and may be used as consultants to private enterprise.

Since polygraph ("lie detector") tests were first submitted as evidence in an Illinois court in 1964, their use in law enforcement and in the private sector has been controversial. Some states prohibit use of the polygraph or PSE for employment screening, but many corporate executives and security directors feel such instruments are valuable for screening.

Using the polygraph for preemployment became strictly regulated through the Employee Polygraph Protection Act (EPPA) signed into law by President Reagan, effective December 1988. This law, according to Bailey et al. (1989, p. 1):

> . . . prohibits the use of all mechanical lie detector tests in the workplace, including polygraphs, psychological stress evaluators, deceptographs, and voice stress analyzers. . . .
>
> EPPA allows for one type of lie detector test—the polygraph—to be used by private sector employers for certain types of pre-employment screening . . . [including] employers whose primary business is the provision of certain types of security services. . . .
>
> Where the particular employer is the United States government or any state or local government, EPPA does not apply. Government employers may use any lie detector test without complying with any of EPPA's procedures or

---

*Underwriter's Laboratory sets standards for various appliances and types of equipment.

restrictions. The FBI, the CIA, firms doing sensitive defense work, and companies who manufacture, distribute, or dispense controlled substances are also exempted.

In addition to doing background checks on employees, sometimes using deception detection instruments, consultants also can provide advice on risk management, loss prevention, and crime prevention systems design and evaluation; architectural liaison; and security ordinance compliance.

## ☐ EQUIPMENT AND PROCEDURES

In addition to security personnel, other security measures include physical controls, such as locks, lighting, alarms, surveillance systems, etc. (discussed in Chapter 6), and procedural controls, such as hiring procedures, access control, accounting and receiving procedures, etc. (discussed in Chapter 7). The entire second section of this book will expand on the equipment and procedures used to achieve security.

## ☐ REGULATION OF PRIVATE SECURITY

Since private security has become "big business," efforts have been made to regulate it. The reasons behind such efforts are fairly obvious (*Private Security*, 1976, Foreword):

> In many large cities, the number of private security personnel is considerably greater than the number of police and law enforcement personnel. Of those individuals involved in private security, some are uniformed, some are not; some carry guns, some are unarmed; some guard nuclear energy installations, some guard golf courses; some are trained, some are not; some have college degrees, some are virtually uneducated.

Although criticism of increased government regulation of business and industry has generally heightened, many favor regulation of private security because of the preceding disparities, and because of the nature of the field itself. First, private security services are important and expensive. Consumers should be assured that they are receiving the services they are paying for. Second, private security personnel come into daily contact with the public as authority figures. Control of these contacts must be ensured. Third, many private security personnel carry weapons that can kill or inflict great bodily harm. Use of such weapons must also be controlled.

The Task Force Report provides examples of what has happened without regulation (*Private Security*, 1976):

> A tragic example of lax supervision of private police occurred here in July. Sidney Bennett Jr. was hired as a private security guard and given a gun. His employer, National Industrial Security Corp., did not know Bennett had confessed to the 1970 sniper killing of two Chicago police officers but was freed when he was found mentally incompetent.
>
> Three days after he was hired, Bennett was accused of fatally shooting a 19-year-old youth without provocation (while on duty) and was indicted for murder (Chicago *Sun-Times*, Sept. 28, 1975).

In October, it [California Bureau of Correction and Investigative Services] revoked the licenses of 41 persons engaged in security guard work. Of these 28 related to robbery or burglary on the part of the licensee, two were for other forms of dishonesty, and 11 involved improper use of weapons including two cases where deaths resulted (Pasadena *Star-News,* November 26, 1975).

In spite of such findings, licensing and regulation of security personnel is a highly controversial issue. With the national emphasis on *de*regulation, care must be taken not to be overly restrictive. For example, the governor of Ohio vetoed a bill that mandated 120 hours of training for Ohio security officers. The added paperwork and excessive cost of such training was felt to be prohibitive.

After much deliberation by numerous experts in law enforcement and private security, the Task Force established recommended standards for regulating private security (*Private Security,* 1976, pp. 282–306).

Regulation of the private security industry should be performed at the *state level** through a regulatory board and staff.† Regulation can be achieved by requiring licensing of contract security services and by requiring registering of all persons specifically performing private security functions.

The Task Force recommended that the regulatory board consist of representatives from private security, local police departments, consumers, and the general public. Various departments are responsible for regulating private security at the state level, as indicated in Table 2-4.

These state regulatory bodies should establish licensing and registering requirements and a mechanism for resolving consumer complaints. To fulfill their responsibilities, they should have access to all criminal history record information to check applicants for licenses and registrations.

Basically, the Task Force favors *licensing* private security businesses and *registering* "every person who is employed to perform the functions of an investigator or detective, guard or watchman, armored car personnel or armed courier, alarm system installer or servicer, or alarm respondent . . ." (Standard 11.1).

Such a procedure would be costly given the vast number of individuals involved; hence the controversy remains. Whether the benefits might justify the cost by eliminating undesirable personnel and professionalizing the private security field has not yet been resolved. The majority of states have legislation requiring licensing of guards, investigators, and alarm systems and setting forth the major qualifications for the license, as summarized in Table 2–5.

## ☐ REGULATION OF PRIVATE INVESTIGATORS

Most states and some cities provide some form of government regulation of the formation and operation of private investigation agencies, but

---

*Standard 9.1.
†Standard 9.2.

**Table 2–4 State regulatory bodies.** This chart lists the regulatory bodies within each state charged with licensing and regulating the private security industry. One should also be aware of changing county and city regulatory agencies and should watch carefully for these.

| State | Agency |
|---|---|
| Alabama | — |
| Alaska | State Troopers |
| Arizona | Department of Public Safety |
| Arkansas | Board of Private Investigators and P.S.* Agencies |
| California | Department of Consumer Affairs |
| Colorado | — |
| Connecticut | Department of Public Safety |
| Delaware | Board of Examiners, State Police |
| District of Columbia | Metropolitan Police Department |
| Florida | Department of State |
| Georgia | Board of Private Investigators and Private Securities Agencies |
| Hawaii | Board of Private Detectives and Guards |
| Idaho | — |
| Illinois | Department of Registration |
| Indiana | State Police |
| Iowa | Department of Public Safety |
| Kansas | — |
| Kentucky | — |
| Louisiana | — |
| Maine | State Police |
| Maryland | State Police |
| Massachusetts | Department of Public Safety |
| Michigan | State Police |
| Minnesota | Board of Private Detectives and Protective Agent Services |

*P.S. = Private Security

only a few states have enacted laws controlling the investigative employees of private contract agencies. In addition, state laws regulating security, private investigators, and related enterprises vary in content and application.

Most states that regulate the private investigative business require the licensing of individuals, partnerships, and corporations providing private contract investigative services, and most have established a variety of standards to obtain a license.

The cost of such a license and the provisions for renewing it also vary from state to state.

**Table 2–4** *continued*

| State | Agency |
|---|---|
| Mississippi | — |
| Missouri | — |
| Montana | Department of P.S., Patrol, and Private Investigators |
| Nebraska | — |
| Nevada | Private Investigators Licensing Board |
| New Hampshire | Department of Safety |
| New Jersey | State Police |
| New Mexico | Bureau of Private Investigators |
| New York | Department of State |
| North Carolina | Private Protective Services Board |
| North Dakota | Department of State |
| Ohio | Department of Commerce |
| Oklahoma | — |
| Oregon | — |
| Pennsylvania | — |
| Rhode Island | — |
| South Carolina | Law Enforcement Division |
| South Dakota | — |
| Tennessee | — |
| Texas | Board of Private Investigators and Private Securities Agencies |
| Utah | Department of Public Safety |
| Vermont | Board of Private Detective Licensing |
| Virginia | Department of Commerce |
| Washington | — |
| West Virginia | Secretary of State |
| Wisconsin | Department of Regulations and Licensing |
| Wyoming | — |

*P.S. = Private Security

In addition to state and city statutes and regulations, federal laws such as the Fair Credit Reporting Act affect private investigators and their activities. Although the act was passed originally to regulate and control mercantile credit, insurance, employment, and investment agencies, recent interpretations of this law have resulted in its being applied to many facets of the private investigative function. Requirements for a private investigator's license vary from state to state, with some states being much more restrictive than others.

Requirements for a private investigator's license usually include state residency, U.S. citizenship, training and/or work experience as a police officer or investigator, a clean arrest record, the passing of a background investigation, and the passing of an oral or written examination.

# Table 2–5 States requiring licensure of guard, investigator, and alarm systems and major qualifications.

| | AK[A] | AZ | AR | CA | CT | DE | FL | GA | HI | IL | IN | IA | KS | KY | ME | MD | MA | MI | MN |
|---|---|---|---|---|---|---|---|---|---|---|---|---|---|---|---|---|---|---|---|
| *Areas Regulated* | | | | | | | | | | | | | | | | | | | |
| Contract guards | X | X | X | X | X | X | X | X | X | X | X | X | | | X | X | X | X | X |
| Proprietary guards | | | | | | | | X | | | | | | | | | | | |
| Private investigators | | X | X | X | X | X | X | X | X | X | X | X | X | | X | X | X | X | X |
| Alarm system contractors | | | X | X | | | | | | | | | | | | | | X | |
| *Licensure Requirements* | | | | | | | | | | | | | | | | | | | |
| No felony convictions | | X | X | X | X | | | B | | B | X | X | X | X | X | | X | X | X |
| US citizenship | | C | X | | X | | | X | X | X | X | X | X | X | C | X | X | X | |
| Written examination | | | X | X | | | | X | X | X | | X | X | | | | | | |
| Minimum age | | D | E | D | G | G | D | D | F | E | E | D | E | E | D | G | G | G | D |
| Experience | | X | X | X | X | X | | X | X | H | X | D | E | | X | X | X | X | X |
| Education | | | X | | | | | | X | | | | | | | | | X | |
| Training | X | X | X | X | X | X | X | X | X | X | X | X | X | | | | X | X | X |
| Licensing period | X | X | X | X | X | X | X | X | X | X | X | X | X | E | X | X | X | X | X |
| *Revocation Grounds* | | | | | | | | | | | | | | | | | | | |
| Violations of license law | X | X | X | X | X | X | X | X | | X | X | X | X | | X | | X | X | X |
| False statements | X | X | X | X | X | | X | X | | X | X | X | X | | X | X | | X | X |
| Felony conviction | X | X | X | X | X | | X | X | | X | | X | | | | | | X | |
| Dishonesty/fraud | X | | X | X | X | | X | X | | X | X | X | | | X | | | X | |
| Impersonating police officer | X | X | X | X | | | | X | | | X | | | | X | | | X | |
| Insolvent bond | | | | | | | X | X | | X | X | X | X | | | | | | |
| Release confidential info | | | | X | X | | | | | X | | X | | | | | | X | |
| Fail to render service | | X | | X | | | | X | | | | | | | | | | | |
| Violate court order | | X | | X | | | X | X | | | | | | | | | | | |
| False advertising | | X | | X | | | | | | X | | | | | X | | | | |
| Incompetency | | | X | | X | X | X | | | X | | | | | | | | X | |
| *Miscellaneous* | | | | | | | | | | | | | | | | | | | |
| Application fee | X | X | X | X | X | X | X | X | X | X | X | X | X | X | X | X | X | | X |
| Fingerprints/photograph | X | X | X | X | X | X | X | X | X | X | X | X | X | X | | X | | X | X |
| Fingerprint check | X | | X | | | X | X | X | | | | | | | | | | | X |
| Personal references | X | | | | | | | | X | | | X | X | | X | X | X | X | X |
| Criminal record | X | X | X | X | X | X | X | X | | | | X | X | | X | X | X | X | X |

# Table 2–5 continued

| | MT | NE | NV | NH | NJ | NM | NY | NC | ND | OH | PA | RI | SC | TX | UT | VT | VA | WV | WI |
|---|---|---|---|---|---|---|---|---|---|---|---|---|---|---|---|---|---|---|---|
| *Areas Regulated* | | | | | | | | | | | | | | | | | | | |
| Contract guards | X | | X | X | X | X | X | X | X | X | X | | X | X | X | X | X | X | X |
| Propriety guards | | X | | | | | | | | | | | X | | | | | | |
| Private investigators | X | X | X | | X | X | X | X | X | X | X | | X | X | | X | X | X | X |
| Alarm system contractors | X | | | | | | | X | | | | X | | X | | | | | X |
| *Licensure Requirements* | | | | | | | | | | | | | | | | | | | |
| No Felony convictions | B | B | X | | X | X | X | B | X | B | X | B | X | X | X | | B | X | B |
| US citizenship | X | X | X | | X | X | X | X | | X | X | | X | X | X | | | X | |
| Written examination | X | | X | | | X | X | X | X | X | | X | X | X | X | X | | | X |
| Minimum age | D | E | E | | G | D | | D | | | G | D | D | D | D | D | D | D | D |
| Experience | X | | X | | X | X | X | X | | X | X | X | X | X | X | X | X | X | X |
| *Revocation Grounds* | | | | | | | | | | | | | | | | | | | |
| Violation of license law | X | X | X | | X | X | X | X | X | X | X | X | X | X | X | X | X | X | X |
| False statements | X | | X | | X | X | X | X | X | | | X | X | X | X | | X | X | X |
| Felony conviction | X | | X | | | X | | X | | X | | X | X | X | | | | X | X |
| Dishonesty/fraud | X | X | X | | X | X | X | | X | | X | | X | | X | | X | X | |
| Impersonating police officer | X | | X | | | | | X | X | | | X | X | X | X | | X | X | X |
| Insolvent bond | | | | | X | | | X | | X | | X | | | | | | | |
| Release confidential info | | | | | X | | | X | | | | | | X | | | | | |
| Fail to render service | X | X | X | | | X | | X | | | | | X | | X | X | | X | X |
| Violate court order | X | | X | | | X | | X | | | | | X | | | | | X | |
| False advertising | | | | | | | | X | | | | | X | X | | | | | |
| Incompetency | | | | | X | | X | X | | | X | | X | X | | | | | |
| *Miscellaneous* | | | | | | | | | | | | | | | | | | | |
| Application fee | X | X | X | | | X | X | X | X | X | X | X | X | X | X | X | X | X | X |
| Fingerprints/photograph | X | X | X | | X | X | X | | X | X | X | X | X | X | | X | X | X | X |
| Fingerprint check | | | | | | | X | | | | X | X | | | | X | X | X | |
| Personal references | X | X | X | | X | X | X | X | | X | X | X | X | | X | X | | X | |
| Criminal record | X | | | | | | X | X | | | X | X | X | X | | X | | | |

A Standard used by the US Postal Department for abbreviation of states.
B Time limit exemption or other qualifying expression.
C 18 years old.
D 21 years old.
E 22 years old.
F 25 years old.
G Education allowable substitute for experience.

SOURCE: Security Management, January 1984, pp. 40–41. Reprinted by permission.

Usually applicants must meet all or most of the preceding requirements to obtain a license. In addition, applicants must usually pay an initial license fee and must obtain a specific amount and type of insurance.

## □ CODE OF ETHICS

Even without legislative guidance from the state level, private security directors can set their own standards for conduct and service to increase the professionalism of the field. Both those hired and those hiring should adhere to a code of ethics similar to that guiding professionals. In fact, a self-enforcing code of ethics is required to meet the definition of a true profession.

A code of ethics sets forth self-enforcing moral and professional guidelines for behavior in a given field.

Just as physicians take the Hippocratic Oath, private security personnel and management should agree on guidelines to achieve the desired goals. Codes of ethics have been developed and adopted by numerous organizations, including the American Society for Industrial Security, the Council of International Investigators, the National Council of Investigation and Security Services, the National Burglar and Fire Alarm Association, Inc., the World Association of Detectives, Inc., and the Law Enforcement/Private Security Relationship Committee of the Private Security Advisory Council.

Private security directors may want to obtain copies of several of these codes of ethics and draw from them those guidelines that seem most relevant to their particular situations. The code of ethics of the Law Enforcement/Private Security Relationship Committee in Figure 2−1 is offered as one example of a set of guidelines that might be *adapted* for use (Goal 3.1 *Private Security,* 1976, p. 124).

## □ CERTIFIED PROTECTION PROFESSIONAL (CPP)

In 1977 the American Society for Industrial Security (ASIS) organized the Professional Certification Board to grant a designation of *Certified Protection Professional (CPP)* to individuals meeting specific criteria of professional protection knowledge and conduct.

The CPP program gives special recognition to those security practitioners who have met certain prescribed standards of performance, knowledge, and conduct and who have demonstrated a high level of competency by improving the practices of security management. It also encourages security professionals to continue to develop professionally by requiring continuing education to renew the certification.

The program is administered by a board appointed by the president of the ASIS. Applicants must meet specific experience and education requirements to be eligible to take the written exam.

> ## Code of Ethics for Private Security Employees
>
> In recognition of the significant contribution of private security to crime prevention and reduction, as a private security employee, I pledge:
>
> I To accept the responsibilities and fulfill the obligations of my role: protecting life and property; preventing and reducing crimes against my employer's business, or other organizations and institutions to which I am assigned; upholding the law; and respecting the constitutional rights of all persons.
>
> II To conduct myself with honesty and integrity and to adhere to the highest moral principles in the performance of my security duties.
>
> III To be faithful, diligent, and dependable in discharging my duties, and to uphold at all times the laws, policies, and procedures that protect the rights of others.
>
> IV To observe the precepts of truth, accuracy and prudence, without allowing personal feelings, prejudices, animosities or friendships to influence my judgements.
>
> V To report to my superiors, without hesitation, any violation of the law or of my employer's or client's regulations.
>
> VI To respect and protect the confidential and privileged information of my employer or client beyond the term of my employment, except where their interests are contrary to law or this Code of Ethics.
>
> VII To cooperate with all recognized and responsible law enforcement and government agencies in matters within their jurisdiction.
>
> VIII To accept no compensation, commission, gratuity, or other advantage without the knowledge and consent of my employer.
>
> IX To conduct myself professionally at all times, and to perform my duties in a manner that reflects credit upon myself, my employer, and private security.
>
> X To strive continually to improve my performance by seeking training and educational opportunities that will better prepare me for my private security duties.

Figure 2–1 Code of ethics (officers).

A Certified Protection Professional (CPP) has met specific experience and educational requirements and has passed a common knowledge examination as well as an examination in four speciality subjects.

## Education and Experience

To be eligible to take the CPP examination, candidates must meet the following basic standards:

> ➤ No degree     and     10 years' experience
> ➤ Associate degree     and     8 years' experience
> ➤ Bachelor's degree     and     5 years' experience
> ➤ Master's degree     and     4 years' experience
> ➤ Doctoral degree     and     3 years' experience

At least half the experience must be in "responsible charge" of a security function.

## Behavior and Endorsement

In addition to meeting the experience and education requirements, candidates must affirm adherence to the CPP Code of Professional Responsibility and be endorsed by a person already certified as a Protection Professional. If these basic requirements are met, the person is eligible to take the written examination.

## The Examination

The CPP examination is a one-day objective, multiple-choice test consisting of two parts, a Mandatory test administered in the morning and Speciality Subjects administered in the afternoon. According to the ASIS (1989, p. 4): "The Mandatory or Common Knowledge examination contains 200 questions covering basic knowledge applicable in the field of security and loss prevention. The speciality examinations test knowledge through four optional 25-question examinations, chosen by the candidate from fifteen subjects on security and loss prevention practice in special areas." The Mandatory and Speciality Subject areas are:

➤ **Mandatory Subjects**
➤ Emergency Planning
➤ Investigations
➤ Legal Aspects
➤ Personnel Security
➤ Physical Security
➤ Protection of Sensitive Information
➤ Security Management
➤ Substance Abuse
➤ Loss Prevention
➤ Liaison

➤ **Speciality Subjects**
➤ Banking & Financial Institutions
➤ Computer Security
➤ Credit Card Security
➤ Department of Defense Industrial Security Program Requirements
➤ Educational Institutions Security
➤ Fire Resources Management
➤ Health Care Institutions Security
➤ Manufacturing Security
➤ Nuclear Power Security
➤ Public Utility Security
➤ Restaurant & Lodging Security
➤ Retail Security
➤ Transportation & Cargo Security
➤ Oil & Gas Industrial Security
➤ Telephone & Telecommunications Security

After successfully passing the examination, a person is certified a CPP, which is valid for three years. Recertification is contingent on accumulating nine professional credits. The recertification program is designed to encourage individuals to keep current in new security developments and active in security programs.

The ASIS (1989, p. 1) says: "The Certification of protection professionals benefits the individual practitioner, the profession, the employer and the public. The evidence of competency in security protection furnished by certification will improve the individual, raise the general level of competency in the security profession, promote high standards of professional conduct, and provide evidence to management of professional performance capability."

The ASIS also notes that many companies are now requiring applicants for employment to have a CPP and suggests that this trend will continue as the program becomes more widely known.

## ☐ PRIVATE SECURITY AND MANAGEMENT

Effective management practices are integral to private security, whether it is proprietary or contractual, and regulated by the state or not. It is management that decides what money is spent where, what rules and procedures are established *and* enforced, and who has specific responsibilities for given assignments. Finally, it is management that is responsible for ensuring security. If an organization has a security problem, it has a management problem.

---

Private security should be a priority concern of top-level management of businesses, industries, and institutions.

---

Those in charge of security must be given the necessary authority to fulfill their responsibilities and must have access to top-level management. Lines of communication must be kept open. Planning, evaluating, and updating must be continuous to ensure the full benefits of private security equipment, procedures, and personnel.

The relationship of management to private security is aptly expressed by John P. Sopsic, previous manager of security services for Oscar Mayer & Company (1977, p. 66):*

> As business failures rise, profits shrink, government regulation increases and anti-big business feelings are generated by pressure/interest groups, management quarterbacks are deliberately searching for game plans to alleviate and minimize the anxiety and frustrations indigenous to threat and risk management. Rising expenditures in the security field in the range of many billions of dollars each year corroborate this phenomena. . . .
>
> The functional catalyst for developing and maintaining adequate security programs largely lies with the more professional security manager. Perhaps we may suggest an alternative definition of the security function, the antithesis of traditional concepts. The security function must be a sophisticated, dynamic, flexible, responsive and integrated function of upper management. In addition to protecting the people, property, product, assets and good name of the corporation, the security manager's program must possess the capacity to provide the decision-making leadership with problem solving,

---

*© 1977 *Security Management,* American Society for Industrial Security. Reprinted by permission.

trouble shooting and threat identification information vital to safety, security and profitability. . . .

If the security function is accepted as an artful and valid management process which is involved with and complements every other aspect of the management process, positive change is inevitable.

This is the focus of the next chapter.

## SUMMARY

**P**rivate security is a profit-oriented industry that provides personnel, equipment, and/or procedures to *prevent* losses caused by human error, emergencies, disasters, or criminal actions. The primary function of private security personnel is to prevent loss by (1) gathering information, (2) controlling access to and maintaining order on private property, and (3) protecting persons and property against crime and disaster.

Security services may be proprietary or contracted. Proprietary services are in-house, directly hired and controlled by the company or organization. In contrast, contract services are outside firms or individuals who provide security services for a fee. Both arrangements present advantages and disadvantages to the security manager. The primary types of private security personnel are guards, patrols, investigators, armed couriers, central alarm respondents, and consultants.

Although not all agree, the Task Force recommends that private security be regulated at the state level through a regulatory board and staff that requires licensing of contract security services and registration of all persons specifically performing private security functions.

Most states that regulate the private investigative business require the licensing of individuals, partnerships, and corporations providing private contract investigative services, and most have established a variety of standards to obtain a license. Requirements usually include state residency, U.S. citizenship, training and/or work experience as a police officer or investigator, a clean arrest record, the passing of a background investigation, and the passing of an oral or written examination.

With or without such state regulation, to be considered a profession, private security should develop a code of ethics that sets forth self-enforcing moral and professional guidelines for behavior in the field of private security. One important step toward the professionalization of private security is the establishment of a Certified Protection Professional program by the American Society for Industrial Security. A Certified Protection Professional (CPP) has met specific experience and educational requirements and has passed a common knowledge examination as well as an examination in four speciality subjects.

Private security should be a priority concern of top-level management of businesses, industries, and institutions.

## APPLICATION

1) Reread the code of ethics (Figure 2–1). Does it apply equally to proprietary and contractual private security officers? If not, how might it be changed?

**2)** Discuss with a friend what his or her image of a private security officer is, and what rights and restrictions are normally present in carrying out the responsibilities of a private security officer. Then arrange for a similar discussion with a person in public law enforcement and one in private security.

## DISCUSSION QUESTIONS

**1)** Is licensing of private security agencies and/or officers an advantage or disadvantage to private security agencies?

**2)** Why is supervision so important to a private security agency?

**3)** With or without specific regulations of private security officers in some states, what is the best way to ensure the maximum performance of these officers?

**4)** Do you think private investigators enjoy more status than individuals in the private security work force?

**5)** Consult your Yellow Pages. What security listings are given? Is there a listing for *polygraph services? Lie detection services? Surveillance?*

## REFERENCES

American Society for Industrial Security (ASIS). Certification procedure and examination information for Certified Protection Professional: CPP. Arlington, VA: American Society for Industrial Security, 1989.

Bailey, F. Lee; Zuckerman, Roger E.; and Pierce, Kenneth R. *The employee polygraph protection act: A manual for polygraph examiners and employers.* Severna Park, MD: American Polygraph Association, 1989.

Cunningham, William C.; Strauchs, John J.; and Van Meter, Clifford W. *Private security trends, 1970 to 2000: The Hallcrest report II.* Stoneham, MA: Butterworth-Heinemann, 1990.

Cunningham, W. C. and Taylor, T. H. *The Hallcrest report: Private security and police in America.* Portland, OR: Chancellor Press, 1985.

*The Figgie report on fear of crime: Part II. The corporate response to fear of crime.* Willoughby, OH: The Figgie Corporation, 1981.

How Brink's guards its profits, too. *Business week.* February 6, 1964, pp. 14–15, 58.

Kakalik, J. S. and Wildhorn, S. *The private police.* New York: Crane Russak, 1977 (The Rand Corporation).

Paine, D. *Basic principles of industrial security.* Madison, WI: Oak Security Publications, 1972.

*Private security.* Report of the Task Force on Private Security, National Advisory Committee on Criminal Justice Standards and Goals. Washington, DC: U.S. Government Printing Office, 1976.

Sopsic, J. P. Security in its proper management perspective. *Security management,* May 1977, p. 66.

U.S. Army, FM 1930. *Physical security,* March 1979, pp. 1–7, 293–98.

## Chapter Three

# The Private Security Professional

➤ Where in an establishment's organizational structure private security fits?

➤ What roles a security director fills?

➤ What administrative, investigative, and managerial responsibilities a security director has?

➤ What the primary goal of a private security system is?

➤ What a SMART objective is?

➤ How employees and management can be educated about the security/safety system?

➤ What basic principles make learning more effective?

➤ What positive and negative reinforcements can enhance educational and training efforts?

➤ What the basic investigative skills are?

➤ What areas security directors are responsible for investigating?

➤ What theories of management have been proposed by Maslow, Herzberg, McGregor, Likert, Argyris, Blake-Mouton, and Skinner?

➤ What the managerial responsibilities of security directors are?

➤ What preemployment qualifications should be met by private security personnel?

➤ What constitutes adequate preemployment screening?

➤ How effective job performance of security officers can be increased?

➤ When training of security officers should occur?

➤ What progressive discipline is?

## ☐ INTRODUCTION

"Security," states Wainwright (1984, p. 295), "is the most exciting profession in industry today. The practitioner is required to focus on the entire spectrum of corporate activity as well as on the environment in which corporations operate. While both conflict and opportunity can be found in the security field, it is safe to say there is more opportunity than conflict. Security professionals must not only capitalize on the opportunities of today, but also identify, understand, and manage the opportunities that will arise in the future."

The security director is an executive with the responsibility to protect corporate/organizational assets, to predict where they are at risk, and to take steps to reduce these risks.

Security directors must keep within budget. They must also ensure that the organization has the most qualified and efficient services at the best price. Whether the services are proprietary or contracted, staff must meet the highest standards.

Directors must also be able to deal in liability-prone areas in ways that are not only correct, but also documented and defensible. If they fail to do so, insurance may rise, legal fees may escalate, and the organization's reputation may be damaged.

Security directors must also be aware of what is going on within the organization—who has the power, who gets things done, and who the troublemakers are. They should avoid getting involved in the politics of the organization, but they must, nonetheless, be politically aware of what is happening.

The position of security director has taken on increased importance in the past decade. Some reasons for this are:

➤ The increasing size of both contractual and proprietary security organizations.

> The demand for specialization, such as patrol officers, investigators, equipment installers, computer technicians, consultants, and the need to coordinate their efforts.
> The growing emphasis on private security because of fiscal problems in many cities.

The net effect of these changes has been to place even greater emphasis on the intangible elements of management, particularly the ability to work with and through people. Although *management* is a commonly used term with relatively broad agreement on its meaning, managers may perhaps be seen most appropriately as those who have the responsibility of getting things done through other people. This may happen through a three-tier system consisting of the manager, supervisors, and on-line workers. In small organizations the same person may function in all three capacities.

## □ RESPONSIBILITIES OF THE SECURITY DIRECTOR

Sopsic (1977, p. 66) summarized the function served by today's private security professional:

> The security manager of today and tomorrow must possess those qualities and characteristics of an upper management executive with the ability to relate to all levels of employees. He must bridge the gap between law enforcement and functional security methodology yet complement the organizational image and corporate profile.
>
> The time for molding a new concept of the security function and for building acceptance of the security profession will never be better. It is, however, the emphasis on program management, a systematic approach to problem solving, that security and safety management must embrace.

Whether proprietary or contractual, security managers have a vast array of responsibilities to meet.

> Develop security guidelines and standards.
> Develop short-range and long-range plans.
> Develop and periodically review goals and objectives, policies and procedures.
> Develop emergency contingency plans.
> Conduct risk analysis.
> Establish an annual budget.
> Develop job descriptions and hiring guidelines.
> Hire and train security personnel.
> Evaluate security personnel.
> Conduct investigations.
> Conduct inspections, audits, and evaluations.
> Procure needed security hardware, install and inspect regularly.
> Educate all members of the business/organization about the security program and their responsibilities in it.
> Attend designated meetings.
> Prepare required reports.

➤ Establish working relationships with other departments.
➤ Provide liaison with other managers, the CEO, union representatives, auditors, personnel department, engineers and architects, city inspectors, local police, the fire department, health officials, insurance companies, and the press, as needed.

# □ THE PLACE OF PRIVATE SECURITY IN THE ORGANIZATIONAL STRUCTURE

In many establishments the security function evolved from simple reliance on locks and alarms to a complex, comprehensive system that grew primarily in response to losses that occurred. This reactive response often resulted in a disorganized security approach rather than in an integrated service department. The need for a security system as an integral component of the organizational structure has been recognized by growing numbers of establishments. Usually such departments are headed by a specialist in private security.

Heads of security departments have varying titles, including Chief of Security, Director of Security, Executive Security Officer, Security Director, Security Manager, and Security Supervisor. Whatever their title, to be effective, security directors must have a position of authority within the organization, and they must have the support of top management. Whether this is the president or a vice president will depend on the availability of these executives. Although ideally the security director would report directly to the president, in large organizations the president may be too busy to effectively communicate security needs and concerns to the security director. In such organizations, a vice president may be designated the responsibility and may, in fact, do a better job than the president.

Security directors must be given authority and have access to top management. They must communicate with and coordinate the security efforts of all departments within the organization.

As noted by Gallati (1983, p. 46):

The enormous importance of appropriate role and status for the security manager is highlighted by the fact that the morale of all the security manager's subordinates will undoubtedly be directly affected, constructively or destructively, by the status accorded their superior. Also the quality, cost-effectiveness, and ultimate success of the security operation, and perhaps, the success of the company itself, will depend upon the role and status accorded to the security manager.

If security is to be effective, the cooperation of all departments is essential. This can best be accomplished by private security directors who are not only knowledgeable in their field, but also innovative; who can deal forcefully yet tactfully, objectively yet imaginatively, flexibly yet systematically with people and with security problems. Security directors must establish rapport with top management and with other departments, enlisting their cooperation by helping each meet their own objectives. A positive attitude toward the budgetary and personnel problems of each department helps foster such rapport.

Because private security is a rapidly changing field, it is important to communicate with others in the field, to read professional journals, to join professional associations, and to maintain outside contacts with other private security professionals.

Security directors must also understand and function not only within the formal structure depicted in the corporate organizational chart, but also within the informal organization that exists in any establishment.

A security director's primary roles are those of loss prevention specialist, administrator, investigator, and manager.

## □ LOSS PREVENTION SPECIALIST RESPONSIBILITIES

The appropriate physical and procedural controls discussed throughout this book are selected by security directors in conjunction with top management. Because no individual security director can be knowledgeable in every aspect of private security, and because the expenditures involved are sometimes large, consultants are often used in such areas as electronic or audio surveillance, protective lighting, protective fencing, alarm systems, locking systems, master keying and key control, and security training. As private security becomes more specialized, use of security consultants is likely to increase.

Once the appropriate physical and procedural controls have been established, security directors delegate responsibility for maintaining the controls to each department and maintain liaison with each department to ensure that the controls are properly used. The loss prevention responsibility is the focus of Chapter 4 and Sections Two and Three.

## □ ADMINISTRATIVE RESPONSIBILITIES

Security directors are responsible for security goals; policies, procedures, and daily orders; financial controls and budgets; educational programs; and the image of security within the organization.

### Establishing Goals

Management's philosophy and the desired overall atmosphere greatly influence the security goals that are established. Some managements strive for a very open environment; others, for a very rigid one. Security goals are easier to set if a proper balance is maintained between openness and rigidity.

$\mathsf{T}$he ultimate goal of private security is loss prevention—resulting in maximum return on investment.

As emphasized throughout this book, security measures are aimed at deterring crime, reducing risks, and making the establishment less attractive to would-be criminals. Different establishments obviously have different needs that must be discussed with top management before specific security goals can be established.

The goals should be measurable—for example, reducing shrinkage by a certain percent, or eliminating a certain number of risks identified during a security survey. Once the goals are stated, specific steps to accomplish the goals can be listed, ranked in order of priority, and set into a time frame.

According to Blanchard (1988, p. 14), SMART objectives can ensure that goals are met.

$\mathsf{S}$MART objectives are:

➤ **S**pecific.   ➤ **R**elevant.
➤ **M**easurable.   ➤ **T**rackable.
➤ **A**ttainable.

To establish an objective of eliminating *all* accidents on the job is probably not realistic. To establish an objective of reducing accidents by 50 percent might be.

## Establishing Policies, Procedures, and Daily Orders

Managers also use three kinds of instructions: policies, procedures, and daily orders.

*Policies* are general guidelines or underlying philosophies of the organization. They help ensure that an organization runs efficiently and effectively and meets its goals and objectives. They are the basic rules of the organization and are seldom changed without a basic change in organizational philosophy. For example: All visitors must check in at the reception area.

*Procedures* are the general instructions detailing how employees are to conduct various aspects of their job. Most procedures are aimed at achieving a reasonable, acceptable level of security in as unobtrusive and cost-effective way as possible. For example: When visitors check in at the reception area, they will sign in, including who they are representing, who they are visiting, and the time. They will be given a badge. The person they are visiting will be called to escort them to his or her office. Visitors will be instructed to return the badge and sign out at the conclusion of the visit.

*Daily orders* are temporary instructions or informational items. They are usually dated and last for only a few days. For example: A list may be provided to the receptionist indicating specific individuals who may be allowed to go directly to the person they are visiting without an escort on a specific day or days.

## Establishing Financial Controls and Budgets

One of the most difficult administrative responsibilities is establishing a budget, including costs of equipment, equipment maintenance, and security personnel. Cost for security personnel should be carefully considered. Cohen (1980, p. 18) notes the importance of paying a reasonable wage:

> Given that security involves both contact with the public and the protection of assets, a company may want a security officer who looks like Paul Newman and has the law enforcement background of J. Edgar Hoover. But if they are willing to pay only low wages, they are more likely to get a security officer who looks like J. Edgar Hoover and has the law enforcement background of Paul Newman.
>
> A company, in giving the keys of their facilities to a security officer, should be realistic about the calibre of that individual, determined in part by wages paid to that individual. Every manager should ask himself if he is remiss in leaving his assets in the hands of low paid personnel.

Ideally, security directors are allowed to prepare their own budgets for management's consideration. Justifying expenses for security is extremely difficult if results cannot be proven. Ironically, if security efforts are effective, nothing happens. This may lead top management to the erroneous conclusion that security efforts are no longer critical. Baseline data illustrating what existed before specific security measures were instituted will help to justify security expenses.

Security directors must also be realistic in their budget preparations. Security is one department among many, all vying for limited resources. Priorities must be set, because everything cannot be accomplished at once. Rather, an effective security system is built logically and systematically as resources become available.

## Establishing Educational Programs

People are many companies' most important assets, but they also can be great threats to the companies' other assets. Educational programs to promote safety, to implement security procedures, and to reduce losses from internal theft are critical to an effective security system.

A security system is not established or operated in a vacuum. It requires the informed cooperation of management and all employees. Security directors are often directly or indirectly involved in such education. Sometimes they are given the responsibility to educate personnel on security equipment and procedures. At other times, especially in large companies, training departments are responsible for educating employees. Even in such instances, however, security directors may provide valuable assistance.

Education can enhance the image of private security by showing management and employees that the primary function of security is to ensure a safe place to work and to protect the company's assets so all can benefit. Losses from internal or external theft make raises and/or other benefits less likely. Safety programs can serve a positive public relations function as well. A cardio-pulmonary resuscitation (CRP) program, for example, can make employees feel secure and prepared. Such a program can make them feel they are of value to the company and to one another. If someone does have a heart attack, those in the best position to help will be prepared.

Visitors and the public can also be educated as restrictions and safety procedures to be followed are explained. Effective educational programs can change the image that some people have of security officers from negative to positive.

Personnel can be educated about the security/safety system through posters, signs, manuals, training sessions, drills, and the suggestions and examples of security officers.

Signs and posters can be an effective educational tool and can also heighten awareness. Although permanent signs are cost-effective, they lose their impact after a time; therefore, they should be used only to give directions rather than to educate. Educational posters and displays should be bright, attractive, and changed frequently.

Training manuals are helpful because management is forced to put the procedures into writing, which usually requires careful consideration of what is important. Although preparing a security/safety manual is a good idea, it is *not* sufficient by itself. Employees may not read it; they may not understand it; not wanting to appear ignorant, they may not ask questions or ask for clarification. The manual might also be simply put away and forgotten. Another hazard inherent in training manuals is that frequently they are not kept current.

Training programs or workshops are excellent means of educating. However, it is often hard to get the employees together at one time. In addition, turnover may leave some employees without needed training until the next training session is conducted.

## Employee Awareness Programs

The Department of Defense is a leader in mandatory security awareness programs to safeguard national energy and industrial secrets. Security managers in other areas should follow this lead, using such mechanisms as videotapes, newsletters, posters, and safety/crime prevention activities to accomplish the following:

➤ Explain important security programs and help gain their acceptance.
➤ Stimulate employees to be aware of security measures directly in their control.
➤ Give the security department the additional eyes and ears needed to combat crime.
➤ Help reduce problems in high-crime areas such as computer rooms, parking areas, storage rooms, or docks.

Information about "intellectual property" and property information security to preserve trade secrets should be an integral part of a security awareness program.

## Basic Principles of Learning

Whether the educational efforts are formal or informal, some basic principles of learning can make the education more effective.

Learning is more effective if it is:

► Practical.
► Presented in short segments.
► Clearly explained by examples or demonstrations.

► Practiced and evaluated.
► Reinforced.
► Periodically reviewed.

**BE PRACTICAL** Training should be job related or of personal importance. Employees do not need to know how bombs are made, but they should know what to do if they come across a suspicious object or receive a bomb threat call. They do not need to know about the fire triangle, but they should know what they can do to prevent fire and, should fire occur, what procedures to follow.

**KEEP IT SHORT** A three-day (15-hour) seminar on security and safety is less likely to be effective than ten $1\frac{1}{2}$-hour sessions or fifteen 1-hour sessions. People can absorb only so much information at once. Establish priorities. Some things, such as keeping keys secure, using required safety equipment, wearing badges, and honoring restricted areas, must be taught immediately. Other information can be delayed; for example, the likelihood of sustaining personal or property loss from fire or riot is usually much less than that of sustaining loss from an employee's failure to lock a door or to use safety equipment.

**CLEARLY EXPLAIN** Lecturing or presenting material in a pamphlet or handout is seldom sufficient. If you are teaching someone how to use a fire extinguisher, don't just explain: *show* the right and wrong way. Demonstrate what happens when the wrong type of extinguisher is used. Naturally, needed safety precautions must be taken when the "wrong way" is demonstrated.

**PRACTICE** Give all employees a chance to try newly learned procedures. Let them use a fire extinguisher, respond to a hypothetical bomb threat, or evacuate the premises. "Dry runs" remain in the memory longer and lessen the chance of panic should an emergency occur.

**EVALUATE** After a learning session, evaluate the results. For example, if you have just explained the procedures for evacuating during a fire, conduct a dry run and time how long it takes. Note any incorrect or dangerous actions taken. Let the employees know how well they did. Suggest ways to improve next time.

**REINFORCE** Although reinforcement is usually thought of as something positive, it can also be negative. People may do as you want either to obtain praise *or* to avoid disapproval, to get a reward or to avoid punishment.

---

Positive reinforcers include success, praise, incentives, and rewards. Negative reinforcers include failure, disapproval, threats, and punishment.

---

Although learning theorists disagree on which is more effective, positive or negative reinforcement, most favor the positive. For one thing, it is a more pleasant system within which to operate. People feel better about themselves and what they are doing when they are praised and rewarded for their efforts. And the educators usually do, too.

Unfortunately, not all people learn this way. They take advantage of the "system" and see it as loose and permissive. Often a combination of positive and negative reinforcement is most effective. The incentive programs discussed previously can serve as positive reinforcement for learning and applying security principles and practices. Negative reinforcement might include prosecution for stealing, a reprimand or fine for poor housekeeping, or a bill for ruining something due to carelessness.

Be selective in using reinforcement. You cannot praise people every time they do something right, especially if it is expected, such as arriving on time, wearing safety equipment, and locking doors. But you can reinforce people who promptly report losses or unsafe conditions. Use common sense; too much praise becomes meaningless.

**REVIEW** All procedures should be periodically reviewed. Make a schedule for review and carry through with such things as poster campaigns, audiovisual presentations, guest speakers, and drills.

All newly assigned or employed personnel need education initially and periodically. Follow-up instruction and reinforcement are keys to any good educational program. Additionally, the person responsible for the educational program should be clearly defined or no one may take the initiative or follow through.

## Establishing Image

Security directors also establish the image of the security department. Many security directors are retired police, FBI, or military officers who once served in an apprehension function; that is, they were primarily reactive rather than preventive in their responsibilities. This difference in purpose and authority has posed problems for some security directors, making it difficult for them to become an integral, accepted part of the organization. An authoritarian image will perhaps deter a few dishonest employees, but it is also likely to make other employees resentful and uncooperative. The influence of security should be pervasive, but not suffocating. Security directors can set this tone by example.

Decisions must also be made as to whether security officers will be uniformed and whether they will be armed. Factors influencing these decisions include the product produced or sold, the type of security interest involved, the number and type of employees, and the area in which the establishment is located. Other important considerations are the availability of local police, past experience, and hazards inherent in foreign locations. If security officers are armed, strict regulations regarding the issuing, use, and care of weapons must be established and enforced.

## ☐ INVESTIGATIVE RESPONSIBILITIES

Investigation is both a science and an art, requiring very specific skills. Proficiency comes through practice and experience. The primary activity of investigators is to acquire information, so it is logical that the ability to elicit or obtain such information is critical to a successful investigation.

---

The basic investigative skills are communication skills and surveillance capabilities.

---

Effective investigators are able to elicit information from all types of people, including those who are uncooperative and belligerent. They must also be able to communicate effectively in writing. Their investigative reports must be accurate, clear, and readable. In addition, investigators are often called on to follow and observe persons and activities inconspicuously, so they must develop skill in surveillance techniques.

---

Security directors are responsible for investigating the potential for loss (risk analysis), for investigating actual occurrences of loss, and for conducting background checks and periodic audits.

---

### Conducting Security Surveys

The foundation of a security system is the security survey and resultant risk analysis, discussed in Chapter 4. To determine existing and potential problems, security directors survey the physical facility, the procedures used in each department, and the internal and external traffic patterns during open and closed periods. They may need to know basic principles of accounting and computer operations in some instances. They must also understand and have access to company statistics, computer operations, personnel department operations and records, and the operations of every other department, including accounting (petty cash, cash handling, refund procedures, check cashing, accounts receivable, accounts payable, payroll, etc.), purchasing, shipping, and receiving.

Security directors should be involved in top-management discussions and decisions in any area that might affect security and safety, especially any building or remodeling plans, *before* final decisions are made.

## Investigating Losses

Any losses or accidents that occur should be thoroughly investigated. This sometimes involves cooperation with local authorities, with police and fire departments, and with OSHA representatives. Careful records of losses should be kept so that problems can be more easily identified. Security files should be well organized and current. Internal data on losses can be used to develop, improve, and evaluate the security system.

## Conducting Background Checks and Audits

Security directors may also conduct employee security clearances, either before employment or when employees are being considered for promotion to sensitive positions or positions with access to valuable assets. Conducting a background check on a long-time employee is a sensitive but important responsibility that requires tact and diplomacy.

Security directors also conduct or assign someone else to conduct periodic, unannounced audits to verify cash-handling, refund, check-cashing, accounting, shipping, and receiving procedures.

## ☐ THE SECURITY DIRECTOR AS MANAGER

Management is a complex relationship among employees of different levels, ranks, authority, and responsibilities. It is often a person-to-person relationship, working within the organizational framework.

Security directors must support the development of *individual* responsibility, encouraging all personnel to achieve maximum individuality and potential while simultaneously supporting the organization's needs. The sum total of individual energy is transformed into organizational energy needed for success.

Because management is an area many private security professionals have limited experience in, a brief summary of important theories of management as well as the language it uses follows before specific managerial responsibilities are discussed.

## ☐ THEORIES OF MANAGEMENT

Several theories of management have been developed to guide those in positions of authority. Among the most well known are those based on Maslow's hierarchy of needs, Herzberg's two-factor hygiene/motivation theory, McGregor's Theory X/Theory Y, Likert's four-system approach, Argyris's mature employee theory, Blake-Mouton's Managerial Grid®, and Skinner's reinforcement theory.

## Maslow's Hierarchy of Needs

According to Maslow, people have a range of needs going from basic physiological needs such as food and shelter to high-level, complex needs such as self-actualization. Needs must be met at the most basic level before the next level of needs becomes important.

Maslow's hierarchy of needs consists of basic physiological needs, safety/security needs, social needs, esteem needs, and the need for self-actualization. Lower-level needs must be met before higher-level needs.

Basic physiological needs on the job might include base salary, heat/air-conditioning, cafeteria/vending machines, working conditions, rest periods, efficient work methods, labor-saving devices, and comfortable uniforms.

Safety/security needs on the job might include safe working conditions, fringe benefits, seniority, proper supervision, sound company policies, protective equipment, general salary increases, job security, and a feeling of competence.

Social needs on the job might include quality supervision, compatible coworkers, professional friendships, and organizational pride/spirit.

Esteem needs on the job might include merit pay raises, titles, status symbols/awards, recognition, the job itself, responsibility, and sharing in decisions.

Self-actualization on the job might include challenging tasks, creativity, achievement in work, advancement, involvement in planning, freedom to make decisions, and chances for growth and development.

## Herzberg's Two-Factor Hygiene/Motivation Theory

Herzberg's hygiene factors are similar to Maslow's lower-level needs. Hygiene factors are things employees expect. If they do not get them, they are dissatisfied. Supervision, a basic salary, safe working conditions, and the like are extrinsic conditions that do not necessarily motivate people to do a good job; but if they are absent, employees will be unhappy. Hygiene factors explain why people stick with a job. They are not dissatisfied with the tangible rewards, even though they may find the work itself unsatisfying.

Motivation factors, in contrast, are like Maslow's higher-level needs. They include praise, recognition, opportunity to grow, satisfying work, and the like.

Herzberg's hygiene factors are tangible rewards that cause dissatisfaction if lacking. Motivation factors are intangible rewards that cause satisfaction. Hygiene factors must be provided; motivation factors are where managers should concentrate their efforts.

## McGregor's Theory X/Theory Y

McGregor's theory focuses on what management thinks about employees. Under Theory X the manager assumes that employees need control by coercion, threats, and punishment. The average employee has an aversion to work. Management makes all decisions and directs employees to carry them out. Employees are dull and lazy and desire secure jobs above all else.

Under Theory Y the manager assumes that employees can be trusted to do a good job, they are willing workers, they can be given reasonable goals to accomplish, and they should share in decision making.

---

McGregor's Theory X maintains that employees are basically lazy and do not like to work; they need close supervision and should not participate in decisions. Theory Y maintains that employees are willing workers, are motivated by growth and development opportunities, and should share in decisions.

---

Table 3–1 summarizes McGregor's assumptions of Theory X and Theory Y.

Given these assumptions, management's responsibility under Theory X is to provide constant supervision. Employees do not want responsibility; they are mainly interested in salary, fringe benefits, and avoiding punishment. In contrast, under Theory Y management's responsibility is to encourage self-motivation and use fewer outside controls. Contemporary management practices would favor Theory Y.

## Likert's Four-System Approach

Likert divided managerial approaches into four systems. The first, similar to McGregor's Theory X, was a traditional, dictatorial approach that used coercion. The second system was like the first except that economic rewards replaced coercion. System 3 was more liberal, using employee initiative and giving employees more responsibility. System 4 was participatory, the opposite of System 1.

---

Likert's four-system approach to management goes from System 1, which is a traditional, authoritarian style, to System 4, which is a participative management style.

---

Participative management is closely allied with the democratic approach, except that employees do not vote. System 4 also promotes team management, widely used in businesses today. Characteristics of Likert's System 1 and System 4, the two extremes, are illustrated in Table 3–2.

## Argyris's Mature Employee Theory

Argyris's theory emphasizes employees' growth and development as a means to increase their contributions to the job. Argyris analyzed the relationship between the organization's demands and those of employees. He felt both have a mutual effect on the end result.

## Table 3–1 McGregor's Theory X and Theory Y assumptions.

| Theory X | Theory Y |
| --- | --- |
| 1. The average person inherently dislikes work and will avoid it when possible. | 1. The expenditure of physical and mental effort in work is as natural as the expenditure of physical and mental exertion in play or rest. |
| 2. Most people must be coerced, controlled directed, or threatened with punishment to get them to put forth adequate energy in achieving organizational goals. | 2. An employee will exercise self-direction and self-control in the service of objectives to which he or she is committed. |
| 3. The average person prefers to be directed, wishes to avoid responsibility, and has relatively little ambition; he or she wants security above all. | 3. Commitment to objectives is a function of the rewards associated with their achievement. |
| 4. The average person is inherently self-centered and indifferent to organizational needs. | 4. The average person learns, under proper conditions, not only to accept but also to seek responsibility. |
| 5. The average person is by nature resistant to change. | 5. The capacity to exercise high degrees of imagination, ingenuity, and creativity in solving organizational problems is widely, not narrowly, distributed in the population. |
| 6. The average person is gullible, not very bright, the ready dupe of the charlaton and the demagogue. | 6. The intellectual potentialities of the average person are only partially utilized under the conditions of modern industrial life. |
|  | 7. The essential task of management is to arrange organizational conditions and methods of operation so people can achieve their own goals best by directing their own efforts toward organizational goals. |

McGregor/*The Human Side of Enterprise.* 1960. Reprinted with permission of McGraw-Hill, Inc.

Argyris's mature employee theory views employees and their organization as interdependent.

Organizations and employees are interdependent because organizations provide jobs and people perform them. Neither can exist well without the other.

## Blake-Mouton's Managerial Grid®

The Managerial Grid, republished as The Leadership Grid Figure in 1991, maps management approaches based on whether the focus is on con-

**Table 3–2  Likert's System 1 and System 4 management styles compared.**

| System 1 (Traditional) | System 4 (Participative) |
|---|---|
| **Leadership** is not based on confidence and trust. Subordinates don't feel free to discuss ideas with managers, and the managers don't use subordinates' opinions in decision making. | **Leadership** is based on confidence and trust in subordinates. Subordinates discuss their ideas with managers, and their ideas and opinions are used in decision making. |
| **Motivation** is based on fear, threat, punishment, and some rewards. Responsibility for achieving goals decreases down the hierarchy. | **Motivation** is through economic rewards and involvement in setting goals. People at all levels feel a responsibility for reaching goals. |
| **Communication** flows downward from the top of the hierarchy and is viewed with suspicion. There is little feedback. | **Communication** flows freely throughout the organization. Feedback is accurate. |
| **Interaction** between managers and employees is minimal and is viewed with fear and distrust. There is little teamwork. | **Interaction** between managers and employees is extensive, friendly, and based on a high degree of confidence and trust. There is a great deal of teamwork. |
| **Decision making** takes place primarily at the top of the hierarchy with little subordinate involvement. Acceptance of the decision is usually not considered. | **Decision making** is dispersed but linked through teamwork. Subordinates are fully involved in decisions relating to their work. |
| **Goals** are set at the top of the organization. Goals are resisted. Performance goals are relatively low. | **Goals** are set through participation at the level where they will be achieved. Goals are accepted. Performance goals are high. |
| **Controls** are concentrated in top management and are used in a punitive way. | **Controls** are widespread and are used for self-guidance and for coordinated problem solving. |

Likert/*The Human Organization: Its Management and Values,* 1967. Reprinted with the permission of McGraw-Hill, Inc.

cern for people or on concern for production. The "ideal" management style would be to integrate the two equally, the upper right corner of the Grid, using a team approach.

The lower right corner is the authority-compliance management style. The manager is a taskmaster who uses a no-nonsense approach. Concern is for manager authority, status, and running the organization. Production is the only concern—get things done.

The upper left corner is the opposite, the country club style. Managers are overly concerned with keeping employees happy at the expense of reasonable productivity. The lower left corner illustrates Impoverished Management style, permitting workers to do just enough to get by. This is sometimes called laissez-faire management. Managers and employers put in their time and look ahead to retirement. Little concern for employees or production exists.

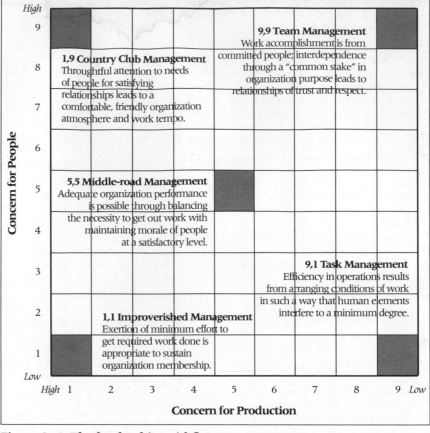

**Figure 3–1 The leadership grid figure.**
*Source: The Leadership Grid® Figure from **Leadership Dilemmas—Grid Solutions**, by Robert R. Blake and Anne Adams McCanse. Houston: Gulf Publishing Company, p. 29. Copyright © 1991, by Scientific Methods, Inc. Reproduced by permission of the owners.*

In the middle is the middle of the road management style, with managers showing some concern for both employees and productivity, but in a low key that does not really accomplish much. The manager is a fence straddler, appeasing both sides, avoiding conflict, and seldom satisfying anyone.

The Blake-Mouton Managerial/Leadership Grid maps management styles based on their emphasis on people and production. The "ideal" management style is an integration of high concern for both people and productivity, resulting in an energetic team approach.

In a team approach, managers work with employees, providing information, caring about their feelings, assisting, coaching, advising. Employees are committed to their jobs and to the organization. Goals are achieved as a team.

## Skinner's Reinforcement Theory

B. F. Skinner, known for his work on behavior modification, suggested that behavior can be shaped by what happens immediately after the behavior occurs. If something positive happens after the behavior, the behavior is likely to be repeated. If something negative happens after the behavior, the behavior is not likely to be repeated.

---

Skinner's reinforcement theory suggests that positive reinforcement increases a given behavior and that negative reinforcement decreases a given behavior.

---

Both positive and negative reinforcement can be used on the job. Praise, bonuses, and awards are examples of positive reinforcers. Criticism and docks in pay are examples of negative reinforcers. Another important principle of reinforcement theory relevant for managers is that positive reinforcement is usually more effective than negative reinforcement. (Some people, however, respond only to punishment.)

## The "Best" Approach

Each management theory provides some insight into how a person might "manage" employees. What is probably of most importance, however, is that all employees are individuals. What works with one employee may not work with another. Managers must be sensitive and responsive to each employee for whom they are responsible.

## ☐ THE LANGUAGE OF MANAGEMENT

In addition to being expert and current in all areas of loss prevention/asset protection, security managers must also be familiar with the language of business management if they are to effectively interact with other business executives and overcome the stereotypical image of the "company cop." Most security managers must vie with other top executives for personnel and budget. To successfully compete, they must be familiar with "management jargon" such as the following:

➤ *Affirmative action*—actions to eliminate current effects of past discrimination.
➤ *Agenda*—items to be accomplished, usually during a meeting.
➤ *Authoritarian*—manager who uses strong control over personnel; also called autocratic.
➤ *Authority*—right to give orders.
➤ *Bureaucratic*—reliance on rules and regulations.
➤ *Delegation*—assigning tasks to others.
➤ *Democratic*—manager who involves personnel in decision making.
➤ *Dictatorial*—manager who is close-minded and uses threats with personnel.

➤ *Discipline*—actions taken to get personnel to follow rules and regulations.

➤ *Equal Employment Opportunity Commission (EEOC)*—commission set up to enforce laws against discrimination in the workplace.

➤ *Goal*—end result desired.

➤ *Grievance*—a complaint, usually written, made to one's supervisor.

➤ *Hierarchy*—levels; management hierarchy goes from the CEO to vice presidents (managers) to supervisors to on-line personnel.

➤ *Hierarchy of needs*—human needs identified by psychologists, placed in order from lower-level needs (food, shelter, etc.) to higher-level needs (self-actualization).

➤ *Job description*—statement of duties and responsibilities for a specific position.

➤ *Management*—the "bosses" in an organization.

➤ *Management by Objectives (MBO)*—management and staff set goals and time lines within which to accomplish the goals.

➤ *Manager*—one who accomplishes things through others.

➤ *Mentor*—teacher, role model.

➤ *Morale*—how a person feels; the general mood of an organization or company (e.g., morale is high/low).

➤ *Motivate*—encourage, inspire.

➤ *Occupational Safety and Health Act of 1970 (OSHA)*—makes employers responsible for providing a safe workplace.

➤ *On-line personnel*—those who do the work (e.g., security guards and patrols).

➤ *Performance appraisal*—evaluation of an employee's work.

➤ *Permissive*—manager who has or exercises little control over personnel.

➤ *Span of management (or control)*—number of people for whom a manager is responsible.

➤ *Supervisor*—directly oversees the work of on-line personnel; usually reports to a manager.

➤ *Unity of command*—people have only one supervisor.

## □ MANAGERIAL RESPONSIBILITIES

Security directors are responsible for hiring, writing job descriptions, training, issuing equipment, scheduling, supervising, taking corrective action, and evaluating security personnel.

### Hiring Security Personnel

When security directors are responsible for hiring security officers, they should keep in mind the vicious circle described by Anthony Potter in an address to the First Annual Conference on Private Security in 1975 (*Private Security*, 1976, p. 13) (Figure 3–2).

The first step in breaking this vicious circle is to hire qualified people who will perform effectively and who will make private security their career.

**P**rivate security personnel should meet the following minimum preemployment standards:

- ➤ Minimum age of eighteen.
- ➤ High-school diploma or equivalent written examination.
- ➤ Written examination to determine the ability to understand and perform the duties assigned.
- ➤ No record of conviction (of a serious crime).

- ➤ Minimum physical standards: Armed personnel—vision correctable to 20/20 (Snellen) in each eye; capable of hearing ordinary conversation at a distance of ten feet with each ear without benefit of a hearing aid. Others—no physical defects that would hinder job performance (Private Security, 1976, p. 82).

These are minimum requirements; others may be established depending on the position to be filled.

**AGE**   Police departments have traditionally required that applicants be twenty-one years of age, a restrictive requirement that need not apply to private security. A mature eighteen-year-old, given proper training, can function effectively as a security officer, as evidenced by the military services, which have used people under age twenty-one for years. The age requirement should be low enough that qualified applicants can enter the field before they are committed to other careers. By the time a person is twenty-one, he or she usually has made a career decision that is not readily changed.

**EDUCATION**   Applicants should demonstrate that they have mastered the basic skills taught in high school, either by having a high-school diploma or by having passed an equivalent written examination. Additionally, a valid test should be given to assess the applicant's ability to learn the information required to effectively fill the role of security officer.

**CONVICTION RECORD**   Because security officers are in a position of extreme trust, they should have a clean record. This means that criminal history records should be available to employers of private security officers, a key issue in many states today. Current rules and regulations do not authorize dissemination of nonconviction data to private security personnel, but do authorize release of conviction data. Additionally, criminal history record information, including arrest data on an individual currently being processed through the criminal justice system, may be restricted. It is up to individual states whether to allow other than criminal justice agencies to have access to such records. Therefore, private security professionals should encourage their state officials to specifically allow private security employers access to nonconviction data to assist in screening potential employees.

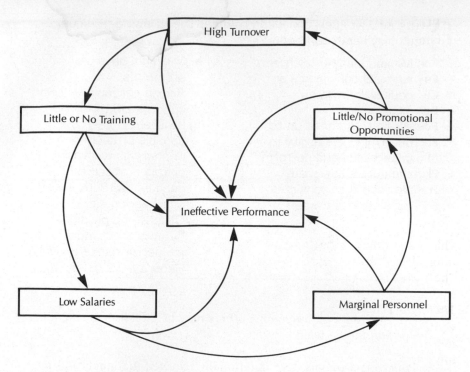

Figure 3–2 **Private security vicious circle.**

An arrest or conviction record does not necessarily mean the person should not be hired, but the employer should be provided this information so an informed decision can be made.

**PHYSICAL REQUIREMENTS** Physical requirements should be based on the specific type of job the person is expected to perform. Height and weight are often relevant, and vision and hearing are almost always relevant, especially if the person will be armed.

**STATE REQUIREMENTS** Different states have different personal qualifications for licensing private security personnel. The same requirements might be considered for each individual security officer being considered for a position.

Applicants for security positions should complete an application and should be carefully screened using such methods as an interview, a background check, and other tests as appropriate to the job.

Unfortunately, because of the high turnover rate in security personnel, management is sometimes unwilling to invest much time or money in screening security personnel. This decision can accelerate the "vicious circle" so frequently encountered in the security field.

**APPLICATION** All applicants should complete a form that contains, at minimum, the following information:

- ➤ Full name
- ➤ Current address and phone number
- ➤ Date of birth
- ➤ Education
- ➤ Previous employment
- ➤ Military record, if any
- ➤ Physical conditions as they relate to the job
- ➤ Personal references
- ➤ Fingerprints*

The application should contain a statement to the effect that incorrect information can be used as the basis for dismissal from employment. The form should be signed by the applicant.

**BACKGROUND CHECK** The information on the application should be verified. This is particularly true if the person was formerly employed in a security position. If employers would cooperate in exchanging information on the previous work of their employees, the overall personnel quality would improve substantially. Because the movement of individuals from one employer to another in the security field is extremely high, cooperation among employers helps eliminate unqualified, untrustworthy personnel. Records waivers should be obtained from all applicants.

Personal references listed by the applicants should also be contacted and interviewed.

**INTERVIEW** Personal interviews with the applicant can help clarify any missing or vague information on the application form and can provide an opportunity to observe the applicant's appearance and demeanor. Questions can be geared to probe the applicant's honesty, dependability, judgment, and initiative. For example, applicants might be asked why they want the job, what their goals are, why they left their last job, etc. When permitted by law, information on such items as arrest record, use of drugs and/or alcohol, credit, and interpersonal relations with fellow workers should be obtained. Psychological stress interviews are sometimes used, but their value is controversial.

**OTHER TESTS** Other job-related tests, psychological tests, and detection of deception (honesty) tests are sometimes used by employers when they hire security personnel. Where permitted by law, polygraph examinations are sometimes required. Use of such examinations is highly controversial.

---

*Local fingerprint and police checks should be made because national agency checks often overlook important data.

To increase effective job performance, security directors should provide security personnel with a job description, basic training, a security manual or handbook, and the necessary equipment.

## Writing Job Descriptions

Because private security is a complex, diverse field, personnel are assigned to many kinds of security functions. Carefully prepared job descriptions help ensure that each function is properly carried out. The job description can also help in the selection process, increase productivity and promotability, and ensure that training programs are job related.

Most job descriptions specify the type of work involved and the type of employee who would be best suited for this work. The description should include a summary of the major functions of the job; a description of the training, experience, skills, and equipment needed; physical requirements, if any; a specific listing of the activities performed; and the relationship of this job to other jobs in the department. Many job descriptions also include the normal working hours, the pay range, and the name of the supervisor.

In addition, new personnel need an orientation to the company—its philosophy, organization, goals, and operating procedures and policies. They should know the location of all stairways and where they lead, all emergency exits, fire alarm boxes, fire-fighting equipment, telephones, emergency switches, water sources, and the like. They should be taught the operation of any security equipment for which they may be responsible.

## Training

As with screening, management is frequently unwilling to devote much time or expense to training security personnel because of the high turnover rate. Untrained security officers are not only a waste of money, but also may be a direct threat to themselves and to the company.

Both basic preassignment training and ongoing training should be provided.

**PREASSIGNMENT TRAINING**  The preassignment training will depend on the type of job to be performed and the existing level of training of the applicant. As soon as possible, new employees should receive training in the following areas:

➤ *Access control*—employee IDs, visitor IDs, contractors, surveillance cameras, sign-in/out log, after-hours access.
➤ *Alarms*—operation, controls, panels, actions to take for each alarm state.
➤ *Communications*—telephones (directory of critical numbers, professional answering), walkie-talkies, radios.

- *Package control*—what to accept, procedures for accepting, what to allow out, procedures for packages leaving premises.
- *Passes*—property passes, camera passes.
- *Emergency procedures*—bomb threats, weather emergencies, earthquake.
- *Parking*—security, permits, traffic control.

Each security employee should have a policy and procedures manual and become thoroughly familiar with it. The manual should be kept current.

**ONGOING TRAINING**  In addition to preassignment training, security directors should provide security personnel with continuous training, the content of which would depend on the specific company and the job. Such ongoing training can keep personnel informed on things such as issues, changes in company policies, updates in criminal law, and technological improvements in the system. This ongoing training is not classroom-oriented like the preassignment training, but rather is individualized and job related. Job descriptions are often the basis for ongoing training. These steps are necessary to establish an ongoing, individualized, job-related training program:

1) Analyze job descriptions and identify the specific skills/knowledge needed to perform effectively. Determine the frequency and importance of each skill identified. Establish priorities and a timeline.
2) Write objectives to be met and how each will be evaluated.
3) Implement the training. This may be through audiovisual resources, practical exercises, case studies, roll-call sessions, training bulletins, and the like.
4) Evaluate the results. Job performance, not test performance, should determine the effectiveness of the training.

## Issuing Equipment

After basic preassignment training is completed, security directors should give security officers the necessary equipment to perform their job. This might include a watch-clock, flashlight, pocket pager or two-way radio, nightstick, pen and pad, handcuffs, and, in some instances, a weapon. If a weapon is issued, appropriate training must be provided.

**FIREARMS TRAINING**  The serious consequences for both employers and employees when untrained security officers are assigned to take jobs that require firearms include:

- Self-injury because of the mishandling of the weapon.
- Injury to others, often innocent bystanders, because of the lack of skill when firing the weapon.
- Criminal and/or civil suits against both employers and employees resulting from the above actions (*Private Security*, 1976, p. 107).

To reduce such consequences, the Task Force makes this recommendation in Standard 2.6 (p. 107):

Equipment for a security officer patrolling a high-crime area may include handcuffs and a gun.

All armed private security personnel, including those presently employed and part-time personnel, should:

1) Be required to successfully complete a twenty-four-hour firearms course that includes legal and policy requirements—or submit evidence of competence and proficiency—prior to assignment to a job that requires a firearm;
2) Be required to requalify at least once every twelve months with the firearm(s) they carry while performing private security duties (the requalification should cover legal and policy requirements).

## Scheduling

Security directors are also responsible for determining where personnel are to be assigned—for example, a fixed post, patrol, or reserve. They must also decide whether to change assignments and rotate responsibilities. Such changes can keep personnel from getting too familiar with the people with whom they work, and thereby decrease the possibility of corruption. But there is a disadvantage in that they must then learn a new position.

Scheduling personnel is time consuming, yet critical to accomplishing goals and objectives. Scheduling is usually done according to the following priorities:

1) Cover the shift; ensure that competent staff is available and trained to provide an acceptable level of security at each post.
2) Provide this coverage in the most cost-effective way (avoiding overtime when possible).
3) Use personnel effectively and fairly.

**4)** Train and assign personnel to achieve the best balance of capability and desire.

Efficient scheduling begins with a permanent schedule showing all employees when and where they will be working. In some instances employees might be designated as on "standby" in case of illness or other reasons assigned employees cannot fulfill their assignment.

Effective managers are sensitive to the needs of regular part-time employees who are likely to be working under the demands of another regular part-time commitment such as school or another job. Once part-time employees are trained, retaining them is important. They allow managers to have additional personnel on hand when the need is there. They also make scheduling more flexible.

Security directors may also direct undercover operations within the organization to detect internal thefts and rule violations. Or they may hire honesty shoppers to perform the same functions.

## Supervising

In larger organizations and companies, the security director/manager may have several supervisors to directly oversee security personnel. In smaller organizations, the security director may also function as the supervisor. The basic differences between the executive security director/manager and the security supervisor are as follows:

| Manager | Supervisor |
|---|---|
| Goal oriented | Task oriented |
| Long-term planner | Short-term planner |
| Mission oriented | Program oriented |
| Works in future | Works in present |
| Represents whole | Represents unit |
| Concept oriented | Data oriented |
| Establishes policies and procedures | Enforces policies and procedures |
| Internal and external politics | Internal politics |

In either case, supervisors must have a basic knowledge of the facility and of the duties of all personnel under their supervision. They must also know the basic policies and procedures of the security department. One primary responsibility of security supervisors is to conduct inspections.

## Inspections

Random inspections of individual facilities and officers during regular shift assignments might include the following:

➤ Presence of all required personnel and equipment.
➤ Personal appearance and behavior of security personnel.
➤ Orderly appearance of site.
➤ Operability of equipment.

➤ Assessment of potential problems or hazardous situations.
➤ Preparation of reports of inspections.

The objective of such inspections is to ensure that time, equipment, and personnel are being used as effectively and efficiently as possible.

## Taking Corrective Action

If security personnel are not performing as expected, corrective action must be taken. In most instances, security directors or supervisors use *progressive discipline,* going from the mildest reprimand to the most severe—termination.

*Progressive discipline* goes from the least severe reprimand, a warning, to the most severe, termination.

Progressive discipline usually involves the following actions:

1) *Warning*—This may be verbal or written, formal or informal. It should always be given in private and should always be documented.
2) *Reprimand*—This is a formal, written statement of an unacceptable behavior, the time line for correcting it, and perhaps an offer of assistance.
3) *Suspension*—This should be preceded by a reprimand in all but the most serious problems. Review and appeal procedures should be available.
4) *Demotion or termination*—This should be a last resort. The reasons and previous corrective actions taken should be carefully documented.

In most instances, managers who are skilled at effectively giving warnings will need go no further. They will accomplish the desired behavior change if they fit the warning to the individual and the situation. The purpose should be to change behavior, not to embarrass the person. Effective warnings usually meet the following criteria:

➤ They are based on facts—*all* the facts. And they stick to the facts, not to personalities.
➤ They are conducted privately, *never* in front of others.
➤ They avoid abuse, sarcasm, anger, and threats.
➤ They seek causes—why did the employee do what he or she did?
➤ They are suited to the individual.
➤ They end on a friendly, constructive tone.

The effectiveness of warnings can be judged by a simple test. Did the warning correct the problem?

## Evaluating Security Personnel

Security directors evaluate their personnel, provide feedback on how well they are performing, and determine what is being done well and what can be improved. They provide nonthreatening evaluation, recognize accomplishments, and recommend pay raises and promotions.

Factors managers might use in performance evaluations of security personnel include the following:

➤ Quality of work/technical skills
➤ Quantity of work
➤ Attendance/punctuality
➤ Organization
➤ Cooperation
➤ Problem-solving ability
➤ Communication skills
➤ Initiative
➤ Attitude

## ☐ GUIDELINES FOR EFFECTIVE MANAGEMENT

To manage effectively and to obtain the most from a security staff, security directors must:

➤ Create a good work environment—safe, pleasant.
➤ Be open to suggestions and input.
➤ Give credit to others when deserved.
➤ Keep employees informed—let them know what is expected, when it is or is not accomplished; let them know of changes, etc.
➤ Be fair and impartial.
➤ Act when necessary, but know your authority.
➤ Set a good example.

## ☐ MANAGEMENT CODE OF ETHICS

Just as security officers should follow a code of ethics, security managers should also follow such a code. The following code of ethics of the Law Enforcement/Private Security Relationship Committee is one example of a set of guidelines that might be adapted for use (Gold 3.1, *Private Security,* 1976, p. 124).

## SUMMARY

**P**rivate security has come into its own during the past decade. Security directors must be given authority to act and have access to top management. They must communicate with and coordinate the security efforts of all departments within the organization. Their primary roles are those of loss prevention specialist (the focus of the entire book), administrator, investigator, and manager.

As administrators, security directors are responsible for security goals; policies, procedures, and daily orders; financial controls and budgets; educational programs; and the image of security within the organization. The ultimate goal of private security systems is loss prevention—thereby maximizing return on investment. One way to achieve this goal

---

### Code of Ethics for Private Security Management

As managers of private security functions and employees, we pledge:

I  To recognize that our principal responsibilities are, in the service of our organizations and clients, to protect life and property as well as to prevent and reduce crime against our business, industry, or other organizations and institutions; and in the public interest, to uphold the law and to respect the constitutional rights of all persons.

II  To be guided by a sense of integrity, honor, justice and morality in the conduct of business; in all personnel matters; in relationships with government agencies, clients, and employers; and in responsibilities to the general public.

III  To strive faithfully to render security services of the highest quality and to work continuously to improve our knowledge and skills and thereby improve the overall effectiveness of private security.

IV  To uphold the trust of our employers, our clients, and the public by performing our functions within the law, not ordering or condoning violations of law, and ensuring that our security personnel conduct their assigned duties lawfully and with proper regard for the rights of others.

V  To respect the reputation and practice of others in private security, but to expose to the proper authorities any conduct that is unethical or unlawful.

VI  To apply uniform and equitable standards of employment in recruiting and selecting personnel regardless of race, creed, color, sex, or age, and in providing salaries commensurate with job responsibilities and with training, education, and experience.

VII  To cooperate with recognized and responsible law enforcement and other criminal justice agencies; to comply with security licensing and registration laws and other statutory requirements that pertain to our business.

VIII  To respect and protect the confidential and privileged information of employers and clients beyond the term of our employment, except where their interests are contrary to law or to this Code of Ethics.

IX  To maintain a professional posture in all business relationships with employers and clients, with others in the private security field, and with members of other professions; and to insist that our personnel adhere to the highest standards of professional conduct.

X  To encourage the professional advancement of our personnel by assisting them to acquire appropriate security knowledge, education, and training.

---

**Figure 3–3  Code of ethics (management).**

is through SMART objectives, objectives that are specific, measurable, attainable, relevant, and trackable.

Other employees and staff can be educated about the security/safety system through posters, signs, manuals, training sessions, drills, and the suggestions and examples of security officers. Such learning will be more effective if it is practical, presented in short segments, clearly explained by examples or demonstrations, practiced and evaluated, reinforced, and periodically reviewed. Positive reinforcements include success, praise, incentives, and rewards. Negative reinforcements include failure, disapproval, threats, and punishment.

Security directors are responsible for investigating the potential for loss (risk analysis), for investigating the actual occurrences of loss, and for conducting background checks and periodic audits. The basic investigative skills are communication skills and surveillance capabilities.

As managers, security directors should be familiar with the best-known theories of management, including Maslow's hierarchy of needs,

Herzberg's two-factor hygiene/motivation theory, McGregor's Theory X/Theory Y, Likert's four-system approach, Argyris's mature employee theory, Blake-Mouton's Managerial Grid, and Skinner's reinforcement theory.

As managers, security directors are responsible for hiring, writing job descriptions, training, issuing equipment, scheduling, supervising, taking corrective action, and evaluating security personnel.

If the vicious circle leading to high rates of turnover is to be broken, private security personnel selected for employment should meet minimum employment standards, including being at least eighteen years old, having a high-school diploma or equivalent written examination, passing a written examination to determine the ability to understand and perform the duties assigned, having no criminal record, and meeting minimum physical standards. All applicants for security positions should complete an application and should be carefully screened using such methods as an interview, a background check, and other tests appropriate to the job to be performed.

To increase effective job performance, security directors should provide security personnel with a job description, training, a security manual or handbook, and the necessary equipment. Both preassignment training and ongoing training should be provided. If personnel do not perform up to standards, progressive discipline should be used. Progressive discipline goes from the least severe reprimand, a warning, to the most severe, termination.

## APPLICATION

1) As a security supervisor, you are aware that the security director is considering arming his proprietary security force. List the advantages and disadvantages of having armed proprietary security officers.
2) List as many factors as you can that contribute to the image of a private security officer.
3) Write a job description for a private security supervisor.

## DISCUSSION QUESTIONS

1) How can private security directors enhance the image of the private security officer?
2) List the resources one might use to obtain qualified people to hire as security officers.
3) What are three characteristics of a good training program?
4) What are the minimum requirements for an effective security officer?
5) What additional qualifications are required for a security supervisor? A security director?

## REFERENCES

Blanchard, Kenneth. Getting back to basics. *Today's office*, January 1988, pp. 14, 19.
Cohen, Joseph. Security forum. *Security world*, December 1980, p. 18.

Gallati, Robert J. *Introduction to private security*. Englewood Cliffs, NJ: Prentice-Hall, 1983.

*Private security*. Report of the Task Force on Private Security, National Advisory Committee on Criminal Justice Standards and Goals. Washington, DC: U.S. Government Printing Office, 1976.

Sopsic, J. P. Security in its proper management perspective. *Security management*, May 1977, p. 66.

Wainwright, O. O. Security management of the future. *Security management*, March 1984, pp. 47–51, 295.

## ☐ INTRODUCTION

When the contract security operations manager for a five-hundred-room hotel in the Midwest was informed that one of two grand master keys for the hotel was missing, it was a crisis. The security guard was doubled until the entire hotel could be re-keyed, a process that cost $500,000. The hotel manager responsible for the key's security lost his job. That single, lost key created an extreme risk that had to be dealt with immediately.

Risk management, however, is much more than dealing with crises. In fact, effective risk management should greatly reduce such crises. The purpose of risk management is to make an organization's environment secure, yet consistent with its operations and philosophy. Consequently, risk managers must consider not only the possible targets of attack and existing security measures as they relate to profits, but also the aesthetic and operational needs of the enterprise. Efficiency, convenience, appearance, and profit are all important factors as security systems are planned.

Effective risk management should provide an integrated, comprehensive approach to a secure environment. As noted by Foster (1978, p. 3): "Patchwork security is dangerous and lacks the elements necessary for long-range problem solving. Risk management provides both a logical and systematic approach to problem solving by causing the handling of the most serious vulnerabilities first."

# Chapter Four

# Loss Prevention through Risk Management

## DO YOU KNOW

➤ The difference between pure and dynamic risk?

➤ What risk management is?

➤ What is included in a systematic approach to preventing loss through risk management?

➤ Whether risk management is a moral or a legal responsibility?

➤ What three factors are considered in risk analysis?

➤ What a security survey is?

➤ How the information needed for a security survey is obtained?

➤ What alternatives exist for handling risks?

➤ When components of the security system should be evaluated?

## ☐ RISKS AND RISK MANAGEMENT DEFINED

The concept of risk is familiar to most people. A risk is a known threat that has effects that are not predictable in either their timing or their extent. The effects can include actual losses, interruption of production cycles, reduction of sales opportunities, injury to persons, liability claims, and property damage.

The National Crime Prevention Institute (NCPI) identifies two types of risks existing in any enterprise: pure risk and dynamic risk.

Pure risk is the potential for injury, damage, or loss with no possible benefits. Dynamic risk, in contrast, has the potential for both benefits and losses.

Pure risks include crimes and natural disasters. These offer no benefit to management—only added cost. Also included within the category of pure risks is the employer's liability to protect employees, customers, and visitors. People have a right to be reasonably safe when on the property of business or organizations. Recall several years ago when a popular night club entertainer was assaulted, raped, and robbed in a hotel where she was staying during her singing engagement. The singer sued the hotel for negligence and won the case. Lawsuits based on inadequate security have increased. Stenno (1981, p. 35) suggests that among the reasons for this increase are "rising expectations of the public with regard to the quality of services" and the "rise of consumerism, with citizens demanding protection of their rights."

In contrast to pure risks, dynamic risks result from a management decision and may result in both benefits and losses. For example, management personnel decide to accept checks because doing so stimulates business; at the same time, they recognize that some losses may occur from the pure risk of check fraud. Or, they decide to hire security personnel. They are then liable for the actions of such personnel. Among charges sometimes brought against security personnel are improper detention or search, false arrest, injury resulting from excessive force, slander, and the like, as discussed in Chapter 5.

Both pure and dynamic risks must be recognized and dealt with in a systematic approach to private security.

Risk should not be viewed as all negative. Change necessitates taking risks. As knowledge proliferates and organizations restructure, security managers must deal with the inevitable uncertainty that results from change. They should not be bound by tradition, but rather be willing to take some risks. Security managers who fail to take risks have a rigid, inflexible approach, perceiving change as a threat. Such security managers tend to seek stable, unchanging environments in which they feel safe, but also in which obsolescence and stagnation are found.

---

Risk management is anticipating, recognizing, and analyzing risks; taking steps to reduce or prevent such risks; and evaluating the results.

---

Risk management is sometimes referred to as loss prevention or loss prevention management. The following discussion provides an overview of risk management. What is important at this point is the overall security system and how it is developed. Specific risks and alternatives to eliminating or reducing them are the focus of Sections Two and Three.

## ☐ RISK MANAGEMENT: THE TOTAL PICTURE*

Risk management is a complex challenge to security managers. In the market economy a company must take risks; this situation has always

---

*Adapted from Statsföretag AB, Skandia Insurance Co. and Skandia Risk Management Ltd., Stockholm, Sweden.

existed. But given our sophisticated technology and the demand for high production, even a minor disturbance can cause a substantial economic setback. Consequently, security managers must define and analyze all risks companies may encounter to make it possible to restrict the number and the scope of such disturbances. Risk management is a comprehensive system of measures aimed at achieving that end.

## The Risk Management Circle

In Figure 4–1, the outer area shows a company's risk environment—all the risks that affect the company. These will, of course, vary from business to business. The second circle shows the various components of the protection a company can include. The third circle shows the positions involved in a company's protection plan and each individual's areas of responsibility. At the center of the risk management circle is the coordinator, the person who manages the entire security effort and all its components.

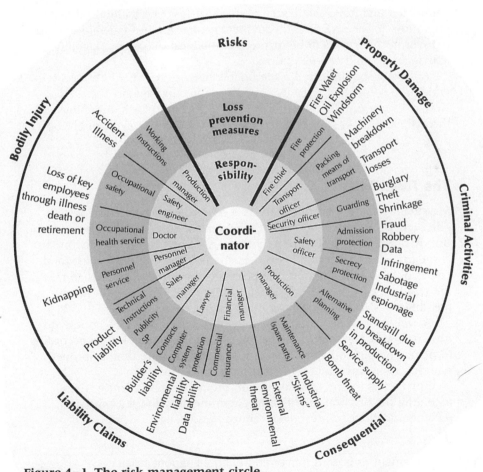

**Figure 4–1 The risk management circle.**
*Adapted from Statsföretag AB, Skandia Insurance Co. and Skandia Risk Management Ltd., Stockholm, Sweden.*

## The Risk Cycle

An efficient, effective, non-crisis-oriented security system does not just happen. Developing such a system involves critical observations and judgments.

A systematic approach to preventing loss through risk management includes risk analysis, policy formulation, specification of a protection plan, and follow-up.

The purpose of the *risk analysis* is to create an awareness within a company of any risks and to elucidate as far as possible their potential influence on the business.

After the risk analysis is completed, *policy* is formulated. The necessary security measures are arranged in order of importance, the cost of such measures is computed, and management determines the level of protection the company should choose.

Next a *protection plan* is specified that includes which risks are to be eliminated and how; the degree of need for loss prevention and loss limitation, for protective company health care, and for training in company protection; risks to be insured; and allocation of responsibility, management, and coordination.

*Follow-up* should insure a reasonable balance between the risks with which the company has to live and the protection against these risks. New risks can rapidly materialize (e.g., as a result of a kidnapping threat). Other risks may become less serious. The risk cycle might be diagrammed as in Figure 4–2.

## The Risk Balance

Risk management seeks to establish a cost-efficient protection system. The higher the protection costs, the lower the costs for loss and damage. But as can be seen in Figure 4–3 there is a point in the protection cost curve that should not be passed, i.e., the point where the lowest total cost is obtained. In addition, the protection must be organized so that the requirements prescribed in state law are fulfilled. It is not always possible to calculate the cost of these requirements.

A well-functioning company protection system means that few disturbances will arise and thus the operations can be carried on according to plan. Consequently, management can devote more time to proper working tasks. Investment in such protection is profitable.

Key factors in any loss prevention program are to identify risks, including the physical opportunity for crime, and to then prepare recommendations to prevent or reduce these risks.

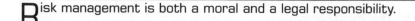

Risk management is both a moral and a legal responsibility.

**Figure 4–2 The risk cycle.**
*Adapted from Statsföretag AB, Skandia Insurance Co. and Skandia Risk Management Ltd., Stockholm, Sweden.*

Organizations that do not have a comprehensive risk management program in place leave themselves open to disgruntled employees/customers as well as to potential civil liability, as discussed in Chapter 5.

## ☐ RISK ANALYSIS

As noted by Green (1987, p. 115): "If security is not to be one-dimensional, piecemeal, reactive, or pre-packaged, it must be based upon analysis of the total risk potential."

---

Three factors to consider in risk analysis are (1) vulnerability, (2) probability, and (3) criticality.

---

Establishing **vulnerability** involves identifying threats. Where could losses occur? How? What types of thefts might occur? What safety hazards exist? Security managers should consider their vulnerability to such risks as accidents, arson, assault, auto theft, bombs, burglary, fraud (including credit card and check fraud), kidnapping, larceny/theft (both internal and external), robbery, sabotage, sex crimes, shoplifting, and

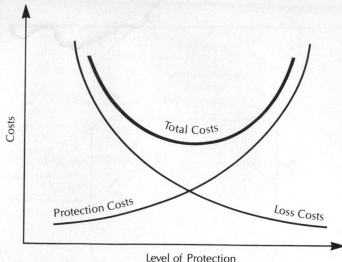

**Figure 4–3  Cost vs. level of protection.**
*Adapted from Statsföretag AB, Skandia Insurance Co. and Skandia Risk Management
Ltd., Stockholm, Sweden.*

vandalism. They should also consider their vulnerability to natural disasters such as earthquakes, floods, tornadoes, fires, and the like.

Establishing **probability** involves analyzing the factors that favor loss. Is the establishment located in a high- or low-crime area? How tight is existing physical security? Records of past losses help establish probability. Where is a shrinkage occurring? Is it primarily due to internal or external causes? Where is it most likely to occur? Are OSHA* requirements being met? How likely are civil disturbances in the area? Would the establishment be a probable target?

Establishing **criticality** involves deciding whether a loss, if it occurs, would be of minimum or maximum consequence. How serious would it be? Pilferage may appear to be of negligible seriousness, but if it is continuous and engaged in by many employees, it may be more costly than a robbery or burglary. According to Green (1987, pp. 117–118), criticality "has been defined to mean the impact of a loss as measured in dollars." He cautions: "The dollar loss is not simply the cost of the items lost." It also includes:

➤ Replacement cost (including delivery and installation costs).
➤ Temporary replacement (for example, if a main computer goes down and must be temporarily replaced until new equipment can be bought and installed).
➤ "Down time" (including not being able to continue doing business and having employees idled).
➤ Insurance rate increases.

Of course, when considerations such as human life or the national security are involved, cost becomes secondary.

---

*Occupational Safety and Health Act, discussed in Chapter 8.

Management makes the preliminary decisions on the degree of security desired or required. Common sense plus the establishment's past history are key ingredients in stating security objectives. Security measures should neither obstruct operations nor be neglected; rather, they should be an integrated part of the establishment's operations.

To determine what risks exist and what approach to use in dealing with them, security managers frequently rely on conducting a security survey.

## ☐ THE SECURITY SURVEY

A **security survey** is an objective but critical on-site examination and analysis of a business, industrial plant, public or private institution, or home. Its purpose is to determine existing security, to identify deficiencies, to determine the protection needed, and to recommend improvements to enhance overall security.

"A security survey," says Green (1987, p. 122), "is essentially an exhaustive physical examination of the premises and a thorough inspection of all operational systems and procedures. Such an examination or survey has as its overall objective the analysis of a facility to determine the existing state of its security, to locate weaknesses in its defenses, to determine the degree of protection required, and, ultimately, to lead to recommendations establishing a total security program."

Risk analysis involves developing (or adapting) the security survey, conducting the survey, and assessing the results.

### Developing the Security Survey

Kingsbury (1973, pp. 27–28) outlines the following topics to consider in developing a security survey:*

**A)** Planning (purpose): What and how much security?—Degree
    1) Physical security (property, etc.)
    2) Personnel (background, etc.)
    3) Information (files, records, etc.)
    4) Security survey/consultant
**B)** Responsibilities: Who?
    1) Administrative authority (Vice-President level, etc.)—Security organization
    2) Budget/scheduling
**C)** Area (duties): Where will the security emphasis be placed?
    1) Parking
    2) Visitor control
    3) Hazards (man-made and environmental)
    4) Employee pilferage
    5) Outside losses

---

*From A. A. Kingsbury, *Introduction to Security and Crime Prevention Surveys*, 1973. Courtesy of Charles C. Thomas, Publisher, Springfield, Illinois.

6) Disaster planning/civil disturbance
7) Fire/safety responsibility
8) Special events
**D)** Issues (policy—procedure): When? Why?
1) Legal basis
2) Education/training
3) Manuals (general/specific)
4) Intelligence gathering
5) Contract guard vs. in-house
6) Side arms vs. none
7) Extra chores (escort, lock-up, room checks, protect transfer of monies)
8) Guard force vs. hardware
9) Uniform vs. nonuniform
10) Contract with local law enforcement
11) Security cadets
12) Consultant (outside)
13) Consultant (staff member)—contract guard

The actual survey can be in the form of a checklist, prepared with adequate space between entries for detailed notes. Often aerial maps or diagrams of the facility are included with the security survey. The amount of detail in the survey will vary depending on the degree of security required. A thorough security survey would include the general area, as well as all roads and/or streets leading to the facility; the perimeter, including fencing, warning signs, and No Parking signs; the buildings, including construction and possible points of unauthorized entry, entrances and exits, entry control, locks and keys, alarm systems, and lighting; identification of restricted areas, including computer rooms; procedures to control theft or pilferage of property or information; employee safety, including fire protection and emergency plans; security personnel required, including needed training and responsibilities; and security indoctrination of all employees.

All potential targets of attack should be identified and the means for eliminating or reducing the risk to these targets specified. Pure risks should also be identified. For example, is the facility susceptible to accidents, arson, auto theft, bombs, burglary, fraud, kidnapping, larceny, sabotage, theft, or vandalism? For each pure risk identified, appropriate security measures should be recommended.

---

The security survey (audit) is a critical, objective, on-site analysis of the total security system.

---

The survey lists the components of the security system to be observed and evaluated. Many such surveys exist. Figure 4–4 illustrates a security survey.

The Mecklenburg County Police Department has developed a graphic checklist for security measures to prevent burglary (Figure 4–5).

**J&B Innovative Enterprises, Inc.**
**12908 Revere Lane, Champlin MN 55316, (612)427-9645**
**HOLIDAY/WEEKEND SECURITY CHECKLIST**

*Instructions:* Check all items, ensure each area has been inspected for general safety, see GENERAL SAFETY checklist.** **DO NOT leave this facility unattended if ANY of the *Bold* items on this checklist cannot be checked.** Refer to the emergency personnel list at the receptionist desk, contact one of the persons on the list for further instructions. Minor problems that can be resolved the next working day should be logged under comments. This checklist must be submitted to the plant manager the next working day.

**\*\*GENERAL SAFETY** (check each area)

- ☐ *\*All cigarettes extinguished*
- ☐ *\*All roof access doors locked*
- ☐ *\*All water faucets closed*
- ☐ *\*Flammable spills which may ignite*
- ☐ *\*Obvious frayed/defective wiring*
- ☐ *\*All Fire Doors secured*
- ☐ Floors condition okay
- ☐ Aisles clear
- ☐ Stairways clear
- ☐ Lights (no burned-out bulbs)
- ☐ First Aid kits visible & stocked
- ☐ Fire extinguishers visible & charged

**PRODUCTION AREA** (Do not power down any equipment, unless specified)

- ☐ *\*Windows secured*
- ☐ *\*Compressor off, relief valve open*
- ☐ *\*Fans & Machinery off*
- ☐ Compressor room locked
- ☐ Air hose service lines bled
- ☐ Rest rooms empty
- ☐ Lights off/night lights on

**SHIPPING & RECEIVING AREA**

- ☐ *\*Fans & machinery off*
- ☐ *\*Garage doors secure*
- ☐ *\*Battery chargers turned off*
- ☐ Rest rooms empty
- ☐ Forklift secure
- ☐ Windows secure
- ☐ Lights off/night lights on

**STOCK/CRIB ROOM**

- ☐ *\*Stock room locked*
- ☐ *\*Crib window locked*
- ☐ Rest room empty
- ☐ Lights off/night lights on

**OFFICE AREA** (Do not power down any equipment including computers)

- ☐ *\*Safe Locked*
- ☐ *\*File cabinets locked*
- ☐ All office doors closed
- ☐ Lights off/night lights on

**BUILDING EXTERIOR**

- ☐ *\*All external doors & windows locked*
- ☐ Outside lights switch on, timer set
- ☐ Parking lot empty
- ☐ Gates in parking area locked

**COMPUTER ROOM** (do not power down any equipment)

- ☐ *\*Door locked, alarm set*

**CHECKLIST COMPLETED** (minor problems logged under comments)

- ☐ *\*Plant secured*
- ☐ *\*Security alarm tested & armed*

I understand and have completed the preceding checklist. It will be submitted to the plant manager the next working day.

Name_____

Time _____ Date_____

Comments:_____
_____

**Figure 4–4 Basic security survey.**
*Courtesy of J & B Innovative Enterprises, Inc.*

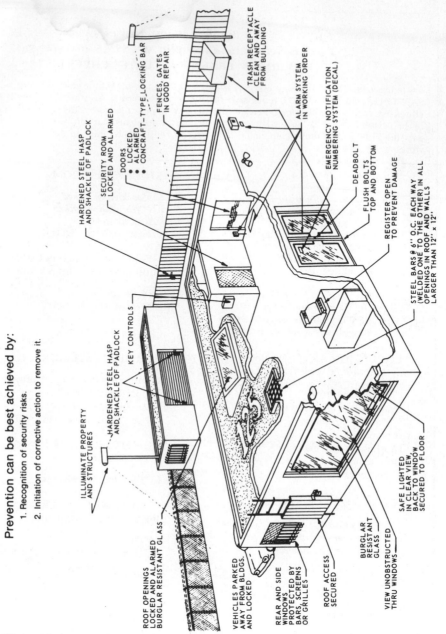

**Figure 4–5  Sample security survey.**
*Courtesy of Mecklenburg County Police Department, Charlotte, N.C.*

The Mecklenburg County Police also have developed a checklist to assess vulnerability to crime that could be adapted to suit a given establishment (Figure 4–6).

## Conducting the Security Survey

After the survey is developed, someone should physically walk through the establishment, observing and talking to personnel to obtain the

---

**HOW VULNERABLE IS YOUR BUSINESS?**

➤ Are you and your employees careful and alert when opening and closing your place of business?

➤ Do you keep a record of equipment and merchandise serial numbers?

➤ Are your employees thoroughly screened before hiring?

➤ Do you keep more than a minimum amount of money on hand?

➤ Is your alarm system checked regularly?

➤ Do you have a key control system?

➤ Are locks re-keyed after an employee leaves your employment?

➤ Is your safe combination changed periodically?

➤ Are any company vehicles parked where they block the view of doors and windows, or can be used for climbing onto the roof?

➤ Do you vary your route and schedule of banking?

➤ Are your employees trained in procedures for a robbery, burglary, shoplifter, short change, check, and credit card artist?

➤ Have you participated in Operation Identification?

---

**Figure 4–6 Sample security survey.**
*Courtesy of Mecklenburg County Police Department, Charlotte, N.C.*

required information. Usually the survey is conducted by the security director, but it may be conducted by an outside consulting firm.

---

The information needed for a security survey is obtained by observing and by talking to personnel.

---

Evaluation may be inherently threatening to employees. No one wants to be found responsible for a breach in security. But employees must be honest in their responses if the results of the survey are to be valid. Therefore, the correct climate must be established so that employees will cooperate and answer questions honestly. Of utmost importance is explaining the purpose of the survey to those from whom information is requested. Without such an explanation, the people interviewed may feel they are "under suspicion" for their actions. Many of the interviewing techniques discussed in Chapter 11 are applicable when conducting a security survey.

## ☐ SELECTING ALTERNATIVES TO HANDLE IDENTIFIED RISKS

Once risks are identified, alternatives are selected to reduce vulnerability to them. Inherent in risk management is a logical, systematic approach to deal with the recognized hazards.

---

Alternatives for risk handling include the following:

➤ Risk elimination.          ➤ Risk transfer.
➤ Risk reduction.           ➤ Risk acceptance.
➤ Risk spreading.           ➤ combonation

**RISK ELIMINATION**  The best alternative, if realistic, is to eliminate the risk entirely. For example, the risk of losses from bad checks or credit card fraud can be avoided if the business does not accept checks or credit cards. The risk of employees till tapping is eliminated if they are denied access to the cash register. Dynamic risks can be avoided or eliminated. They exist because of a management decision and can be eliminated by a change in management decision.

**RISK REDUCTION**  Pure risks will always exist and cannot be completely eliminated, and some dynamic risks cannot be avoided without incurring some other type of loss. Frequently, the best alternative is to establish procedures and use physical hardware to reduce or minimize the risk. For example, establishing and implementing check-cashing policies can reduce the risk of loss from bad checks. Installing locks, security lighting, and alarm systems can reduce the risk of loss from burglary by helping delay and/or detect intruders. If the assets at risk are of high value, such risk-reducing methods should be considered.

**RISK SPREADING**  Closely related to risk reduction is the practice of risk spreading. This approach uses methods that ensure that the potential loss in any single incident is reduced (for example, placing expensive jewelry in separate display cases). Such risk spreading further reduces exposure to threats after risk-avoidance and risk-reduction measures have been instituted.

**RISK TRANSFER**  If risk elimination, risk reduction, and risk spreading do not bring the risk to an acceptable level, the risk may be transferred either by taking out insurance or by raising prices. Most establishments carry insurance against fires and other types of natural disasters, as well as liability insurance in case an employee or other person is injured on the premises.

Rising insurance costs, however, can drastically affect reliance on insurance as a way to guard against unforeseen business losses. In addition, some losses are virtually impossible to insure against, for example, loss of customer confidence, lowered employee morale, and loss of reputation.

Clearly, insurance can never be a substitute for a security program. Another alternative to effective risk reduction is price raising, which also has obvious drawbacks. Most retail establishments raise prices to cover shoplifting losses. The key element of this method is the absorption of the loss by a third party.

**RISK ACCEPTANCE**  It is never cost-effective, practical, or, indeed, possible to provide 100 percent security for an establishment. Risks can never be entirely eliminated. Some must simply be accepted. If the security survey has been completely conducted and the results competently analyzed, the greatest risks will be identified and dealt with by the appropriate alternative or combination of alternatives. The remaining risks will be accepted as part of the "cost of doing business."

**COMBINATION**  Usually a combination of alternatives provides the best risk management.

# REPORTING THE RESULTS

Once the survey is conducted, the risk analysis is completed, and the alternatives for handling the risks are selected, the information must be communicated to individuals who can act on the findings. The information should be written into a comprehensive report that includes, at minimum, the following sections:

I) Introduction—a brief summary of the purpose of the survey, the anticipated risks, and the identified needs and objectives of the total security system; also, a description of the survey developed and conducted to assess the system. Include a copy of the survey in an appendix at the end of the report.

II) A discussion of the risk analysis.
   A) Strengths of the system—what is working well.
   B) Weaknesses of the system—areas of vulnerability and potential risk, arranged in order of priority.

III) Recommendations for alternatives for managing the risks, including the estimated cost and savings and who should be responsible for making the changes.

The completed security survey, the security report, and any copies of these documents should be treated as *confidential* documents.

# IMPLEMENTING THE RECOMMENDATIONS

Implementing the recommended changes is management's responsibility. Changes might include modifying procedures, improving or upgrading security equipment, or adding additional security equipment or personnel.

Budgeting is always an important consideration in implementing any recommended changes. Budgeting efforts may be facilitated by dividing costs into specific categories, as illustrated in Figure 4–7. Budget requirements may limit somewhat the extent of implementation. Some changes may not be made for weeks or months, but a schedule should be established so that high-priority changes are made first.

Implementing the recommendations also frequently requires tact and diplomacy. Security managers must recognize their establishment's overall plan, goals, and needs. The security system does not operate in a vacuum, but relies on the understanding and support of all persons involved in the business or industry. Consequently, security managers must build acceptance and trust, and they must act as professionals who understand and respect the needs and wants of others.

# EVALUATING THE SECURITY SYSTEM

Evaluation of security should be ongiong. The effects of any changes made as a result of the security survey should be studied. For example, if a need for personnel training is identified and a program instituted, the effectiveness of that training should be assessed. Periodic, unannounced audits should be conducted of security procedures, such as cash handling or check cashing.

| | Investment | | Operating Costs | | |
|---|---|---|---|---|---|
| | Prevention | Loss Limitation | Prevention | Loss Limitation | Insurance |
| *Work Protection* | | | | | |
| Common equipment | x | | x | | |
| Individual equipment | x | | x | | |
| *Surveillance* | | | | | |
| Identity card | | | x | | |
| Personnel | | | x | | |
| Technical | x | | x | | |
| Fencing, locks | x | | | | |
| *Fire Service* | | | | | |
| Prevention | x | | x | | |
| Extinguishing | | x | x | | |
| *Company Health Care* | | | | | |
| Sick care | x | x | x | x | |
| *Insurance* | | | | | |
| Company insurance | | | | | x |
| Personal insurance | | | | | x |
| Products liability | | | | | x |
| Labour market no-fault | | | | | x |
| Liability insurance | | | | | |
| *Reserve Equipment* | | | | x | |
| *Training and information in company protection questions* | | | x | x | |
| **Total Sum** | | | | | |

**Figure 4–7 Example of the arrangement of the budget.**
*From Statsföretag AB, Skandia Insurance Co. and Skandia Risk Management Ltd., Stockholm, Sweden.*

Each component of the security system should be periodically evaluated and changes made as needed.

Some aspects of the security system, such as closing procedures, are checked daily. Other components should have a regular schedule of inspection.

The needs and objectives of the entire security system should be reevaluated annually. Security needs change as an establishment grows or as the neighborhood changes. If the city installs street lights or provides routine patrol by local police, the establishment may need less of its own external security. However, if the neighborhood deteriorates and vandalism and crime increase, it may need more security.

## SUMMARY

**P**rivate security managers must recognize and deal with both pure risks—risks with the potential for injury, damage, or loss with no possible benefits—and dynamic risks—risks that have the potential for both benefits and losses. They do so through risk management: anticipating, recognizing, and analyzing risks; taking steps to reduce or prevent such risks; and evaluating the results.

A systematic approach to preventing loss through risk management includes risk analysis, policy formulation, specification of a protection plan, and follow-up. Risk management is both a moral and a legal responsibility. Risk analysis focuses on three factors: vulnerability, probability, and criticality. A key tool in risk analysis is the security survey. The security survey is a critical, objective, on-site analysis of the total security system. The information needed for a security survey is obtained by observing and by talking to personnel.

Once risks are identified, alternatives to handle these risks must be selected. Alternatives for risk handling include risk elimination, risk reduction, risk spreading, risk transfer, and/or risk acceptance.

In addition to the comprehensive security survey that may be conducted yearly or at even more lengthy time intervals, periodic audits should be made of each component of the security system, and changes should be made as needed.

## APPLICATION

1) List the pure and dynamic risks in your own daily life. Then indicate whether you have taken steps to reduce these risks and, if so, how.
2) As the security manager for a local hotel, list the dynamic and pure risks that could affect the operation and rank them in order of priority.
3) As security manager in charge of organizing company protection, list the statutes in your state that affect a cost-effective security program, e.g., licensing, bonding, training requirements, and the like.

## DISCUSSION QUESTIONS

1) What types of programs would you implement to eliminate pure risks in a company?
2) How much responsibility and authority should be placed at the security supervisory level to cope with dynamic risks?

3) What could cause the needs and objectives of a security system to change? Elaborate.
4) In developing a security survey, what areas should receive high priority?
5) Is it better for security managers to develop their own security survey or to use one developed by someone else?

## REFERENCES

Foster, O. C. Introduction to risk management. *The practice of crime prevention* Vol. 1, *Understanding crime prevention*. Louisville, KY: The National Crime Prevention Institute, School of Police Administration, University of Louisville, 1978.

Green, Gion. *Introduction to security,* 4th ed. Revised by Robert J. Fisher. Stoneham, MA: Butterworth Publishers, 1987.

Kingsbury, A. A. *Introduction to security and crime prevention surveys.* Springfield, IL: Charles C. Thomas, 1973.

Stenno, D. Be sure your security is legally secure. *Security world,* June 1981, p. 35.

# ☐ INTRODUCTION

Security managers must be concerned with their own loss prevention program and the individuals hired to implement it, but they must also know how the private "policing" function differs from that of the public police, how they might contribute to public policing efforts, and in numerous instances, how they might benefit from public policing efforts.

They must also be completely familiar with the legal authority they and their employees have and the restrictions on this authority. Finally, they must know what civil lawsuits they must protect against and how to most effectively do so.

These aspects of the total context within which private security operates must be kept in mind throughout the remainder of the book as specific security responsibilities and security systems are discussed.

## Chapter Five

# The Public/Private Interface, Legal Authority, and Civil Liability

### DO YOU KNOW

- How private security officers and public police officers are alike?
- How private security officers differ from public police officers?
- What authority private security officers have? How they are restricted?
- How private security officers compare in numbers with public police officers?
- How private and public security officers might work together?
- What advantages private security offers public police and vice versa?
- What a tort is?
- What a nondelegable duty is?
- For what actions security officers are most frequently sued?
- How civil liability can be reduced?

## ☐ THE PUBLIC/PRIVATE INTERFACE

Loss prevention, security, privacy—such goals are not the sole domain of private security. They have been of concern since recorded time. Recall from Chapter 1 that the history of public policing and private security is intertwined.

According to Shearing and Stenning (1987, p. 15):

> With contemporary corporations as the modern-day equivalents of feudal lords, reigning supreme over huge feudal estates, the search for a historical parallel leads us back beyond frankpledge to more ancient concepts of private peaces and conflicting private authorities. Indeed, the very distinction between private and public takes on a new significance that blurs, and contradicts, its liberal meanings. This is true not only because private "individuals" are engaged in the maintenance of public order but also because more and more public life is nowadays conducted on privately owned and controlled property.
>
> Corporate orders are defended on the grounds that corporations, like any other "persons," have the right to a sphere of private authority over which they have undisturbed jurisdiction. Furthermore, this right is sacrosanct, for to encroach upon it would undermine the very freedoms that are definitive of liberal democracy.

This "right to a sphere of private authority" has long been recognized by governments and by the wide variety of policing mechanisms they have established, with public and private policing continuing to coexist, as noted by Bayley (1987, p. 6):

> Policing has been done under an enormous variety of auspices—national and local governments, revolutionary and nonrevolutionary parties, neighborhoods, churches, landowners, workers, peasants, businesses, and professional associations. Even more interesting, varieties of policing are complexly mixed. . . . Although the proportions in the mixture vary, similar forms appear again and again. In particular, "public" and "private" policing never wholly supplant one another. Indeed, the distinction itself becomes problematic in many circumstances. Public and private police institutions cooperate, sometimes interpenetrate, and often share modes of operation. . . . Policing is a reciprocating engine in that groups regulate individuals but individuals collectively regulate groups.

As noted by the United Way Strategic Institute (1989, p. 3): "There will be a blurring of the boundaries that have traditionally defined the roles of the public sector versus the private sector, as well as individual versus institutional responsibilities."

Shearing et al. (1980, p. 14) describe private policing as a continuum going from one end representing those who have special powers and public accountability to the other end representing no special powers and accountability only to private interests:

> Where on this continuum any given security employee should be placed depends, we believe, not only on who his immediate employer is but also on what legal powers he possesses and to whom he is accountable for the exercise of those powers.

Marx (1987, p. 187) lists a series of questions to be asked in determining if policing is public or private:

➤ Where does the policing occur—in public, private, or mixed space?
➤ Whose interest is served by the policing—the general public, a private interest, or both?
➤ What is the function of the policing?
➤ Who pays for, or sponsors, the policing—public or private interests, or both?
➤ Who carries it out—regular sworn agents of the state with full police powers, special-purpose deputies with more limited powers, or citizens with no official powers?
➤ Who controls and directs the policing?
➤ Where the policing involves data collection and investigation, who has access to the results?
➤ What popular and self-definitions characterize those doing the policing?
➤ What organizational form does the policing take?
➤ To what extent are social control agents linked together in informal networks that transcend their nominal definition as public or private?

Answers to these questions will call attention to certain basic similarities and differences between the private and the public "policing" efforts.

## Similarities Between Private and Public Officers

Private and public officers do have many things in common, including wearing a uniform and badge, being trained to compel obedience to their authority, and being liable for their actions. Both private and public officers seek to prevent losses from criminal actions and, if such losses occur, to investigate and apprehend the person responsible.

---

Private and public police officers may wear uniforms and badges, are trained in compelling obedience, and are apt to be sued. Both also seek to prevent crime and to apprehend criminals.

---

Both public and private officers may receive respect and cooperation from those they work with or may face hostility and aggression. In addition, both public and private officers have a tremendous influence on the image of those for whom they work. Their every action has an impact on public relations, as discussed in Chapter 12.

## Differences Between Private and Public Officers

Four basic differences exist between private and public officers: (1) the financial orientation, (2) the employer, (3) the specific functions performed, and (4) the statutory power possessed.

---

| Private Security: | Public Law Enforcement: |
|---|---|
| ➤ Profit-oriented enterprise. | ➤ Nonprofit, governmental enterprise. |
| ➤ Serving specific private clients. | ➤ Serving the general public. |
| ➤ To prevent crime, protect assets, and reduce losses. | ➤ To combat crime, enforce laws, and apprehend offenders. |
| ➤ To regulate noncriminal conduct not under the authority of public police. | ➤ Statutory authority. |

---

Other basic differences between private and public officers exist in the authority they have and the restrictions placed on them.

## □ LEGAL AUTHORITY

Because they wear uniforms, often carry weapons, and have been placed in a position of authority by their employer, private security officers may appear to have more legal authority than private citizens. This is not always the case, however.

---

Private security officers usually have no more powers than private citizens. As citizens, they have the power to arrest, to investigate, to carry weapons, to defend themselves, and to defend their property or property entrusted to their care.

---

Often private security officers conduct periodic inspections of personal items such as briefcases, purses, and lunch boxes as directed by management and specific policy. Generally, private security officers have no police authority. Their authority does not go beyond that of a private citizen. Nonetheless, because they wear uniforms and may be armed, they are likely to give the *appearance* of authority. In addition, their training and experience makes it more likely that they will be able to exercise this authority.

They can deny access to unauthorized individuals into their employers' business or company, and they can enforce all rules and regulations established by their employers. They can also search employees and question them without giving the Miranda warning in most states.

Private security officers *do* have the authority to prevent access of unauthorized individuals into a business or company and to enforce those rules and regulations established by their employer.

In *Bowman v. State* (1983), an Indiana court ruled that private security officers, unlike public law enforcement officials, are *not* required to issue Miranda warnings. Giving warnings, the court observed, is required only in cases involving state action.

## Restrictions on Private Security Officers

Laws governing the conduct of private security officers are derived from several sources: tort law, state statutes, criminal law, constitutional guarantees, and contract law.

Private security officers cannot invade another's privacy, electronically eavesdrop, trespass, or wear a uniform or badge that closely resembles that of a public police officer.

Because of actions they must perform in fulfilling their responsibilities, private security officers are more open to civil lawsuits than most other citizens.

Many of the restrictions on private security officers come from the tort law of each state. (Tort law defines citizens' responsibilities to each other and provides for lawsuits to recover damages for injury caused by failing to carry out these responsibilities.) Civil liability is discussed later in this chapter.

State and federal criminal laws prohibit security officers from committing crimes such as assault. Other state and federal laws regulate wiretapping, surveillance, gathering information on individuals, impersonating public police officials, and purchasing and carrying firearms. For example, in *National Labor Relations Board v. St. Vincent's Hospital* (1977), the U.S. Court of Appeals held that the interrogation of hospital employees by their supervisors in connection with several thefts does *not* constitute coercive action. The court did, however, observe that placing hospital employees who were engaged in union activities under surveillance did violate the National Labor Relations Act.

Although it is well known that the U.S. Constitution places the major legal limitations on police powers, such restrictions are applied only to state activities. However, the distinction between state and private activity is not always clear-cut. This is true, for example, when a private security officer is hired by a public institution or when a private security officer is deputized. In such instances, it is often felt that the constitutional restrictions *do* apply to those private security officers.

Usually private security officers who are deputized or are contracted by a public authority are subject to the same restrictions as public officers. In addition, public police officers who work during off-hours in private security positions are considered to be public law enforcement officers in many states. Consequently, many police departments do not allow their officers to "moonlight" in private security positions. Two states, Connecticut and Kansas, specifically deny a private security license to anyone vested with police powers.

Clearly, the distinction between public and private police is not always black and white, but various shades of gray. In some states shopkeeper statutes and other similar legislation dealing with railroad officers, nuclear facility officers, bank security officers, and the like give private security officers greater powers than those of the general public. A few jurisdictions recognize private security officers who have total public police authority based on compliance with certain legal and training requirements.

State laws also regulate the arrest powers of private security officers. In the majority of thirty-one states surveyed, private security officers can arrest for a misdemeanor. In all thirty-one states they can arrest for a felony, but in none of the states are they granted police arrest powers.

Other restrictions are placed on private security officers by local ordinances and state statutes that establish licensing regulations. These restrictions vary greatly from state to state.

Finally, most security officers are further restricted by the contract they sign to provide their services to an agency or to an employer.

The similarities in goals and objectives of private and public policing and the differences in their legal authority suggest that in many ways public and private policing efforts are complementary.

## ☐ THE COMPLEMENTARY ROLES OF PRIVATE AND PUBLIC OFFICERS

Private and public security forces frequently engage in similar activities and have similar goals, including prevention of crime. However, private security officers also perform functions that cannot be performed by public law enforcement officers, which makes their roles complementary.

Security officers provide services the public police cannot either because of legal constraints or because of limited resources. Law enforcement officers usually cannot be spared to investigate suspected crimes such as employee pilferage. Nor are they legally responsible to enforce the private rules and regulations of businesses and organizations. In fact, public police officers often have no jurisdiction inside premises until after a crime has been committed.

Promoting cooperative interaction between private and public police officers is of utmost importance, as noted by Charles Connally, chairperson of the American Society for Industrial Security's (ASIS) Law Enforcement Liaison Council at a national conference (Bocklet, 1990 p. 59):

> Many private forces are far ahead of police departments in technology and available security resources. Their training has improved, some meet state standards and experienced retired law enforcement officers are often employed as directors. In fact, security management is becoming a real profession with 200 colleges giving courses, 25 offering BAs, ten offering MAs, and the University of Michigan even starting a doctorate program.
>
> ASIS's major task this year is to develop operational guidelines for the burgeoning security industry to link up with local law enforcement.

Connally noted that 80 percent of the nation's police departments have a dozen or fewer officers and could especially profit from linking up with private security:

> Police can save time and manpower by training private security to gather evidence and do preliminary investigations, become better courtroom witnesses, take crime and accident reports, carry out tedious surveillance procedures, and even giving lectures that police usually do.
>
> Large industrial plants can loan smaller departments listening devices, communications equipment, trucks, rovers, helicopters and planes. And since corporations maintain top-grade lawyers, they might provide useful legal advice on cases as well. The gains in working with private security are multiple.

Although public police officers also seek to prevent crime, a large portion of their time is devoted to enforcing laws, investigating crimes, and apprehending suspects. Their presence may serve as a deterrent to crime, but they cannot be everywhere at once. The vital role played by private security in preventing crime was clearly stated in the preface of the Task Force Report on Private Security (*Private Security*, 1976):

> The application of the resources, technology, skills, and knowledge of the private security industry presents the best hope available for protecting the citizen who has witnessed his defenses against crime shrink to a level which leaves him virtually unprotected.
>
> Underutilized by police, all but ignored by prosecutors and the judiciary, and unknown to corrections officials, the private security professional may be the one person in this society who has the knowledge to effectively prevent crime.

In 1978 the *Police Chief*, the official publication of the International Association of Chiefs of Police (IACP), devoted an entire issue to private security. An editorial in that issue by the president of the IACP reiterated the importance of private security in relation to public law enforcement (Shook, p. 8):

Today, more than ever, private security forces are contributing to the public safety and security. Their omnipresence in business, industry, transportation, and government relieves public police from many of the order maintenance duties that are so vital to the public safety.

Likewise, a key finding of the Hallcrest Report was the need for private security (Cunningham and Taylor, 1985, p. 275):

> Citizen fear of crime and awareness that criminal justice resources alone cannot effectively control crime has led to a growing use of individual and corporate protective measures, including private security products and services and neighborhood-based crime prevention programs. . . . Law enforcement resources have stabilized and in some areas are declining. This mandates greater cooperation with the private sector and its private security resources to jointly forge a partnership on an equal basis for crime prevention and reduction. Law enforcement can ill afford to continue isolating and, in some cases, ignoring this important resource. . . . The creative use of private security, human resources and technology may be one viable option left to control crime in our communities. . . .
>
> As long as law enforcement maintains the posture that they should bear the primary burden for protection of the community, then creative alternative solutions will be limited in the midst of dwindling public resources.

Chapter Five
The Public/Private
Interface, Legal
Authority, and
Civil Liability

103

One area that police seem willing to let private security personnel handle is "economic crime." Crimes such as shoplifting, employee theft and pilferage, and credit card and check fraud are usually a low priority with public police and are usually well developed by the time the police are notified. In addition, management is usually more interested in the deterrent value of prosecution and is usually more interested in plea bargaining than in a conviction. Cunningham and Taylor (1985, p. 245) comment on this area: "Since employee theft is the largest single problem in business and institutions and is resolved largely through private justice systems, private security removes a tremendous burden from the public criminal justice system and contributes greatly to crime prevention, detection, and deterrence."

Bottom (1986, p. 13), reporting on the Hallcrest survey of police attitudes on transferring police responsibilities to private security companies, says: "In general, police executives said yes, police will be happy to yield burglar alarm response (57 percent); incident report completion for insurance purposes (68 percent); preliminary investigation (40 percent); and misdemeanor incident reports (45 percent)." Unfortunately, however, friction often exists between private and public officers. Historically, public and private security have seen themselves as being in competition, with private security usually coming out on the "short end of the stick." A police sergeant was quoted as saying (Remesch, 1989, p. 32): ". . . to state that the only difference between a police officer and a security officer is the title 'security,' is like comparing a surgeon to a butcher since they both cut meat." According to Remesch (1989, p. 33):

> Much of the problem centers on the still-evolving nature of the private security industry. Like a grown sibling, the older, wiser, public police officer wants the private police officer to just follow his lead in the path he's trav-

eled a million times. But like the younger sibling who has finally reached the age of maturity, members of private security are saying to their brethren: "We've grown up. Give us some respect."

That private security has, indeed, "grown up" is highlighted by Bocklet (1990, p. 54):

Today private security plays a major role in the national scene, employing an estimated two million people, and is growing. By contrast, there's about 600,000 police officers, experiencing zero growth over the last two decades and apparently stabilizing at that level. In 1986, private protection services spent $22 billion, while the police budgets came in at $13 billion.

There are now almost twice as many people employed in private security as there are public police.

Trojanowicz and Bucqueroux (1990, p. 131) note the "dramatic and far-reaching change, for good or ill, taking place during this past decade . . . the continued and increasing privatization of public justice. . . . Almost invisibly, private for-profit and nonprofit corporations have been assuming roles that were once almost exclusively the province of the public criminal justice system."

## Public/Private Interdependence

Marx (1987, pp. 172–173) discusses five forms of "interdependence between public and private police" in undercover work:

➤ Joint public/private investigations.
➤ Public agents hiring or delegating authority to private police.
➤ Private interests hiring public police.
➤ New organizational forms in which the distinction between public and private is blurred.
➤ The circulation of personnel between the public and private sector.

Public and private officers may work together, may hire or delegate authority to each other, or may move from one sector to the other.

Marx gives as an example of joint public/private investigations an FBI-IBM sting involving "perhaps the largest industrial espionage case ever in the United States," the sale of computer secrets in Silicon Valley.

Bocklet (1990, pp. 58–59) describes a joint effort between public and private police in Tacoma, Washington, where drug trafficking was a major problem at downtown intersections. Businesses banded together, taxed themselves, and hired fifteen private security guards who became community service representatives (CSRs), patrolling the streets and providing escort services to those who wanted it. They also provided much valuable information about drug trafficking to the public police, serving as "extra sets of eyes and ears" (p. 58). According to an officer involved with the program: "The heavy security presence has driven the druggies out of the downtown area and a better business climate has ensued" (pp. 58–59).

To illustrate public hiring of private police Marx (1987, p. 178) notes that in 1984: "Approximately 36,000 of the nation's 1.1 million private security guards worked for government. . . . They serve as U.S. marshals in federal courthouses, and guard military bases, nuclear facilities, NASA, and various public building, including city halls and public housing projects. They also provide security at airports."

Private sector hiring of public police can be seen in such efforts as trade associations and chambers of commerce cooperating in sting operations. For example: "In operation 'mod-sound' the recording industry contributed $100,000 to an FBI investigation of pirated records and tapes" (Marx, 1987, p. 178).

New quasi-public or quasi-private organizations include the Law Enforcement Intelligence Unit (LEIU), "founded as a private organization for local and state police to share intelligence files. The private nature of the organization apparently permits the exchange of information that would not otherwise be possible by agents acting strictly in a public capacity" (Marx, 1987, p. 179). Another example is the National Auto Theft Bureau, a private, nonprofit organization that serves as a clearinghouse for law enforcement agencies seeking information on vehicle thefts.

Finally, the exchange of personnel also is occurring frequently, with people using security jobs as stepping-stones into law enforcement and law enforcement officers moonlighting or retiring to go into private security or to become security directors for corporations.

According to Burden (1989, p. 92): Today, in some city precincts, there are more moonlighters than on-duty officers on the streets."

Chapter Five
The Public/Private
Interface, Legal
Authority, and
Civil Liability

105

## Mutual Advantages

The advantages of private police using public police, according to Marx (1987, p. 183), include the benefits of "the power of state agents to arrest, search, interrogate, carry weapons and use force and electronic surveillance, and gain access to otherwise protected information. Their legal liability may also be reduced or eliminated. The training, experience, skill, and backup support that public police can offer are other factors."

Public police offer private security the power of interrogation, search, arrest, and use of electronic surveillance. They may reduce or eliminate their legal liability, and they offer training, experience, and backup.

The advantages of public police using private police, says Marx (1987, p. 183), include: "Information. Sworn agents cannot be everywhere and they face restrictions on access to private places. . . . But private agents, operating on private property and in contexts where persons appear voluntarily, are granted wide authority to carry out searches, to keep people under surveillance, and to collect and distribute extensive personal information." In addition: "Private police vastly extend surveillance and reduce demands on public police. In addition . . . they may offer public police a way to get things done that the former are prohibited from doing," such as interrogating without giving the Miranda warning and conducting searches and seizures without warrants. Private police are not bound by the Exclusionary Rule, which would make inadmissible any evidence obtained by means violating a person's constitutional rights.

Private security officers offer the public police information, access to private places, and extended surveillance and coverage. In addition, they are not bound by the Exclusionary Rule, so can question without giving the Miranda warning and can search without a warrant.

In fact, employees' obligations to their employers may sometimes allow public police greater freedom in their investigations. In *United States v. Cockery* (1984), for example, this was true.

A bank employee who was suspected of embezzlement submitted to questioning by FBI agents under instructions from her employer. Her attorney later argued that her confession should be barred. The U.S. Court of Appeals for the 8th Circuit disagreed. It observed that the statements had been made voluntarily, and the suspect had consented to the interview as part of her obligation to her employer.

Although not as rigidly controlled as public police, private security officers must still respect the rights of others. Failure to do so can and often does result in civil lawsuits.

## □ CIVIL LIABILITY

Private security officers are responsible for their actions. If such actions are unlawful, they may be sued. The unlawful action is technically called a *tort*.

A *tort* is a civil wrong for which a person can be sued.

Civil actions may be brought against any private security personnel who commit an unlawful action against another person. Often, the officer's employer is sued as well the officer.

In *Granite Construction Corp. v. Superior Court* (1983), for example, a California court held that the term *person* includes corporations and that therefore a corporation *can* be prosecuted for manslaughter.

In addition, as noted by Schnabolk (1983), a "revolutionary theory" affecting private security is the "concept of a nondelegable duty":

Under the principles of agency law, an independent contractor relationship relieves the one who hired the independent contractors of liability because no control is exercised over the activities of the contractor. Thus, a motel owner, for example, could employ a security agency to protect the motel. If an incident occurred that resulted in an injury, the motel owner would claim he/she was not responsible for the injury because the duty to provide protection had been given to the guard service. Under the concept of a nondelegable duty, however, the motel owner would remain liable. Some duties rightfully belong to certain individuals, according to the courts, and the law will not permit these individuals to escape liability by delegating the duty to someone else. The law allows a delegation of authority, but not of responsibility for the performance of a legal duty.

---

A **nondelegable duty** is one for which authority can be given to another person, but responsibility cannot. Civil liability remains with the person who has the legal duty to act.

---

Chapter Five
The Public/Private
Interface, Legal
Authority, and
Civil Liability

107

Civil liability has become of increasing concern in the private security profession. As noted in the Hallcrest Report II (Cunningham et al., 1990, pp. 33–34):

> Perhaps the largest indirect cost of economic crime has been the increase in civil litigation and damage awards over the past 20 years. This litigation usually claims inadequate or improperly used security to protect customers, employees, tenants, and the public from crimes and injuries. Most often these cases involve inadequate security at apartments and condominiums; shopping malls, convenience and other retail stores; hotels, motels, and restaurants; health care and education institutions; office buildings; and the premises of other business or government facilities.

One expert has estimated that U.S. corporations pay in excess of $20 billion annually to litigation lawyers (Allison, 1990, p. 166).

The Hallcrest Report II goes on to note (p. 36): "All indications point to more security-related lawsuits and more $11 million-plus awards than ever before." In addition, the report says:

> Growing concern over lawsuits was expressed by virtually all of the corporate and contract security managers in the Hallcrest 1989 reconnaissance interviews. . . . [The concern was] manifest in a variety of security management issues such as hiring, training, equipment (armed vs. unarmed), personnel deployment, crime incident response, supervision, and security systems (locking, lighting, fencing, access control, etc.).

Schnabolk (1983) suggests not only that lawsuits have increased, but that judicial and legislative sanctions against the security industry have increased as well. He gives several reasons for this increase:

➤ The exceptional growth of the industry.
➤ The rising expectations of the public.
➤ The quality of security services.
➤ The increase in the number of new laws and lawyers.

➤ The availability of liability insurance.
➤ The increased sophistication of individuals regarding legal matters and their rights.

Security managers and those they employ must be aware of those actions that are most likely to put them at risk of a civil lawsuit or criminal charges.

## Common Civil Lawsuits Brought Against Private Security

The most common civil suits brought against private security are for assault, battery, false imprisonment, defamation, intentional infliction of emotional distress, invasion of privacy, and negligence.

**Assault** is an intentional act causing reasonable apprehension of physical harm in the mind of another. An example is threatening someone, with or without a weapon, into obeying your demands.

**Battery** is the unconsented, offensive touching of another person, either directly or indirectly. An example is touching a person or his/her clothing in an angry or rude manner. Use of bodily force should be avoided whenever possible. At times, however, security officers may have to use force to defend themselves or others from serious bodily harm.

**False imprisonment** is unreasonably restraining another person using physical or psychological means to deny that person freedom of movement. An example is requiring someone to remain in a room while the police are being called. If a person *is* detained, there must be reasonable grounds to believe that a crime was committed and that the person being detained actually committed it. *Mere suspicion is not enough.*

**Defamation** is injuring a person's reputation, such as by falsely inferring, by either words or conduct, in front of a third disinterested party, that a person committed a crime. An example is to falsely accuse someone of shoplifting in front of friends or to falsely accuse an employee of pilferage in front of coworkers or visitors.

**Intentional infliction of emotional distress** refers to outrageous or grossly reckless conduct intended to and highly likely to cause a severe emotional reaction. An example is to threaten to have an employee fired because he/she is suspected of stealing.

**Invasion of privacy** refers to an unreasonable, unconsented intrusion into the personal affairs or property of a person. An example would be searching an employee's personal property outside of search guidelines established by the employer.

**Negligence** occurs when a person has a duty to act reasonably but fails to do so and, as a result, someone is injured. An example is failing to correct a dangerous situation on the premises or failing to give assistance to an employee in distress.

Negligence suits are common, as illustrated in the following cases.

**TAYLOR V. CENTENNIAL BOWL, INC. (1966)** The plaintiff was attacked in a bowling alley's parking lot. Earlier in the evening, while she was in a cocktail lounge on the premises, a man had been bothering her, and she had asked the bouncer to keep him away from her. When the business closed for the evening, the bouncer warned her not to go out to her car because the man was in the parking lot. The plaintiff left anyway and was attacked by the man. The court held that the proprietor's knowledge of a threat of harm gave rise to a duty to take positive action to prevent the attack. A warning alone was not sufficient.

**KLINE V. 1500 MASSACHUSETTS AVENUE CORP. M. (1970)** The plaintiff was assaulted and robbed in the hallway outside her apartment. The premises had been the site of an increasing number of criminal attacks during the years of the plaintiff's residency, but despite this clear trend, the owner/landlord made no effort to maintain or continue the security devices that had been in place when the tenant moved in. The court found the landlord liable for the injuries suffered in the criminal attack.

**PICCO V. FORD'S DINER, INC. (1971)** The plaintiff in this case presented no evidence of prior criminal acts on the premises. The plaintiff, a customer at the diner, was assaulted in an unlighted parking lot at the diner's rear. The court held that it is common knowledge that lighting an area during nighttime hours deters criminal activity. Therefore, the proprietor was found liable, even though no prior criminal acts had occurred on the premises.

**ATAMIAN V. SUPERMARKETS GENERAL CORP. (1976)** Three men raped the plaintiff in a grocery store parking lot. Prior to the rape, five assaults had occurred on the premises, and the store had employed a security guard. However, the court reasoned that where a proprietor has knowledge of previous criminal attacks on its premises, a security guard might not be enough. The proprietor has the duty to ensure adequate lighting and other preventive measures to protect customers from criminal assaults. Trying to give content to the nebulous standard of "reasonable care" is, at best, difficult and often impossible.

**TRENTACOST V. BRUSSEL (1980)** A tenant was robbed and beaten in the unlocked hallway of her apartment. The court held that the landlord/tenant relationship carries with it an implied warranty that the premises will be safe, even without requiring proof of notice of dangerous neighborhood conditions.

**SORICHETTI V. CITY OF NEW YORK (1984)** A New York Court of Appeals held that the failure to provide adequate police protection by a government unit *is* a basis for liability. The defendants had a reasonable duty to provide adequate protection, especially because the plaintiff had notified them she had been threatened and assaulted. The court awarded the plaintiff $2 million in damages.

Chapter Five
The Public/Private
Interface, Legal
Authority, and
Civil Liability

109

**MEYERS V. RAMADA INN (1984)** An Ohio court held that hotel owners *can* be held liable for any injuries a guest suffers as a result of a criminal assault. However, the court stated that the guest must first demonstrate that the defendant should have anticipated the assault.

**PITLARD V. FOUR SEASONS MOTOR INN (1984)** A New Mexico court held that a hotel *can* be held liable if one of its employees assaults a guest, provided the injured party could demonstrate that the hotel had notice of similar past conduct by the employee in question.

**KOLOSKY V. WINN DIXIE STORES, INC. (1985)** A Florida court awarded $80,000 to a woman who was knocked to the floor while at a supermarket and injured by an unruly customer. The court observed that a supermarket has an obligation to take all necessary steps to ensure the security and safety of its customers.

## ☐ REDUCING LIABILITY

One extremely important way to reduce liability is to hire trustworthy, qualified individuals, whether they be proprietary or contractual. The following cases, although not pertaining specifically to private security employees, illustrate clearly the serious consequences of not hiring carefully.

**TOLBERT V. MARTIN MARIETTA (1985)** A federal court allowed a secretary to sue her aerospace company for hiring a janitor who abducted her and raped her on company premises while she was walking to lunch. The janitor had a criminal record.

**CRAMER V. HOUSING OPPORTUNITIES COMMISSION (1985)** Maryland's highest court ruled that a nighttime break-in and a rape of a public housing tenant *was* caused by the housing agency's earlier decision to hire the rapist as a building inspector. A new trial was ordered.

**MALORNEY V. B & L (1986)** The Illinois Appellate Court ruled that because B & L should have known that "truckers" are prone to give rides to hitchhikers despite rules against such actions, the general duty to hire competent employees could be extended to checking for criminal convictions.

**SHEERIN V. HOLIN (1986)** The Iowa Supreme Court ruled that the estate of a waitress stabbed to death by a cook could sue the motel-restaurant that employed them, where the murder took place during working hours.

Gallagher (1990, p. 18) suggests that liability might be lessened by setting minimum standards, establishing clear policies, and providing effective basic training. He suggests the following (p. 26):

> Consider undertaking a liability assessment—a comprehensive review of all policies, procedures, rules, regulations, operations, records and training—

with an eye to uncovering the potential areas of liability and finding ways to decrease that liability. . . .

Whatever is done to decrease liability simultaneously increases professionalism.

---

Civil liability might be reduced by hiring wisely, setting minimum standards for job performance, establishing clear policies, and providing effective training and supervision.

---

Laws regarding civil liability vary from state to state. Nonetheless, certain guidelines will usually help reduce civil liability of on-line security personnel:

Chapter Five
The Public/Private
Interface, Legal
Authority, and
Civil Liability

111

## DO
➤ Consistently and fairly enforce policies and procedures regarding all security matters and employee safety.
➤ Know and understand your duties and responsibilities.
➤ Always identify yourself as a security officer before taking any actions involving an employee or visitor.
➤ Know the limits of your authority and recognize the authority of others. If you do not have authority to act, go to someone who does.
➤ Ask for help if you are unsure and do not feel confident to handle a problem.
➤ Maintain a helpful, courteous attitude when assisting employees and visitors.
➤ Always be aware of and sensitive to individuals' privacy.
➤ Guide your behavior by the standard of *reasonableness*. Make every effort to act objectively and fairly in all situations.
➤ Maintain high visibility in common areas to deter crime.
➤ Be alert to and remedy any safety risks or potential safety hazards you observe.
➤ Remain calm at all times to perform your duties efficiently and safely.
➤ Cooperate fully in investigations or inquiries.
➤ Know who to call in emergencies and keep names and telephone numbers easily accessible.
➤ Consciously observe and promptly record your observations in a clear, concise, complete report.
➤ Following any incident, immediately record all information on an incident report form. Include all facts. Avoid conclusions and opinions.

## DO NOT
➤ Forcefully detain someone.
➤ Cause an employee or visitor to believe they are not free to leave, whether it be through physical restraint or words.
➤ Make physical contact either directly or indirectly with employees, visitors, or intruders while questioning them or escorting them to an exit.
➤ Use unnecessary force.

➤ Search any person, purse, lunch box, or toolbox unless the search is specifically authorized by management and the search guidelines have been communicated to all employees.

➤ Search employees or visitors selectively.

➤ Issue a statement or opinion or discuss any issue associated with your duties with any reporter.

➤ Question individual employees or visitors in front of others. If you must ask sensitive questions, ask the person to accompany you to a private area.

➤ Discuss sensitive information with people who do not have a genuine *right* or *need* to know.

➤ Accuse an employee or visitor of committing a crime.

➤ Deviate from actions authorized by your security manual.

Some good may come from civil lawsuits, as suggested by the Hall-crest Report II (Cunningham et al., 1990, p. 38):

> Perhaps during the 1990s, as a secondary outcome of litigation, we will see evaluative research into the crime prevention effectiveness of security guards, alarms, locks, cameras, lighting, and employee training. The litigation explosion may also be the catalyst for long overdue security standards and/or codes which should help reduce the claims of inadequate security and ultimately may improve security services and products.

## A Liability Checklist

☐ Have potential liabilities been identified?

☐ Have ways to reduce these risks been implemented?

☐ Are there clear policies on:
   a. Detaining
   b. Searching
   c. Arresting
   d. Emergencies
   e. Using force
   f. Carrying a weapon

☐ Have all employees been trained in these areas?

☐ Has a record of such training been kept?

☐ Are there clear, stringent employment standards?

☐ Are employees evaluated periodically?

☐ Are supervisors adequately trained?

☐ Are employees properly supervised?

☐ Are all incidents having potential civil liability properly reported and investigated?

☐ Are all incidents resulting in civil liability investigated and remedial actions implemented?

Properly reporting all incidents is critical. Lawsuits can be filed several years after an incident. Information from reports can be critical to refreshing the memory of those involved or if those involved are no longer employed there.

# SUMMARY

**P**rivate security officers and police officers have both similarities and differences. They both may wear uniforms and badges, are trained in compelling obedience, and are apt to be sued. Both also seek to prevent crime and to apprehend criminals, with private security focusing efforts more on prevention than apprehension.

Private security officers differ from public police officers in that private security officers operate in a profit-oriented enterprise serving specific private clients to prevent crime, protect assets, and reduce losses and to regulate noncriminal conduct not under the authority of law enforcement. They are given their authority by their private employers. Public police officers, in contrast, operate in a nonprofit, governmental enterprise serving the general public to combat crime, enforce laws, and apprehend offenders. They have statutory authority.

The amount of authority and the restrictions placed on both also differ. For example, private security officers usually have no more powers than private citizens. As citizens, they have the power to arrest, to investigate, to carry weapons, to defend themselves, and to defend their property or property entrusted to their care. They can deny access to unauthorized individuals into their employers' business or company, and they can enforce all rules and regulations established by their employers. They can also search employees and question them without giving the Miranda warning in most states.

Private security officers cannot invade another's privacy, electronically eavesdrop, trespass, or wear a uniform or badge that closely resembles that of a public police officer.

There are now almost twice as many people employed in private security as there are public police. Their roles are complementary. They may work together, may hire or delegate authority to each other, or may move from one sector to the other. Public police offer private security the power of interrogation, search, arrest, and use of electronic surveillance. They may reduce or eliminate their legal liability, and they offer training, experience, and backup. Private security officers offer the public police information, access to private places, and extended surveillance and coverage. In addition, they are not bound by the Exclusionary Rule, so can question without giving the Miranda warning and can search without a warrant.

Although private security officers are given authority to enforce the rules and regulations of their employers, they must still be mindful of the rights of those with whom they interact. If they ignore those rights, they can be sued. A *tort* is a civil wrong for which a person can be sued. Not only the individual security officer, but also the employer can be sued under the concept of nondelegable duty. A nondelegable duty is one for which authority can be given to another person, but responsibility cannot. Civil liability remains with the person who has the legal duty to act—and this can include a company, business, organization, or corporation. The most common civil suits brought against private security are for assault, battery, false imprisonment, defamation, intentional infliction of emotional distress, invasion of privacy, and negligence.

Civil liability might be reduced by hiring wisely, setting minimum standards for job performance, establishing clear policies, and providing effective training and supervision.

Chapter Five
The Public/Private
Interface, Legal
Authority, and
Civil Liability

113

# APPLICATION

1) Look for instances of private/public cooperation in your community. For example, at major sporting events, are both used? If so, how?
2) Reread the security officer's code of ethics. What sections of this code would help reduce civil liability?

# DISCUSSION QUESTIONS

1) What are the advantages and disadvantages of private security officers not being restricted by the U.S. Constitution (not having to give the Miranda warning, for instance)?
2) How do private security officers assist public police officers in your community? Vice versa?
3) Have there been any civil lawsuits against private security officers or providers in your community within the past few years?
4) Do you feel police officers should be allowed to moonlight as private security providers? Why or why not?
5) Who do you feel has more status, private or public officers? Why? Do you foresee a change in status for either group in the future?

# REFERENCES

Allison, John. Five ways to keep disputes out of court. *Harvard business review,* January-February 1990, p. 166.

Bayley, David H. Foreword. In *Private policing,* by Clifford D. Shearing and Philip C. Stenning, eds. Beverly Hills, CA: Sage Publications, 1987, pp. 6–8.

Bocklet, Richard. Police-private security cooperation. *Law and order,* December 1990, pp. 54–59.

Bottom, Norman R., Jr. Privatization: Lessons of the Hallcrest report. *Law enforcement news,* June 23, 1986, pp. 13, 15.

Burden, Ordway P. Rent-a-cop business is booming. *Law and order,* August 1989, pp. 92–94.

Cunningham, William C.; Strauchs, John J.; and Van Meter, Clifford W. *Private security trends, 1970 to 2000: The Hallcrest report II.* Stoneham, MA: Butterworth-Heinemann, 1990.

Cunningham, W. C. and Taylor, T. H. *The Hallcrest report: Private security and police in America.* Portland, OR: Chancellor Press, 1985.

Gallagher, G. Patrick. Risk management for police administrators. *The police chief,* June 1990, pp. 18–29.

Marx, Gary T. The interweaving of public and private police in undercover work. In *Private policing,* by Clifford D. Shearing and Philip C. Stenning, eds. Beverly Hills, CA: Sage Publications, 1987, pp. 172–193.

*Private security.* Report of the Task Force on Private Security, National Advisory Commission on Criminal Justice Standards and Goals. Washington, DC: U.S. Government Printing Office, 1976.

Remesch, Kimberly A. Shared responsibility. *Police,* November 1989, pp. 32–35, 67.

Schnabolk, Charles. *Physical security: Practices and technology.* Woburn, MA: Butterworth Publishers, Inc., 1983.

Shearing, Clifford D.; Farnell, M.; and Stenning, Philip C. *Contract security in Ontario.* University of Toronto: Centre for Criminology, 1980.

Shearing, Clifford D. and Stenning, Philip C. Reframing policing. In *Private policing,* by Clifford D. Shearing and Philip C. Stenning, eds. Beverly Hills, CA: Sage Publications, 1987, pp. 9–18.

Shook, H. C. Police and private security. *Police chief,* June 1978, p. 8.

Trojanowicz, Robert and Bucqueroux, Bonnie. The privatization of public justice: What will it mean to police? *The police chief,* October 1990, pp. 131–135.

United Way Strategic Institute. Nine forces reshaping America. Bethesda, MD: World Future Society, 1989.

Chapter Five
The Public/Private
Interface, Legal
Authority, and
Civil Liability

115

# Section Two

# Basic Security Responsibilities

Security considerations affect every facet of a business or organization. Sometimes security measures are viewed as unnecessary expenses or even as impositions that lessen efficiency and lower the organization's public image. With careful planning and education, however, such negative effects can be avoided. Management, employees, customers, and all who use the facility can be made to feel more comfortable, knowing they are being protected against intruders and/or harm from natural disasters.

Effective security involves all aspects of a facility, whether internal or external, whether occupied or not, as well as all individuals within the facility and all who might seek to gain illegal entrance.

One primary security responsibility is to prevent loss by ensuring physical and environmental controls (Chapter 6). But physical security in itself is rarely sufficient; the human factor must inevitably enter the picture. Therefore, security procedures are required to further prevent loss (Chapter 7). In combination, security personnel, equipment, and procedures can be used to prevent or reduce losses resulting from accidents, natural disasters, violence, and emergencies (Chapter 8), and those resulting from criminal actions (Chapter 9). They can also enhance computer security (Chapter 10).

PRIVATE PROPERTY
AUTHORIZED PARKING ONLY! ALL OTHERS
WILL BE TOWED AWAY AT OWNERS EXPENSE
FOR TOWED VEHICLES CALL
S.F.P.D. KL.3-1235

In addition to all these responsibilities, most security officers will find that they spend a lot of time writing reports and that they may need to testify in court (Chapter 11). Finally, private security officers also play an important role in any organization's public relations efforts (Chapter 12).

Although specific security responsibilities will depend on the needs of the establishment, these basic responsibilities and alternatives to fulfill them are generally present in every establishment. Using analytic creativity, security managers can select and adapt those physical and procedural controls relevant to their individual situation. Possible applications in security systems for commercial, industrial, and retail establishments and institutions are discussed in Section Three.

## ☐ INTRODUCTION

Throughout the centuries, people have sought to protect themselves and their property by physical controls. Among other things, they have built their dwellings on poles, constructed high fences, rolled boulders in front of doors, buried money, tied gaggles of geese where an intruder would startle them, stationed lookouts, built fires to frighten away wild animals, and the like. Although modern physical security controls are usually much more sophisticated, the intent is the same: to prevent any intruder from harming the owner or the owner's property.

The Hallcrest Report (Cunningham and Taylor, 1985, p. 41) says: "Physical security concerns the physical means used to (1) control and monitor the access of persons and vehicles; (2) prevent and detect unauthorized intrusions and surveillance; and (3) safeguard negotiable documents, proprietary information, merchandise, and buildings. . . ." For certain entities, such as banks, the Defense Industry Security Program, and nuclear plants, the minimum standards of protection are mandated by a governing authority." Such standards may also enhance employee safety.

# Chapter Six

# Enhancing Security through Physical Controls

## DO YOU KNOW

➤ What four purposes are served by physical controls?

➤ What three lines of defense are important in physical security?

➤ How the perimeter of a facility can be made more secure? The building exterior? The interior?

➤ What the two common types of safes are and why the distinction is important?

➤ What constitutes basic security equipment?

➤ What kinds of locks are available? What type of key lock is recommended?

➤ What functions are performed by lighting?

➤ What the components of a total lighting system are?

➤ What types of alarms are available for the three lines of defense?

➤ Where alarms may be received?

➤ What factors must be balanced in selecting physical controls?

➤ What two factors are critical in establishing and maintaining physical controls?

Physical controls serve to reduce risk of loss by:

*THE 5 D'S*

➤ Denying unauthorized access.
➤ Deterring or discouraging attempts to gain unauthorized access.
➤ Delaying those who attempt to gain unauthorized access.
➤ Detecting threats, both criminal and noncriminal.
➤ *Detain*

The emphasis on physical controls has had an impact on architects and contractors and has resulted in the emerging discipline of *Crime Prevention through Environmental Design* (CPTED). The primary goals of CPTED are to anticipate and to prevent crime through physical and environmental planning.

As stated in the Task Force Report, *Private Security,* Standard 5.4 (p. 188): "Architects, builders, and/or their professional societies should

**119**

Fencing can protect pedestrians on an overpass.

continue to develop performance standards of crime prevention in design with advice from law enforcement agencies and the private security industry." Some cities now include crime prevention measures in existing building codes. Others have established specific building security codes that must be adhered to. Ideally, physical security controls would be included when a facility is constructed. For example, the National Advisory Commission on Criminal Justice Standards and Goals in a 1973 report, *Community Crime Prevention*, recommended that: "Careful considerations should be given to the design and placement of doors, windows, elevators and stairs, lighting, building height and size, arrangement of units, and exterior site design, since these factors can have an effect on crime." To add physical security controls to existing facilities is almost always more expensive; yet, such controls can pay for themselves in a short time by preventing loss of assets.

As noted by the National Crime Prevention Institute (NCPI) (1986, p. 57) in discussing the wide variety of natural and human-made physical and perceptual barriers that may be part of a physical security system:

> Security factors must compete with other functional and cost considerations. Inevitably in barrier design some sort of balance must be struck among the various needs for security, convenience, utility, illumination, access, climate control, and pleasing appearance. The objective is to design the barrier so that security features are compatible with all other considerations, are cost effective, and provide the needed degree of protection. . . .
>
> The primary functions of a barrier are to delay the intruder as much as possible and to force him to use methods of attack that are highly conspicuous or noisy. . . .
>
> As the value of the target increases, however, the strength of the barrier must increase proportionately. . . .

The trade-off between delay time and detection time is perhaps the single most important consideration in designing a barrier.

The National Crime Prevention Institute (1986, p. 59−60) also stresses "circles of protection":

> In security design, the concept of concentric barrier circles should be extended in depth as much as possible. Not only might there be an outer protective ring (such as a fence) at the property line and a second ring consisting of the building shell, but also within the building there might be one or more additional barriers to protect specific targets. . . .
>
> A single barrier ring (particularly in the case of commercial or industrial establishments) may be both ineffective and dangerous, because once an intruder penetrates it, he may be free to do as he wishes, screened from observation by the barrier that was intended to keep him out in the first place.

4

The three basic lines of physical defense are the perimeter of a facility, the building exterior, and the interior.

Sometimes all three lines of defense are available, as in, for example, a manufacturing firm situated on its own acreage. Other times only one line of defense is available, for example, the interior of a small business occupying a single room in a large office complex. Although the office manager can bring pressure to bear on the office complex manager to ensure security, the individual office manager has very limited control.

## ☐ THE PERIMETER

The location of a facility influences its security needs. When selecting a site for a new plant, managers should carefully consider security needs in the decision. Is the area a high-crime area? Is there ample public lighting? Do local law enforcement officers patrol there? If a facility has grounds around it, security measures can be used to protect this perimeter.

*Perimeter barriers,* according to the NCPI (1986, p. 62), are: "any obstacle which defines the physical limits of a controlled area and impedes or restricts entry into the area. It is the first line of defense against intrusion. . . . At a minimum, a good perimeter barrier should discourage an impulsive attacker. At the maximum, when used in conjunction with other security measures, it can halt even the most determined attack."

The NCPI (1968, p. 60) stresses that:

> The growing weight of evidence, however, suggests that no boundary barrier can serve as anything more than a perceptual barrier, because it has been demonstrated that even the relatively unskilled attacker can go over, under or through any boundary barrier in a matter of seconds. Hence, fences, boundary walls, hedges and other such obstacles are referred to by NCPI as *boundary markers* to make it clear that boundary marking is their major function. If boundary markers can also provide a degree of perceptual security, so much the better, but in no event should they be considered as physical security systems.

The perimeter can be physically controlled by fences, gates, locks, lighting, alarms, surveillance systems, signs, dogs, and security personnel. Physical layout and neatness are other important factors.

### Fences — *may be included as perimeter*

*protection only from 4-12 seconds*

*doesn't provide protection*
*must have other factors*
*even w/ barbed wire your still not protected*
*7-15 seconds*

Some facilities are protected by a natural barrier, such as the water surrounding Alcatraz. Usually, however, a barrier must be constructed as a physical and psychological deterrent to intruders.

According to the NCPI (1986, p. 6), three types of boundary marker fencing are currently used: wood stockade fence, barbed wire, and chain link. All provide about equal protection and cost less than concrete or masonry walls. The NCPI says chain link is the most commonly used, is "relatively attractive, low in maintenance cost, simple to erect and less of a safety hazard than barbed wire."

Fences should be straight, taut, and securely fastened to metal poles; they must extend to the ground or below. Sometimes a **header** or **top guard** is used. This added protection consists of strands of barbed wire extending outward from the top of the fence at a forty-five degree angle. A double top guard that extends both outward and inward is also available.

Chain-link fencing allows an unobstructed view both for security officers inside the perimeter and for private or public patrol cars passing on the outside. To provide adequate security, the chain link should be #11 gauge or heavier, with not larger than two-inch mesh, and the fence should be at least eight feet high. However, some building codes do not allow such tall fences in certain areas.

*standards*

*rod underground should link poles of fence, bottom of fence should be embedded at least 2 ft. underground in soft.*

Objections are sometimes raised to the institutional look of chain-link fences. Such objections can be overcome by planting vines and/or bushes to conceal the fence, but the advantage of an unobstructed view is then negated. If a facility's appearance is high priority, masonry or brick walls are sometimes constructed. Such barriers are more attractive, but they obstruct the view and are often easy to climb. To thwart climbers, a barbed-wire top guard is sometimes used.

When appearance is not a concern, a barbed-wire fence is often used. Such fences are usually at least eight feet tall and have the strands of barbed wire no farther than six inches apart, and two inches apart at the bottom. Many types of barbed wire or barbed tape are available, including one very aptly named "razor ribbon." After a trucking firm in Phoenix, Arizona, installed barbed tape on top of its existing ten-foot chain-link fence, its severe losses from stolen parts and vandalism dropped to zero.

Concertina, rolls of barbed wire fifty feet long and three feet in diameter, provides the strongest barrier. Placing one roll on another creates a formidable six-foot-high barrier. Concertina is used primarily in emergencies when a fence, gate, or building entrance is no longer secure.

Fences can also be electrified, but use of either an electrified fence or one with barbed tape has the potential for lawsuits from injury, especially if children are likely to be injured by the security devices.

Fences should be inspected periodically. Attention should be paid to telephone poles, trees, or other objects close enough to the fence to

A security officer inspects the security fence.

allow an intruder to use them in climbing the fence. Care should be taken so that vehicles cannot be driven beside a fence and used as an aid in climbing it.

A minimum number of entrances and exits should be used. Gates are usually locked with a post-locking bar and a padlock. If a gate is locked from the inside, a metal shield can be welded to the gate and the chain pulled through an opening in the shield and then locked on the inside. Although the shield offers greater security, it cannot be used if the gate has to be opened from the outside. Some businesses use electrically controlled gates operated by pushbuttons or a card-key. Pedestrian traffic can be controlled by turnstiles. In addition, a guard house located at major arteries can serve as a central security command post to monitor all entrances and exits.

For tight security, *all* perimeter openings must be secured, including not only gates, but also air-intake pipes, coal chutes, culverts, drain pipes, exhaust conduits, sewers, sidewalk elevators, and utility tunnels. Perimeter openings that cannot be permanently sealed because they serve a function should be barred or screened if they are larger than ninety-six square inches. *or if 6 in around*

Often the fence, the gates, and all perimeter openings are wired into an alarm system. They may also be monitored by a surveillance camera and may be patrolled by dogs or security personnel.

## Perimeter Lighting   *Lighting is a psychological deterrent — they are afraid of being detected.*

Adequate lighting on the perimeter is another prime consideration. An unobstructed view is of little consequence in complete darkness.

*pedestrian gates and vehicle entrances. should be lit separately w/ diff illumination*

Four types of lights are commonly used:

➤ **Floodlights** form a beam of concentrated light for boundaries, fences, and area buildings and, positioned correctly, produce a desired glare in the eyes of persons attempting to see in.

➤ **Streetlights** cast a diffused, low-intensity light evenly over an area and are often used in parking lots and storage areas.

➤ **Fresnal units** provide a long, narrow, horizontal beam of light ideally suited for lighting boundaries without glare.

➤ **Searchlights,** both portable and fixed, provide a highly focused light beam that can be aimed in any direction and are ideal for emergencies requiring additional light in a specific area.

Boundary lighting is often provided by floodlights that create a barrier of light, allowing those inside to see out, but preventing anyone on the outside from seeing in. Although the glare may deter intruders, it can also pose a traffic hazard or annoy neighbors; therefore, the technique is not always possible to use.

Inside the perimeter, lights are usually positioned thirty feet from the boundary, fifty feet apart, and thirty feet high, depending, of course, on the size of the area to be lit. All storage areas, thoroughfares, entrances and exits, sides and corners of buildings, alleys, and accessible windows should be adequately lit. A guideline for determining if the lighting is adequate is to see if enough light is available to read the subheads of a newspaper.

The illumination inside a guard house should be less than that outside so security personnel can see out, but others cannot see in. All electrical wires should be buried, if possible, to secure the source of power. The lights themselves should be protected with metal screens so the elements cannot be broken by vandals or intruders.

## Physical Layout and Appearance

A clear zone of at least twenty feet on either side of the perimeter should be maintained when possible. Neatness is important not only for appearance, but also for security. Ladders and piles of debris or merchandise close to fences or buildings could easily be used to an intruder's advantage. Bushes and hedges should be no more than two feet tall and should be kept away from the boundary and buildings. Weeds

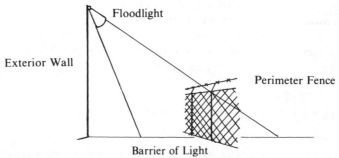

Figure 6-1 **Barrier of light.**

should be cut, hedges and bushes trimmed, and all discarded material or merchandise properly disposed of. Trash and boxes strewn around the premises not only are a safety hazard, but also can provide hiding places for intruders.

Buildings can be connected by tunnels or walkways, reducing the number of main entrances to be made secure. A utility building can centralize utilities, such as an emergency electric generator, emergency water tanks and pumps, gas valves and regulators, the main switch and power controls, and the transformers. Whether in a separate building or located around the premises, all main-control valves, regulators, and switches must be protected from vandalism, tampering, and sabotage.

*Parking lots* often present a security problem. When possible, privately owned vehicles should be parked outside the perimeter in a parking lot with its own fence, gate, and lights. Employees or visitors who park adjacent to a loading dock or warehouse doors present a security risk. Many thefts are committed by friends or family waiting in the parking area for an employee to get out of work. Some security managers feel that if employees and/or visitors must walk a long distance to their vehicles, the chances of theft are reduced. Others argue that a lengthy walk to a vehicle needlessly exposes people to the possibility of being the victim of an assault, robbery, or rape.

When possible, all privately owned vehicles should be parked in a common parking lot on only one side of the building, thus reducing the number of common entrances to the building. Parking lots should have proper drainage and lighting, as well as appropriate marking and signing, including pedestrian crosswalks, if needed. Sometimes stickers or parking permits are used to identify vehicles with legitimate access to parking areas.

## ☑ THE BUILDING EXTERIOR

The first line of defense for some facilities is the building exterior, also called the building **envelope** by some architects and security planners.

Strong, locked doors and windows, limited entrances, secured openings (if larger than ninety-six square inches), alarms, surveillance, and lighting help establish the physical security of a building's exterior.

In the majority of break-ins, entrance is gained through windows. The next most common method of entrance is through doors, followed by roof hatches, skylights, vents, and transoms. A few break-ins have involved chopping or cutting holes through walls, floors, and ceilings.

### Doors

The vulnerable parts of a door are the lock, frame, hinges, and panels. Not too many newer locks are picked, but many are pulled or "slipped," as discussed later.

Door with security screen.

*consider these*

*The door frame* should be heavy so it cannot be sprung with a crow-bar or jack. Experts recommend two-inch-thick solid wood or a frame covered with sixteen-gauge sheet steel if the wood is 1⅜ inches or less. Strong frames thwart jamb-pulling (Figure 6–2).

*The hinges* should be inside, if possible. The pins should not be removable, but should be welded in (Figure 6–3).

*The door panels* should be solid, meeting the same specifications as the door frame stated above. If the panels are glass, they should be protected by bars or a screen on the inside. Often sheet metal is installed on the inside and outside of basement doors.

Doors should have a minimum of sixty-watt illumination above them and should be wired into the alarm system to add further protection.

Although door transoms are seldom built into newer buildings, they exist in many older buildings. If they cannot be sealed because they are needed to provide ventilation, they should be fitted with locks on the inside and secured when the room is unoccupied.

Many facilities have installed hardware, for example, chains and pad-locks around the door exit bar, that makes it impossible for a "hide-in" thief to exit the building after hours. However, some city ordinances prohibit such hardware, viewing it as a safety hazard.

The number of doors and their placement is extremely important to physical security. The number of personnel entrances should be limited to control access and to reduce thefts while the building is open. In some instances guards or receptionists are stationed at the entrance. All doors not required for efficient operation should be locked. If a door is required as an emergency exit, it can be equipped with emergency exit

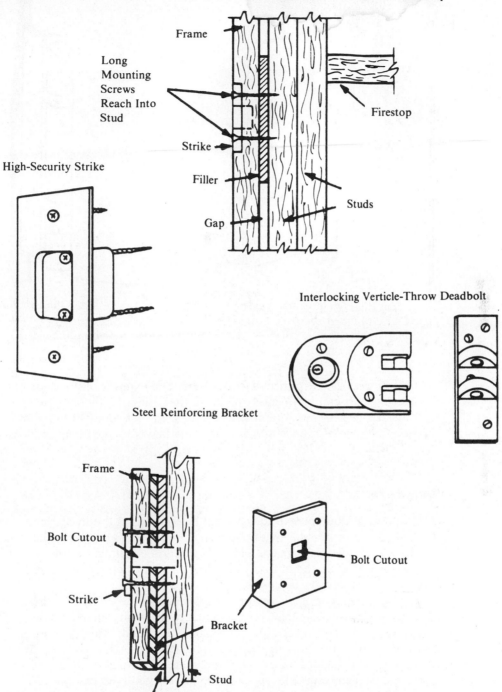

Filler Plates Used to Close Frame-Structure Gap

Frame

Long
Mounting
Screws
Reach Into
Stud

Firestop

Strike

High-Security Strike

Filler

Gap

Studs

Interlocking Verticle-Throw Deadbolt

Steel Reinforcing Bracket

Frame

Bolt Cutout

Bolt Cutout

Strike

Bracket

Stud

Filler

**Figure 6–2 Measures used to protect against door frame spreading.**
*From "Understanding Crime Prevention," by the National Crime Prevention Institute.*

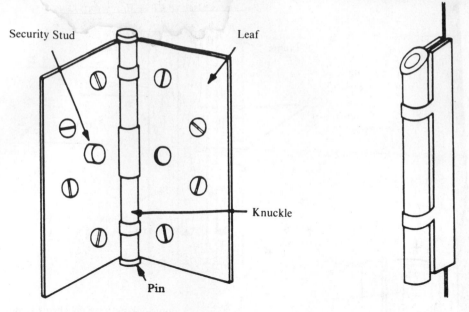

Security Stud                    Leaf

Knuckle

Pin

Leaf Hinge With Security Stud                    Fixed Pin Leaf Hinge

**Figure 6–3  Standard security hinges.**
*From "Understanding Crime Prevention," by the National Crime Prevention Institute.*

locking devices called **panic** or **crash bars.** The exterior of the door has
no hardware. It can be opened only from the inside. Many emergency
exit locking devices are equipped with an alarm that sounds if the door
is opened. Some also have a lock so that if a key is used, the alarm does
not sound.

## Windows   50%

If windows can be opened, they should be secured on the inside by a
bolt, slide bar, or crossbar with padlock. Window glass can be broken or
cut by an intruder, so bars or steel grills should be installed inside the
windows. However, the hazard this might present to employees should a
fire occur must always be considered.

About 50 percent of all criminal intrusions are achieved by breaking
window glass. Any opening larger than ninety-six square inches and less
than eighteen feet from the ground should be protected. If the window is
not needed for ventilation, the panes can be replaced with glass block. If
the likelihood is high of the glass being broken, security glass should be
considered. This is especially applicable to display windows that are vulnerable to the "smash and grab" thief. Although security glass generally costs ·
twice as much as regular glass, it can effectively thwart intruders.

Security glass meets the standards of the Underwriters Laboratories
in resisting heat, flames, cold, hammers, picks, and rocks. It is usually
two hundred to three hundred times stronger than tempered or plate
glass and is practically impenetrable, although it may crack. Older security glass usually consists of five or more layers of glass that have been

*can do glazing plex glass*
*beware — bars mesh due to escape problems. if you use make sure they have a crashbar*

A heavily protected security door.

laminated to create a sheet 5/16 inch thick. Newer, synthetic types of glass are rapidly replacing these heavier, more expensive types of glass.

## Other Openings

Any accessible openings larger than ninety-six square inches should be protected the same way as windows. Utility tunnels, elevator shafts, ventilation openings, skylights, and the like should all have protective screens or metal bars to prevent access to the building's interior. Such openings can also be connected to the alarm system.

## The Roof, Floor, and Walls

The roof is a favorite entry point for many intruders. A building's roof is usually not lit, is not visible to passing patrols, is not strongly constructed, is not built into the alarm system, and often has unsecured openings such as skylights or ventilation ducts. If no such openings exist, an intruder can often simply drill four holes arranged in a square and then saw out the square to gain access to the building. A facility in a row of buildings with connecting roofs is especially vulnerable. Roof intrusion can be deterred by a chain-link fence topped with a double barbed-wire header as long as zoning regulations allow this.

A common wall or floor between two buildings or establishments is also a potential entry point. An intruder may break into a nonsecure building having a common wall with a secure building, and then break through the common wall with leisure. This same hazard exists when there are secure areas above and/or below nonsecure areas.

Fire escapes pose another problem. They often provide access to doors or windows that should be accessible only from the inside of the building. Counterbalanced fire escapes are preferable to stationary ones because the counterbalanced stairs are suspended until the weight of a person descending is on the last section.

## Lighting

Lights should be mounted on the sides and corners of buildings, with the illumination cone directed downward and away from the structure to prevent shadows and glare. The alley, the rear of the building, and all entry points should be lit. The lights can be turned on by an automatic timer if desired.

 **THE BUILDING INTERIOR**

Because no perimeter or building exterior can be 100 percent secure, internal physical controls are usually required as well.

---

Interior physical controls include locked doors, desks, and files; safes and vaults; internal alarms and detectors; lighting; mirrors; bolt-down equipment; dogs; security personnel; and communication and surveillance systems.

---

The physical layout of a building's interior directly affects its security. Secure areas should be separate from nonsecure areas and should be located deep within the interior so no windows, exterior doors, or walls are in common with another building. Cashier offices, research laboratories, storage rooms, and rooms containing classified documents or valuable property often require extra security.

The interior construction of the building is also important. The ceiling in many modern buildings is simply acoustical tile laid in place with a crawl space above it that provides access to any room on that floor. Older buildings are better constructed from this perspective, but they often have door transoms and inferior glass and locks.

## Storing Assets    *computer rooms*

Assets requiring security include cash, stocks, inventory, and records. The National Fire Protection Agency classifies business records into four classes: vital, important, useful, and nonessential. Usually only 1 percent to 2 percent of an organization's records are classified as vital. Specific types of records to be protected and the means of doing so are discussed in Chapter 9. Generally, however, such records are kept in file cabinets with lock bars having combination padlocks. Sometimes they are kept in a vault. The National Fire Protection Association defines a vault as a "completely fire-resistive enclosure to be used exclusively for storage." Work should not be performed inside a vault. Because vaults are primarily for fire protection, many contain a burglar-resistant safe.

**M**ost safes are *either* fire resistant *or* burglar resistant, but *not* both.

A burglar-resistant safe must have an Underwriters Laboratories (UL) listed combination lock. It almost always has a very limited capacity, and it does not protect against fire. The UL classifies the fire resistance capacity of a safe as *A*, *B*, or *C*. Safes with an *A* classification resist up to 2000°F for four hours; those classified as *B* resist up to 1850°F for two hours; those classified as *C* resist 1700°F for one hour. Alarms and time locks are often additional security precautions in safes.

Although some controversy exists over whether a safe should be hidden or in clear view, most experts feel that hiding a safe just helps the burglar. It is better to have it located where it is plainly visible from the outside and clearly lit at all times. It should always be locked and the combination secured.

*2 best ways to protect records.*  *① have a duplicate stored elsewhere*  *② safe or file cabinet*

*various ratings*
*papers 350-4   2000°F 4 hr*
*↑  -3*
*-2*
*350-1   1700°F  1 hr*
*computer tapes*
*150-4*

## ☐ BASIC SECURITY EQUIPMENT

At all three lines of defense, certain basic equipment can add considerable security.

**B**asic physical security equipment consists of locks, lights, and alarms.

The degree of physical security required will determine which of the basic components is used. In some instances, locks may be all that are required. In other instances, lights and/or alarms may also be needed (Figure 6–4).

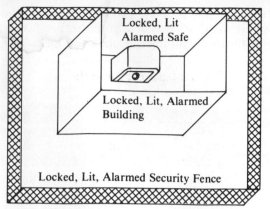

**Figure 6–4 Basic security equipment at the three lines of defense.**

## ☐ LOCKS

A beam across a door was one of the oldest security devices used for protection against an intruder. Locks were used in Egypt over four thousand years ago, and they have been important security devices ever since. Locks are, in fact, one of the oldest, most commonly used, cost-effective means to physically control access to an area, a building, a room, or a container.

The primary function of a lock is to deter or deny access into a protected area. Although any lock can be opened by a determined, skilled person, locks are valuable because they increase the amount of time an intruder must spend gaining access, thereby increasing the probability of being detected. Additionally, locks frequently provide evidence of forced entrance, evidence that may be required to collect insurance.

The better the hardware's quality, the longer it will withstand physical abuse, and thus the more likely it will show signs of being forced.

Usually, with locks come locksmiths. As noted by Cunningham et al. (1990, p. 188): "Locksmiths primarily serve a security function. However, they generally operate outside of conventional security circles, with their own trade associations and journals." The Hallcrest staff estimates revenues from the locksmith segment of security grew at an annual rate of 10 percent, with annual revenues by 1990 at $2.9 billion. The number of firms increased to twelve thousand, employing almost seventy thousand people. Hallcrest projects that by 2000, revenues will increase at an average annual rate of 7 percent to $5.7 billion and that seventeen thousand lock shops will employ eighty-eight thousand people (p. 189).

Available types of locks include key operated, combination, card activated, and electronically operated.

### Key-Operated Locks  *most common    problem: must control key access*

Key-operated locks are most frequently used and are simple to operate. A **key** is inserted into a **keyway** and turned to insert or withdraw a

**bolt** from a **strike.** The keyway contains obstacles that must be bypassed to withdraw or insert the bolt. It can be housed in a doorknob or in the door itself. The key is notched so that when it is inserted into the keyway it either bypasses or arranges the tumblers (or other obstacles) so that it can be turned to insert or withdraw the bolt from the strike.

The keyway may be warded or cylindrical. **Warded locks,** commonly used up to the 1940s, have an open keyway (keyhole) that can easily be opened with a skeleton or pass key or picked with a wire. Warded locks also allow a view into the room's interior. Warded locks are often used on file boxes, suitcases, and handcuffs.

**Cylindrical locks** may use disc tumblers or pin tumblers. Disc tumbler locks, commonly used in cars, desks, files, and cabinets, are not too effective because they usually cause only a two- to four-minute delay in gaining access to the protected areas. Pin tumbler locks are usually preferred for business and industry because they can create up to a ten-minute delay in gaining access.

The lock's bolt can be either spring loaded or dead bolt (Figure 6–5). **Spring-loaded bolts** (sometimes called latches) automatically enter the strike when the door is closed. When locked, they can often be opened by inserting a plastic credit card or a thin screwdriver above the bolt and forcing it downward, releasing the spring. Such **slipping**

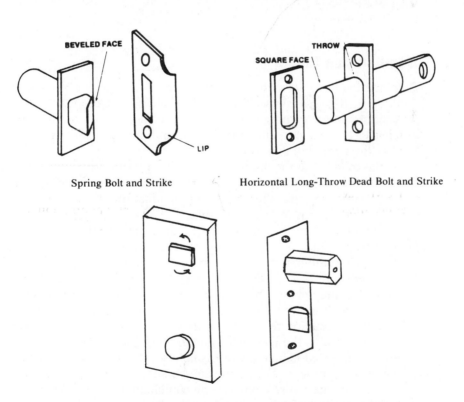

Spring Bolt and Strike        Horizontal Long-Throw Dead Bolt and Strike

Interconnected Spring Bolt and Dead Bolt

**Figure 6–5  Basic types of bolt mechanisms.**
*From "Understanding Crime Prevention," by the National Crime Prevention Institute.*

can be deterred, however, by a latch guard, a metal plate extending from the strike area to the door frame.

**Dead bolts** are non-spring-loaded metal bars that are manually inserted into or withdrawn from a strike. Dead bolts are usually from ½ to 1¼ inches long and offer greater protection than spring-loaded bolts.

A dead-bolt lock with a one-inch throw and an antiwrenching collar or a secondary dead bolt with a one-inch throw offers the best protection if a key-operated lock is used.

In a key-operated **padlock**, the same basic principles apply except that the bolt is replaced by a **shank** that can be secured or released by turning the appropriate key in the keyway.

The primary disadvantages of key-operated locks are that many locks can be picked, keys can be stolen or obtained by unauthorized people, and keys may be duplicated. Another disadvantage is that some individuals may have to carry many keys, but this can be overcome by using a master keying system, discussed in the next chapter.

Whether keys should contain identification is debatable. Identified keys can be returned to the owner if they are lost, but they can also be used to gain unauthorized access. Key identification is an important management decision.

## Combination Locks

Combination locks are often used on padlocks as well as on safe and vault doors. **Dial combination locks** usually have from two to six notched tumblers. Turning the dial to prespecified numbers align the notches to create a slot, allowing an arm to drop into it so that the locking bar can be withdrawn from the strike.

Some combination locks are operated by **pushbuttons** rather than dials. One or more buttons are pushed, either in sequence or simultaneously. Such locks are often used on individual rooms or on entrances to semiprivate rooms in large buildings.

Combination locks cannot be picked, and they use no keys that can be lost, duplicated, stolen, or borrowed. The probability of someone randomly trying combinations and hitting on the correct one is extremely low. Nonetheless, combination locks are also vulnerable to unauthorized entry. A thief may obtain the combination from a disloyal employee or may even find it written down somewhere close to the combination itself. The combination to a lock should never be written down and kept in the same area as the lock. Combination locks should not be opened when unauthorized people might casually see what numbers are being dialed. If someone who knows the combination is fired or resigns, or if there is the slightest suspicion that the combination might be known to unauthorized people, the combination should be changed.

**Padlocks,** whether key or combination operated, should have a short shank to thwart prying and should be made of hardened steel to prevent cutting. The hasp through which the shank is inserted must also be strong and nonremovable. An unlocked padlock is an open invitation to would-be intruders to substitute the padlock with one of their own. Consequently, padlocks should be distinctive so that any replacement can be easily detected.

## Card-Operated Locks *state of the art*

Card-operated locks are inserted into a card reader installed near a door or passageway that is restricted. When an authorized card is inserted into the slot, a minicomputer activates the locking device, thereby opening the door, traffic control arm, gate, or turnstile. Some card-operated locks are also equipped so that the identification of the person operating the lock and the time it was operated are automatically recorded.

The card itself is usually plastic and resembles an ordinary credit card. It is invisibly coded in a way that makes every card or group of cards identifiable, yet impossible to duplicate.

Card-operated locks are often used when areas are restricted to the general public, but accessible to large numbers of employees. In fact, a single card can be used to control access to parking, turnstiles, elevators, files, computer rooms, copy machines, fuel pumps, restrooms, and executive offices. The same card could provide time and attendance reporting information.

Card-operated systems can be easily programmed to reject cards that are no longer valid.

According to Naudts (1987, p. 169): "[In] 1000 BC the Chinese required servants at the Imperial Palace to wear rings engraved with unique and intricate designs identifying palace areas they were permitted to enter. Historians credit this method by the Chinese as the first comprehensive access control system."

Access control systems came into use in the early 1960s and have evolved into highly advanced, widely used security technology. Naudts (1987, p. 170) says that card manufacturers are producing systems that can control from eight card readers and one thousand cards up to several thousand readers and more than sixty thousand cards.

A typical system has the user insert, place, or swipe a card into or by a reader. The reader determines if the card is valid and if access is to be granted. Many systems not only grant or deny access but also record information such as the card number, the door for which entry was requested, the time, the date, and if entry was allowed.

Some systems can be programmed to lock and unlock doors at specific times of the day or specific days such as weekends or holidays.

**ACCESS CONTROL CARD OPTIONS** Various options from which to choose are described by Naudts (1987, pp. 171–172). *Magnetic stripe cards* use a strip similar to those used on credit cards. Magnetic stripe cards can be encoded on site, but they can easily be copied or modified. *Watermark cards* also use a magnetic strip and can be encoded on site. They also have a permanently encoded number that cannot be changed or copied, making them more secure than magnetic stripe cards. *Barium* *ferrite cards* contain information encoded in a soft pliable magnetic material sandwiched between layers of plastic.

*Wiegand cards* have metallic rods or wires embedded in the card that are not visible to the unaided eye. *Infrared cards* use a pattern of shadows inside the card and a low-level infrared light in the reader to detect the pattern and determine if entry is to be granted. *Proximity cards* use radio frequency signals to gain entry.

Access control systems may also use a keyless system activated by a personal identification number (PIN), which allows access to individuals having the correct six- or seven-digit access number. Some automobiles have such a system as an option.

Electronic access control cards provide a vast array of potential uses for employers and security professionals, including time and attendance, purchases, inventory, and after-hours entry records.

*Card Access* Can program what you want into it.
*Adv.* Can monitor these both internally or externally
can control who goes in and out of where.
can also get a printout of who was in the building.

## Electronic Locks
*buzzer locks*

Electronic locks are frequently used in apartment buildings and in offices where strict physical security is required. For example, in an apartment building, the doorway between the foyer and the hallways to the apartment can be electronically locked. A person who has no key can gain an unforced entrance only by contacting someone within the building by a phone or buzzer system and then having that person unlock the door by pressing a button.

Electronic locks are also often used on gates as well as on doors where tight security is required; for example, computer rooms or the room in a bank containing safety deposit boxes or the cash.

## Biometric Security Systems

Technological advances in security include biometric security systems that can recognize unique physical traits such as fingerprints, voices, and even eyeballs. Says Hof (1988, p. 109): "Forget your key chain . . . computerized security guards are fast becoming the modern 'open sesame.' " Such systems are being used at the Los Alamos National Laboratory in New Mexico to protect high-security areas of the nuclear research lab, the wine cellar of the La Reserve Hotel in White Plains, New York, and a jewel vault in Dallas, Texas. According to Hof (1988, p. 129): "Beginning in 1991, fingerprint or retina readers will be used in a federal program to keep truckers with poor driving records from obtaining licenses in other states. . . . The microchip has made security machines smaller, cheaper, faster, and more reliable."

## Other Locks

In addition to the preceding types of locks, clamshell locks (such as those used on windows), bars, bolts, chains, and time locks can also be used to provide additional security. Whatever type of lock is used, it will be only as secure as the material into which it is mounted and the integrity of the unlocking mechanism, be it a key, combination, code, or card.

## ⊠ SECURITY LIGHTING

The importance of lighting the perimeter and the building's exterior has already been stressed.

Adequate light inside as well as outside a building enhances safety, deters would-be intruders, and makes detection of actual intruders more probable.

Intruders prefer the cover of darkness to conceal their actions. The majority of nonresidential burglaries occur at night. In fact, three out of four commercial burglaries are committed within buildings with little or no light.

Standard 5.2 of the Private Security Task Force Report (1976, p. 182) emphasizes adequate security lighting: "Where appropriate, property should be adequately lighted to discourage criminal activity and enhance public safety." The report presents evidence on relighting programs that have had significant success in reducing crime (p. 192):

> As a result of a relighting program, the City of Indianapolis, Ind., reported crime reductions of as much as 85 percent in specified neighborhood areas. An added plus accompanying the lowered incidence of crime was a reduction in accidents. A 40.9 percent reduction in crimes against persons, a 28 percent reduction in auto thefts, and a 12.8 percent reduction in burglaries were reported in St. Louis, Missouri, one year after the implementation of a new lighting system.

A total lighting system includes four types of lighting:

➤ *Continuous* on a regular schedule, for secure areas.
➤ *Standby*, for occasions when more light is needed.
➤ *Moveable*, for when light is needed in areas not usually lit.
➤ *Emergency*, to be used as an alternate power source when the regular power source fails.

How much light is enough? Most authorities contend that adequate lighting should provide visibility and allow surveillance without creating excessive glare or shadows.* In our energy-conscious society, care must be taken not to waste energy when using security lighting. The American Society of Industrial Security suggests that improving the efficiency of lighting systems can preserve lighting as a security aid. Use of high-efficiency fluorescent tubes can result in immediate energy and operating cost savings of 14 percent. An effective lighting system modification would be to install new, high-efficiency ballasts that can reduce energy consumption by as much as 7 percent without loss of light. High-

---

* The specific lighting needs for a facility can best be determined by contacting the Illuminating Engineering Society, which publishes *The American Standard Practice for Protective Lighting*. They can also suggest consultants to assist in planning for security lighting of a specific facility.

efficiency lamp/ballast combinations can reduce energy consumption by as much as 20 percent without loss of light.

## ☒ ALARMS

Alarm systems date back to at least 390 B.C., when squawking geese alerted the Romans to surprise attacks by the Gauls. Centuries later geese were used to protect the perimeter of the Ballantine Scotch distillery in Scotland. Many homeowners depend on their dog's sense of smell and hearing to detect intruders and to then warn them by barking. Alarms have always been an effective supplement to locks, especially if the locks do not stop a persistent intruder.

Lewin (1990, p. 69) cites a March 1990 study reporting that "monitoring alarm systems is now big business, an 'industry' that has grown an average of 17% per year since 1987." Recent studies indicate that a typical city of twenty-five thousand to forty thousand population will have between 650 and 1,600 alarm installations that will generate 100 to 150 alarm calls per month (Lewin, 1990, p. 67).

Alarms are available for all three lines of defense:

➤ *Perimeter alarms* protect fences and gates, exterior doors, windows, and other openings.
➤ *Area* or *space alarms* protect a portion of or the total interior of a room or building.
➤ *Point* or *spot alarms* protect specific items such as safes, cabinets, valuable articles, or small areas.

Statistics indicate that alarm systems affect crime. For example, the burglary rate has been significantly reduced in communities where alarm systems are used extensively (*Private Security,* 1976, p. 135). Many federally insured institutions, such as banks, are required by law to install alarm systems. Additionally, many insurance companies offer lower premiums to businesses protected by alarm systems.

Alarms are used not only to detect intruders, but also to detect fires (to be discussed in Chapter 8), and in some instances, may monitor physical conditions such as temperature, humidity, water flow, electrical power usage, and machinery malfunction.

### Alarm Respondents

An important decision facing a security manager who selects an alarm as one means of reducing risk is where the alarm should be received.

Alarm systems may be local, proprietary, central station, or police connected.

**Local alarms** sound on the premises and require that someone hears the alarm and calls the police. Such alarms are the least expensive, but are also the least effective because no one may hear them; they may be heard but ignored; and they are easily disconnected by a knowledgeable intruder. In addition, they are extremely annoying to others in the area.

**Proprietary alarms** use a constantly manned alarm panel which may receive visible and/or audible signals to indicate exactly where the security break has occurred. Such systems are owned and operated by the owner of the property.

**Central station alarms** are similar to the proprietary system, except that observation of the control panel is external to the alarm's location and is usually under contract with an alarm agency. The central station can receive alarms from hundreds of different businesses. When the central station receives an alarm, it usually will dispatch its guard to the location of the alarm, notify the owner, and notify the police.

**Police-connected** systems direct the alarm via telephone wires to the nearest police department.

Trade magazines can provide current information on specific alarm systems' characteristics and capabilities. Standards for alarm systems are also issued by the Burglary Protective Department of the Underwriters Laboratories.*

## Three Basic Parts of an Alarm System

Alarm systems consist of three basic parts:

- A *sensor*, a triggering device that detects a condition that exists or changes.
- A *circuit*, a communication channel activated by the sensor that provides the power, receives the information, and transmits the required information.
- A *signal*, a visible or audible signal activated by the circuit that alerts a human to respond.

**SENSORS** Sensors in alarm systems range from simple magnetic switches to sophisticated ultrasonic Doppler and sound systems, as illustrated in Figure 6–6. The simplest sensors are electromechanical devices in which an electric circuit is broken or closed, including switches, window foil, and screens. These sensors are also the easiest to thwart.

Some sensors are pressure devices that respond to the weight of a person, similar in principle to automatic door openers under mats. Taut wire detectors are often used on the top of fences. Any change in the

---

\* The following bulletins, available from the Underwriters Laboratories, describe the *minimum* standards for specific alarm systems:

| #609, 610 | Burglar Alarm Systems, Local |
| #611–1968 | Burglar Alarm Systems, Central Station |
| #636 | Hold-up Alarm Systems |
| #681 | Installation, Classification, and Certification of Burglar Alarm Systems |

Magnetic contacts are attached to doors, windows, etc. so that when the door is opened the contacts are separated.

Pressure mats are usually placed under carpets and react to pressure from footsteps.

Foil is attached to glass or other surfaces and breaks when the surface is broken.

Photoelectric beams cast an invisible infrared light beam across doorways, etc. and react when the beam is interrupted.

Plunger contacts operate in the same way as the light switch on a refrigerator door.

Motion detectors transmit and receive patterns of ultrasonic or microwave radiation. The pattern is changed when a person enters it, causing the detector to react.

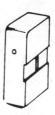

Electric and magnetic field devices create stable fields close to specific targets such as safes and react when a person or object enters the field.

Vibration detectors are attached to surfaces and react to vibrations caused by attempts to break through the surface.

**Figure 6–6  Typical sensors.**
*"From "Understanding Crime Prevention," by the National Crime Prevention Institute.*

tension of the wire activates the alarm. Photoelectric sensors are activated when a light beam is interrupted. Such sensors are frequently used in the entrance to establishments where a single clerk may leave the customer area unattended when no customers are present.

Other sensors detect sound, temperature, electrical capacitance, vibration, or motion by using radio frequency transmissions or ultrasonic wave transmission.

An analogy can be drawn between sensor devices and the human senses. The sense of *touch* includes the more common electromechanical devices and a few electronic devices that function by breaking a conductor, moving an object, vibrating, applying pressure, and sensing temperature. *Smell* includes those devices that sense ionized particles or products of combustion. *Hearing* covers those devices that use airborne sound in their sensing functions, including devices that transmit sound and listen for a reflected sound and those that simply receive the sounds. *Sight* includes devices that use electromagnetic radiation, regardless of frequency, including all photoelectric, microwave, electrical field, and magnetic field devices.

**THE CIRCUIT** The circuit is the communication channel that conveys the information from all sensors in the system to the signal by means of wire, radio waves, existing electrical circuits, or a combination of these. Fiber-optic lines, dedicated leased lines, and satellite dishes have also become popular means of conveying signals. The circuit is like the network of nerves that run from the human senses to the brain and is usually the most vulnerable component of the alarm system. Power sources should be hidden, protected, checked, and tested regularly.

Some alarms have a fail-safe feature that activates the signal when the power line is cut. In fact, that is the principle behind **capacity alarms.** Such alarms are universally used for point protection of specific objects requiring a high degree of security. The protected object is part of the circuit's capacitance. If a change occurs in the region of the protected object, a change in the system's capacitance sets off the alarm.

Many alarm systems use an automatic **telephone dialer** that sends a recorded message or signal to a central station, the establishment's owner or manager, or to the police station. Although this type of alarm is relatively inexpensive, it has several weaknesses. The dialer could call an answering service and be put on hold, allowing the tape to play itself out before the operator heard the message. Telephone lines can be cut. The telephone line of the person to receive the call may be busy, or the telephone line of the establishment where the sensor is located can be tied up by someone calling in.

**THE SIGNAL** The actual alarm may be audible or silent, a bell, buzzer, phone ringing, or a flashing light. Opinions vary as to which signal is more effective. An audible alarm may frighten intruders away, or it may simply hasten their activity. A silent alarm is unlikely to prevent a theft, but it is more likely that the thief can be apprehended while committing the crime.

# Table 6–1 Detectors—an interior space protection review.

| Device | Application | Operation | False-Alarm Potential | Advantages | Disadvantages |
|---|---|---|---|---|---|
| Contact Switches | Doors and windows to detect opening | Metallic contact held in place by magnet; removal of which causes spring to open contact, triggering an alarm. Mechanical contact switches operate on similar principle, but without magnet. | Basically stable. Environmental conditions may cause gap between magnet and contact to widen | Wide variety of applications and types, i.e. plunger, recessed, leaf, wide gap, overhead door, mercury, tilt, tamper, reed. | Surface-mounted contacts subject to internal sabotage. Reed switches may "lock-up" if put on seldom-used door. |
| Shock Sensors | Mounted on surfaces subject to forced entry: doors and window frames, walls, safes, cabinets, roofs | Electronically analyzes shocks or vibrations in terms of frequency and intensity. | When sensitivity is improperly adjusted | Adaptable to various construction materials. Processor enables analysis of signal from sensor, ignoring ambient vibrations or shocks. | Relatively expensive |
| Traps | Duct work, skylights, air conditioning sleeves, above false ceilings | A cord held under tension, when loosened, tightened or cut will open circuit. | Stable | Ideal for protection of unusual points of entry where other types of devices are impractical or ineffective. | When activated or tripped manual reset is required. |
| Foil | Mounted on glass, laced inside doors | Metallic tape, which carries current, is applied under tension to glass or wood. Forced entry severs tape and opens circuit. | Hostile environment like heavy traffic, temperature, wind may cause hairline cuts and intermittent opens | Reliable and stable. Visible deterrent. Low material cost | Easily damaged in a hostile environment. Installation is labor intensive. |
| Glass Break Sensors (vibration) | Mounts directly on glass | Mechanically responds to the frequency of breaking glass. | When the sensitivity is improperly adjusted | Relatively inexpensive. Covers large area of continuous glass. Unit does not need power to operate | Potential false alarms from ambient vibrations. |
| Audio Discriminators | Glass protection | Capable of detecting selected frequencies, such as the airborne sound of breaking glass. | When the sensitivity is improperly adjusted | Omni-directional and can protect several hundred square feet. Can protect several windows as well as multi-pane windows. | Many false alarms due to ambient sources. |
| Glass Break Sensors (piezoelectric) | Mounts directly on glass | Electronically detects the intermolecular noises of breaking glass. |  | Covers large area of continuous glass. Fairly stable device | Unit needs power to operate. Relatively expensive when compared to other types of glass protection. |
| Vibration Contacts | Mounted on surfaces subject to forced entry: doors, window frames, walls, safes, and ceilings | Vibration/shock causes two touching pieces of metal to separate upon impact and open the circuit. | When the sensitivity is improperly adjusted | Inexpensive unit cost | Limited sensitivity adjustment potential. |

ERENCE SOURCE     NO TEST

## Table 6–1 Detectors—an interior space protection review (continued).

| Device | Operational Theory | Application | Characteristics | Considerations |
|---|---|---|---|---|
| Ultrasonics | Transmits and receives sound waves. Transmitted sound waves, upon striking a moving object, return to the receiver at a different frequency; frequency difference (or Doppler Shift) trips an alarm. | Volumetric coverage<br>Warehouse<br>Schools<br>Municipal buildings | Easily contained; will not penetrate most materials, but may be absorbed.<br>Sound waves will bounce off hard surfaces to fill protected area. | Avoid:<br>Areas with air turbulence<br>Noisy areas, phones, machinery<br>Moving signs, displays, drapes, plants, etc.<br>Severe humidity fluctuations<br>Changing configuration of area (moving stock or equipment) without a corresponding sensor adjustment. |
| Microwave | Radio waves transmission and reception; also works on the Doppler Shift principle. | Volumetric coverage<br>Large open areas<br>Factories<br>Warehouses | Will penetrate most nonmetallic materials, but will be reflected off metal surfaces.<br>Reflected waves may "leave" protected area.<br>Can be mounted in false ceilings for covert detection or to protect unit from tampering. | Avoid:<br>Aiming at vibrating or moving metal surfaces<br>Unwanted signal penetration<br>Fluorescent lighting (at least by 3 feet) |
| Passive Infrared | Receives only infrared energy or heat. Unit constantly looks for a relative rapid change in temperature between two separate zones. If intruder enters one zone, the relative change in temperature is sensed and an alarm occurs. | Pattern or array of beams<br>Large open areas<br>Hallways or aisles<br>Offices | Infrared energy will not penetrate most materials.<br>Needs a clear line of sight. | Avoid:<br>Hot or cold drafts on unit<br>Pointing at areas where animals may move<br>Aiming at moving signs, plants<br>Hot environment, above 95°F<br>Moving stock, furniture or equipment that may block unit |
| Photoelectric | Transmission of a pulsed infrared light beam is focused on a receiver (photoconductive cell), causing current to flow. Interruption of this beam stops the current flow and causes an alarm. | Channel protection<br>Main access areas or corridors<br>Long hallways or warehouse aisles<br>Long unobstructed walls or row windows | Needs a clear line of sight<br>Range 300 to 800 feet<br>Use of mirror allows beam to go around corners | Avoid:<br>Moving objects that may cross beam<br>Areas where animals may move.<br>Moving stock, furniture, or equipment that may block beam. |
| Mats | When pressure is applied to two metal strips (or electrodes) separated by sponge rubber, they touch and short out the system and cause an alarm. | "Spot" protection<br>Any place where intruder is likely to enter & walk: under windows, in front of safes, cabinets, doors and along corridors | Inexpensive protection<br>Covert detection, used under carpets<br>Pressure sensitive | Avoid:<br>Moving furniture or equipment onto mats<br>Heavy traffic area<br>Wet or moisture prone areas |

*System needs extensive walk-testing due to penetration potential.

*Aim to force intruder to walk across zones.

*Alignment critical, use "guard rail" to protect unit.

NOTE: All devices should be mounted on stable, vibration-free surfaces.
SOURCE: Security World, Jan. 1985, pp. 44–45.

# The False-Alarm Problem

Although alarm systems are important means of physical control, they also pose a very serious problem: false alarms. Over 90 percent of all intrusion-alarm signals are false alarms, resulting in needless expense, inappropriate responses, and negative attitudes toward alarm systems.

Because of this high percentage of false alarms, many cities prohibit alarms directly connected to the police department. Even with such restrictions, however, local law enforcement officers are usually called to respond to alarms received by central stations or proprietary centers. Department policy usually dictates that a burglary or robbery-in-progress call be treated as an emergency and that officers respond as rapidly as possible, presenting possible danger to the responding officers and any individuals along the route to the scene.

An additional hazard of the possible false alarm is that responding officers may not take the call seriously, may not respond as rapidly as they should, and may not be on their guard when they approach the scene, leaving themselves exposed to a potentially dangerous situation.

The Hallcrest Report (Cunningham and Taylor, 1985, p. 269) states that studies by the National Burglar and Fire Alarm Association (NBFAA) and other groups studying false alarms indicate three major and several minor causes: "(1) between 40% and 60% are caused by customer (and their employees) misuse and abuse of their alarm systems; (2) between 15% and 25% are caused by alarm company personnel in the installation and servicing of alarm systems; and (3) between 10% and 20% involve faulty equipment. Lesser causes of false alarms include telephone line problems and stormy weather conditions."

Lewin (1990, p. 67) suggests that most alarm systems now being installed are "so reliable and user-friendly that they cause less than one alarm annually." He also suggests that the number-one cause of false alarms is *people*. They either do not know their systems or they install systems that are far more sophisticated than they need.

No matter what the cause of false alarms, the end result is the same: great amounts of patrol time expended in responding to these calls.

However, alarm systems do deter and detect crimes. Burglary data, for instance, consistently indicates that three-fourths of burglaries involve forced entry—what alarm systems were designed to detect. Two police department studies of alarm system effectiveness found that homes with alarm systems were six times less likely to be burglarized than homes without such systems. Furthermore, one of the studies found that the burglary rate for commercial establishments with alarm systems was half that of non-alarmed establishments. The Hallcrest Report (Cunningham and Taylor, 1985, p. 269) notes this success: "Studies by the NBFAA and the Western Burglar and Fire Alarm Association also indicate that alarm systems annually are responsible for the capture of tens of thousands of suspects, resulting in high conviction-to-arrest ratios, thus offsetting additional criminal justice expense and resolving a large number of other burglaries through 'clearance by arrest.' "

The report goes on to note (p. 270):

Efforts to control the false alarm problem have primarily involved enactment of alarm control ordinances and development of customer education and awareness programs by alarm companies. The NBFAA estimates over 2,000 communities with alarm control ordinances which generally have the following characteristics: (1) allowance for three to five false alarms per system per year, (2) punitive action in the form of graduating scales of fines, and ultimately nonresponse to problem locations, and (3) alarm system permits.

Hallcrest Systems surveyed two police departments on their opinions regarding the false-alarm problem and possible deterrents and found the most popular sanction was graduated subscriber fines.

Hallcrest's review of alarm control programs found that (p. 270): "The most effective programs appear to be those which were initially developed in conjunction with the alarm companies, and those which continue to involve the alarm companies in follow-up customer training."

## ☒ SURVEILLANCE SYSTEMS

Some companies use surveillance systems in place of or to supplement security officers. These systems may be used at any of the three lines of defense: the perimeter, the entrance/exit to a building, or a specific location within the building.

Many forms of surveillance are available. One of the simplest and most commonly used is the convex mirror, which allows clerks to see areas that are not observable from a checkout station. More complex forms of surveillance include closed-circuit television and videotape, still, still sequence, and motion picture cameras. Surveillance systems can operate continually or on demand. They can be monitored or unmonitored.

Closed-circuit television (CCTV) can be used in corridors, entrances, and secured areas. Although expensive, it saves personnel costs because one person can monitor several locations at one time. When combined with videotape capabilities, CCTV need not be continuously monitored because of its playback capabilities.

Although less expensive than CCTV, motion picture cameras are not as effective because they require light and almost always make noise. Infrared film can be used if night-only picture taking is anticipated. Sequence cameras can take still pictures at regular intervals or be activated to take pictures when a switch is thrown.

Each system has specific advantages and disadvantages, as illustrated in Table 6–2.

Security managers are cautioned to remember the restriction on surveillance and appropriate legal/privacy issues that might arise.

## ☐ OTHER MEANS TO ENHANCE SECURITY THROUGH PHYSICAL CONTROL

In addition to locks, lights, alarms, and surveillance systems, numerous other alternatives are available to security managers to reduce losses through the use of physical controls.

**Table 6–2 Selection and application guide to fixed surveillance cameras LEAA – National Institute of Law Enforcement and Criminal Justice.**

| | Still Demand Cameras | | | Still Sequence Cameras | | | Motion Picture Cameras (Demand) | TV Cameras | TV Camera and Videotape |
|---|---|---|---|---|---|---|---|---|---|
| | 8mm | 16mm | 35mm | 8mm | 16mm | 35mm | | | |
| EVIDENCE QUALITY | Fair | Good | High | Fair | Good | High | Variable | None | Poor |
| OPERATOR REQUIRED | Yes | Yes | Yes | No | No | No | No | Yes | No |
| CONTINUOUS COVERAGE | No | No | No | Partial | Partial | Partial | Yes | Yes | Yes |
| IMMEDIATE RESULTS | No | No | No | No | No | No | No | Yes | Yes |
| POSSIBLE PERSONNEL HAZARD | Yes | Yes | Yes | No | No | No | No | No | No |
| LIGHT VARIATION TOLERANCE | Low | Low | Low | Low | Low | Low | Low | High | High |
| LIGHT LEVEL REQUIRED (FC) | 50–75 | 50–75 | 50–75 | 50–75 | 50–75 | 50–57 | 50–75 | 20 | 20 |
| AGAINST BURGLARY | Poor | Poor | Poor | Fair | Good | High | High | None | Good |
| AGAINST ROBBERY | Fair | Good | High | Fair | Good | High | Variable | None | Poor |
| AGAINST EMPLOYEE THEFT | None | None | None | Good | High | High | None | None | High |
| AGAINST SHOPLIFTING | None | None | None | Poor | Fair | Good | None | Good | Good |
| AGAINST BAD CHECKS | High | High | High | High | High | High | High | None | Poor |
| EQUIPMENT FIRST COST | Very low | Low | Medium | Low | Medium | Medium | Medium | High | Very high |
| SUPPLIES COST | Very low | Very low | Very low | Very low | Low | Medium | Medium | None | Low |
| PERSONNEL COST | None | None | None | None | None | None | None | High | None |

Quality of motion picture camera output will vary by film size, just as still cameras.
EVIDENCE QUALITY comparisons are based on prints from single frames.
LIGHT LEVEL REQUIRED is based on ASA 250 film exposed at 1/125 second, F2.8.
Effectiveness AGAINST BURGLARY comparisons assume use of available accessories including scanners on motion picture and TV cameras.
Effectiveness AGAINST SHOPLIFTING assumes that television monitors are constantly watched.
Effectiveness AGAINST BAD CHECKS assumes use of equipment to the passer with check in court.
All demand camera systems are assumed to be properly activated by some means, whether by personnel, sensors, or burglar alarm tie-in.
NOTE: Do not rely on the chart alone. Details are contained in the text.

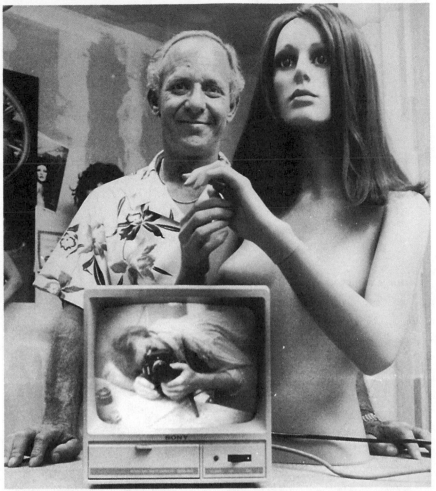

Inventor F. Jerry Gutierrez demonstrates one of his surveillance mannequins designed to watch for shoplifters. They are being photographed by the photographer shown on the TV monitor.

## Other Security Devices

Other security devices available are paper shredders, used to make certain no classified information is improperly discarded; lock-down devices for office machines and other valuable equipment such as microscopes; mirrors in hallways to reveal if anyone is lurking around corners and in retail stores to detect shoplifting; metal detectors; electronic price tags; and computerized telephone systems that automatically route outgoing calls over the least expensive lines and that detect and control long-distance phoning abuses and the like.

Other devices range from such basic items as bulletproof vests to such sophisticated items as bug detection systems that protect privacy during personal conversations in offices, hotels, and at home; a bionic briefcase that contains a bomb and bug detector and is wired to prevent theft; and an electronic handkerchief that allows a person to disguise his or her voice over the telephone.

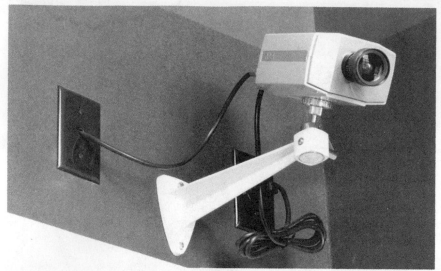

Interior surveillance.

Convex mirror.

New security devices are constantly being produced and marketed. Magazines such as *Security Management* and *Security World* can help security managers keep abreast of new developments in security hardware.

## Signs

Signs can be used to provide instructions and warnings; for example, "Restricted Area," "No Unauthorized Personnel Beyond This Point," "No Admittance," "One Way," "This Building Protected by an Alarm," "Caution: Attack Dog," "All shoplifters will be prosecuted to the full extent of

The traditional watch clock was carried by the security officer. Modern watch clocks operate by keys being inserted into them, which sends a record of when the check was made back to the central control panel.

the law," "No Smoking," and so on can effectively improve safety and discourage crime. In most jurisdictions signs are a legal requirement for trespassing prosecutions.

## Dogs

Security dogs may be classified as **patrol dogs** or **guard dogs**. Sentry or **patrol dogs** are usually leashed and make rounds with a security officer, providing companionship and protection. Because of their keen sense of smell and hearing, they can easily detect intruders. Sentry dogs, frequently German Shepherds or Doberman Pinschers, are the most expensive security dogs.

**Guard dogs** roam alone inside a perimeter or building to deter intruders. They may be alarm dogs whose growl and bark are intended to frighten intruders away, or they may be attack dogs, trained to physically restrain any intruders. Guard dogs are frequently used by the military, by some contract security firms, by car dealers, by junk dealers, by warehouse operators, and in large stores. Often the dogs are leased from a security dog contractor. Such dogs usually respond to only one handler and therefore pose a potential risk, especially for police officers or fire fighters who might be called to the premises in an emergency.

Although security dogs are expensive and do present a potential risk for lawsuits, and although they can be shot, hit, anaesthetized, or poisoned, they remain a viable alternative for many establishments. According to Spurlock (1990, p. 94), the greatest expense is training. Budget reports for five small- to medium-sized police departments indicate that the highest annual maintenance cost was $800.

Guard dog patrolling an industrial facility.

## Security Officers

Many establishments depend on the presence of a uniformed security officer, perhaps armed, as a deterrent to most would-be offenders. In addition, security officers can perform the numerous functions discussed in Chapter 2, and they can ensure the effectiveness of security equipment.

Some establishments have their security patrols carry watch clocks on their rounds. Watch clocks are seven-day timepieces. Keys are located at various stations in a facility, and the security officer simply inserts the key into the watch clock at each station. A record is automatically made of the time the location was checked. Any stations not visited at the appropriate time can be monitored.

The beat clock is becoming a relic, however. Bar-coding devices now allow security personnel to check hazardous areas, inventory items, inspect fire equipment, and produce neatly printed reports by simply attaching the bar-code wand to a desktop computer with a printer.

Some facilities have sophisticated automatic guard-monitoring systems that transmit a message to the central security office if a guard does not arrive at the appointed time. The central security office is thus alerted to any illness, accident, or crime-related problems. One disadvantage of this system, however, is that an established patrol pattern can be learned by unauthorized people and used to their advantage.

## Communication Systems

Numerous types of communications are available, including telephones, public address or loudspeaker systems, intercoms, radios or walkie-talkies, pagers, tape recorders, and teletypes. Although means of communication are often taken for granted, they are vital in situations such as emergencies or natural disasters.

## The Command Center

Ideally, the communication center should be linked to the security control center and should be in a controlled area. The communication center area might receive any alarm signals and might be the control for the switchboard, a closed-circuit television monitoring system, and a public address system.

## □ THE PHYSICAL SECURITY SYSTEM

All too often, managers concentrate on appearance, efficiency, and convenience to the neglect of security and safety.

Aesthetic, operational, safety, and security needs must be balanced.

The key factors in any physical security program are to identify risks and then to alleviate them when possible. The security survey discussed in Chapter 4 allows managers to assess the vulnerability of assets as well as the criticality of their loss and then to select physical controls to meet the needs of their particular facility. Providing either more or less physical security than is needed is never desirable.

The following security checklist (Figure 6–7) summarizes the key physical controls used to provide security.

It is common sense that a locked, well-lit building equipped with an alarm system will be less attractive to a thief than an unfenced, unlocked, unlit building with no alarm system. But locks, lights, alarms, and other security equipment must be properly maintained and used to be effective.

Common sense and attention to detail are critical factors in establishing and maintaining physical controls.

Because security hardware has become increasingly complex and sophisticated, the Private Security Task Force Report recommends that security consultants be used for specialized areas such as alarm systems, anti-burglary strategies, personnel control techniques and systems, security hardware for access points, security lighting techniques, and special security needs such as those required for computers. This chapter has presented only an overview of the physical security control options available.

## SUMMARY

One important responsibility of security managers is to provide security through physical controls. Physical controls serve to reduce risk of loss by denying unauthorized access, by deterring or delaying those who attempt to gain unauthorized access, and by detecting threats, both criminal and noncriminal.

**PORTLAND POLICE BUREAU COMMERCIAL SECURITY SURVEY**

Business Name _____ File No. _____

Address _____ Date _____

Name of Person Contacted _____ Position _____

Type of Premise _____ Phone No. _____

KEY:   STND = STANDARD          REC = RECOMMENDATION          COMM = COMMENTS

| 1. BUILDING FRONT | STND | REC | COMM | 4. BUILDING LEFT SIDE | STND | REC | COMM | 7. ALARMS | STND | REC | COMM |
|---|---|---|---|---|---|---|---|---|---|---|---|
| DOORS | — | — | — | DOORS | — | — | — | AUDIBLE | — | — | — |
| LOCKS | — | — | — | LOCKS | — | — | — | SILENT | — | — | — |
| WINDOWS | — | — | — | WINDOWS | — | — | — | OTHER | — | — | — |
| LIGHTS | — | — | — | LIGHTS | — | — | — | | | | |
| VENTS | — | — | — | VENTS | — | — | — | ALARM PERMIT # _____ | | | |
| MISC. | — | — | — | MISC. | — | — | — | | | | |

| 2. BUILDING RIGHT SIDE | STND | REC | COMM | 5. BUILDING ROOF | STND | REC | COMM | 8. SAFES | STND | REC | COMM |
|---|---|---|---|---|---|---|---|---|---|---|---|
| DOORS | — | — | — | ROOF ACCESS | — | — | — | ANCHORED | — | — | — |
| LOCKS | — | — | — | ROOF | | | | SHIELDED | | | |
| WINDOWS | — | — | — | SKYLIGHT | — | — | — | DIAL | — | — | — |
| LIGHTS | — | — | — | ROOF | | | | VISIBLE | — | — | — |
| VENTS | — | — | — | VENTS | — | — | — | LIGHTED | — | — | — |
| MISC. | — | — | — | MISC. | — | — | — | MONEY CHEST | — | — | — |
| | | | | | | | | FILE | — | — | — |

| 3. BUILDING REAR | STND | REC | COMM | 6. LOADING DOORS | STND | REC | COMM | 9. MISCELLANEOUS | STND | REC | COMM |
|---|---|---|---|---|---|---|---|---|---|---|---|
| DOORS | — | — | — | OVER HEAD | — | — | — | KEY CONTROL | — | — | — |
| LOCKS | — | — | — | SLIDING | — | — | — | FENCING | | | |
| WINDOWS | — | — | — | SIDEWALK | | | | LIGHTING | — | — | — |
| LIGHTS | — | — | — | ELEVATOR | — | — | — | LANDSCAPING | — | — | — |
| VENTS | — | — | — | ROLLER | — | — | — | OFFICE | | | |
| MISC. | — | — | — | | | | | EQUIPMENT | | | |
| | | | | | | | | ENGRAVED | — | — | — |

COMMENTS: _____
_____
_____
_____
_____
_____
_____
_____
_____
_____
_____
_____
_____

This report is advisory only and does not purport to list all hazards or the adequacy of present hazard controls.

| OFFICER: | NO. | PREC/DIV: | DISTRICT: |
|---|---|---|---|

PRECINCT

**Figure 6–7 Security checklist.**
*Courtesy of the Portland Police Bureau.*

The three basic lines of physical defense are the perimeter of a facility, the building exterior, and the interior. The perimeter can be physically controlled by fences, gates, locks, lighting, alarms, surveillance systems, signs, dogs, and security personnel. Physical layout and neatness are other important factors.

The physical security of a building's exterior can be established by strong, locked doors and windows, limited entrances, secured openings (if larger than ninety-six square inches), alarms, surveillance, and light-

## FOLLOW-UP INTERVIEW

First Follow-Up

1. Have you improved your security based upon what you have learned from the survey? Yes ___ No ___ What have you done?

2. Were you burglarized since your inspection? Yes ___ No ___

3. Was the burglary reported to the police? Yes ___ No ___

4. Would compliance with security recommendations have prevented the burglary? Yes ___ No ___

5. Have you engraved your property? Yes ___ No ___

6. Is the emergency sticker posted? Yes ___ No ___

Comments: _____

| Officer | No. | Date | Prec. | District |
|---------|-----|------|-------|----------|

Second Follow-Up

1. Have you improved your security base upon what you have learned from the survey? Yes ___ No ___ What have you done?

2. Were you burglarized since your inspection? Yes ___ No ___

3. Was the burglary reported to the police? Yes ___ No ___

4. Would compliance with security recommendations have prevented the burglary? Yes ___ No ___

5. Have you engraved your property? Yes ___ No ___

6. Is the emergency sticker posted? Yes ___ No ___

Comments: _____

| Officer | No. | Date | Prec. | District |
|---------|-----|------|-------|----------|

**Figure 6–7 Security checklist** (*continued*).
*Courtesy of the Portland Police Bureau.*

ing. Interior physical controls include locked doors, desks, and files; safes and vaults; internal alarms and detectors; lighting; mirrors; bolt-down equipment; dogs; security personnel; and communication and surveillance systems. Most safes are either fire resistant or burglar resistant, but not both.

From the above, it can be seen that basic security equipment at any of the three lines of defense includes locks, lights, and alarms. Available locks include key operated, combination, card activated, and electronically operated. If a key-operated lock is used, the best protection is offered by a dead-bolt lock with a one-inch throw and an antiwrenching collar, or a secondary dead bolt with a one-inch throw.

Adequate light inside as well as outside a building enhances safety, deters would-be intruders, and makes detection of actual intruders more probable. A total lighting system includes four types of lighting: (1) continuous—on a regular schedule for secure areas, (2) standby—for occasions when more light is needed, (3) moveable—for when light is needed in areas not usually lit, and (4) emergency—to be used as an alternate power source when the regular power source fails.

Alarms are also available for all three lines of defense: perimeter alarms, to protect fences, gates, exterior doors, windows, and other openings; area or space alarms, to protect a portion of or the total interior of a room or building; and point or spot alarms, to protect specific items such as safes, cabinets, valuable articles, or small areas. Alarm systems may be local, proprietary, central station, or police connected.

When selecting physical controls to reduce losses from recognized risks, security managers must balance aesthetic, operational, safety, and security needs. Once physical controls have been selected and installed, common sense and attention to detail are critical factors in establishing and maintaining the physical controls.

## APPLICATION

1) The Ace Industrial Company is faced with the problem of saving on lighting to conserve energy without sacrificing its security. The company's president instructs the security manager to research the problem. If you were in this manager's position, what suggestions might you make to reduce the cost of lighting, conserve energy, and yet maintain security?

2) Design a 50-foot-by-100-foot storage building that will contain heavy equipment, parts, and a repair area for the equipment. Include locks, lighting, and alarms that would be appropriate and justify each installation you recommend.

3) Obtain from several police departments statistical data regarding responses to false alarms in the community. Also obtain a copy of the community's false-alarm ordinance, if available, and bring it to class for a discussion and analysis of the ordinance's effectiveness in bringing the consumer, the law enforcement agency, and the alarm company together to curb the false-alarm problem.

## DISCUSSION QUESTIONS

1) Most adults have several keys in their possession. How many keys are in your possession? What types of locks do they fit? Compare the different types of keys that others have with your own.

**2)** Local communities frequently pass ordinances to curtail false-alarm responses by the public police. From the user's standpoint, is this an advantage or a disadvantage?

**3)** Despite the numerous advantages offered by a reliable surveillance system, what disadvantages might be expected?

**4)** Security managers frequently overcompensate in protecting areas with fencing. List some guidelines you would consider before recommending any type of outside security fencing.

**5)** In providing for security needs, why are aesthetics important to the security manager?

# REFERENCES

Broder, J. F. *Risk analysis and the security survey.* Boston: MA: Butterworth, 1984.

Crime Analysis Center. *Serious crime survey: 1982 update.* Executive Department, State of Oregon, September 1982.

Cunningham, William C.; Strauchs, John J.; and Van Meter, Clifford W. *Private security trends, 1970 to 2000: The Hallcrest report II.* Stoneham, MA: Butterworth-Heinemann, 1990.

Cunningham, W. C. and Taylor, T. H. *The Hallcrest report: Private security and police in America.* Portland, OR: Chancellor Press, 1985.

Gigliotti, R. and Jason, R. *Security design for maximum protection.* Boston, MA: Butterworth, 1984.

Hill, Col. T. J. *The security manager's handbook.* Waterford, CT: Bureau of Business Practice, 1981.

Hof, Robert D. Forget the I.D.—Let's see your eyeball. *Business week,* November 21, 1988, pp. 109–112.

Kakalik, J. S. and Wildhorn, S. *The private police.* New York: Crane Russak, 1977 (The Rand Corporation).

Lewin, Thomas M. Plagued by false alarms? *Law and order,* December 1990, pp. 67–69.

National Advisory Commission on Criminal Justice Standards and Goals, Programs for Reduction of Criminal Opportunity. *Community crime prevention.* Law Enforcement Assistance Administration, Washington, DC: U.S. Government Printing Office, 1973.

National Crime Prevention Institute. *Understanding crime prevention.* Stoneham, MA: Butterworth Publishers, 1986.

Naudts, John. Access control: It's in the cards. *Security management,* September 1987, pp. 169–173.

*Private security.* Report of the Task Force on Private Security, National Advisory Committee on Criminal Justice Standards and Goals. Washington, DC: U.S. Government Printing Office, 1976.

Spurlock, James C. K-9. *Law and order,* March 1990, pp. 91–96.

## □ INTRODUCTION

The BuildMore Construction Company has installed a sophisticated alarm system, the most modern security lighting, and the best locks available. Management is confident that the facility is secure. It is unaware, however, that Employee A is taking small tools home in his lunch pail almost daily; Employee B is placing several lengthy personal long-distance calls a month; Employee C is loading extra lumber on his truck and using it to build his own garage; Employee D is falsifying her time card regularly; and Employee F is submitting false invoices to be paid to his wife under her maiden name. In addition, the typewriter repairer who just carried out a new electric typewriter is not really a technician but a thief.

Locks, lights, and alarms cannot protect the BuildMore Construction Company from such losses. Physical controls must be complemented by procedural controls to establish security. The facility itself and the degree of security required will, of course, determine the extent of the physical and procedural controls. The following discussion presents general procedures that might apply in most facilities. Additional procedures frequently required in industrial, retail, commercial, and other specific types of establishments are discussed in Section Three.

Numerous books on private security differentiate between the "enemy from without"—the robber and burglar—and the "enemy from within"—the dishonest employee who systematically depletes a company's assets and causes **shrinkage.**

---

*Shrinkage* refers to lost assets.

---

Klump (1983, p. 63) suggests that: "To security professionals, shrinkage is a polite term for employee theft." He further suggests: "In tackling employee theft, security managers actually face two separate

## Chapter Seven

# Enhancing Security through Procedural Controls

### DO YOU KNOW

➤ What shrinkage is?

➤ What hiring procedures can help reduce shrinkage and negligence lawsuits?

➤ What educational measures can help promote security?

➤ How most procedural controls seek to prevent loss?

➤ What specific procedures can be used to control access to an area?

➤ What characterizes an effective employee badge or pass?

➤ What constitutes effective key control?

➤ What an effective closing procedure ensures?

➤ When opening and closing is a two-person operation?

➤ What areas are particularly vulnerable to theft?

➤ What accounting procedures can help prevent shrinkage?

➤ What procedures can help detect theft or pilferage?

➤ When searches of lockers, vehicles, packages, and persons are acceptable?

➤ What procedures to use when transporting valuables?

➤ What additional protection against financial loss is available to owners/managers?

157

problems—keeping thieves out and weeding them out." Wise hiring can eliminate the second problem.

Internal theft may account for up to 70 percent of all shrinkage. Such thefts may be of cash, merchandise, industrial tools and supplies, office supplies, time, and/or vital information. According to the U.S. Commerce Department, employee theft costs the nation's businesses over $40 billion each year.

There is another problem with the "enemy from within." Many businesses are finding that they are legally liable for any misdeeds of their employees, particularly if they did not exercise "reasonable care" in their hiring procedures. For example, the owner of an apartment complex was sued by a tenant who had been sexually assaulted by the apartment manager (*Ponticas* v. *K.M.S. Investments*—Minn. 1983). The manager was on parole at the time he applied for the job and gave as his two references his mother and sister. The court ruled that the preemployment screening was insufficient given the responsibility associated with the job.

Schubb and Connelly (1985, p. 27) note that such lawsuits are becoming more common:

> Charges of negligence and negligent hiring are reported to be the bases for most business liability suits. Lawyers in many states say the number of negligence suits being filed against businesses is growing at a geometric rate. . . . In addition to the increase in the number of suits, the amount of damages being awarded in these cases has also been climbing. According to a study of cases reported by the American Trial Lawyers Association, between 1967 and 1982, the average major damage award increased from $20,333 to $1,048,063, more than a 5,000 percent increase.

## ☑ HIRING PROCEDURES AND EMPLOYMENT PRACTICES

*one of the most critical aspects a co. can do.*

One way to reduce shrinkage and avoid negligence suits is to improve the quality of personnel hired. Kuhn (1990, p. 23A) notes that security and human resources personnel have several trends working against them:

➤ A shrinking pool of qualified workers.
➤ Diminished employee loyalty.
➤ Tougher legislation surrounding employee selection practices.
➤ Defamation of character suits brought against employers who provide references on ex-employees.
➤ Increasing workplace theft and drug use.
➤ Growing number of vicarious liability and negligent hiring suits.

The difficulty in finding honest, trustworthy, reliable employees is reiterated by Schubb and Connelly (1985, p. 24): "In most firms today, the demand for employees is often great and continuous, especially where low wages have effected maximum turnover, where responsibilities are great and temptations even greater, and where an indifferent society no longer believes in the work ethic." (Schubb and Connelly (1985, p. 27) go on to note:

Lawyers also agree that even a *hint* of negligence is sometimes enough to launch a suit that could win a large award from a business or force a substantial out-of-court settlement.

The development of business security systems is partly responsible for the increase in negligence suits; and the court's definition of "reasonable care" is toughening.

---

**Job applicants should be screened, including a background check, examination of past work record, and contact with references.**

---

**THE RESUMÉ**  Schafer (1990, p. 17A) cautions: "One mistake in the hiring process can cost an employer millions in negligent hiring or retention lawsuits." Steps employers might take to avoid resumé fraud, according to Schafer, include the following:

➤ Establish and publish requirements within the company that background investigations must be completed on all new hires.
➤ Verify educational backgrounds.

Often those who make the best impression during a job interview are actually those who are the most skilled in lying.

**THE INTERVIEW**  Jayne (1990, p. 18A) describes the *integrity interview* as a "face-to-face, nonaccusatory interview consisting of a series of questions that address issues such as significant thefts from prior employers, use of illegal drugs during work hours, participation in criminal activities, falsification of the application form, and similar job-related concerns." All questions asked must be job related and nondiscriminatory.

**THE INTEGRITY TEST**  Harris (1990, p. 21A) suggests that integrity tests are valuable tools but must be used "prudently and judiciously." Such tests are supposed to predict an individual's potential to commit job-related theft.

**PSYCHOLOGICAL TESTS**  Such tests are also valuable and, according to Kuhn (1990, p. 23A), can be used to measure "various mental characteristics such as intelligence, aptitude, attitude, personality types, knowledge, and skills."

A wide range of other tests are available for preemployment screening, including tests that measure job aptitude, job abilities, emotional stability, and mental health. A test should be *valid*, that is, it should measure attitudes or skills that are directly related to the position. Test publishers should supply such validity data. Some publishers, in fact, have compiled national norms that provide standards against which to compare applicants' scores.

A conscientious background and reference check should be made on every new employee for the best security. Although it is not permissible to ask a job applicant about prior arrest or prison records (EEO ruling), gaps in employment history may indicate such records. Any unexplained time periods may be asked about.

**BACKGROUND INVESTIGATIONS** In *High Tech Gays v. Defense Industrial Clearance Office* (1990), the U.S. Ninth Circuit Court ruled that the U.S. Department of Defense did have the authority to conduct expanded background investigations of gay applicants who were candidates for secret and top secret clearance. The court observed that homosexuals are part of a "quasi-suspect" class that should receive heightened security.

**USE OF THE POLYGRAPH** As noted in Chapter 3, use of the polygraph as a preemployment tool has become severely restricted. In 1987, in *Texas State Employment Union v. Texas Department of Mental Health*, the Texas Supreme Court declared unconstitutional a state law requiring the state department of health's employees to take a polygraph test as a condition of employment. The court observed that polygraph tests constitute an unwarranted intrusion of privacy.

In 1988, as previously discussed, the Employee Polygraph Protection Act (EPPA) was signed into law prohibiting employers from using lie detector tests for preemployment screening or during employment except in certain instances. Recall that one of the exceptions was prospective employees of private armored car, security alarm, and security firms. Rea (1989, p. 51) cautions that:

> There is not a blank exemption for security companies to administer lie detector tests. The exemption only applies to companies that derive 50 percent of their business from armored car, security alarm, and security guard business. Thus, a company that simply provides security services for its own use does not qualify to use lie detector tests for screening employees.

In 1989, in *Mest v. Federated Group, Inc.*, a California court awarded $12 million in damages to fifteen thousand job applicants who alleged that a retailer had violated their privacy rights by compelling them to take a polygraph. Although honest, reliable employees are desirable at all levels, the extensiveness of the personal background investigation will depend on the job and type of security required. Noncritical clearances may involve completion of an application form with name, address, telephone number, education, past work record, and references. Even these noncritical clearances should be checked.

Critical clearance for positions involving large sums of cash, valuable merchandise, or trade secrets goes further and may include a polygraph examination (where it is legal) and/or a psychological stress examination. At least the last five years' employers and three references should be checked. It is often advisable to talk to neighbors as well, because most job applicants will list as references only those individuals who will speak favorably of them.

**NATIONAL INVESTIGATION AGENCIES** Hill (1990, p. 16A) contends:

> The need for thorough pre-employment screening is receiving more attention now that the courts have started to hold companies—and in some cases individuals—liable for negligent hiring procedures. To meet the screening demand, nationwide private investigation agencies have started using new approaches and the latest technology. These agencies provide background

investigation reports that are not only fast, accurate, and cost-effective but also viable to this modern-day employer problem. . . .

A national investigation agency specializing in employment screening provides services and benefits otherwise unobtainable:

➤ Quick turnaround.
➤ Legal accuracy.
➤ Thoroughness.
➤ Analysis—and experienced judgments.

Hill notes (p. 16A) that national private investigation agencies use computers and street investigators to search public records such as criminal records, federal records, workers' compensation records, driving records, credit records, and quasi-public records such as medical and military records.

Any persons being considered for promotion into positions of trust should also be checked carefully from a security point of view. Despite careful screening and checking of job applicants, some dishonest people are likely to be hired. Klump (1983, p. 63) discusses the need to minimize such hiring:

> Weeding out people who have become problem employees requires careful management of the available resources. If a company were to hire at random, most surveys show it would wind up with a few employees who are virtually incorruptible, a few more who would steal at the first opportunity, and a substantial number in the middle who are basically honest, but who could become a problem under a given set of circumstances. Put a thief in their midst and some will join him out of greed, fear, spite, or anger. If the problem continues for just a little while, others will join in because "everyone else is doing it." Workers conclude the company doesn't care or the company "deserves" to suffer the losses. Isolating and perhaps eliminating a dishonest employee, if done promptly, will often save many others who may be tempted to steal.

Hire good people and then maintain the climate that will keep them honest. For example, an organization of fast-food restaurants was noted for its good employee relations. Management treated people fairly and displayed faith in their integrity and ability, but also provided uniforms without pockets. When the opportunity to steal is removed, half the battle is won. Nothing can substitute for rigid, well-implemented preventive measures.

Owner/managers should have a continuing program of investigation and training on ways to eliminate stock shortages and shrinkage. For example, one small retailer trained his employees to record each item, such as floor cleaner, taken out of stock for use in the store. Unless recorded, it was an inventory loss, even though it was a legitimate store expense. Management must let employees know that it is always aware and always cares.

Employees should be accountable for all assets entrusted to them.

Educate all employees as to their responsibilities and restrictions. Establish reasonable rules and enforce them.

Make clear that certain areas are off-limits, that supplies are to be used only for job-related activities, that personal long-distance phone calls are not to be made on company phones, that periodic inspections will be held, and that any thefts will be prosecuted.

Policies must not be stated as suggestions but rather as rules that are and will be enforced. In addition, posters might be strategically placed emphasizing "Zero Shrinkage." A more negative but possibly effective poster might illustrate frequently pilfered items, a price tag attached to each, and a caption reading, "Is your future worth more than this?"

## ☑ CONTROLLING ACCESS TO RESTRICTED AREAS

Many facilities require strict access control. In such cases they may require that all employees (including security), contractors, and visitors sign in/out and may in addition require them to have identification badges. The only exceptions may be emergency service personnel such as fire, police, and ambulance responding to a call for assistance.

The purpose of access control is to facilitate authorized entry and to prevent the unauthorized entry of those who might steal material or information, or might bring harmful devices onto the premises.

Most physical controls are aimed at limiting access to restricted areas, particularly during the time when an establishment is not conducting business, that is, after hours. During business hours, however, access cannot be completely limited, or the company could not function.

Most procedural controls seek to prevent loss by limiting access to specific areas by unauthorized personnel.

Sometimes it is necessary to limit access to nonemployees only. Other times, however, even employees are denied access to certain areas of a facility. From a security standpoint, it is best to limit the number of people having access to cash, important documents, valuable merchandise, and areas where these are stored.

Access control includes identifying, directing, and/or limiting the movement of vehicles, employees, contractors, vendors, and visitors.

Procedural controls to limit access to specified areas include stationing guards, restricting vehicle traffic, requiring registration and sign-outs, requiring display of badges or passes, ensuring key control, and using effective opening, closing, and after-hours procedures.

Even in retail establishments where traffic flow is encouraged, certain areas are usually off-limits to nonemployees and perhaps even to some employees. A uniformed security guard, especially if armed, may be a psychological deterrent to a would-be thief, whether internal or external. Restricted areas and boundaries should be clearly specified and the restrictions unconditionally enforced.

## Vehicle Control

Vehicle traffic can be restricted in several ways. The simplest way is to have only one gate, with a card-key system or a guard to check identities and allow or refuse admittance to drivers seeking entrance to the premises. Sometimes stickers on the bumper or windshield constitute the necessary identification for admittance.

Another method is to have two parking lots, both equipped with traffic control arms. Employees can gain entrance to their parking lot by use of a card-key. Visitors can gain entrance to their parking lot simply by driving in, but they cannot exit without a token obtained from the receptionist. This system is sometimes used at drive-in restaurants to prevent teenagers from cruising around the parking lot and not making a purchase. Without a purchase, the driver has no token and cannot exit without a confrontation with the manager.

## Check-in/out Register

A check-in/out register can be used with employees as well as with vendors, contractors, and visitors. This system requires the person seeking entrance to sign in with a receptionist or security guard, present identification, state the purpose of the visit, and sign out before leaving. The date, time of entrance, and time of leaving are recorded. The person may then be directed to the desired location, may be given a badge or pass, or may be met in the reception area by the person he or she is visiting. Either the business can be conducted there or the visitor can be escorted to an office. Sign-in/out logs such as that shown in Figure 7–1 are commonly used for after-hours entrance.

## Badges and Passes

Sometimes supervisory personnel and/or security guards know all the employees, at least by sight, and the areas they are authorized to enter. Often, however, in large establishments, employees are required to wear badges or to carry passes that identify them. Although some employees object to wearing badges, feeling they are impersonal, unsightly, and damaging to clothing, with the proper type of badge and the proper orientation, the badge can be established as a status symbol, an indication that the person is "part of the team."

Some badges are simply name plates and serve little security function.

At minimum, effective employee badges and passes display the employee's name, employment number, signature, and photograph as well as an authorizing signature. They are sturdy, tamper-proof, and changed periodically.

Effective badges or passes should also use a distinctive, intricate background design difficult to reproduce; use a code denoting the area(s) for which the badge or pass is valid; contain an easily recognized serial

| SIGN IN LOG | | | | DATE _____ | |
|:---|:---|:---|:---|:---|:---|
| **Please print** | | | | POST _____ | |
| | | | | SHEET NO. _____ | |
| **NAME** | **EMPLOYEE NO.** | **DEPT.** | **PHONE EXT.** | **TIME IN** | **TIME OUT** |
| | | | | | |
| | | | | | |
| | | | | | |
| | | | | | |
| | | | | | |
| | | | | | |
| | | | | | |
| | | | | | |

**Figure 7–1  After hours sign-in/out log.**

number; be resistant to fumes inherent in the facility; and have some secret characteristic known only to management.

The issuing of badges and passes should be carefully controlled. They should be issued only after the employee is cleared by the supervisor. Then the reason for the badge or pass and its importance to security must be carefully explained to the employee.

The system should specify when, where, how, and to whom identification is displayed; what is to be done if the identification is lost or damaged; and procedures to follow if an employee is terminated. Employees should be instructed to report lost or damaged passes or badges immediately. Temporary badges may be provided for employees who lose theirs or who forget them at home. Such passes should be valid for only one day and should be turned in at the end of the day. A log such as that shown in Figure 7–2 should be kept of these badges to maintain effective security.

Procedures for canceling and/or reissuing identification passes or badges must be clearly established. For example, if employees lose an ID badge, they must report the loss immediately to their supervisor, fill in a form authorizing a new badge to be issued and have that form approved, and, perhaps, pay a fee for the replacement.

Security officers should be given a "hot sheet" of lost or stolen badges or passes, as well as those of terminated employees who have retained theirs. Security officers should also compare the photographs, signatures, and descriptions with those of the wearer. They should *not* assume the pass or badge is valid, but should periodically check their "hot sheet."

*Visitor badges or passes,* often used for security purposes, should be distinct from employee badges and passes. If both employees and non-employees are required to have a badge or pass, supervisors and security personnel can immediately ascertain whether a specific person is authorized to be in a specific location.

## Temporary Badge Sign In/Out

**Please print**                                              DATE _____

| TEMP. BADGE NO. | NAME | EMPLOYEE NO. | PHONE EXT. | TIME IN | TIME OUT | APPROVED BY |
|---|---|---|---|---|---|---|
| | | | | | | |
| | | | | | | |
| | | | | | | |
| | | | | | | |
| | | | | | | |
| | | | | | | |
| | | | | | | |
| | | | | | | |
| | | | | | | |

**Figure 7–2  Temporary badge sign-in/out log.**

## VISITOR REGISTRATION LOG

Welcome To *J&B Innovative Enterprises, Inc.*

**Please print**

| DATE | NAME | BADGE NO. | VEHICLE LICENSE | REPRESENTING | EMPLOYEE SPONSOR | TIME IN | TIME OUT |
|---|---|---|---|---|---|---|---|
| | | | | | | | |
| | | | | | | | |
| | | | | | | | |
| | | | | | | | |
| | | | | | | | |
| | | | | | | | |
| | | | | | | | |
| | | | | | | | |
| | | | | | | | |
| | | | | | | | |
| | | | | | | | |

**Figure 7–3  Visitor register log.**

Visitors are often required to sign in, as previously described. If the visitor is issued a pass or badge, the number should be recorded in the check-in/out register. The visitor should return the badge or pass when signing out. If the visitor retains the pass, a serious breach in security is created. Visitor register logs such as that shown in Figure 7–3 are used in many establishments.

If employees wish to have guests (relatives, children, friends) visit, some facilities require prior approval, using a form such as that shown in Figure 7–4.

*Tour groups* may present a special security problem in that a would-be thief, terrorist, or industrial spy may join a tour group with the intention of slipping away and gaining access to a restricted area. Passes or badges can help prevent such illegal activity. Ideally, every

## NON-BUSINESS VISITORS ACCESS REQUEST

Requests for any visit to the facility by individuals not conducting company business must be approved by your supervisor before the visit.

Visitors are not allowed in any restricted or hazardous area.

The host employee must maintain control and responsibility for visitors and their actions.

Employee Name _____

Employee Number _____    Phone Extension _____

Date of Visit _____

Guests' Names

_____    _____

_____    _____

_____    _____

_____    _____

Approximate Time _____

Manager's Approval _____
                                    Signature

**Figure 7–4  Nonbusiness visitor access request.**

member of a tour group should sign in with the receptionist or security guard and be issued a pass or badge that is clearly marked "Tour Group." The members should be required to stay together and be accompanied by a uniformed guard. When the tour is over, a head count should be done, all badges collected, and all members signed out. Even though the tour will not be likely to go into restricted areas, these measures will deter anyone from leaving the group to gain access to restricted areas or will detect such illicit activity early.

*Contractors and vendors* are frequently treated like visitors; that is, they sign in and receive a temporary badge or pass that identifies them as nonemployees and indicates the area(s) to which they have access.

Employees using contracted services often must arrange for badges to be issued to the individuals who will be providing the services. The form in Figure 7–5 serves this purpose.

Some regular contractors and vendors may be issued long-term passes, but caution should be exercised in using such passes. Holders of permanent passes should be required to use only one entry/exit, and the security guard should have a list of those with permanent passes, along with their signatures, to compare when they sign in. Contractors and vendors should be required to give their name, company, purpose, vehicle license number, and badge number, and to sign in. The date, time in, and time out should always be recorded. Such permanent passes should be reissued periodically, just like those of employees.

## Key Control

Another procedure important in controlling access to restricted areas is adequate key control. As noted earlier, a lock is only as secure as the key or combination that operates it.

## CONTRACT EMPLOYEE ACCESS REQUEST

Complete this form if you want a contracted employee to be issued a badge. Allow three days for processing.

A contracted badge will be issued for the requested individual each day at the gate designated. They will sign in on the Visitor Register at that time. The badge must be returned at the end of the day.

Contract Company _____

Contact Company Telephone Number _____

Contact Employee (s) Name _____

Dates of Contract Employment:   from_____ to _____

Type of Employment _____

      ☐ Overload/Temporary Help

      ☐ Service/Maintenance

      ☐ Construction Work/Mover

Facility Required _____ Gates Required _____

Supervised by _____

Telephone Extension _____ Mail Station _____

Restrictions (if any) _____

Department Manager Authorization _____

Contrator badges are generally issued only during working hours unless other arrangements are made with the security office.

| CONTRACTOR BADGE SIGN IN/OUT | | DATE _____ | | | |
|---|---|---|---|---|---|
| NAME | BADGE NO. | REPRESENTING (COMPANY) | CALLING ON | TIME IN | TIME OUT |
| | | | | | |
| | | | | | |
| | | | | | |
| | | | | | |
| | | | | | |
| | | | | | |
| | | | | | |
| | | | | | |
| | | | | | |
| | | | | | |

**Figure 7–5  Contract employee access request.**

Having a key is often a status symbol. In small businesses, it is common for every employee to have a key, but from a security standpoint, this is unsound. The only reason for having a key should be *job necessity*. The greater the number of people having keys, the greater the security risk.

A written record should be kept of all keys in use. The record might look like the one shown in Figure 7–6.

A key control system limits the number of persons having keys, establishes a master list of all existing keys and to whom they are assigned, keeps all duplicate keys secure, and requires a physical audit periodically.

To eliminate the inconvenience of a person having to carry several keys, perhaps even hundreds, a **master keying system** is sometimes used. Under this system, a **change key** opens only one specific door. A **sub-master key** opens the locks in a specific area. A **master key** opens the locks in the entire building. Sometimes the system extends even further if multiple buildings are concerned, with a **grand master key** opening all locks in two or more buildings.

Although master keying offers advantages to the user, it also is much less secure. If the master key falls into the wrong hands or is duplicated, the system poses a much greater security risk than a single key system; it is also much more costly to rekey an entire building should such a risk be discovered.

All keys, but especially master keys, should be stamped "Do Not Duplicate." This does not, however, guarantee that duplication is prevented. Some security experts recommend scratching off the serial numbers on keys and padlocks because locksmiths can make duplicates if given the make and number.

Though marking keys "Do Not Duplicate" may seem futile, it will have some effect. The best way to hamper key copying, however, is to purchase locks that use restricted keys. These are particularly secure because lockmakers limit the distribution of restricted key blanks, even among reputable locksmiths.

Some security managers use an inexpensive method to reduce unauthorized key duplication by having keys made on "neuter" head blanks. These blanks have the same grooving as common blanks, but the heads have an unusual shape and contain no embossed stock numbers of coin-

| Name/Department | Exterior | Office | Store Room | Supply Room |
|---|---|---|---|---|
| H. King/Accounting | | 8/86 | | |
| S. Lewis/Administration | 9/88 | 9/86 | | |
| B. Jones/Purchasing | | 5/85 | 5/85 | 8/85 |
| T. Hall/Administration | 1/84 | 1/84 | | |
| Etc. | | | | |

**Figure 7–6 Sample record of keys in use.**

ing marks, so a catalog cannot be used to identify the correct blank. This feature prevents the nonprofessional from duplicating the keys.

Keys should not be left lying around or left in desk drawers, in purses, or in coat pockets. Such abuse is cause for revoking the key. Lending keys should also be strictly forbidden. Any employee found lending keys should lose the privilege of having a key. In rare instances when management loans a master key, care should be exercised that a duplicate is not made.

Do not give custodians keys, especially master keys. Because the turnover in custodial services is extremely high, it is preferable to have a guard or employee grant custodians entrance and exit. Otherwise, a custodian may have master keys to several buildings, have duplicates made, and then several months later commit a series of burglaries. Likewise, do not give entrance keys to tenants of an office building. Establish procedures whereby they can be admitted by a security guard or receptionist.

When any employee having a master key leaves or is terminated, the locks should be changed, as should combinations of safes and/or vaults if the terminated individual knew them. It is also a good security practice to periodically change locks, even if no employee having a key has been terminated.

A key depository is an important part of key control. Duplicate keys should be stored in a secure place, such as a safe or vault.

In addition, periodic key audits should be conducted to ensure that those to whom keys have been issued still have the key(s) in their possession. Auditing key inventories requires physical verification that each assigned key is actually in the possession of the specified person. If it is discovered that a key to a critical area has been lost, the door should be immediately rekeyed.

Keys to internal areas of the building should be controlled in the same way as external keys. Only those who really need the keys should have them.

Curtis (1977, p. 3) makes the following recommendations regarding key control:

> To keep keys from falling into the hands of burglars, issue as few keys as possible. Keep a record on the keys you issue. Exercise the same care with keys as you would a thousand dollar bill by doing the following:
>
> 1) Avoid the danger of key duplication. Caution employees not to leave store keys with parking lot attendants, or in a topcoat hanging in a restaurant, or lying about the office or stockroom.
> 2) Keep your records on key distribution up to date so that you know what keys have been issued and to whom.
> 3) Whenever a key is lost or an employee leaves the firm without turning in his key, re-key your store. [Even if the key is turned in, there is no assurance that a duplicate was not made.]
> 4) Take special care to protect the "master key" used to remove cylinders from locks.
> 5) Have one key and lock for outside doors and a different key and lock for your office. Don't master-key because it weakens your security.
> 6) Have a code for each key so that it does not have to be visibly tagged and only an authorized person can know the specific lock that key fits.

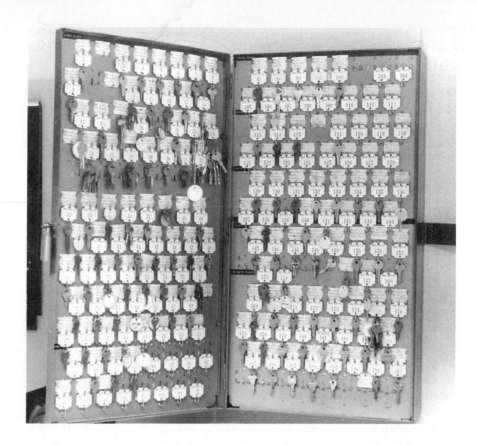

**7)** Take a periodic inventory of keys. Have employees show you each key so you will know it has not been lost, mislaid, or loaned to someone.

A checklist such as that illustrated in Figure 7–7 can help ensure effective key control. The same principles apply if a card-key system is used.

## Opening, Closing, and After-hours Procedures

Controlling access after hours is a critical part of any security system. Usually physical controls are heavily relied on, but certain procedures are required to ensure that these physical controls are effective.

Effective closing procedures include checking all restrooms and areas where someone might be concealed, turning off all unnecessary lights and machinery, opening cash registers and placing money in the safe, locking the safe as well as all windows and interior doors, turning on security lighting, activating the alarm, and securing all exterior doors.

Cash registers should be left empty and open to prevent costly damage caused by a burglar forcing the register open.

| Items with Locks | Number of Locks | Items with Locks | Number of Locks | Items with Locks | Number of Locks |
|---|---|---|---|---|---|
| Access Space | | Dispensers | | Mail Bags | |
| Air Conditioning | | Sanitary Napkins | | Mail Boxes | |
| Alarms | | Soap | | Money Bags | |
| Automotive | | Towel | | | |
| | | | | | |
| | | Doors (Exterior) | | Penthouse | |
| Bulletin Boards | | Entrance | | Plan Case | |
| | | Exit | | | |
| | | Doors (Interior) | | | |
| | | Cafeteria | | Refrigerators | |
| | | Closet | | Rolling Grills | |
| | | Connecting | | Roof Vents | |
| Cabinets | | Elevator | | | |
| Electric | | Elevator Corridor | | | |
| Filing | | Fan Room | | Safe Compartments | |
| Key | | Fire | | Safe Deposit Boxes | |
| Medicine | | Garage | | Screens | |
| Storage | | Office | | Stop Sink Closet | |
| Supply | | | | Switch Key | |
| Tool | | | | | |
| Wardrobe | | | | | |
| | | Drawers | | Tanks (Oil & Gas) | |
| | | Cash | | Thermostat | |
| | | Lab. Table | | Trucks & Trailers | |
| | | Safe | | Trucks | |
| | | Tool & Bench | | | |
| Cash Boxes | | | | | |
| Cash Registers | | | | | |
| Chute Doors | | Gas Pump | | Valves | |
| Clocks | | Gates | | Vaults | |
| | | | | | |
| | | Lockers | | Watchman's Box | |
| Dark Rooms | | Employee | | | |
| Desks | | Paint | | | |
| Display Cases | | Tool Room | | | |

**Figure 7–7  Key control checklist.**
*Courtesy of TelKee Inc., Subsidiary of Sunroc Corp., Glen Riddle, PA 19037.*

These procedures help ensure that no unauthorized persons remain on the premises and that all physical security measures are operative.

Opinions vary on whether blinds and/or shades should be drawn during closing procedures. Drawn blinds or shades do prevent intruders from seeing available "targets" inside, but they also give privacy to a successful intruder.

In an establishment where the risk of burglary is high and no security guard is on night duty, opening and closing should be a two-person operation.

Opening and closing procedures with specific assigned responsibilities should be written out. Before someone opens an establishment, it is prudent to drive by the entrance at least once before parking. If anything looks suspicious, the police should be called. If everything looks normal, one person should unlock the exterior door that is most exposed to public view and traffic, enter, check the alarm and premises to ensure that everything is as it should be, and then signal the person waiting some distance away from the premises. The time this takes is preestablished; the person outside waits until the ''all clear'' is given. If it is not given on schedule, the outside person notifies the police.

Periodically store management should be reminded to be alert to strangers in nonpublic areas immediately after opening or before closing.

The closing procedure is similar to the opening procedure, with one person waiting some distance away while another person makes a routine check of the premises, paying particular attention to areas where someone might hide, such as washrooms, perimeter stock areas, fitting rooms, and the maintenance department. This person then checks and activates all security measures and joins the person waiting outside to lock up.

Procedures for admittance after hours should also be established and strictly enforced. The security officer should have a list of the individuals authorized to be in the building after hours, whether they stay late, arrive early, or return after the building is closed. If an authorized person is in the building after hours, a record should be made of the reason for the person's being there, the time in, and the time out. Employees who consistently arrive early or stay late with no good reason may be doing so to steal or to use company equipment without authorization.

## ☑ CONTROLLING ACCESS TO VULNERABLE AREAS AND EQUIPMENT

Particularly vulnerable to theft or employee pilferage are storage areas; areas where cash, valuables, records, and forms are kept; mail rooms; supply rooms; duplicating rooms; and computer rooms.

All of these areas should have limited access and should be kept locked or have an authorized person in attendance at all times to monitor the activities of others present.

*Warehouses* and *stockrooms* are particularly vulnerable to theft, and there physical and procedural controls are especially important. Such areas should be locked or have an attendant on duty. In addition, high-value rooms or cages should be used for small, valuable items vulnerable to theft. Temporary help should work with a regular, full-time employee to prevent the temptation to steal.

Forklifts should be kept locked when not in use. In one warehouse burglary, the burglar gained access through the roof, but was unable to exit the same way. Alertly, he used the forklift that had been left with the key in the ignition to pry open the warehouse door. He then used the forklift to transport large quantities of merchandise to his pickup truck parked outside.

Limit access to important *documents* as well as to *business forms* such as purchase orders, checks, vouchers, and receipts. Such forms, in the wrong hands, can cost a business thousands of dollars. Important papers and records that are no longer needed should not be discarded in the trash, but incinerated or shredded.

*Mail rooms* should have one person in charge to handle all incoming and outgoing mail. A postage meter eliminates the possibility of stamps being stolen. This meter should be kept locked when not in use. The practice of having routine outgoing mail unsealed, so that contents can be checked to ensure that the letter is indeed business related, can eliminate personal use of company postage. Of course, confidential or sensitive correspondence should be sealed and marked as such. Periodic checks should be made of unsealed letters and packages before they are sealed, stamped, and sent.

Some mail rooms have a separate mailbox for the personal letters and packages of employees. Although the employees pay for their postage, they see this as a service provided by their employer.

*Supply rooms* are very susceptible to pilferage and should, therefore, be restricted to authorized personnel. One individual should be in charge of the supply room. Employees should obtain supplies by filling in a requisition, not by simply going to the supply room and helping themselves or asking for the supplies. An inventory should be taken regularly.

*Copy machines* may be a source of shrinkage if employees use them for making personal copies. Given that a single copy usually costs from three to ten cents depending on the system used, excessive personal use of copiers can cost an establishment hundreds, even thousands of dollars a year. Some establishments have attempted to alleviate the problem by having the copy machine locked and issuing keys to only a few authorized individuals. Others have machines installed that have an element bearing a coded number that must be inserted into the machine before it will run, or use a card-key system for access. In either case, the code and number of copies made are automatically recorded. Other companies have only one person authorized to run the copy machine and require that a work order or copy requisition be completed before copies can be made by the authorized person (see Figure 7–8).

Some companies recognize that being able to make copies of documents for personal use is appreciated by employees and, consequently, allow their employees to use the copy machine and pay for their copies. Such a practice is good public relations, but it can easily be abused if individuals are placed on the "honor system," as is frequently the case.

*Computers* can also be a source of shrinkage if employees use them for personal benefit, at substantial cost to the company. In some instances, employees have been discovered to have established their own sideline computer business, using the company's computer after hours and on weekends. One such employee rationalized the use by saying, "It was just sitting there, going to waste. I wasn't hurting anyone." Computer security is discussed in Chapter 10.

```
┌─────────────────────────────────────────────────────────────────┐
│                    REPRODUCTION WORK ORDER                        │
│                                                                   │
│   Name _____                                   │
│   Cost Center Code _____     Assembled _____   │
│   Date & Hour Received _____     Back to Back __ Not Back to Back __ │
│   Date & Hour Due _____      Total Number of Originals _____ │
│   Number of Copies _____     Other _____      │
│   Color of Paper/Card Stock _____  _____       │
│   Special Instructions:                                           │
│                                                                   │
│   ----------------------------------------------------------------│
│   Return to _____       Will pick up in duplicating _____ │
│   Secretary _____                                   │
└─────────────────────────────────────────────────────────────────┘
```

**Figure 7–8 Sample reproduction work order.**

## ☐ PROPERTY CONTROL

Property control is of concern in most security systems. Control may be exercised over the employer's property as well as the property of individual employees, vendors, contractors, or visitors.

### Employer Property

Any property of the employer that is to be taken from a facility may require a pass such as that illustrated in Figure 7–9. Property passes play a major role in property control. A log such as that shown in Figure 7–10 should be kept of all property that is signed out.

### Nonemployer Property

If employees, contractors, visitors, or others bring personal property into a secured facility, they might be required to register it so that when they leave there is no question as to their legitimate right to remove the property. A form such as that in Figure 7–11 might be used for this purpose. Such passes are not usually necessary for briefcases, purses, or lunch boxes.

## ☐ INFORMATION PROTECTION

Frequently security personnel have access to trade secrets, product data, and information that is proprietary and confidential. Specific actions security managers might take to safeguard sensitive information and trade secrets include the following:

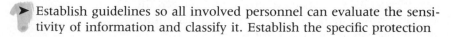 Establish guidelines so all involved personnel can evaluate the sensitivity of information and classify it. Establish the specific protection

# PROPERTY PASS

\# \_\_\_\_

PROPERTY PASSES ARE RETURNED TO THE
APPROVING MANAGER FOR VERIFICATION
OF ITEMS REMOVED FROM THE BUILDING.

| MANAGER NAME |
| --- |
| TELEPHONE EXT. |

| DESCRIPTION OF ITEMS TO BE TAKEN FROM THE BUILDING (INCLUDE MODEL, SERIAL AND TAG NUMBER) | TO BE RETURNED | | DATE TO BE RETURNED |
| --- | --- | --- | --- |
| | YES | NO | |
| | | | |
| | | | |
| | | | |
| | | | |
| | | | |
| | | | |

| FROM (BUILDING) | TO (BUILDING OR HOME) | CHECKED EMPLOYEE NAME AGAINST BADGE OR I.D. | |
| --- | --- | --- | --- |
| EMPLOYEE (PRINT OR TYPE) AND SIGNATURE | EMPLOYEE NUMBER | RECEPTIONIST OR GUARD | DATE OUT |
| MANAGER SIGNATURE | RECEPTIONIST OR GUARD | | DATE IN |

## FOLLOW-UP

☐ EQUIPMENT RETURNED

☐ EQUIPMENT NOT RETURNED

| COMMENTS |
| --- |
| |
| SIGNATURE                              DATE |

**Figure 7–9  Property pass.**

required for each classification and ensure that classifications are
clearly marked on documents.

➤ Use appropriate techniques to safeguard such information as passwords, coding, and locking file cabinets.

➤ Keep records of who has received sensitive information and why.

➤ Share sensitive information only with individuals who have a genuine need to know. Make clear what security measures are expected.

➤ Establish procedures for disposing of sensitive information when it is no longer needed.

PLEASE PRINT

| NAME | PROPERTY | PASS NUMBER | DATE REMOVED | DATE RETURNED |
|---|---|---|---|---|
|  |  |  |  |  |
|  |  |  |  |  |
|  |  |  |  |  |
|  |  |  |  |  |
|  |  |  |  |  |
|  |  |  |  |  |
|  |  |  |  |  |
|  |  |  |  |  |

Figure 7–10  Property check-in/out log.

## PERSONAL PROPERTY REGISTRATION

Complete this form if you wish to bring personal property into the building.

| QUANTITY | DESCRIPTION OF MATERIAL |
|---|---|
|  |  |
|  |  |
|  |  |
|  |  |
|  |  |
|  |  |
|  |  |
|  |  |
|  |  |
|  |  |
|  |  |
|  |  |

PLEASE PRINT

| NAME | REPRESENTING | DEPARTMENT OR PERSON VISITED |
|---|---|---|
|  |  |  |

I understand that items are to be removed from the plant only at the gate of entry, unless other arrangements are made at the gate of entry. This is not a property pass and applies only to people, vendors, or employees who have a reason to bring in material.

| SIGNATURE | GUARD SIGNATURE | TIME ENTERED | DATE |
|---|---|---|---|
|  |  |  |  |

Figure 7–11  Personal property registration.

# ☐ USE OF CAMERAS OR VIDEO EQUIPMENT ON SITE

Many facilities do not allow cameras or video equipment to be brought into the facility without prior approval. This restriction may apply to all employees, contractors, visitors, and even security personnel. A form such as that in Figure 7–12 might be used for this purpose. After the form is approved, the person authorized to take pictures or videos might be issued a pass such as that illustrated in Figure 7–13.

# ☐ ROUTINE SEARCHES

Individual facilities may adopt policies and procedures to allow searches to examine work areas including lockers, desks, files, and items being brought into or removed from the facility, including packages, briefcases, purses, and boxes. Searches are usually allowable if:

➤ All employees and visitors are notified about the program before it is implemented.

## REQUEST FOR AUTHORIZATION TO TAKE PICTURES

Date and time equipment will be used

Date (s) _____    Time _____

_____    _____

Purpose of pictures _____

_____

_____

_____

Location/Area pictures will be taken_____

_____

_____

_____

Person (s) taking pictures

| Name | Company Name | Employee # |
|------|--------------|------------|
| _____ | _____ | _____ |
| _____ | _____ | _____ |
| _____ | _____ | _____ |

Requested By _____

Approved By _____

**Figure 7–12 Request for authorization to take pictures.**

**CAMERA PASS**

_____ IS AUTHORIZED TO TAKE

PICTURES OF _____

ON _____ , IN _____
       (date)                  (plant)

_____
                          (area)

COMPANY REPRESENTED _____

ESCORT _____

PURPOSE _____

DEPT. MANAGER _____

SECURITY OFFICER _____

**Figure 7–13  Camera pass.**

➤ The program itself is courteous, fair, and nondiscriminatory, that is, it includes all employees/visitors.

Notices such as those in Figure 7–14 might be used to inform employees and visitors of a search policy.

   Searches are extremely sensitive. Security personnel must be courteous and nonthreatening. Each inspection should be entered in the officer's daily log, including the person's name and time of the inspection. If the person refuses, policies should be in place as to whether the security officer confiscates the package, calls a supervisor, or simply records the person's name and employee number or company represented and allows the person to leave. Security officers should not argue or forcefully attempt to conduct a search.

   If security officers find during an exit search that a person has property that belongs to the facility, they should ask for a completed property pass authorizing removal of the property as discussed previously. If no pass has been filled in, it should be completed on the spot, or the person should write out an explanation as to why the property is being removed.

   Likewise, if security officers find unauthorized property such as alcohol or illegal drugs during a routine search of a work area, such employees might be asked to submit to their manager a written explanation of why the property was in their possession.

## ☐ MAKING ROUNDS

Often security personnel are responsible for _making rounds_, that is, for conducting a visual check of the facility to observe conditions. Security

## WORK AREA SEARCH NOTICE
## TO ALL EMPLOYEES

Effective _____ , 19__ we are establishing work area search procedures to improve security.

Work areas will be subject to search at our discretion. We will post the following notice in conspicuous places informing people of this policy.

> WE RESERVE THE RIGHT TO INSPECT AND SEARCH EMPLOYEE LOCKERS, DESKS, FILES, BOXES, PACKAGES, BRIEFCASES, LUNCHBOXES, PURSES OR BAGS WITHIN THE WORK AREA.

Because this program will increase our work and work area security, we expect and appreciate your full cooperation. Failure to cooperate with this procedure will result in disciplinary action.

THE MANAGEMENT

## ENTRANCE AND EXIT SEARCH NOTICE
## TO ALL EMPLOYEES/VISITORS

Effective _____ , 19__ we are establishing new entry and exit procedures to improve security.

People entering and leaving this facility may be subject to questions at our discretion. Packages, handbags, purses, briefcases, lunchboxes, and other possessions may be subject to search.

The following notice will be posted in conspicuous places informing people of this policy.

> WE RESERVE THE RIGHT TO QUESTION PEOPLE ENTERING OR LEAVING THE PROPERTY AND TO INSPECT ANY PACKAGE, HANDBAG, PURSE, BRIEFCASE, LUNCHBOX, OR OTHER POSSESSION CARRIED INTO OR OUT OF THE COMPANY PROPERTY.

Because this program will increase our work and work area security, we expect and appreciate your full cooperation. Failure to cooperate with this procedure will result in disciplinary action.

THE MANAGEMENT

**Figure 7–14 Sample search notification.**

officers should be alert to hazards that might lead to an accident, such as water or grease on the floor, materials stacked too high, faulty railings and/or stairs, loose carpeting or rugs, and inadequate lighting in walkways. They should also be alert to hazardous weather-related conditions such as slick sidewalks or ice or snow falling from roof and window ledges.

Security officers should also recognize and intervene in any employee behavior that might pose a safety hazard such as "goofing off," working without safety glasses and hard hats where designated, fighting, running, or reckless driving in parking lots.

Being alert to fire hazards is also important. Security officers should note blocked aisles, stairway exits, or fire doors. They should also note uncovered containers of solvent, oily rags, roof leaks, unusual odors, or defective electrical wiring, as well as the operability of fire extinguishers and hoses.

Being alert to opportunities for theft is yet another responsibility of security officers as they make their rounds. They should check for evidence of illegal entry such as broken windows and locks, check that all doors that are to be locked have been, and make certain safes and vaults are locked. They should also check to be sure that sensitive information is not being left out on desks or discarded in the trash.

Another function security officers often fulfill while making their rounds is that of energy conservation. They should be authorized to and responsible for turning off water left running, unneeded lights or equipment left on after hours, including copy machines, typewriters, desk lights, and space heaters. Security officers should *not* turn off any computers or test equipment.

Yet another important function of security personnel making rounds is to ensure access control. They should question suspicious individuals. Suspicious behavior includes a person being in an unlighted area, being in a secured area without authorization, being at someone else's desk or going through someone else's desk drawers or file cabinets, going through wastebaskets, and loitering near a card-controlled entry or a trash container. When security officers observe suspicious behavior, they should request identification from the individual, determine their purpose for being there, and take appropriate action.

While making rounds, security officers are also usually responsible for checking monitoring devices for climate control and responding to any alarms. Last, but of utmost importance, security officers should be helpful and friendly to employees and all others they encounter while conducting their rounds.

If any risk-producing factors are encountered during rounds, security officers should promptly report them to the appropriate person and also make a written report. They should follow up to ensure that the risk has been eliminated.

## ACCOUNTING AND RECEIVING PROCEDURES FOR CONTROLLING SHRINKAGE

Security managers are not expected to be accountants, but they should be aware of where potential security problems exist within the accounting system and the receiving department. Temptation to steal can be reduced by following some basic procedures.

➤ Keep limited cash on hand.
➤ Establish strict procedures for obtaining petty cash.
➤ Keep purchasing, receiving, and paying functions separate.
➤ Use prenumbered purchase orders in sequence.

The limited amount of cash that is kept should be secured in a safe at closing.

People requesting petty cash should have an authorization and a signed voucher or request form before being given the cash. Strict records should account for every cent disbursed. Where possible, receipts should be provided by the person receiving the petty cash.

Whenever possible, purchasing, receiving, and paying functions should be kept separate. Purchasing should be centralized, not only to minimize opportunity for unauthorized purchases, but also because buying in bulk is usually less expensive. Purchase orders should be prenumbered and used in sequence. If more than one department does purchasing, each should be issued a purchase order book and made accountable for every number contained in the book before another is issued. Any purchase orders that are ruined should be marked void, *not* simply discarded. Copies of the purchase orders should be sent to the receiving and the paying department.

The receiving department should check the orders received against the purchase orders on file. Any missing or damaged items or extra items should be promptly reported. The supplier should be notified if a shipment is not received within a reasonable time; it may have been stolen or misrouted. It is usually best to have one central receiving area.

Merchandise should be received in a protected area such as a sheltered inside dock. Only suppliers' vehicles and company cars should be allowed in the receiving area. The receiving area should be physically separated from the shipping area. If a great security risk exists, the hours for receiving should be limited and a security guard assigned during this period. The doors should be kept closed and locked when not in use. A buzzer or bell can be used to alert personnel when a delivery is being attempted.

Suppliers should never leave merchandise unattended on the dock. If they do, the receiver is not legally responsible. Any supplier whose delivery agents simply unload merchandise on the dock and leave should be promptly notified of this break in security.

Train boxcars and truck trailers may use a numbered metal seal bar. In such cases, receivers should check the seal number with the bill of lading. If it appears to have been tampered with, the delivery should not be accepted.

Once a delivery is accepted, it should be unloaded and properly stored as soon as possible. If this cannot be done, the doors on the boxcar or truck trailer should be padlocked or nailed shut.

Receivers should not go by the packing slip (called blind receiving), but should actually count the items delivered. Some purchasing departments omit the quantity on the copy of the purchase order sent to receiving, forcing the receiver to do a careful count. A hazard inherent in this procedure is that an incomplete shipment may be accepted. If a shipment is ordered by weight, the merchandise should be weighed when received. The accuracy of the scales should be checked periodically.

The paying department should issue checks for only those orders for which they have an authorized purchase order and authorized verification from the receiving department that the shipment has arrived as specified on the purchase order.

Keeping purchasing, receiving, and paying functions separate will thwart such dishonest practices as writing purchase orders for nonexistent materials, writing double purchase orders, or making payments for materials that were never ordered. Bill padding can be thwarted by insisting that competitive bids be obtained for any major purchases. Acceptance of gifts or gratuities from suppliers should be strictly forbidden, as this may foster doing special "favors" for each other.

## ☐ TRANSPORTING VALUABLES

Procedures for transporting valuable goods and/or cash should be established and strictly adhered to.

Maintain secrecy when transporting valuables. Vary times, routes, personnel, and vehicles used.

Kingsbury (1973, pp. 278–81) cites several recommendations for maintaining security of cash and valuables in transit:

> Never use new employees whose references have not been authenticated. Change times, routes, and collection or delivery point frequently. If large sums are involved, provide an escort in front and behind. If large sums are involved, divide the delivery into two or three portions. If on foot, walk toward oncoming traffic to lessen the risk of a surprise attack from behind. If in a vehicle, use a closed vehicle and vary the vehicle; be certain all vehicles so used are in good mechanical condition.

Many businesses prefer to use commercial firms for transferring valuable merchandise and cash. When armed courier services are used, employees should be instructed to always check the couriers' credentials carefully before handing over the cash or items to be transported.

## ☐ DETECTING EMPLOYEE THEFT AND PILFERAGE

Accurate records help management discover when and where shrinkage is occurring.

Some thefts can be detected by using a perpetual inventory and periodic internal and external audits.

Although keeping a perpetual inventory requires much time and effort, the benefits are worth it because the owner/manager has up-to-date information on existing supplies and stock and is, therefore, immediately alerted to inventory shrinkage. A perpetual inventory also serves as a psychological deterrent to theft. This is in contrast to the annual inventory system in which an employee may begin stealing shortly after completion of the inventory, knowing that the shortage will not be discovered until almost a year later.

When inventories are taken, care must be exercised not to be fooled by empty cartons or containers. Spot checks should be made to ensure that the merchandise is actually there. In one filling station, an attendant pocketed any cash received for oil and put the empty cans in the storeroom at the back of the shelf.

Careful, periodic internal and external audits also help detect shrinkage. An internal audit of accounting procedures can be conducted by intentionally introducing errors. For example, what does the purchasing department do if a purchase order is submitted without an authorized signature? What does the receiving department do if it is sent a shipment containing extra items? Is the error reported, do the extra items simply disappear, or does the error go unnoticed? What does the paying department do with a bill for which there is no purchase order? Prompt reporting of shortages, losses, and errors should be encouraged and positively reinforced. Periodic external audits are also important to security.

Some thefts can be detected by *inspection* of lockers, packages, vehicles, persons, and trash containers.

Although most employees and visitors are honest, security requires that periodic inspections be made to ensure that theft is not occurring.

Providing employees with *lockers* is a sound security practice because it helps employees keep their personal possessions safe. On the other hand, lockers are also a security risk because employees can conceal stolen property or goods in their lockers until an opportune time comes to remove them from the premises undetected. Employee lockers should be considered a privilege, not a right. They are not the employees' private property. Employees should not be allowed to use their own locks. They should be informed when they are given a locker that the locker is provided by the company as a convenience to the employee and that the company retains the right to inspect the locker at any time. Periodic inspections can and should then be made without fear of legal entanglements.

*Packages* brought into or taken from the premises may also be subject to inspection. Frequently people are required to check all packages prior to entering an area. College bookstores, for example, often require all books to be left in a rack prior to entering the store. Discount stores often require that packages brought into the store be checked. Some stores even require women to check their purses until they are ready to make their purchases. Such requirements may anger customers and/or visitors, but if the procedure is adequately explained, public relations may not suffer.

If people are allowed to take packages, briefcases, or other containers into restricted areas, a receptionist or security guard frequently inspects the contents, lists what is being taken in, and then reinspects the package or briefcase when the person leaves.

If a visitor, employee, or repair worker takes a package or item from a secure area, the person authorizing the removal should sign a removal authorization, in ink, with all uncompleted lines on the form crossed out so the person receiving the authorization cannot add additional items to the pass. Persons authorizing such removals should sign their names in full. Initials can be easily forged.

Because thieves may pose as repair workers and simply walk out of an establishment with expensive recording equipment, televisions, or office machines, strict security procedures should be followed. The person authorizing the removal should check the service person's credentials prior to signing the removal pass and should require the service person to sign a receipt for the items to be removed.

This removal pass system should also be used if it is company policy to lend tools and office machines to employees for personal use after hours or on weekends.

Inspections may also be made of lunch boxes, vehicle interiors and trunks, and individuals, unless expressly prohibited in the labor contract.

Inspections are acceptable if they are done democratically and if the procedure is clearly established and explained prior to the inspection.

Employees should not feel that they are under suspicion or not trusted when a personal inspection is made. The chances of this are lessened if everyone is inspected or a systematic inspection is made (for example, every tenth person is inspected) and if everyone has been informed *prior* to employment that periodic personal inspections are part of the established security system. Likewise, visitors or customers should not be annoyed when their packages are inspected if a sign obviously displayed clearly states: "We reserve the right to inspect all packages," as discussed earlier.

Trash containers and trash removal procedures should be checked periodically. Dishonest employees can hide stolen items in the trash and later retrieve them, or items may be accidentally discarded. In some cases, employee/thieves have worked with trash collectors to steal vast quantities of merchandise.

Given that 70 percent of losses are caused by employees, probabilities are good that some dishonest employees will be caught stealing from the company.

Usually an employee caught stealing from the company should be fired and prosecuted.

Frequently, however, such is not the case. Employees are given second, third, and even fourth chances. Or, if they are dismissed, the reasons for the dismissal is kept secret. When the discharged person seeks employment elsewhere and the new potential employer makes a background check, the reason for the dismissal may be hidden. Such practices only encourage internal theft and should be discontinued.

Because there are degrees of seriousness of crimes and there may be mitigating circumstances, policies should exist setting forth actions to be taken for varying types of criminality, dollar amounts, safety considerations, and the like, with punitive actions ranging from verbal reprimands to criminal prosecution.

An interesting type of justice system operating in the private sector is described in the Hallcrest Report (Cunningham and Taylor, 1985, p. 245):

> In responding to and resolving the criminal behavior of employees, organizations routinely choose options other than criminal prosecution, for example, suspension without pay, transfer, job reassignment, job redesign (elimination of some job duties), civil restitution, and dismissal. . . .
>
> While on the surface it appears that organizations can opt for less severe sanctions than would be imposed by the criminal justice system, in reality, the organizational sanctions may have greater impact on the employee-offender (e.g., loss of job, civil restitution, garnisheed wages). In addition, the private systems of criminal justice are not always subject to principles of exclusionary evidence, fairness, and defendant rights which characterize the public criminal justice systems. The level of position, the amount of power, and socio-economic standing of the employee in the company may greatly influence the formality and type of company sanctions. In general, private justice systems are characterized by informal negotiations and outcomes, and nonuniform standards and procedures among organization and crime types.

Firing *security* personnel who are discovered to be dishonest is a must. If the security profession is to grow and build respect, dishonest security personnel must be weeded out.

## ☐ INSURANCE AND BONDING

Recall that one of the means to deal with risk is to *transfer* it. If the risk is still unacceptable after all measures to eliminate or reduce it are completed, insurance and bonding are viable alternatives.

---

Insurance and bonding of specific employees may help reduce losses.

---

Most managers carry insurance on their buildings and on expensive equipment. If the risk is great that, despite effective physical and procedural controls, large value losses might be sustained by employee dishonesty or external crime, many security managers recommend that the company take out insurance and have individuals in key positions bonded. Fidelity bonds protect a company from losses suffered from dishonest employees. Most insurance companies require that all reasonable preventive measures be instituted before they will insure a company against crime. When such security devices and procedures exist, significant savings in insurance premiums often result—sometimes as high as a 70 percent reduction.

"The most recent security development in the insurance industry," say Bottom and Kostanoski (1990, p. 54), "involved providing expanded risk assessment (survey) services for clients. Insurance employees visit clients, perform security surveys, and evaluate the data so that loss-control recommendations can be made. There is a growing number of security opportunities in today's insurance world.''

## SUMMARY

A prime responsibility of security is to prevent or reduce *shrinkage*, defined as lost assets. Good security can also help to prevent negligence lawsuits. An important first step is to screen all job applicants. This should include a background check, examination of past work record, and contact with references. All employees should then be educated as to their responsibilities and restrictions. Reasonable rules should be established and enforced.

Most procedural controls seek to prevent loss or shrinkage by limiting access to specific areas by unauthorized personnel. Procedural controls to limit access to specified areas include stationing guards, restricting vehicle traffic, requiring registration and sign-outs, requiring display of badges or passes, ensuring key control, and using effective opening, closing, and after-hours procedures. Effective employee badges and passes display the employee's name, employment number, signature, and photograph as well as an authorizing signature. They should be sturdy, tamper-proof, and changed periodically. An effective key control system limits the number of persons having keys, establishes a master list of all existing keys and to whom they are assigned, keeps all duplicate keys secure, and requires a physical audit periodically.

Effective closing procedures include checking all restrooms and areas where someone might be concealed, turning off all unnecessary lights and machinery, opening cash registers, locking the safe, locking all windows and interior doors, turning on security lighting, activating the alarm, and securing the exterior doors. In an establishment where the risk of burglary is high and no security guard is on night duty, opening and closing should be a two-person operation.

Particularly vulnerable to theft or employee pilferage are storage areas; areas where cash, valuables, records, and forms are kept; mail rooms; supply rooms; duplicating rooms; and computer rooms.

In addition to procedures for controlling access to certain areas, accounting and receiving procedures can help control shrinkage. A limited amount of cash should be kept on hand. Strict procedures for obtaining petty cash should be established. Purchasing, receiving, and paying functions should be kept separate. Prenumbered purchase orders should be used in sequence.

When valuables are being transported, secrecy should be maintained and the times, routes, personnel, and vehicles used should be varied.

Despite effective security procedures, thefts may still occur. Such thefts can be detected by using a perpetual inventory, periodic internal and external audits, and periodic inspection of lockers, packages, vehicles, persons, and trash containers. Inspections are better accepted if they are done democratically, and if the procedure is clearly established and explained prior to the inspection.

Insurance and/or bonding of specific employees may help reduce financial losses.

# APPLICATION

Read the following rules from *Preventing Employee Pilferage* by S. D. Astor (1977, pp. 4–5):

Company rules are important in setting up a strong loss-prevention program. Here are some rules which will help to insure against employee theft.

➤ Make a dependable second check of incoming materials to rule out the possibility of collusive theft between drivers and employees who handle the receiving.

➤ No truck shall approach the loading platform until it is ready to load or unload.

➤ Drivers will not be allowed behind the receiving fence. (Discourage drivers from taking goods or materials from the platform by the following devices: heavy-gauge wire fencing between bays, with the mesh too fine to provide a toehold; closed-circuit television cameras, mounted overhead so as to sweep the entire platform; and locating the receiving supervisor's desk or office to afford him an unobstructed view of the entire platform.)

➤ At the loading platform, drivers will not be permitted to load their own trucks, especially by taking goods from stock.

➤ Every lunchbox, toolbox, bag, or package must be inspected by a supervisor or guard as employees leave the plant.

➤ All padlocks must be snapped shut on hasps when not in use to prevent the switching of locks.

➤ Keys to padlocks must be controlled. Never leave the key hanging on a nail near the lock where a crooked worker can "borrow" it and have a duplicate made while he is away from his work.

➤ Trash must not be allowed to accumulate in, or be picked up from, an area near storage sites of valuable materials or finished goods.

➤ Inspect disposal locations and rubbish trucks at irregular intervals for the presence of salable items when you have the slightest reason to suspect collusion between employees and trash collectors.

➤ Trash pickups must be supervised. (Companies have been systematically drained over long periods by alliances between crooked employees and trash collectors.)

➤ Rotate security guards. (Rotation discourages fraternizing with other employees who may turn out to be dishonest. Rotation also prevents monotony from reducing the alertness of guards.)

➤ Never assign two or more members of the same family to work in the same area. (You can expect blood to be thicker than company loyalty.)

➤ Key men will be kept informed about the activities and findings of the man who is in charge of security. (Thus weak points in security can be strengthened without delay.)

➤ Control receiving reports and shipping orders (preferably by numbers in sequence) to prevent duplicate or fraudulent payment of invoices and the padding or destruction of shipping orders.

➤ Receiving reports must be prepared immediately upon receiving a shipment. (Delay in making out such reports can be an invitation to theft or, at best, result in record keeping errors.)

➤ Employees who are caught stealing will be prosecuted. (Settling for restitution and an apology is inviting theft to continue.)

Green and Farber (1978, pp. 146–47) describe numerous types of employee dishonesty that account for between 7 and 10 percent of business failures annually. Read the list, keeping in mind the preceding rules to thwart pilferage.*

➤ Payroll and personnel employees collaborating to falsify records by the use of nonexistent employees or by retaining terminated employees on the payroll.

➤ Padding overtime reports, part of which extra unearned pay is kicked back to the authorizing supervisor.

➤ Pocketing unclaimed wages.

* Reprinted with permission of the publisher from Green and Farber, *Introduction to Security,* revised edition, Woburn, Mass.: Butterworth Publishers, Inc., 1978.

➤ Splitting increased payroll which has been raised on checks signed in blank for use in authorized signer's absence.
➤ Maintenance personnel and contract servicemen in collusion to steal and sell office equipment.
➤ Receiving clerks and truck drivers in collusion on falsification of merchandise count. Extra unaccounted merchandise is fenced.
➤ Purchasing agents in collusion with vendors to falsify purchase and payment documents. Purchasing agent issues authorization for payment on goods never shipped after forging receipt of shipment.
➤ Purchasing agent in collusion with vendor to pay inflated price. Split profit.
➤ Mailroom and supply personnel packing and mailing merchandise to themselves for resale.
➤ Accounts payable personnel paying fictitious bills to an account set up for their own use.
➤ Taking incoming cash without crediting the customer's account.
➤ Paying creditors twice and pocketing the second check.
➤ Appropriating checks made out to cash.
➤ Raising the amount of checks after voucher approval or raising the amount of vouchers after their approval.
➤ Pocketing small amounts from incoming payments and applying later payments on other accounts to cover shortages.
➤ Removal of equipment or merchandise with trash.
➤ Invoicing goods below regular price and getting a kickback from the purchaser.
➤ Under-ringing on a cash register.
➤ Issuing (and cashing) checks on returned merchandise not actually returned.
➤ Forging checks, destroying them when returned with statement from the bank, and changing books accordingly.

Which rules in the first selection might thwart specific dishonest practices in the second selection? What other rules might be required?

# DISCUSSION QUESTIONS

1) Why is curbing pilferage so important to a security manager?
2) What factual information should be obtained to make the decision to employ or not to employ an applicant?
3) What procedures can be used regarding employee coats, purses, and packages to deter internal theft?
4) What are some rationales frequently given by employees for stealing from their employers?
5) What employee actions might lead security personnel to suspect dishonesty?

# REFERENCES

Astor, S. D. *Preventing employee pilferage.* Small Business Administration. Management Aids No. 209. Washington, DC: U.S. Government Printing Office, 1977.

Bottom, Norman R., Jr. and Kostanoski, John I. *Introduction to security and loss control.* Englewood Cliffs, NJ: Prentice-Hall, 1990.

Cunningham, W. C. and Taylor, T. H. *The Hallcrest report: Private security and police in America.* Portland, OR: Chancellor Press, 1985.

Curtis, S. J. *Preventing burglary and robbery loss.* Small Business Administration. Small Marketers Aids No. 134. Washington, DC: U.S. Government Printing Office, 1977.

Green, G. and Farber, R. C. *Introduction to security.* Los Angeles: Security World Publishing Company, 1978.

Harris, William G. The integrity test. *Security management: Special supplement — The ways and means of screening,* 1990, pp. 22A–23A.

Hill, William T. Getting help from the outside. *Security management: Special supplement — The ways and means of screening,* 1990, pp. 15A–16A.

Jayne, Brian C. The interview. *Security management: Special supplement — The ways and means of screening,* 1990, pp. 18A–19A.

Kingsbury, A. A. *Introduction to security and crime prevention surveys.* Springfield, IL: Charles C. Thomas, 1973.

Klump, C. S. Honest employees: Find them and keep them. *Security management,* August 1983, pp. 63–64.

Kuhn, Ryan A. The psychological test. *Security management: Special supplement — The ways and means of screening,* 1990, p. 23.

Rea, Kelly V. EPPA: The fine print. *Security management,* May 1989, pp. 49–55.

Schafer, June P. The resumé. *Security management: Special supplement — The ways and means of screening,* 1990, p. 17A.

Schubb, A. N. and Connelly, W. M. In search of an honest employee. *Security management,* August 1985, pp. 24–30.

## □ INTRODUCTION

Preventing losses from accidents and emergencies is a critical responsibility of security managers. Despite the best efforts to reduce the possibility of accidents or emergencies occurring, they will happen. Security managers and personnel must be prepared to deal effectively with them. The simple fact that an accident or emergency happened might be the basis for a lawsuit. How the accident or emergency is dealt with might also be cause for civil action against security personnel and their employers.

As stressed by Gallati (1983, p. 27): "Alert patrols and constant checking for possible dangers can often prevent a hazard from developing, or nip a lethal situation in the bud before it causes irreversible damage."

Security managers are often responsible for accident prevention programs as one means to prevent losses and protect assets.

It is not only common sense to protect against accidents, but also federally mandated that such protection be provided.

## □ THE OCCUPATIONAL SAFETY AND HEALTH ACT

**DO YOU KNOW**

➤ Why accident prevention is often part of a security manager's responsibility?

➤ What OSHA is and how it relates to private security? What records it requires?

➤ What causes the vast majority of accidents? How they can be prevented or reduced?

➤ What the security manager's role is during civil disturbances, riots, and strikes?

➤ What the primary defenses against bombs are?

➤ How a bomb threat can be prepared for? Received? Acted on?

➤ What three elements are required for a fire to occur?

➤ How fires are classified?

➤ How fires can be prevented?

➤ What equipment can help protect lives and assets from fire?

➤ What types of fire detectors are available?

➤ When water or a Class A fire extinguisher should *not* be used?

➤ What procedures help protect against loss by fire?

➤ What the security manager's responsibilities are in the event of a fire?

➤ What natural disaster plans should be formulated?

Traditionally, loss prevention has focused on preventing and minimizing losses from internal and external crime. However, since the passage of the Occupational Safety and Health Act, the security function has gradually expanded to include specific safety responsibilities. Security managers involved in these safety programs often have titles such as Director of Loss Prevention, Director of Security and Prevention, or Director of Safety and Security, reflecting the dual functions of security and safety.

Because of a disturbing pattern of increasing occupational injuries, in 1970 Congress enacted Public Law 91-596, the Occupational Safety and Health Act. The Occupational Safety and Health Administration (OSHA),

**191**

a federal agency within the Department of Labor, was established to administer this act. The stated purpose of the act is "to assure so far as possible every working man and woman in the nation safe and healthful working conditions and to preserve our human resources." In essence, the act requires every employer covered by the act to furnish employees with a place of employment that is free from recognized hazards that cause or are likely to cause death or serious physical harm.

---

OSHA, the Occupational Safety and Health Administration, was established to administer the Occupational Safety and Health Act, which seeks to ensure safe and healthful working conditions for every employee in the nation.

---

The act applies to every employer who is engaged in interstate commerce or whose business affects interstate commerce and who has at least one employee. The vast majority of employers in the nation are, therefore, under the jurisdiction of OSHA. The act excludes employees of federal, state, and local governments and those protected under federal occupational safety and health laws, such as the Atomic Energy Act of 1954 or the Federal Coal Mine Safety and Health Act.

## OSHA Standards

OSHA has established three types of standards: initial, emergency temporary, and permanent.

**Initial standards** include the general rules for avoiding known hazards, such as having employees wear safety glasses, hard hats, and face shields; having exits clearly marked and aisles and walkways to these exits free of obstacles or obstructions; providing an adequate supply of drinking water and adequate toilet facilities; and having fire protection and suppression equipment readily available and in good operating condition.

**Emergency temporary standards** are issued by the Department of Labor as needed when a new danger or hazard is recognized. These emergency temporary standards can remain in effect for six months, but they must then be either replaced by a permanent standard or rescinded.

**Permanent standards** include all new requirements since the initial set of standards was established. Many of these standards are quite controversial and are seen as unnecessarily restrictive. Given the current emphasis on deregulation, many OSHA standards may be modified or eliminated in the near future.

Employers can request a *variance* if a specific standard seems to be unnecessarily restrictive or impossible to comply with as specified. Four types of variances may be requested. A *permanent variance* may be obtained if an employer can prove that current conditions and processes are as healthful and safe as those established under a specific standard. A *temporary variance* may be obtained if the employer needs more time to comply with a standard, either because it is impossible to meet the

requirements immediately or because the employer is financially incapable of making the required changes immediately. A temporary variance may be granted for up to two years. An *experimental variance* may be obtained if an employer wants to try out and validate new equipment or techniques. In rare cases, if the country's security is threatened, a *national defense variance* may be obtained.

## Complying with OSHA Requirements

The act requires employers to post a notice informing employees of their protection under the act. In addition, all employees must have access to OSHA regulations and standards. Employees can request an OSHA inspection of their place of work, and they can request medical tests to determine if they are being exposed to unhealthy conditions.

To comply with OSHA requirements, security managers' responsibilities might include the following:

- ➤ Knowing the act and its initial standards and requirements.
- ➤ Understanding what OSHA standards apply to the specific facility.
- ➤ Keeping informed of and enforcing specific OSHA regulations.
- ➤ Posting all necessary notices.
- ➤ Keeping or supervising the retainment of all required OSHA records.
- ➤ Setting specific safety goals and measuring progress toward these goals.
- ➤ Conducting safety audits and surveys.
- ➤ Examining current unsafe or hazardous conditions and correcting them.
- ➤ Developing in-house safety programs and educating management and labor personnel.
- ➤ Dealing with OSHA representatives and inspectors.
- ➤ Seeing that OSHA violations are corrected.

OSHA requires employers covered by the act to keep a log of all occupational injuries, accidents, and illnesses, as well as an annual summary of the log's information.

The annual summary must be compiled and posted within one month after the close of the year and left up for thirty days. The act also requires employers to keep the detailed safety and health records for five years, subject to OSHA review at any time.

## Inspections

To ensure that its requirements are fulfilled, the act stipulates that OSHA inspectors can investigate any facility subject to OSHA standards to see that they are in compliance. Inspectors can appear at any reasonable hour and should be allowed to inspect the facility. If they request an employee to accompany them, this request should also be honored.

Until recently, OSHA representatives and inspectors could enter an employer's premises without advance notice. These surprise visits were extremely unpopular and were viewed by some as a violation of their protection against unreasonable searches guaranteed by the Fourth Amendment of the United States Constitution.

In 1978, a small businessman refused to allow an OSHA inspector on his premises without a warrant, contesting such surprise inspections. In *Marshall v. Barlow's Inc.,* (1978) the Supreme Court ruled, in a five-to-three decision, that government agents checking for safety and health hazards cannot make spot checks without a warrant. Such inspections, they contended, did amount to a violation of the Fourth Amendment, which protects not only private homes, but commercial premises as well. Certain establishments were held exempt from the warrant requirement, including those engaged in the production of liquor and firearms.

Unlike other search warrants, however, a warrant to check for safety and health hazards does *not* have to be based on the probable cause that unsafe conditions exist. Therefore, the surprise nature of the inspections, a necessary feature to avoid cosmetic changes, remains intact.

Representatives from management, employees, or both have the right to accompany an OSHA inspector and to see the results of that inspection.

The U.S. Department of Labor is responsible for enforcing OSHA standards and proposing penalties for violators. The penalties apply *only* to the employer. Although the act requires employee compliance with all safety and health standards and regulations, the employer is responsible to see that the employees comply. For example, if a worker is seen without a hard hat in an area where such safety equipment is required, it is the employer, not the employee, who gets the citation.

Various types of violations might be found. They are usually classified as serious or nonserious, willful or nonwillful. An employer who is found to be in violation is cited and allowed a reasonable time to comply with a specific standard. The citation must be posted on the premises and corrective action taken. Failure to comply with a citation can carry a fine of $10,000 and/or a jail sentence of six months. Employers can also be fined up to $1,000 per day for serious violations of OSHA standards. If an imminent danger to workers is discovered, a facility can be shut down immediately.

Additional information on OSHA and specific standards for a given type of facility can be obtained from the state labor departments or from the United States Labor Department in Washington, D.C.

In addition to OSHA inspectors, premises are often subject to safety and fire inspections by insurance underwriters and city and state inspectors.

## ☐ ACCIDENT PREVENTION

Often safety hazards such as toxic chemicals and hydraulic presses, saws, grinders, and punches are very apparent. Although accidents are commonly associated with heavy industry, the National Safety Council reports that more accidents occur in wholesale and retail businesses than in heavy industry. Accidents take an enormous human and economic toll each year. The National Safety Council also makes this statement:

*(know)*

Ninety-five percent of all accidents (on or off the job) are caused by human error, especially lack of safety consciousness.

*(Know)*

The vast majority of accidents result from carelessness, failure to have and/or follow safety rules and regulations, or engaging in horseplay. The remaining 5 percent result from mechanical failures or natural disasters.

*(Know)*

Careless accidents may result from improperly handling objects, slipping or falling, colliding with someone, being hit by a falling object, receiving an electric shock, or being injured by machinery.

Accidents can be prevented by removing hazards, using protective equipment, making employees aware of hazards that cannot be removed, and following good housekeeping practices.

To prevent injuries from electric shock, employees should be alert to and report hazardous conditions such as frayed electric cords on office equipment or lighting; assume that wires and cables, whether indoors or outdoors, are "hot"; lock circuits when working on electric connections; and wear rubber gloves when working on wires, circuits, or electric lines.

Employees should be constantly aware of potential hazards when working around machinery. Safety equipment should be used when available. Employers should, for example, install hoods, canopies, and/or ducts to exhaust noxious fumes and chemicals; they should install machine guards such as shields over grinding wheels and sweep arms that pull an operator's arms free from punch presses. Employees are also often required to wear personal protective equipment such as safety glasses or goggles, face shields, hard hats, safety shoes, rubber aprons, and rubber gloves.

The government publication *Preventing Illness and Injury in the Workplace* (1985, p. 190) describes a "fundamentals program" in existence at Gray Tool company, Houston, Texas, manufacturer of heavy machinery. This company trains its eight hundred workers and all supervisors in basic techniques to prevent injuries. The program emphasizes being aware of hazards and having each individual take responsibility for his or her own safety and that of fellow employees. The program is intended to help employees (1) perform the job while avoiding injury, (2) learn emergency procedures, (3) adopt proper hygiene and health care, and (4) use protective devices and techniques. To accomplish the preceding, the health and safety staff instructs workers in proper lifting techniques, eye protection, use of respirators, hoist operating training, and sling inspection training.

Accidents are more apt to occur in cluttered areas, so good housekeeping practices are essential. Trash and rubbish accumulations not only are unsightly, but also can block fire exits, extinguishers, and alarm boxes. Neatness provides a safer working environment and usually increases efficiency as well.

When accidents or injuries do occur, they should be reported, recorded, and investigated. An effective accident investigation determines why and how the accident happened and includes the date of the accident, the name and occupation of the person injured, details of the accident, identification of the hazard or cause, and the corrective action taken.

Many managers use safety incentive plans such as cash or merchandise awards for employees with the best safety record. Trucking companies often provide awards for drivers who reach one hundred thousand miles without an accident.

## ☐ PROTECTING AGAINST AIDS AND HEPATITIS B

According to Bigbee (1987, p. 17): "Today, with AIDS and hepatitis B infections virtually epidemic, investigators and crime scene technicians are more likely than ever before to encounter violence involving blood and other body fluids of persons with infectious diseases. It is also likely that the patrol officer will encounter these infectious body fluids during his routine activities." The same is true of security personnel who deal with accident victims. Blood is frequently present, often in great quantity. Security personnel should take precautions because blood can transmit not only the deadly AIDS virus but also hepatitis B virus and tuberculosis. Bigbee (p. 20) suggests:

> The first line of defense against infection . . . is protecting the hands and keeping them clean and away from the eyes, mouth, and nose. The best protection is to wear disposable gloves. Any person with a cut, abrasion, or any other break in the skin on the hands should never handle blood or other body fluids without protection.

The AIDS virus can survive at least fifteen days at room temperature in dried and liquid blood. Those responsible for cleaning up any blood at an accident scene should be cautioned about the potential hazard and provided with appropriate protection such as gloves.

Accidents are not the only situation in which security personnel might have to deal with blood. Several other types of emergency situations and other security problems may also present this hazard.

## ☐ GENERAL GUIDELINES FOR DEALING WITH EMERGENCIES

Security managers and their staff may be faced with a variety of emergencies including medical emergencies; civil disturbances, riots, and strikes; bombs and bomb threats; hazardous material spills; fire; and natural disasters. Every emergency presents a unique security challenge. Nevertheless, several guidelines can help ensure the most effective response possible.

## Before the Emergency

➤ Be prepared. Be proactive. Anticipate the emergencies and the personnel needed to deal with them.

➤ Have written plans in place. Specify *in writing* who does what, how, and when. The more common elements there are among the plans for different types of emergencies the better. This should include posting evacuation routes and emergency phone numbers for different types of emergencies. It should also include determining who will communicate with the media and what kind of information will be communicated.

➤ Identify the equipment and resources required and make certain they are either available or immediately accessible.

➤ Know how to use the emergency equipment: fire protection systems, first-aid equipment, hazardous material control equipment, communications systems.

➤ Inspect emergency equipment at least monthly. Check batteries in flashlights.

➤ Practice when possible.

## During the Emergency

➤ Take time to assess the situation. Do not make the situation worse by acting without thinking.

➤ Keep the channels of communication open and the information flowing as required to those who need it.

➤ Keep as many options open as possible. Avoid "either/or" thinking.

➤ Do not get sidetracked by personal, individual requests for help, but rather focus on the "big picture," routing individual requests to the appropriate source of assistance.

➤ Involve key personnel as rapidly as possible. Do not hesitate to call for help from the police, fire department, medical centers, and any other assistance that might be needed. When calling for help:
  ➤ Speak slowly and clearly.
  ➤ Give your name, position, company name, address, and location of the emergency.
  ➤ Answer any questions.
  ➤ Do *not* hang up until directed to do so.

➤ Accept the fact that security cannot do everything. The security manager must prioritize and delegate responsibilities quickly. Mistakes probably will happen.

➤ Keep top executives fully informed of progress and problems.

➤ Ensure that someone is tending to "normal" security needs during the emergency.

➤ Maintain control of the media. Follow established procedures.

## After the Emergency

➤ Get back to normal as soon as possible.

➤ *Document* everything that happened and was done. Accurate records are critical. (Expect that lawyers will get into it at some point.)

> Evaluate the response after the situation has returned to normal. Look at "mistakes" as the "least effective alternative" as well as learning opportunities. However, as May (1990, p. 99) cautions: "Nothing should be written down during these critiques that you wouldn't want to discuss in court if the material is subpoenaed."

> Modify any identified risks remaining and modify emergency-preparedness plans as needed based on what was learned.

Emergency procedures are designed to save lives; minimize injury, loss, or damage; and get back to normal as rapidly and safely as possible. In most instances the primary responsibility of security personnel is to respond rapidly and appropriately and to maintain control of the situation until support professionals such as police, fire fighters, or medical specialists arrive.

## Evacuation

If evacuation is required, an announcement such as the following should be made over the public address system:

> Attention. Please turn off all equipment and machines and leave the building through the nearest exit immediately. Move 200 feet away from the building. Stay there. Do not leave the premises unless directed to do so.

This message should be repeated at least three times. People should not leave the premises so that a check can be made of all personnel to determine if anyone is still inside the building.

## ☐ MEDICAL EMERGENCIES

If the security personnel responding to a medical emergency have the necessary training, such as first aid or CPR, they should render aid. If they do not have such training, they should wait for trained personnel to arrive. Responding security personnel *must not* do more than they are trained to do. Any injured or seriously ill person should *not* be moved unless to leave them would put them in greater danger than if they were not moved. Improper moving can cause further injury or even death and could easily result in a civil lawsuit.

Facilities should have a wheelchair, stretcher, and basic first-aid equipment readily available.

## ☐ CIVIL DISTURBANCES, RIOTS, AND STRIKES

Some types of violence can also pose a threat to safety and property. As with other types of emergencies, the key to preventing or reducing losses is to *be prepared* with a written plan detailing who does what and when.

In the event of civil disturbances, riots, or strikes, the security manager is responsible for maintaining order and protecting lives and assets.

## Civil Disturbances

Protests, demonstrations, sit-ins, picket lines, blockades, and confrontations can threaten the safety of employees and assets. Demonstrators often use abusive language and attempt to provoke security officers. Although nonviolent demonstrations are usually legal, a company may protect its rights, its personnel, and its property. If demonstrators act illegally (for example, by destroying property), they should be charged and arrested. Often the assistance of the public police is requested in civil disturbances.

## Riots

Some civil disturbances erupt into full-blown riots, causing tremendous destruction, as vividly demonstrated during the Watts riots of 1965, when thirty-six people were killed, seven hundred were injured, and property losses estimated at half a billion dollars were incurred.

Retail stores are usually the hardest hit during riots, but wholesalers, manufacturers, and institutions such as hospitals and colleges may also be involved.

Access control is critical in a riot situation. It is best to lock up and sit tight. Protecting personnel and assets becomes a proprietary responsibility because police and fire fighters are usually busy and cannot respond to private calls for assistance.

Management may seek to hire supplemental security forces, but often such forces are unavailable during a riot. Some establishments have paid a retainer to private contract security forces to ensure their availability in an emergency situation. Others have their own "auxiliary" security force.

Demonstrators expressing their First Amendment right to free speech.

If it is safe to do so, employees should be evacuated. The lights should be left on, and store windows and entrances should be barricaded. Some establishments keep rolls of concertina wire on hand for use during riots.

## Strikes

Almost one-fourth of the labor force in our country is now unionized. Though strikes are unpleasant even when nonviolent, they pose an especially difficult situation for security officers who belong to a union themselves. The situation can become next to impossible when labor contracts for employees and security personnel are not separate. As management's representatives, security officers are hired to protect the premises even though the employees are out on strike; they may have to cross picket lines.

Security officers must remain neutral and do the job they were hired to do. Picketing is legal as long as it remains nonviolent and there is no restraining order against the strike. Those who wish to cross the picket line to enter a picketed building must be allowed to do so. Any assaultive action should be prosecuted. As in any other potentially high-risk situation, management should have a preestablished strike plan, including what the consequences will be for security officers who honor the picket line.

## Dealing with Unruly People

Any group gathering near or in an establishment should be reported to the appropriate people and then observed. If the situation warrants, outside doors might be locked.

Any violent disturbance, especially if weapons are involved, is usually the responsibility of law enforcement. It is security's responsibility to protect people and property and to support the police responding to the scene.

Crowds might be classified into four general categories:

➤ Casual—at a shopping mall, at a concert, etc.
➤ Specific purpose—there for one purpose, e.g., accident, fight, fire, etc.
➤ Expressive—there for a religious, political, or other cause.
➤ Aggressive—highly emotional, out to accomplish something.

Any of these types of crowds, especially if an emergency occurs, can turn into a mob—acting without reason, emotionally, sometimes hysterically. Mallory (1990, p. 85) suggests the following for dealing with unruly groups of people:

➤ Have built-in plans, and exercise them periodically. The most important thing is to have a thought-out plan based on realistic capabilities.
➤ Do not overcomplicate the paper plan. Fancy stuff may not work.
➤ Use a phased response, and ask for more help before it is too late.

- Conduct continual risk assessment during the incident, so decisions can be made promptly.
- Always deal with equipment issues in advance. Do not wait until the equipment is needed, then start rounding it up.
- Conduct annual training of your cadre.

## ☑ BOMBS AND BOMB THREATS

Any business, industry, or institution can be the victim of a bomb threat or an actual bombing. Despite the fact that 98 percent of telephoned bomb threats are hoaxes, such a threat is disruptive and disquieting. In addition, the response to the threat may be costly, emotionally charged, and even dangerous. Bomb threats are a major security concern and are also a federal offense.

Several underground publications provide detailed instructions on making bombs. One common type of homemade bomb consists of a lead pipe filled with black powder, caps screwed on either end, and a fuse. Another common type of bomb is made of sticks of dynamite taped together and set off by a timer or a trip wire. Incendiary bombs can consist of a container such as a glass bottle filled with a highly flammable substance, usually gasoline. The wick can be lit and the bomb thrown, or it can be attached to a timing device. Such bombs are frequently referred to as "Molotov cocktails."

Most bomb threats are telephoned and are hoaxes. The caller may simply want the day off if he or she is an employee, or the caller may want to disrupt the business. Few actual bombings are preceded by a warning. When such a warning is given, it is almost always to save lives. Most bombings occur at night for the same reason—to lessen the chance of killing someone.

Common victims of bombings and bomb threats are airlines, banks, hospitals, industrial complexes, utilities, educational institutions, government buildings, and office buildings.

### Preventing Bombings

Access control, orderliness, and regular inspections are the primary defenses against bombs.

Lock storerooms, equipment rooms, and duplicating rooms. Provide adequate lighting. Control entrance into the facility. Conduct periodic inspections of lockers, and have a procedure for checking packages and containers brought onto the premises.

Orderliness, keeping things in their proper places, will make it easier to detect unfamiliar objects that might be bombs. Employees should be instructed to be alert for any suspicious items they come across in their work area. Trash should be stored in metal containers outside the facility. Shipments of merchandise should be checked as soon as possible and then moved promptly to their appropriate locations. Fire doors should be kept shut at all times except for emergency use.

## Responding to a Bomb Threat

A bomb threat is a frightening experience fraught with potential danger, and therefore a response plan must exist *before* such a call is received. Decisions made under the pressure of the moment should be based on previously established guidelines, so being prepared is vital.

To be prepared for a bomb threat, teach personnel how to talk to a person making such a threat and whom to notify. Determine who makes the decision on whether to evacuate and, if so, how personnel are to be informed and what they are to do. Have a plan that specifies how to search for the bomb and what to do if one is found.

All personnel who answer the telephone should be taught to respond appropriately to a telephoned bomb threat. Some phones have tape recorders that can be activated to record the conversation. Others have phone traps that keep the line open until the *receiver* of the call hangs up, allowing the telephone company to trace the call. (Such traps do not work for long-distance calls.)

The receiver of a bomb threat should:

➤ Keep the caller talking as long as possible.
➤ Try to learn as much as possible about the bomb, especially when it will go off and where it is located.
➤ Try to determine the caller's sex, age, accent, and speech pattern, and whether he or she is drunk or drugged.
➤ Listen for any background noises.
➤ Immediately notify the appropriate person(s) of the call.

Many organizations have a report form kept by the switchboard to record information on bomb threats (see Figure 8–1).

After the bomb threat is reported to the appropriate person, usually the chief administrator or manager, this individual decides who else is to be notified as well as whether the call is to be taken seriously. Evaluating the legitimacy of the bomb threat is important. Laughter in the background may indicate that it is a practical joke. Other indications are if the person receiving the call recognizes the voice or knows that the location where the caller claims the bomb is has been tightly secured and that no bomb could possibly have been planted there. Even if the decision is made that the call is a hoax, the police should be notified.

Because any bomb threat may be the real thing, many experts recommend that all such threats be treated as real. Assuming this, the decision must be made as to whether to evacuate. This decision is usually

General Services Administration          Date: _____
              Region 8                         Received        Ended
                                        Time
        BOMB THREAT INFORMATION         Call:

EXACT WORDS OF CALLER:
_____
_____
                    (Continue on reverse)

QUESTIONS TO ASK:
1. WHEN IS BOMB GOING TO EXPLODE? _____
_____

2. WHERE IS BOMB RIGHT NOW? _____
_____

3. WHAT KIND OF BOMB IS IT? _____
_____

4. WHAT DOES IT LOOK LIKE? _____
_____

5. WHY DID YOU PLACE BOMB? _____
_____

DESCRIPTION OF CALLER'S VOICE:            TONE OF VOICE
  ☐ Male   ☐ Female                _____
  ☐ Young  ☐ Middle-Aged  ☐ Old

ACCENT                                  BACKGROUND NOISE

IS VOICE FAMILIAR?                      IF "YES," WHO DID IT
                                        SOUND LIKE?
☐ Yes.   ☐ No.

ADDITIONAL COMMENTS:
_____
_____

Name of Person Receiving Call          Organization & Location

Home Address                           Office Phone

                                       Home Phone

**Figure 8–1  Sample bomb threat form.**
*Reprinted with permission of the publisher from Green and Farber,* Introduction to
Security, *revised edition, Woburn, Mass.: Butterworth Publishers, 1978.*

made by management, often in conjunction with the police. Although
evacuation may seem the safest approach, this is not always true. Moving large groups of people may expose them to greater danger than not
moving them. Evacuating may be exactly what the caller wanted and
may prompt further calls. In addition, it is extremely costly.

Nonetheless, sometimes the best alternative is to evacuate either the
area where the bomb is suspected or the entire building. Total evacuation may cause panic and may expose more people to danger, especially

if the bomber knows the evacuation plan. Sometimes it is thought that evacuation encourages or excites the caller. Planning carefully in advance should result in a safe, orderly evacuation.

Ideally, personnel are informed of a bomb threat over a central public address system rather than by an alarm. If an alarm is used, it should be different from that used for fire because the procedures to be followed are somewhat different. In a fire, windows and doors are closed; in a bomb threat situation, however, windows and doors are opened to vent any explosion.

In both fire and bomb threat evacuations, personnel should *walk* out of and away from the building until they are a block away and then wait until they are informed it is safe to return to the building.

## The Bomb Search

Whether employees are evacuated or not, a search must be conducted if the threat is assumed to be real. A bomb search is an ultrahazardous task and is not to be undertaken lightly. It will be more effectively conducted by those familiar with the facility, so employees are often asked to search their own area before they evacuate.

Areas that are usually unlocked and unwatched are the most common sites for bombs, for example, restrooms, lobbies, lunch rooms, elevators, and stairs. Bombs can be hidden in lunch pails, briefcases, shopping bags, candy boxes, and any number of other types of containers. The key is to look for anything out of place or foreign to the area, for example, a briefcase in the restroom.

A command post should be established as soon as the decision is made to treat the threat as real. The entire building should then be diagrammed and areas crossed off as they are searched. Some security managers have the searchers mark the doors of areas after they have been searched. If enough security guards are available, they should be positioned around the perimeter of the area in which a bomb may be planted to keep curiosity-seekers from endangering themselves.

A system of communicating among searchers must be established, but it must not involve the use of portable radios, as they may detonate the bomb. All searchers should be cautioned not to turn on lights, as this might also detonate the bomb. Searchers should move slowly and carefully, listening for any ticking sounds and watching for trip wires. Sometimes metal detectors or dogs are used to assist in the search.

Do not touch or move any suspicious object found during a bomb search. Provide a clear zone of at least 300 feet around the device and call the nearest bomb disposal specialist or the police.

The following procedures are suggested by Fisher (1979, pp. 320–21) if a suspicious object or a bomb is located:

1) Doors and windows in the vicinity of the bomb should be opened to reduce shock waves in the event of an explosion.

Security officer with bomb-sniffing dog.

2) All available fire extinguishers should be readied and in position to combat any fires caused by the explosion.
3) If time allows, highly flammable objects and liquids should be removed from areas immediately surrounding, or otherwise endangered by the bomb.
4) The bomb should be surrounded with sandbags or similar shock-absorbing objects, such as specially constructed bomb blankets. One of these blankets can cover an area of up to 16 square feet.*
5) Valuable and irreplaceable documents, files, and other papers should be taken from the endangered area.

All procedures for dealing with bomb treats should be practiced, if possible. The operator may be called with a fake bomb threat to see the response. A suspicious container capable of concealing a bomb may be

*Security managers should be aware, however, of the reluctance or possible refusal of many police/military EOD squads to handle any object previously covered by a bomb blanket.

planted and a practice bomb search conducted. The evacuation plan may be practiced as well.

## ☐ HAZARDOUS MATERIALS INCIDENTS

Hazardous materials (H/M) incidents can cause serious, even life-threatening, problems and must be dealt with immediately. Contact with highly toxic chemical liquids, solids, or gases or with highly corrosive materials requires extreme care. Hazardous materials emergencies may involve poor visibility, difficult breathing, fire, hysteria, and lack of information about the substance causing the problem.

Although writing for public patrol officers and their supervisors, May (1990, pp. 85–87) lists some key "dos" and "don'ts" for first responders that apply equally to security officers and supervisors:

➤ Report the incident as a possible hazardous materials accident. Give exact location and approach route, and request assistance.
➤ Stay upwind and upgrade (if the hazard is outdoors).
➤ Clear the area of nonessential personnel.
➤ Avoid contact with liquids or fumes.
➤ Eliminate ignition sources. (Do not smoke or use flares.)
➤ Rescue the injured—only if prudent.
➤ Identify the material(s) involved and determine conditions.
➤ If necessary, initiate an evacuation.
➤ Establish a command post.

Additional steps if the hazard occurs indoors are to isolate and seal off the area by closing doors and to shut down the ventilation system for the area.

If hazardous materials are commonly present at a specific location, they should be clearly labeled as such. In addition, the security manager should consider having an H/M control team trained to respond to those materials that might cause a problem. In some instances special equipment such as chemical suits, gloves, boots, and air packs should be available for emergency use.

## ☐ PREVENTING AND PROTECTING AGAINST LOSS BY FIRE

Fire is probably the single greatest threat security must deal with. Studies show that three out of every five businesses struck by serious fires never open again. Security personnel should be continuously alert to the potential for fire. The ideal time to stop a fire is before it ever starts. Eliminating fire hazards is a prime responsibility of all security personnel and, indeed, of all personnel within a business, company, or organization. Security managers can better prevent and protect against fire loss by understanding how fires occur, what frequently causes them, and what equipment and procedures can help minimize losses.

Knowing how fires burn helps one to understand potential fire hazards and how to control them.

*test*

The *fire triangle* consists of three elements necessary for burning: *heat, fuel,* and *oxygen.*

*eliminate 1 of these*

When a flammable substance is heated to a specific temperature, called its **ignition temperature,** it will ignite and burn as long as oxygen is present. Because oxygen and fuel are always present in business and industry, the potential for fire always exists. If any of the three elements is eliminated, the fire is extinguished. Remove oxygen by smothering, fuel by isolating, and heat by cooling.

The National Fire Protection Association has established four classifications of fires:

*know test*

➤ Class A fires involve ordinary combustible materials such as paper, packing boxes, wood, and cloth.
➤ Class B fires involve flammable liquids such as gasoline and oil.
➤ Class C fires involve energized electrical installations, appliances, and wiring.
➤ Class D fires involve combustible metals such as magnesium, sodium, and potassium. (Class D fires are sometimes called "exotic metals fires.")

Destruction and death are caused not only by flames, but by smoke, heat, gas, and panic. Smoke can blind and choke. Carbon dioxide and carbon monoxide, by-products of burning, can poison and can cause buildings to explode. Intense heat can explode gases, ignite materials, and expand air. Expanded air can exert tremendous pressure, shattering doors and windows. Because smoke, gas, heat, and expanded air all rise, it is possible to determine safe and unsafe areas and to control the direction of a fire if building construction and preplanning are adequate.

## Causes of Fires

The major sources of ignition in industrial fires are electrical circuits, overheating, sparking, friction, chemical reaction, flames, and heat transfer.

Often fires result from carelessness or poor housekeeping practices, such as improperly storing or using flammable liquids; replacing electric fuses with ones having too high amperage, or with coins, wires, or nails; overloading electric circuits; carelessly discarding cigarette butts and/or matches; and allowing oily rags, rubbish, or other materials to accumulate, resulting in spontaneous combustion. Fires have also been caused by faulty wiring and connections, ignition sparks from static electricity, lightning, and arson.

An effective fire safety program has two parts: (1) preventing fires and (2) protecting against losses caused by fires that do occur.

## Preventing Fire

Most fires can be prevented. The greatest single precipitant is carelessness. Factory Mutual estimated that 75 percent of the industrial fires were caused by human error and carelessness and especially by deficiencies in housekeeping practices.

Although many modern buildings are built to be fire-resistive, a fireproof building does not exist. Despite the fact that an exterior of steel and concrete does not burn, the interior contains numerous flammable substances which can burn, causing the building to become like a furnace. Given sufficient heat, the structure can collapse.

Fires can be prevented by reducing fire-loading, properly storing and handling flammable materials, enforcing no-smoking regulations, using proper wiring, and following good housekeeping practices. Access controls can lessen the chance of arson.

**Fire-loading** refers to the amount of flammable material within an area, including flammable rugs, curtains, paper, and liquids such as paints and solvents. To the extent possible, reduce fire-loading by using flame-resistant curtains and furniture.

When highly combustible chemicals, glues, and the like are used, make sure ventilation is adequate. The main supply of such materials should be kept in protective containers stored in properly ventilated areas. Packing boxes containing excelsior and paper materials should be metal and should preferably be equipped with a lead link that causes the lid to drop into place if heat is generated in the metal box, reducing the oxygen supply and smothering a potential fire. Fire-preventive waste receptacles designed to smother a fire are also available. Never allow oily rags and other flammable materials to accumulate.

Good housekeeping is critical; keep areas free of trash and rubbish. Enforce no-smoking regulations. Check wiring periodically. Make employees aware of potential fire hazards and how to guard against them.

Among the most common fire hazards are violations of electrical codes including:

➤ Defective wiring.
➤ Use of long extension cords or wrong size.
➤ Overloading outlets.
➤ Combustibles within three feet of an electrical access box.
➤ Coffee pots, hot plates, and space heaters left on.
➤ Machinery left running.
➤ Typewriters and calculators left running.
➤ Soldering irons left on.

Materials that are a fire hazard include acids, oil, paint, solvents, explosives, flammable or combustible liquids, flammable gases, and materials subject to spontaneous ignition.

## Protecting against Losses from Fire ✓ KNOW

The best way to protect against loss from fire is to prevent fire from ever occurring. In spite of all efforts, however, the potential for a fire is always present. The best protection against loss from fire is to *be prepared.*

Protection from fire losses is provided by detectors and alarms; properly marked and sufficient exits, fire doors, and fire escapes; fire-resistive safes and vaults; and fire extinguishers, sprinkler systems, and an adequate, accessible water supply.

*Fire detectors and alarms* can provide advance notice of a fire, thereby allowing human life and assets to be protected as well as increasing the possibility of bringing the fire under control before it causes extensive damage.

Fire usually progresses through four stages:

KNOW

➤ *Incipient stage*—Invisible products of combustion are given off. No smoke or flames are visible and there is no appreciable heat.
➤ *Smoldering stage*—Combustion products become visible as smoke, but there is no flame or appreciable heat.
➤ *Flame stage*—An actual fire exists. Flame and smoke are visible, but there is still no appreciable heat. Heat follows, however, almost instantly.
➤ *Heat stage*—Heat is uncontrollable and air expands rapidly.

Each stage of fire can be detected by specific types of detectors.

KNOW
& what they respond to

➤ Ionization detectors respond to invisible particles of combustion.
➤ Photoelectric detectors respond to smoke.
➤ Infrared detectors respond to flame.
➤ Thermal detectors respond to heat, usually temperatures in excess of 135°F.

Ionization detectors are most effective because they give the earliest warning, but they are too sensitive for most areas. Therefore, they are usually used only in such areas as computer rooms. Photoelectric detectors, also called smoke or early warning detectors, are commonly found in homes and in many office buildings. Infrared detectors have the disadvantage of responding to sun reflecting off glass or mirrors. Thermal detectors give the least amount of advance warning, but they are needed in areas such as boiler rooms, garages, and manufacturing areas where smoke and flame are commonly present.

Once the detector is activated, an alarm is sounded, locally and/or at a central station. An alarm sounded in a very noisy area should also give a visible warning, for example, a flashing red light.

Other types of alarms are activated by a person seeing a fire and manually activating a pull box that alerts the fire department. Such pull boxes carry labels reading ''In Case of Fire, Pull'' or ''Break Glass.''

*Exits* should be unobstructed and clearly marked. Fire exit doors can be painted red, but often aesthetic considerations prevent this. Exit signs should be lighted and have emergency standby power. Routes to the exits should be well lit and free of obstructions. Building codes establish the minimum number of exits for a specific establishment and also require that provision be made for handicapped individuals. If access control dictates that some exterior doors be locked from the outside, equip them with a crash bar so they can be opened in case of a fire.

*Elevators* should be clearly labeled ''In case of fire, do *not* use.'' An arrow should indicate where the nearest stairs are. Some establishments have their elevators controlled so that if a fire occurs the elevators return to the lobby level and are locked.

talk briefly about
these

Fire pull box.

Three types of fire extinguishers.

*Fire escapes* should be checked to be certain that they are safe and, if operated by a counterbalance, that they are in good working condition.

*Fire doors* provide added protection and help contain a fire. They not only impede the spread of flame and smoke, but can also protect people trapped inside a burning building. Automatic fire doors are available that are held open by a pulley system. When there is combustion, the heat melts a fusible metal link that allows the counterbalanced door to automatically close.

*Fire-resistive safes and vaults* can protect cash and records from being destroyed in a fire, as discussed in Chapter 6. Most such safes provide protection for paper that ignites at 350°F, but they do not usually provide adequate protection for computer tapes, which ignite at 150°.

*Fire extinguishers* should be located throughout the facility, be in good working order, and be of the type appropriate for the kind of fire that might occur in the area.

It is important to know what type of fire is occurring (A, B, C, or D) in order to select the appropriate extinguisher.

Portable fire extinguishers are pressurized cylinders containing materials to cool and/or smother a fire. Among the most common ingredients are the following:

➤ *Soda acid* uses water, bicarbonate of soda, and acid. This type of extinguisher is operated by being turned upside down. Used on Class A fires.
➤ *Foam* smothers fire. Used on Class A and B fires.
➤ *Dry chemical* is usually clearly labeled to indicate what type of fire it will safely extinguish, usually Class B and C fires.
➤ *Carbon dioxide* cools and smothers. Used on Class B and C fires.

In addition, water, transported by hose or bucket, is effective on a Class A fire.

Water or a Class A extinguisher should never be used on energized electric equipment (Class C fires), as the electric charge can follow the water stream to the holder, causing instant electrocution. Water or a Class A extinguisher should not be used in a Class B fire, as it can splatter the burning oil or gasoline, spreading the fire to a larger area instead of extinguishing it.

ABC extinguishers are effective against all except Class D fires. Ideally, several ABC extinguishers should be placed in strategic locations and checked periodically. Employees should be instructed on their use. Unfortunately, many establishments rely almost exclusively on water and hoses or on type A fire extinguishers because they are cheaper and because Class A fires are the most common.

If fire extinguishers are used to fight a fire, they should be laid on the floor, *not* hung back up. They can then be collected and recharged.

*Sprinkler systems* also provide protection against loss from fire. Sprinkler systems use underground and overhead pipes that are activated by heat of a specific temperature, usually from 130 to 165°F. The heads of the sprinklers are plugged with a fusible metal that melts at a specific temperature, allowing water to flow and also activating an alarm. Many unheated establishments in southern states use a dry sprinkler system in which air holds the water pressure back until after the sprinkler head link is melted. A dry system prevents the water pipes from freezing, but it also causes a brief delay in getting the water to the fire.

Although water damage from sprinkler systems may result, the damage is usually considerably less than the damage a fire would cause. Frequently insurance companies give reduced fire insurance rates for establishments that have installed a sprinkler system. As with fire extinguishers and hoses, sprinkler systems should be periodically checked, the water supply must be adequate, and the pipes must be free of corrosion. In addition, nothing should be stacked closer than eighteen inches to the sprinkler heads or the system will be ineffective.

## Procedures for Protecting against Fire Loss

In addition to obtaining and maintaining equipment to help prevent fires, an effective fire safety program establishes specific procedures for protecting life and assets should a fire occur.

Always call for help before attempting to extinguish a fire. Teach employees what to do in case of fire. Other procedures for protecting against fire loss include having and practicing a plan for evacuation, shutting doors and windows, and using stairs rather than elevators.

Employees should know where the exits are and which they are to use, what kinds of fire extinguishers are available and how to use them, how to recognize fire hazards and report them, and what to do if they cannot evacuate the premises.

Security personnel must recognize the different types of fires so they can select the correct method of putting it out if no extinguisher is available. Eliminating any one of the three components of the fire triangle should put a fire out. Table 8–1 summarizes how to extinguish common fires.

The _evacuation plan_ should include how the employees will be alerted. Sometimes this is not by an alarm, but over the public address system. In some institutions a code word is used to indicate fire. For example, many hospitals have established a specific code to indicate that a fire is occurring and where. The use of the code reduces the probability of patients panicking. All employees should know the location of the nearest exit and how to get there *without* using the elevator. They should be instructed to close windows and doors, never to open a door without first touching it (opening a hot door can be deadly), and to *walk* out of the building and continue walking until at least a block away.

If evacuation is impossible, employees should know the following steps: (1) get as far away from the fire as possible, closing doors behind them; (2) if time permits, remove flammable objects from the room in which they seek shelter; (3) barricade the door; (4) open the window or, if necessary, break it to allow smoke and heat to escape and fresh air to enter; (5) hang something in the window to signal fire fighters; and (6) stay low by the window.

When practical, fire drills should be conducted. Although such drills may be costly in time lost from the job, the practice may save lives should a fire occur. Fire drills in skyscrapers can be conducted weekly, one floor per week, to keep people abreast of how to evacuate and yet avoid disrupting the whole building.

Doors and windows should be closed to reduce the oxygen supply and to confine the blaze. If the premises have central air-conditioning, this should be turned off because it will circulate the smoke throughout the building.

| Table 8–1  How to extinguish common types of fires. | |
| --- | --- |
| **Class** | **How to Extinguish** |
| A | Quench or cool with water or water fog. Use soda acid, pump tank (water), or foam. (Smothering is ineffective.) |
| B | Blanket or smother. Use carbon dioxide ($CO_2$), dry chemicals, or foam. |
| C | Use dry chemicals, carbon dioxide ($CO_2$), or vaporizing liquid extinguishers. |

Some establishments have established a fire brigade, but this should be a voluntary assignment. The security manager is usually in charge of such a brigade. The members of the brigade can be given specific responsibilities to assist security personnel.

## The Security Manager's Responsibility in Case of Fire

All security personnel should know the location of fire extinguishers, fire-alarm boxes, sprinkler valve controls, escalator shutoffs, light control panels, emergency lights, wheelchairs, stretchers, and first-aid equipment.

---

Have a plan, take charge, and stay calm. Take immediate action to protect lives first, assets second.

---

Panic can add to the danger and result in needless death. Security personnel might also assume any or all of the following responsibilities:

- Sound the alarm; alert the fire department.
- Attempt to control the blaze if it is not out of hand.
- Turn off the central air-conditioning and machinery, but leave lights on.
- Close all doors and windows.
- Ground all elevators.
- Provide traffic control.
- Direct fire fighters to the location of the fire.
- Time permitting, remove highly combustible stock and valuables.
- Cover expensive merchandise or equipment, such as computers, with a tarpaulin to prevent water damage.
- Move company cars, trucks, and/or boxcars to a safe distance.
- Administer first aid.

Above all else, protect lives, including one's own.

## Computer Rooms

Computer rooms present special fire hazards and require special fire precautions. They often are equipped with an ionization detector and/or a thermal rate of rise detector. They should *not* be equipped with a sprinkler system because steam and water can damage the computer tapes and because water should *not* be used on Class C fires, the type most commonly occurring in computer rooms. Carbon dioxide fire extinguishers can be used without damaging the hardware or the tapes, but the fumes may be hazardous to humans. Therefore, halon is often preferred. Carbon dioxide and halon should *not* be used together: a lethal condition results.

Seek professional advice from the fire department and/or the fire insurance company for special problems regarding fire prevention and protection.

## ☐ NATURAL DISASTERS

As noted by Gallati (1983, p. 27):

> Earthquakes, storms, floods, hurricanes, tornadoes, some types of fires, and building collapse caused by structural weakness are most often beyond the scope of security to control. The role of security in these cases is to provide warning, to implement evacuation procedures (or "take-cover" procedures), and generally to carry out the security manager's disaster plan with as little confusion and hysteria as possible under the circumstances.

Security managers should identify natural disasters that might occur in their geographic location.

Natural disasters necessitating a contingency plan might include floods, tornadoes, hurricanes, and/or earthquakes.

A plan to protect lives and assets in the event of a natural disaster should be developed, written out, distributed, and practiced periodically. A good plan is logical, uncomplicated, yet comprehensive. It stipulates who does what and when; who is to be notified; and what assistance is available. It should also include where a radio is available to be tuned to emergency frequencies.

As many elements as possible should be the same in plans for responding to different natural disasters. For example, procedures for evacuating in the event of a fire might be the same used in evacuating during a flood. In both instances elevators should *never* be used. This

Santa Cruz, California, October 1989, Pacific Garden Mall the day after a 7.1 earthquake.

was tragically illustrated in the 1977 flood in Rochester, Minnesota, when three nursing home residents in wheelchairs were put into an elevator to be sent to higher floors. Unfortunately, the elevator shorted out, carrying them down into the water-filled lower level. All three drowned.

In some situations, however, evacuation is not the proper procedure, as in a tornado or hurricane alert. In such cases the alarm should be different from that used for fires. Employees should be directed to a clearly marked shelter within the facility, usually on the lowest level, in the center of the building, away from glass. The Civil Defense Department* can help security managers to determine the most appropriate locations and to develop effective plans for such disasters.

Two monitoring systems can assist security by alerting them to impending hazardous weather conditions:

➤ A weather alert radio tuned exclusively to the weather bureau's frequency, left on continuously and activated by the weather bureau when conditions warrant.
➤ An AM radio for weather information.

According to Civil Defense authorities, the safest areas in the workplace during some natural disasters such as tornadoes are under office desks, under heavy tables, or in specific shelter areas.

The difference between a *watch* and *warning* is important. A *watch* means that the weather conditions are right for a specific event to occur, for example, a tornado, blizzard, or severe thunderstorm. A *warning* means such a condition has developed and will probably pose a problem for the area. Precautions should be implemented immediately, including a "take-cover" announcement such as the following if the emergency is a tornado or destructive winds warning:

Attention. A tornado warning has been given for our area. Turn off all equipment, extinguish all flames, and take cover immediately under your desk, a heavy table, or in our designated shelter areas. Do NOT go near windows, glass doors, or outside. Stay under cover until the all clear is given.

Repeat this message at least three times.

First-aid equipment should be readily available and emergency telephone numbers for ambulances, fire departments, police, and other available assistance should be posted.

## ☐ OTHER EMERGENCIES

Plans are needed for all other potential emergencies, such as power failures, water main or gas line breaks, and toxic chemical leaks or explosions. The best emergency plans are simple. They specify *in writing* who does what, how, and when. The more common elements there are among the plans for different types of emergencies, the better.

---

*Called Emergency Services and Disaster Agency in many areas.

# SUMMARY

Security managers are often responsible for accident prevention pro-grams as one means to prevent losses and protect assets. OSHA, the Occupational Safety and Health Administration, was established to administer the Occupational Safety and Health Act, which seeks to ensure safe and healthful working conditions for every employee in the nation. OSHA requires employers covered by the act to keep a log of all occupational injuries, accidents, and illnesses, as well as an annual summary of the log's information.

Ninety-five percent of all accidents are caused by human error, especially lack of safety consciousness. Accidents can be prevented by removing hazards, using protective equipment, making employees aware of hazards that cannot be removed, and following good housekeeping practices.

In the event of civil disturbances, riots, or strikes, the security manager is responsible for maintaining order and protecting lives and assets.

Bombs and bomb threats are a serious security concern. Access control, orderliness, and regular inspections are the primary defenses against bombs. To be prepared for a bomb threat, teach personnel how to talk to a person making such a threat and whom to notify. Determine who makes the decision on whether to evacuate, and, if so, how personnel are to be informed and what they are to do. Have a plan that specifies how to search for the bomb and what to do if one is found.

The receiver of a bomb threat should keep the caller talking as long as possible; try to learn about the bomb, especially when it will go off and where it is located; try to determine the caller's sex, age, accent, and speech pattern, and whether he or she is possibly drunk or drugged; listen for any background noises; and immediately notify the appropriate person(s) of the call.

Do not touch or move any suspicious object found during a bomb search. Provide a clear zone of three hundred feet around the device and call the nearest bomb disposal specialist or the police.

Fire is a major threat to life and property. The fire triangle consists of three elements necessary for burning: heat, fuel, and oxygen. The National Fire Protection Association has established four classifications of fires: Class A fires, which involve ordinary combustible materials such as paper, packing boxes, wood, and cloth; Class B fires, which involve flammable liquids such as gasoline and oil; Class C fires, which involve energized electrical installations, appliances, and wiring; and Class D fires, which involve combustible metals such as magnesium, sodium, and potassium.

Fires can be prevented by reducing fire-loading, properly storing and handling flammable materials, enforcing no-smoking regulations, using proper wiring, and following good housekeeping practices. Access controls can lessen the chance of arson. Protection from fire losses is provided by detectors and alarms; properly marked and sufficient exits, fire doors, and fire escapes; fire-resistive safes and vaults; and fire extinguishers, sprinkler systems, and an adequate, accessible water supply.

Fires can be detected by ionization detectors that respond to invisible particles of combustion, photoelectric detectors that respond to smoke, infrared detectors that respond to flame, and thermal detectors that respond to heat.

Water or a Class A extinguisher should never be used on energized electric equipment (Class C fires), as the electric charge can follow the water stream to the holder, causing instant electrocution. Water or a Class A extinguisher should not be used on a Class B fire, as it can splatter the burning oil or gasoline, spreading the fire to a larger area instead of extinguishing it.

Always call for help before attempting to extinguish a fire. Teach employees what to do in case of fire. Other procedures for protecting against fire loss include having and practicing a plan for evacuation, shutting doors and windows, and using stairs rather than elevators. In case of fire, have a plan, take charge, and stay calm. Take immediate action to protect lives first, assets second.

Natural disasters necessitating a contingency plan might include floods, tornadoes, hurricanes, and/or earthquakes.

# APPLICATION

Read the following emergency procedures established for a college faculty and evaluate their effectiveness.

**EMERGENCY PROCEDURES FOR STAFF MEMBERS** (separate procedures have been developed for administrators, switchboard operator and buildings and grounds workers)*

**FIRE ALARM**

1) All alarms should be treated as a real fire.
2) If a fire is spotted, the individual should find the nearest pull station and turn in the alarm.
3) Next, notify the switchboard operator as to the location of the fire.
4) Instructors should direct their students to leave quickly through the nearest safe exit in a safe and orderly manner, to a position at least 250 feet away from the buildings.
5) Instructors should be the last persons to leave their classrooms or other assigned space and should see that the lights are off, the lab gas is shut off and hazardous chemicals secured where possible. All doors should be shut.
6) No one should enter their car to leave the campus. This will affect the ability of fire fighting equipment to reach the scene of the fire.

**POWER FAILURE**

1) The switchboard operator should be notified so that Northern States Power can be contacted.
2) Call Northern States Power (phone #) when switchboard is closed.
3) All students and staff should remain in offices and classrooms unless told otherwise.
4) The maintenance staff will check each building to see if anyone needs assistance. They will also check the elevators.

---

*Staff Handbook of Policies and Procedures, Normandale Community College, Bloomington, Minnesota. Reprinted by permission.

## TORNADO ALERT

1) The switchboard operator will immediately call the administrator on duty and tune to WCCO when the Civil Defense alarm sounds.
2) If the decision is made to take cover, the administrator in charge will make the appropriate announcement over the PA system.
   **Tornado announcement:** We are having a tornado emergency. Please go to the Commons lower level, LRC tunnel or the Activities tunnel. Please stay inside and away from all windows. Wait for the all clear to be given.
3) Once the alarm is sounded, all staff and students should take cover. No one should be in the following areas: gym, theatre, auditorium, LRC reading room and all areas with outside windows.

## WATER MAIN BREAK

*Day*—switchboard open

1) Call switchboard—explain location and nature of break.
2) Move anything which could be damaged by water flow.

*Night*—switchboard closed

1) Call police emergency (911) and explain location and nature of break.
2) Meet emergency crew and direct them to area of break.
3) Notify Bernard Lundstrom (phone #) or Daniel Barnett (phone ).

## GAS LINE BREAK

*Day*—switchboard open

1) Clear immediate area.
2) Call switchboard operator with location and extent of break.
3) If necessary, evacuate the area by pulling the fire alarm.

*Night*—switchboard closed

1) Call the fire department at (phone #). Give location and extent of break.
2) Clear immediate area.
3) Notify Bernard Lundstrom (phone #) or Daniel Barnett (phone #).

## MEDICAL EMERGENCY

1) The switchboard operator should be notified and given as much information as possible. The exact location of the individual needing assistance should be given and an individual sent to the closest main entrance to meet the emergency vehicles.
2) The switchboard operator will then notify the police.
3) When switchboard is closed, call the police at 911 and give them as much information as possible. One individual should stay with the person in need and another should meet the emergency vehicles at the nearest door.

## STUDENT DISTURBANCES

1) The individual witnessing a major disturbance or disorder should notify the Dean of Students or the administrator on duty and give him/her all the important details. It will then be up to the administrator to decide what action is to be taken.
2) At times when an administrator is not present, a staff member should use his/her best judgment. Police can be reached at (phone #). The incident should be reported to the Dean of Students on the next class day.

## BOMB THREATS

1) Keep caller on the telephone as long as possible.

**2)** Try to get as much information as possible regarding the bomb. That is, the bomb's location, type of device, time of detonation and anything else that might be pertinent to the safety of the college and individuals inside.

**3)** Try to remember everything about the call, voice, accent, background noises. These items or anything else you might think of might help identify the caller.

**4)** Report the incident to the president or the administrator on duty.

**5)** The president or administrator on duty will make the final decision on what action is to be taken.

**6)** If the switchboard is closed, call the police at 911 and evacuate the buildings. If necessary, pull the fire alarm.

## DISCUSSION QUESTIONS

**1)** What alternatives are available to security managers in handling personnel conflicts? Are they the responsibility of the security manager?

**2)** What natural disasters are likely to occur in your geographic area, and how should a security manager prepare for an adequate response to them?

**3)** What resources would you contact to counter a series of bomb threats against your facility?

**4)** When a strike is certain to occur, what contingency plans should a security manager be concerned about?

**5)** If a security director notices OSHA violations and reports them to top management, and top management chooses to ignore the violations, what should the security director do?

## REFERENCES

Bigbee, Paul. Evidence handling and infectious diseases. *FBI law enforcement bulletin,* July 1987, pp. 17–21.

Fisher, A. J. *Security for business and industry.* Englewood Cliffs, NJ: Prentice-Hall, 1979.

Gallati, Robert J. *Introduction to private security.* Englewood Cliffs, NJ: Prentice-Hall, 1983.

Mallory, Jim. Demonstrations. *Law and order,* September 1990, pp. 83–85.

May, William A., Jr. Post-traumatic stress after large-scale disasters. *Law and order,* March 1990, pp. 97–99.

May, William A., Jr. Responding to hazardous materials incidents: Formulating a basic response plan. *Law and order,* October 1990, pp. 85–87.

*Preventing illness and injury in the workplace.* Washington, DC: U.S. Congress, Office of Technology Assessment, OTA-H–256, April 1985.

## ☐ INTRODUCTION

Early Saturday morning, June 17, 1972, a private security patrol officer, Frank Wills, was walking his beat on a Washington, D.C., street. He approached the entry door to the Watergate complex and tried the door to see if it was secure. Noticing that the latch had been taped open and that the door swung open freely, the officer immediately called the Washington police. Five men carrying photographic equipment and electronic gear were subsequently arrested for burglarizing the National Democratic Headquarters. Thus came about the most noted political upheaval in the history of our country—Watergate. Officer Wills' watchfulness and the quick actions of the Washington police led to the imprisonment of two top presidential aides, the incarceration of the United States attorney general, and the resignation of the president of the United States.*

The primary role of private security in combating crime is to *prevent* its occurrence by reducing the opportunity for criminal activity. Criminal activity in business and industry takes many forms, ranging from simple property loss through shoplifting or pilfering to property loss by physical violence, as in armed robbery. The impact of burglary and robbery on the business community is substantial.

# Chapter Nine

# Preventing Losses from Criminal Actions

## DO YOU KNOW

➤ How criminal and civil offenses differ?

➤ What crimes are of major importance to private security?

➤ How the risk of these crimes can be reduced?

➤ How to differentiate among theft, burglary, and robbery?

➤ What circumstances can indicate arson?

➤ What white-collar crime is?

➤ What pilferage is?

➤ What drugs are commonly abused in the workplace?

➤ What rights private security officers may be called on to enforce?

➤ When and how private security officers can make an arrest?

➤ When force or deadly force may be justified?

➤ When and how searches of suspects can be conducted?

➤ How interviewing differs from interrogating? How to make such questioning more effective?

According to the Hallcrest Report (Cunningham and Taylor, 1985, p. 18), the most common ways of illegally taking money from a business have been robbery, burglary, larceny, and embezzlement. However, more sophisticated, complicated forms of stealing have emerged, such as falsification of records, leading to payments of goods never received or hours never worked, sometimes to nonexistent employees. Waste and abuse of on-the-job time cost the American economy billions resulting from employee 'time theft'—excessive socializing, conducting personal business on employer time, late arrivals, abuse of sick leave, etc.

---

*One reputable source states that Wills removed the tape the first time he saw it; that it was not until a subsequent round, when he noticed that it was retaped, that he called the police.

In addition to these direct losses, the Hallcrest Report also identifies three absorbers of indirect costs of economic crime against businesses: business, government, and the public (p. 19).

*Effects on BUSINESS include the following:*
➤ Increased costs of insurance and security protection.
➤ Costs of internal audit activities to detect crime.
➤ Costs of investigation and prosecution of suspects measured in terms of lost time of security and management personnel.
➤ Reduced profits.
➤ Increased selling prices and weakened competitive standing.
➤ Loss of productivity.
➤ Loss of business reputation.
➤ Deterioration in quality of service.
➤ Threats to the survival of small business.

*Effects on GOVERNMENT include the following:*
➤ Costs of investigation and prosecution of suspects.
➤ Increased costs of prosecuting sophisticated (e.g., embezzlement) and technology-related (e.g., computer) crime.
➤ Costs of correctional programs to deal with economic crime offenders.
➤ Costs of crime prevention programs.
➤ Costs of crime reporting and mandated security programs.
➤ Loss of revenue (e.g., loss of sales tax, untaxed income of perpetrator, and tax deductions allowed businesses for crime-related losses).

*Effects on the PUBLIC include the following:*
➤ Increased costs of consumer goods and services to offset crime losses.
➤ Loss of investor equity.
➤ Increased taxes.
➤ Reduced employment due to business failures.
  NOTE: These effects are concerned only with nonviolent business crime, but if the total crime environment of institutions (schools, hospitals, museums, etc.) were also considered, the effects on institutions would include the following:
➤ Declining enrollment, attendance, or occupancy due to crime-related incidents.
➤ Employee turnover and recruitment costs due to fear of crime incidents.
➤ Increased costs of service.
➤ Increased costs of insurance and security protection.

The crime problem in the United States is severe, as indicated by figures from the 1990 Uniform Crime Reports:

➤ One murder every 24 minutes.
➤ One forcible rape every 6 minutes.
➤ One robbery every 55 seconds.
➤ One aggravated assault every 33 seconds.

Security managers should carefully analyze the potential for crime in their establishment. What type of crime is likely to occur? At what rate? When? What method of attack is likely to be used? What is it likely to cost? If the risk is high, appropriate security measures should be taken to reduce, spread, or shift the risks.

Keep one thing in mind when discussing the security officer's responsibilities regarding crimes. Although this chapter emphasizes the role of the security officer in dealing with potential and actual crimes, the majority of the security manager's time is spent dealing with noncriminal matters.

## ☐ CRIMINAL AND CIVIL OFFENSES

Our country's laws establish what actions constitute a crime. These laws include all the rules of conduct established and enforced by custom, authority, or legislation of a city, state, or federal government. In the United States, state and federal statutes define each crime, the elements involved, and the penalty attached to each. The elements of the crime are the specific conditions and actions prescribed by law that must exist to constitute a specific crime. These elements vary from state to state.

Crimes and their punishments range in seriousness from pickpocketing to murder. They are classified according to their seriousness as a misdemeanor or a felony. A **misdemeanor** is a minor crime such as shoplifting or petty theft that is punishable by a fine and/or a relatively short jail sentence. In contrast, a **felony** is a serious crime, such as murder, robbery, or burglary, that is punishable by death or by imprisonment in the state prison or penitentiary.

In addition to criminal offenses, security personnel may also have to deal with **civil** offenses—actions prohibited by law, but not classified as crimes. These actions, called **torts**, are governed by civil law and are not under the jurisdiction of public law enforcement as discussed in Chapter 5. They include such offenses as libel, slander, and negligence.

A crime is an offense against the state for which punishment is sought. A tort is an offense against an individual for which restitution is sought.

The distinction between a tort and a crime is described by Sutherland and Cressey (1978, p. 8):

> A particular act may be considered as an offense against an individual and also against the state, and is either a tort or a crime or both, according to the way its handled. A person who has committed an act of assault, for example, may be ordered by the civil court to pay the victim a sum of $500 for the damages to his interests, and may also be ordered by the criminal court to pay a fine of $500 to the state. The payment of the first $500 is not punishment, but the payment of the second $500 is punishment.

## ☐ CRIMES OF CONCERN TO PRIVATE SECURITY

The crimes of most concern to private security are larceny/theft, burglary, robbery, trespassing, vandalism, assault, arson; white-collar crime, including embezzlement, bad checks, and credit card fraud; and drugs in the workplace.

A major source of information on these crimes is the Uniform Crime Reports (UCR).* These are annually compiled by the FBI, which serves as the national clearinghouse for crime-related statistical information. The Uniform Crime Reporting Program provides a yearly, nationwide summary of crime based on the cooperative submission of data by nearly fifteen thousand law enforcement agencies throughout the country. The data contained in these reports can be used by private security managers in making administrative, operational, and management decisions. In addition to the Uniform Crime Reports, security managers should be familiar with their state statutes for the crimes they are most likely to have to deal with. They should be familiar with the elements that must be proven if they are to be of assistance in prosecuting perpetrators of crime. Definitions in the following discussions of specific crimes are based on those used in the Uniform Crime Reports.

## Larceny/Theft**

**Larceny/theft** is (1) the unlawful taking (2) of the personal goods or property of another (3) valued above [grand larceny] or below [petty larceny] a specified amount, (4) with the intent to permanently deprive the owner of the property or goods. This crime includes shoplifting, to be discussed in Chapter 14, and employee pilferage, previously discussed in Chapter 7. It also includes such crimes as pickpocketing, purse-snatching, thefts from motor vehicles, thefts of motor vehicle parts and accessories, and other thefts, where *no* use of force or violence occurs. The person simply takes something that does not belong to him or her.

The value of the property is usually determined by the actual value at the time of the theft or the cost of replacing it in a reasonable time. The value determines if the offense is grand or petty larceny. State statutes establish the dollar amount above which a theft is considered grand larceny, a felony, and below which a theft is considered petty larceny, a misdemeanor.

One form of larceny/theft of special concern to security managers is cargo theft, which costs the business sector billions of dollars annually. Four key industries are affected: air, rail, truck, and maritime. A federal study places the annual losses due to theft of air cargo at $400 million; rail cargo at $600 million; truck-related cargo at $1.2 billion; and maritime cargo at $300 million. Such thefts frequently involve the cooperation of insiders.

These thefts can affect any mode of transportation and type of business. Because cargo thefts require organization and advance planning, organized crime syndicates often play a key role in both planning the theft and distributing the stolen merchandise. Stolen cargo can consist of valuable securities, drugs, precious metals, and even cigarettes and shoes. Stolen cargo is a valuable commodity with a readily available market through a chain of fences. Furthermore, stolen merchandise is usually difficult to trace and identify. The cargo theft problem can involve carriers, shippers, insurers, labor unions, employers, and employees, as discussed in Chapter 13.

---

*These reports are entitled *Crime in the United States* and are published yearly.
**Larceny/theft is used here, as the two terms are interchangeable. Some state statutes refer to larceny, others to theft. The Uniform Crime Reports use larceny/theft.

To prevent or reduce losses from larceny/theft, limit access to assets and use basic security equipment and procedures to deter employee pilferage as well as theft by nonemployees.

Specific types of employee pilferage and nonemployee theft in various businesses are discussed in Section Three.

## Burglary

**Burglary** is (1) entering a structure without the owner's consent (2) with the intent to commit a crime. Usually the crime is theft, but it may be another crime, such as rape or assault. Commercial burglaries are often committed in service stations, stores, schools, warehouses, office buildings, manufacturing plants, and the like. Often burglars specialize in one type of facility.

Entrance can be made in any number of ways, but the most common method is prying open a door or window—the jimmy method. It can also be made by simply walking through an unlocked door, an open window, a tunnel, or a ventilation shaft, or by remaining in a building after closing time. The smash-and-grab burglar breaks a display window and grabs whatever merchandise is available.

In many states, if a person is found in a structure and the person has no legal right to be there at that time, it is *presumed* the person intends to commit a crime, unless the suspect can prove otherwise.

Some states require an actual *breaking* into the structure—that is, a forced entry. Other states require that the structure be a *dwelling* or that the crime occur during the *nighttime*. It is provisions such as these that make it necessary for security managers to be familiar with the statutes of their own state to deal effectively with crimes that are attempted or actually committed.

These steps can prevent or reduce the risk of loss from burglary:

➤ Install and use good locks, adequate indoor and outdoor lighting, and an alarm system. This may be supplemented with security patrols.
➤ Keep valuables in a burglar-resistant safe or vault.
➤ Keep a minimum amount of cash on hand.
➤ Leave cash registers open and empty at closing time.
➤ Be sure all security equipment is functional before leaving.

The security checklist in Figure 9—1 might be used in assessing a facility's protection against burglary.

## Robbery

**Robbery** is (1) the unlawful taking of personal property (2) from the person or in the person's presence, (3) against the person's will by force

NAME: _____ PHONE: _____
ADDRESS: _____
PERSON INTERVIEWED: _____ OWNER ☐ OTHER ☐
CONSTRUCTION: WOOD ☐ METAL ☐ CONCRETE ☐ MASONRY ☐ OTHER _____
CONDITION:            EXCELLENT ☐          GOOD ☐          FAIR ☐

| DOORS | ADEQUATE | WOOD | METAL | GLASS | COMBINATION | NON-REMOVABLE HINGE PINS | |
|---|---|---|---|---|---|---|---|
| FRONT | ☐ YES  NO ☐ | ☐ | ☐ | ☐ | ☐ | YES ☐ | NO ☐ |
| REAR | ☐ YES  NO ☐ | ☐ | ☐ | ☐ | ☐ | YES ☐ | NO ☐ |
| SIDE | ☐ YES  NO ☐ | ☐ | ☐ | ☐ | ☐ | YES ☐ | NO ☐ |
| SIDE | ☐ YES  NO ☐ | ☐ | ☐ | ☐ | ☐ | YES ☐ | NO ☐ |

| LOCKS | ADEQUATE | DEAD BOLT | DROP BOLT | KEY IN KNOB | PADLOCK | SLIDE BOLT | OTHER |
|---|---|---|---|---|---|---|---|
| FRONT | ☐ YES  NO ☐ | ☐ | ☐ | ☐ | ☐ | ☐ | ☐ |
| REAR | ☐ YES  NO ☐ | ☐ | ☐ | ☐ | ☐ | ☐ | ☐ |
| SIDE | ☐ YES  NO ☐ | ☐ | ☐ | ☐ | ☐ | ☐ | ☐ |
| SIDE | ☐ YES  NO ☐ | ☐ | ☐ | ☐ | ☐ | ☐ | ☐ |

| LIGHTS | ADEQUATE | WEAK | NONE | LEFT ON | | LOCATION | |
|---|---|---|---|---|---|---|---|
| INTERIOR | ☐ YES  NO ☐ | ☐ | ☐ | ☐ YES  NO ☐ | | ☐ GOOD | BAD ☐ |
| EXTERIOR | ☐ YES  NO ☐ | ☐ | ☐ | ☐ YES  NO ☐ | | ☐ GOOD | BAD ☐ |
| FRONT | ☐ YES  NO ☐ | ☐ | ☐ | ☐ YES  NO ☐ | | ☐ GOOD | BAD ☐ |
| SIDE | ☐ YES  NO ☐ | ☐ | ☐ | ☐ YES  NO ☐ | | ☐ GOOD | BAD ☐ |
| SIDE | ☐ YES  NO ☐ | ☐ | ☐ | ☐ YES  NO ☐ | | ☐ GOOD | BAD ☐ |
| REAR | ☐ YES  NO ☐ | ☐ | ☐ | ☐ YES  NO ☐ | | ☐ GOOD | BAD ☐ |

| WINDOWS | ADEQUATE | BARS | GATE | MESH | LOCKS | |
|---|---|---|---|---|---|---|
| FRONT | ☐ YES  NO ☐ | ☐ | ☐ | ☐ | ☐ YES | NO ☐ |
| REAR | ☐ YES  NO ☐ | ☐ | ☐ | ☐ | ☐ YES | NO ☐ |
| SIDE | ☐ YES  NO ☐ | ☐ | ☐ | ☐ | ☐ YES | NO ☐ |
| SIDE | ☐ YES  NO ☐ | ☐ | ☐ | ☐ | ☐ YES | NO ☐ |

REMARKS:

| ALARMS | DOORS | | | WINDOWS | | | CEILING | | | WALLS | | |
|---|---|---|---|---|---|---|---|---|---|---|---|---|
| | Adequate | weak | none | Adequate | weak | none | Adequate | weak | none | Adequate | weak | none |
| LOCAL | ☐ | ☐ | ☐ | ☐ | ☐ | ☐ | ☐ | ☐ | ☐ | ☐ | ☐ | ☐ |
| CENTRAL | ☐ | ☐ | ☐ | ☐ | ☐ | ☐ | ☐ | ☐ | ☐ | ☐ | ☐ | ☐ |
| TELEPHONE | ☐ | ☐ | ☐ | ☐ | ☐ | ☐ | ☐ | ☐ | ☐ | ☐ | ☐ | ☐ |

SAFE:          VISIBLE FROM STREET ☐ YES NO ☐          ANCHORED ☐ YES  NO ☐
               LIGHTED ☐ YES NO ☐          ADEQUATE ☐ YES  NO ☐
CASH REGISTER:  VISIBLE FROM STREET ☐ YES NO ☐          ANCHORED ☐ YES  NO ☐
               LIGHTED ☐ YES NO ☐          ADEQUATE ☐ YES  NO ☐

OVERALL EVALUATION:   ☐ EXCELLENT   ☐ GOOD   ☐ FAIR   ☐ INADEQUATE
To the storekeeper:
This is part of a program being conducted by your Fargo Police Department to help you protect yourself against burglars. If you follow the recommendations in this report, you will make it more difficult for a burglar to enter your business.

Investigating officer _____ Telephone number _____
Burglary Prevention Team
Recommendations: _____ Compliance Date _____

**Figure 9–1 Security checklist.**
*Courtesy of Fargo, N.D. Police Department.*

or threat of force. The person from whom the property is taken need not be the owner of the property, but can be someone to whom the property has been entrusted. Usually "from the person or in the person's presence" means the victim actually sees the robber take the property, but this is not always the case. The robber may lock the victim in a room and then commit the robbery. This does not remove the crime "from the presence of the person" if the separation from the property is the direct result of force or threats of force used by the robber.

Most robberies are committed with a weapon or by indicating that a weapon is present and by a command suggesting that if the robber's demands are not met the victim will be harmed. The demands may be given orally or in a note; the threat may be against the victim, the victim's family, or another person with the victim. The possibility of violence and/or a hostage situation must always be considered if a robbery occurs.

These steps can prevent or reduce losses from robbery:

➤ Train employees how to react if a robbery occurs.
➤ Do not build up cash. Use armed couriers to transport cash.
➤ Establish strict opening and closing procedures, and use extreme caution if someone seeks entrance to the facility after hours.

All employees who are in positions where they might be involved in a robbery should know what to do should that occur. It should be stressed that heroics are *not* expected and could, in fact, be a deadly mistake. Robbers are completely unpredictable, but employees should be taught to follow the guidelines below to reduce the risks involved should a robbery occur:

➤ Stay calm.
➤ Do exactly as you are told.
➤ Assure the robber that you will cooperate totally, but do not volunteer to do anything.
➤ Treat any firearm displayed as though it is real and loaded.
➤ Activate alarms only if you can do so undetected.
➤ Try to alert others if possible.

To assist in investigating the robbery, employees should mentally note the robber's appearance, clothing, voice, and unique characteristics—anything distinctive. Some employers place a reference point on a wall or door frame to give employees who might face robbers something to use to estimate the robber's height.

## Correctly Classifying "Unlawful Taking"

The preceding discussions illustrate several types of **"unlawful taking"** security managers may encounter. It is important to keep the basic distinctions among these types of stealing separate.

*Larceny/theft* is the unlawful taking of the property of another without unlawful entrance or confrontation. *Burglary* includes unlawful taking *and* unlawful entry. *Robbery* includes unlawful taking *and* confrontation.

Private security is most often concerned with larceny/theft. However, the amount of losses sustained in a burglary or robbery may be significant if proper precautions are not followed. In addition, robbery carries with it the potential for violence.

## Trespassing and Vandalism

Two frequently encountered problems of private security managers are trespassing and vandalism. **Trespassing** refers to the unlawful presence of a person on the property or inside the premises of someone else. The trespasser may mean no harm; in fact, the trespass may be unintentional if boundaries are not clearly marked and signs are not posted. Often, however, trespassers may smoke where it may be hazardous, or they may intend to steal or to damage property. Trespassing on railroad property can be extremely hazardous. According to an executive of the Association of American Railways in Washington, D.C., some five to six hundred trespassing deaths related to railways occur yearly.

**Vandalism** refers to the malicious or intentional damaging and/or destroying of public or private property. It is also called criminal damage to property or malicious destruction of property.

The gravity of this crime depends on the extent of property damage. In one sense, destruction of property is more serious than theft because it eliminates the possibility of recovering the property. Intent is always a factor in vandalism. School buildings, factories, warehouses, vehicles, and homes are all vulnerable targets for the vandal. How much vandalism occurs internally in business and industry is not documented; however, it is likely to be a great amount. In some instances, vandalism may actually be sabotage. For example, assembly workers who become dissatisfied with their jobs may cause machinery breakdowns (to be discussed in Chapter 13).

Trespassing and vandalism can be prevented or reduced by strict access controls, security lighting, signs, and patrols.

No Trespassing signs can eliminate the excuse that the intruder's presence was "accidental."

## Assault

Some private security managers must face the risks to their employees from verbal or physical assault, including sexual assault. **Assault** refers to an attack upon a person.* It may be committed to cause bodily injury or may result while committing another crime, such as robbery or rape. Establishments having night shifts and those employing large numbers of women are especially susceptible to this risk.

---

*Some states distinguish between assault (threat) and battery (actual physical contact), but the trend is to combine them into a single crime termed *assault*.

The distance to parking lots is a key factor in employees' susceptibility to assault. When practical, this distance should be minimal. Parking areas should be well lit and fenced.

## Arson

**Arson** is the willful, malicious burning of property. It can be committed for financial gain, to hide other crimes such as burglary or embezzlement, for revenge, or as a form of terrorism.

Studies of arrested, institutionalized, and paroled arsonists reveal distinct behavioral categories. The works of Columbia University psychiatrists Nolan Lewis and Helen Yarnell and sociologist James Inciardi, for example, have found that various offender types commit arson for various reasons (Inciardi and Binder, 1983, p. 77).*

1) *Revenge arsonists*, the most prevalent type, are persons who, as the result of arguments or feelings of jealousy or hatred, seek revenge by fire. The victims are typically family members and relatives, employers, or lovers. In retaliation for real or imaginary wrongs, revenge arsonists set ablaze their victims' property or the premises in which they reside. These arsonists appear to be the most potentially dangerous of all types. They set occupied dwellings afire with little thought as to the safety of those within, thinking only of the revenge they must have on their specific victims. Furthermore, they are often intoxicated at the time of the offense. No elaborate incendiary devices are employed, typically only matches and gasoline. Although their crimes are premeditated, they take few steps to conceal their identities and are thus easily detected by alert investigators.

2) *Vandalism arsonists* include teenagers who willfully destroy property solely for purposes of fun and sport, although at times revenge motives may be partially present. As opposed to other arsonists, who work alone, vandalism arsonists usually have at least one accomplice. They tend to set fires at night in churches, school buildings, and vacant structures.

3) *Crime-concealment arsonists* set fire to premises where they have committed other offenses. The crime is usually burglary but sometimes murder, and the arson is an attempt to cover the traces of the criminal or obliterate the proof that another crime has taken place. Such fires are usually set at night in unoccupied dwellings or places of business.

4) *Insurance-claim arsonists* include insolvent property owners, small-business owners, small-business operators, and other individuals who, because of extreme financial pressure, incinerate their own

---

*Adapted with permission of The Free Press, a Division of Macmillan, Inc. from ENCYCLOPEDIA OF CRIME AND JUSTICE, Sanford H. Kadish, Editor in Chief. Copyright© 1983 by The Free Press.

property to collect the insurance on what has been destroyed. As a rule they do not set fire to occupied dwellings, and their offenses generally take place in the daytime.

5) *Excitement arsonists* set buildings ablaze for the thrill connected with fires. Some like setting or watching fires whereas others enjoy viewing the operations of fire fighters and fire equipment. (Occasionally a volunteer fire fighter is found among them.) Their offenses take place at night, they rarely set ablaze anything but uninhabited buildings, and they are usually intoxicated at the time of the offense.

6) *Pyromaniacs* are pathological firesetters. They seem to have no practical reasons for setting the fires and receive no material profit from them. Their only motive seems to be some sort of sensual satisfaction, and the classic "irresistible impulse" is often a factor.

Common sites for setting fires include the basement; stockrooms; duplicating, file, and mail rooms; and utility closets. Access control to such areas is critical to preventing arson.

Security managers might suspect arson in a fire where one of the three elements of the fire triangle is present in abnormal amounts. Greater than normal *oxygen* can come from opened windows, doors, pried-open vents, or holes knocked in walls. Piled-up newspapers, excelsior, or other combustible materials present at or brought to the scene can provide abnormal amounts of *fuel*. Excessive *heat* can be caused by accelerants, including gasoline (the most commonly used), kerosene, turpentine, or paint remover.

Another indicator of arson is an **igniter**, including matches, candles, cigars, cigarettes, cigarette lighters, explosives, and electrical, mechanical, and chemical devices. Time fuses, shorted light switches, electrical devices left in the "on" position, kerosene-soaked papers in wastepaper baskets, magnifying glasses, matches tied around a lighted cigarette, and numerous other igniters have been used to commit arson.

Yet another indication of arson is the presence of **trailers**, paths of paper or accelerants used to spread the fire from one location to another. Arsonists may also set multiple fires to ensure complete destruction, and they may disable the fire-fighting apparatus. Any of the preceding would be strong evidence of arson.

---

Security managers should suspect arson in fires that:

➤ Have more than one point of origin.
➤ Deviate from normal burning patterns.
➤ Show evidence of trailers.
➤ Show evidence of having been accelerated.
➤ Indicate an abnormal amount of air, fuel, or heat present.
➤ Reveal evidence of incendiary igniters at the point of origin.
➤ Produce odors or smoke of a color associated with substances not normally present at the scene.

---

Other suspicious circumstances include goods being removed from the premises shortly before a fire occurs, over-insurance, economic difficulties of the owner, surplus out-of-date or damaged inventory, or needed repairs—perhaps to comply with violations discovered by an OSHA inspector.

According to the UCR Program, arson is the fastest-growing crime in the United States today. In 1989, 99,599 cases of arson were reported.

Every fire, no matter how small, should be investigated and the cause determined so that corrective steps can be taken to prevent a recurrence.

## White-Collar Crime

The Chamber of Commerce of the United States has described **white-collar crimes** as "illegal acts characterized by guile, deceit, and concealment . . . not dependent upon the application of physical force or violence or threats thereof. They may be committed by individuals acting independently or by those who are part of a well-planned conspiracy. The objective may be to obtain money, property, or services; to avoid the payment or loss of money, property, or services; or to secure business or personal advantage."

White-collar crime is business-related crime.

Included among white-collar crimes are bankruptcy fraud; bribery, kickbacks, and payoffs; computer-related crime; consumer fraud; illegal competition and deceptive practices; credit card and check fraud; embezzlement and pilferage; insurance fraud; receiving stolen property; and securities thefts and frauds. Pilferage, a form of larceny/theft, is of prime concern.

According to the Chamber, the yearly cost of embezzlement and pilferage reportedly exceeds by several billion dollars the losses sustained throughout the nation from burglary and robbery.

A special report of the Bureau of Justice Statistics (1987) says:

> Although white collar offenses are less visible than crimes such as burglary and robbery, their overall economic impact may be considerably greater. Among the white collar cases filed by U.S. Attorneys in the year ending September 30, 1985, more than 140 persons were charged with offenses estimated to involve over $1 million each, and 64 were charged with offenses valued at over $10 million each. In comparison, losses from all bank robberies reported to police in 1985 were under $19 million, and losses from all robberies reported to police in 1985 totaled about $313 million.

Pilferage, or internal theft, is an important concern of private security managers.

Gordon (1990, p. 12) notes figures from the U.S. Department of Commerce stating that employees walk off with $40 billion in goods every year. Further, the American Management Association estimates that employee theft causes 20 percent of all business failures.

Gordon (p. 13) urges that the best way to avoid employee theft in the first place is to hire honest employees and maintain an environment that encourages honesty. She suggests that the single best deterrent is fear of being caught.

The Department of Labor says that employees suspected of theft are often involved in other types of misconduct such as unauthorized absences, chronic tardiness, and violation of basic rules (Gordon, p. 13). Many businesses consider internal theft, by an embezzler or a pilferer, their number-one security problem. According to Braithwaite and Fisse (1987, p. 221), "Literature shows us that corporate crime is responsible for more property loss and more injuries to persons than is crime in the streets." They also note (pp. 240–41):

> Companies must be concerned not to put employees under so much pressure to achieve the economic goals of the organization that they cut corners with the law. The role of excessive performance pressures on middle managers in creating corporate crime has been frequently pointed to by the literature. . . .
>
> At one extreme are companies that calculatedly set goals for their managers that they know can only be achieved by breaking the law. Thus, the pharmaceutical chief executive may tell her regional medical director to do whatever he has to do to get a product approved for marketing in a Latin American country, when she knows this will mean paying a bribe. Likewise, the coal mining executive may tell his mine manager to cut costs when he knows this will mean cutting corners on safety.
>
> The mentality of "Do what you have to do but don't tell me how you do it" is widespread in business.

Often computers are involved in white-collar crime. Because this is such a serious problem for many establishments, the next chapter focuses on this relatively recent problem.

## □ ALCOHOL AND OTHER DRUGS IN THE WORKPLACE

Although some drug users report that drugs such as cocaine increase their concentration and improve their performance on a variety of tasks, no concrete evidence supports such statements. Most drugs are short-acting, with the effects wearing off within an hour, leaving the user tired and depressed. In addition, users may steal to support their habit.

Drugs commonly abused in the workplace include alcohol, marijuana, and cocaine—snorted or smoked as freebase or crack.

**Marijuana**, according to Wrobleski and Hess (1990, pp. 413–14), " . . . is probably the most socially acceptable of the illegal drugs. . . . When smoked, marijuana enters the bloodstream quickly, causing rapid onset of symptoms. The effects of the drug on the user's mood and thinking vary widely, depending on the amount and strength of the marijuana as well as the social setting and the effects anticipated. The drug usually takes effect in about fifteen minutes and lasts from two to four hours. 'Social' doses of one or two cigarettes may cause an increased sense of well-being; initial restlessness and hilarity followed by a dreamy, carefree state of relaxation; alteration of sensory perceptions including expansion of space and time; and/or a more vivid sense of touch, sight, smell, taste, and sound; a feeling of hunger, especially craving for sweets; and subtle changes in thought formation and expression."

**Cocaine** is a white crystalline powder extracted from the South American coca plant. Until recently, most users "snorted" cocaine, that is, they inhaled the powdered mixture. The effects appear within minutes, including dilated pupils and increased blood pressure, heart rate, breathing rate, and body temperature. The user initially feels a sense of well-being and may feel more energetic or alert, but within thirty minutes to an hour, is likely to feel down and depressed.

Another form of cocaine is **freebase**, which is made by chemically converting the street drug into a basic form that can be smoked. This is an extremely dangerous, yet popular, practice. Freebase is smoked in a water pipe and is more dangerous than snorting because the cocaine reaches the brain within seconds, producing a sudden, intense high. The symptoms of freebasing cocaine include weight loss, increased heart rate and blood pressure, depression, paranoia, and hallucinations.

The most pressing concern in recent times has been the use of **crack**, the street name given to freebase cocaine that has been processed from cocaine hydrochloride to a base, using ammonia or baking soda and water and heating it to remove the hydrochloride. It resembles hard shavings like slivers of soap and is sold in small vials, folding papers, or heavy aluminum foil. Like freebase, it is smoked in a pipe. Alarmingly, one or two doses of crack can be obtained for from five to ten dollars, making it available to almost everyone. In fact, it has been called the "poor-man's coke."

Bennett and Hess (1991, p. 582) stress that drug addicts frequently become unfit for employment as their mental, emotional, and physical condition deteriorates. They list the following possible symptoms of drug abuse:

➤ Sudden and dramatic changes in discipline and job performance.
➤ Unusual degrees of activity or inactivity.
➤ Sudden and irrational flareups.
➤ Significant change in personal appearance for the worse.
➤ Dilated pupils or wearing sunglasses at inappropriate times or places.
➤ Needle marks or razor cuts, or long sleeves constantly worn to hide such marks.
➤ Sudden attempts to borrow money or to steal.
➤ Frequent association with known drug abusers or pushers.

The addict is generally an unkempt person, appears drowsy, does not feel well, has copious quantities of tears or mucous in eyes and nose, and suffers from alternate chills and fever. Needle marks resembling tattoos may be present in the curve of the arm at the elbow or, after prolonged drug use, in other areas of the body.

Table 9–1 summarizes the physical symptoms, what to look for, and the dangers of the most commonly abused drugs.

**Table 9–1 Common symptoms, what to look for, and dangers of commonly abused drugs.**

| Drug Used | Physical Symptoms | Look For | Dangers |
|---|---|---|---|
| ALCOHOL (beer, wine, liquor) | Intoxication, slurred speech, unsteady walk, relaxation, relaxed inhibitions, impaired coordination, slowed reflexes. | Smell of alcohol on clothes or breath, intoxicated behavior, hangover, glazed eyes. | Addiction, accidents as a result of impaired ability and judgment, overdose when mixed with other depressants, heart and liver damage. |
| COCAINE (coke, rock, crack, base) | Brief intense euphoria, elevated blood pressure & heart rate, restlessness, excitement, feeling of well-being followed by depression. | Glass vials, glass pipe, white crystalline powder, razor blades, syringes, needle marks. | Addiction, heart attack, seizures, lung damage, severe depression, paranoia (see Stimulants). |
| MARIJUANA (pot, dope, grass, weed, herb, hash, joint) | Altered perceptions, red eyes, dry mouth, reduced concentration and coordination, euphoria, laughing, hunger. | Rolling papers, pipes, dried plant material, odor of burnt hemp rope, roach clips. | Panic reaction, impaired short-term memory, addiction. |
| HALLUCINOGENS (acid, LSD, PCP, MDMA, Ecstasy psilocybin mushrooms, peyote) | Altered mood and perceptions, focus on detail, anxiety, panic, nausea synaesthesia (ex: smell colors, see sounds). | Capsules, tablets, "microdots", blotter squares. | Unpredictable behavior, emotional instability, violent behavior (with PCP). |
| INHALANTS (gas, aerosols, glue, nitrites, Rush, White out) | Nausea, dizziness, headaches, lack of coordination and control. | Odor of substance on clothing and breath, intoxication, drowsiness, poor muscular control. | Unconsciousness, suffocation, nausea and vomiting, damage to brain and central nervous system, sudden death. |
| NARCOTICS Heroin (junk, dope, Black tar, China white) Demerol, Dilaudid (D's) Morphine, Codeine | Euphoria, drowsiness, insensitivity to pain, nausea, vomiting, watery eyes, runny nose (see Depressants). | Needle marks on arms, needles, syringes, spoons, pinpoint pupils, cold moist skin. | Addiction, lethargy, weight loss, contamination from unsterile needles (hepatitis, AIDS), accidental overdose. |
| STIMULANTS (speed, uppers, crank, Bam, black beauties, crystal, dexies, caffeine, nicotine, cocaine, amphetamines) | Alertness, talkativeness, wakefulness, increased blood pressure, loss of appetite, mood elevation. | Pills and capsules, loss of sleep and appetite, irritability or anxiety, weight loss, hyperactivity. | Fatigue leading to exhaustion, addiction, paranoia, depression, confusion, possibly hallucinations. |
| DEPRESSANTS Barbiturates, Sedatives, Tranquilizers, (downers, tranks, ludes, reds, Valium, yellow jackets, alcohol) | Depressed breathing and heartbeat, intoxication, drowsiness, uncoordinated movements. | Capsules and pills, confused behavior, longer periods of sleep, slurred speech. | Possible overdose, especially in combination w/alcohol; muscle rigidity; addiction, withdrawal & overdose require medical treatment. |

©1991 "Drug Education Guide," The Positive Line #79930. Positive Promotions, 222 Ashland Place, Brooklyn, N.Y. 11217.

As noted by Wrich (1988, p. 64):

The National Institute on Drug Abuse (NIDA) and the National Institute of Alcohol Abuse and Alcoholism (NIAAA) estimate that at least 10 percent of the workforce is afflicted with alcoholism or drug addiction. Another 10 to 15 percent is affected by the substance abuse of an immediate family member. Still more bear the scars of having grown up with an addicted or alcoholic parent.

All in all, even after eliminating duplicates, at least 25 percent of any given workforce suffers from substance abuse—their own or someone else's.

This is one out of every four employees—certainly of importance to employers. Wrich (p. 64) further notes Alcohol, Drug Abuse and Mental Health Administration figures indicating that alcohol and drug abusers together cost the country more than $140 billion annually, including $100 billion in lost productivity.

Further, in *Largo v. Crespin* (1986), a Colorado Supreme Court ruled that an employer or proprietor could be held liable for the conduct of an intoxicated employee or patron if the drinking occurred at work or at the place of business.

## Drug Testing

Kahler (1991, p. 8D) reports on several studies dealing with drug testing in U.S. businesses:

➤ A 1989 study by the Bureau of Labor Statistics found that 43 percent of the nation's largest businesses, having more than one thousand employees, had drug-testing programs. But since 90 percent of U.S. businesses are small, the bureau estimated that only 3 percent of establishments overall had drug-testing programs.
➤ The Institute for Drug-Free Workplace says 80 percent of *Fortune* 500 companies require preemployment drug testing, although only a few require random testing of their entire work force.

"Tools" of the drug addict and a pipe used to smoke freebase or crack.

➤ The Journal of the American Medical Association (JAMA) reported in November 1990 on a two-year study of more than twenty-five hundred postal workers that found that employees who tested positive for marijuana had 55 percent more industrial accidents, 85 percent more injuries, and 78 percent more absenteeism than those who were free of drugs.

➤ Motorola will spend more than $1 million to implement the program in which every employee is tested for illicit drug use at least once every five years. For that investment, the company believes it will save more than $100 million in lost or unproductive employee time.

Lee Dogoloff, executive director of the American Council for Drug Education, says: "Drug testing has become a fact of life for anyone applying for a job in a major corporation. It's also a fact of life for anyone who holds a safety or security sensitive position in government" (Kahler, p. 8D).

To set up a drug-testing program, Wrich (1988, p. 66) suggests most employers do the following:

➤ Prepare a written policy and procedure statement.
➤ Train supervisors to recognize the signs and symptoms that would justify reasonable suspicion of drug use.
➤ Obtain and test a sample of the employee's urine.
➤ Confirm all positive tests with a second, more accurate test.
➤ Require retesting without notice for those who complete treatment.
➤ Establish serious disciplinary measures, often termination, for those who test positive after undergoing treatment.

To make a drug-testing initiative (DTI) effective, Wrich (p. 68) says an organization should:

➤ Have an effective employee assistance program already in place.
➤ Familiarize itself with the technical and legal limitations of a DTI and consider the possible negative effect on employee relations.
➤ Place control and direction of the DTI in the hands of its human resource department with input from its legal department, not the other way around.
➤ Convince supervisors and employees of the need for drug testing and give them reason to trust and support the program.
➤ Require drug testing of everyone in the organization from the CEO on down.
➤ Establish criteria in advance for maintaining confidentiality and evaluating effectiveness.

**A CASE AGAINST DRUG TESTING**  Bearman (1988, p. 67) makes a case against drug testing, saying:

> Employees have been known to smuggle in clean urine, . . . to drink large quantities of water to dilute their samples, and even to obtain prescriptions for legal drugs known to test positive. . . .
> The mere indication of the drug does not tell us whether the employee has used the drug once or a hundred times. . . .

Ibuprofen, a painkiller found in Advil, Datril, Rufen, and other over-the-counter medications can cause a false positive for marijuana. Ephedrin, an ingredient of Nyquil, can test positive for amphetamines. Dextromathorphon, found in many cough suppressants, has tested positive for opiates. False positives may also result from laboratory errors such as mislabeling urine or transposing results, or from improperly cleaned equipment, incompetence, or out-and-out fraud. . . .

In a litigious society, employers are well-advised to do two confirmatory tests. . . .

Even without litigation, testing is expensive. Most tests range from $7.50 to $70 each and companies must add the costs of administration, supervision, and lost work time. Last but hardly least, the cost to employee morale cannot be measured.

In *Hazlett v. Martin Chevrolet* (1987), an Ohio Supreme Court ruled that an employer did not violate the state's handicap laws by firing an employee addicted to drugs. But in *Glide Lumber Products Company v. Employment Division* (1987), an Oregon court of appeals ruled that a positive drug test, by itself, was not sufficient grounds to fire an employee. The employer must also show that the drug use negatively affected the employee's job performance.

In *National Treasury Employees Union v. Von Raab* (1989) the Court ruled that an employer, the U.S. Customs Service, could require job applicants applying for sensitive positions to undergo drug and alcohol testing. Such testing did not violate an employee's Fourth Amendment privacy rights.

**AN ALTERNATIVE METHOD OF DRUG TESTING**   The Old Town Trolley in San Diego tests strictly for impairment using a thirty-second computer examination that checks hand-eye coordination and psychomotor responses. The test detects motor impairment whether it is caused by drugs, alcohol, stress, or fatigue. It is the impairment, not the cause, that is important. Every employee completes the test every morning.

## □ OTHER CRIMES

Several other crimes, such as shoplifting, bad-check writing, espionage, and sabotage are discussed in following chapters, as they relate more specifically to certain types of establishments.

## □ ENFORCING PROPRIETARY RIGHTS

Not all crimes will be prevented. When they are not, security responsibilities change. According to the Rand Report (Kakalik and Wildhorn, 1977, p. 303):

> While many business organizations hire private policemen for the deterrence effect that results from their mere physical presence, they also expect their private security officers to take certain actions when confronted with disturbances, crimes, and threats to life and property. Therefore private security officers perform various law enforcement and protection functions, including arresting and detaining suspected shoplifters, ejecting persons from private

property, quieting disturbances, and defending against potential attackers. These activities, akin to public police functions, may create a great risk of infringement upon the rights of innocent citizens. . . .

In general the major contract agency will attempt to restrain the apprehension, search, and questioning activities of their personnel . . . whenever possible all matters of arrest and search [are] turned over to the local police authorities.

It is often not possible to simply leave the matter up to local authorities, however. Security managers are expected to *act* to protect the assets of their employers.

Security managers may be called on to enforce the following rights:

- ➤ Prevent trespassing.
- ➤ Control conduct of persons legally on premises.

- ➤ Defend self, others, and property.
- ➤ Prevent the commission of a crime.

How these rights are enforced varies from establishment to establishment. Standards and procedures for arresting, searching, and questioning persons should be clearly defined, because mistakes in these areas can result in either criminal or civil lawsuits, or both. Security managers should be thoroughly familiar with their state laws regarding the enforcement activities of private security. As in other areas of private security, common sense and reasonable actions are critical.

## ☐ EXPELLING, DETAINING, AND ARRESTING

To prevent trespassing or to control the conduct of persons legally on the premises, private security personnel may be used in retail establishments as plainclothes personnel to detect shoplifters; in industrial complexes as patrols to deter burglars; in offices as access control personnel; or at sporting and entertainment events to expel gatecrashers and control or expel unruly spectators. Officers can use reasonable force to do so, if needed. Frequently, however, the person being expelled will consent to leave. In such cases, no force is justified.

In many states, private security personnel can do the following:

- ➤ Detain persons suspected of shoplifting.
- ➤ Make a citizen's arrest of persons who commit a misdemeanor in their presence.
- ➤ Make a citizen's arrest of persons who commit a felony if they have probable cause.

The report of the Task Force on Private Security (1976, p. 391) notes that:

The power of citizen's arrest is not a simple matter. The arrest power is complex and often ambiguous. It may be filled with legal pitfalls and may depend on a number of legal distinctions, such as the nature of the crime being committed, proof of actual presence, and the time and place of the incident.

Because of these difficulties, the private security worker has to know the laws of the local jurisdiction. Improper action in making an arrest can expose the security worker and his employer to civil suits involving charges of false imprisonment, battery, assault, and malicious prosecution. An example of the seriousness of improper arrests by security personnel, as noted in *Security Systems Digest*, is the New York case in which a woman was awarded $1.1 million by the jury in a false arrest and wrongful detention civil suit.

Table 9–2 summarizes the statutory arrest authority of private citizens in the thirty states having such statutes.

Every citizen has the right to arrest a person who is committing or has committed a crime and to turn that person over to the local police. This is called a **citizen's arrest**. However, the extent and power of citizen's arrest authority varies from state to state. Arrest power often depends on whether the offense is a felony or a misdemeanor. In most states, citizens can make an arrest for a misdemeanor only if they actually see the crime committed. They can make an arrest for a felony if they know a felony has been committed and they are reasonably sure the person they arrest committed it.

A citizen's arrest is valid only if the person making the arrest intends to turn the suspect over to local law enforcement officers as soon as possible. The arrested person cannot be detained for questioning or to obtain a confession. Security officers can be sued for an unreasonable delay in turning a suspect over to the police.

In many states, exceptions to the preceding restrictions on arrests are made for instances involving shoplifting. Because most cases of shoplifting are misdemeanors and are not always witnessed by security officers, and because many cases of shoplifting are not prosecuted, several states stipulate that a person suspected of shoplifting can be *detained* for questioning and sometimes for searching. Detention differs from formal arrest in that arrest requires the suspect to be turned over to the authorities.

If an arrest is made, the arrested person must be told the reason for the arrest. Often a citizen's arrest certificate is completed by the arresting citizen (see Figure 9–2).

## ☐ THE USE OF FORCE

Force can be used only when and to the extent that it is necessary. Deadly force can be used only to protect human life.

What is "reasonable" force depends on the nature of the interest being protected, the kind of act being resisted, and the specific facts in a given situation. Additionally, the amount of force allowed often depends on what right is being defended. If property rights are involved, a request for voluntary cooperation should precede any use of force. If only property is involved, the use of deadly force, a gun, for instance, is *not* permitted.

# Table 9-2 Statutory arrest authority of private citizens.*

| | Minor Offense — Type | | | | | | Minor Offense — Knowledge Required | | | | Major Offense — Type | | | | | | | Major Offense — Knowledge Required | | | | | | Certainty of Correct Arrest | | |
|---|---|---|---|---|---|---|---|---|---|---|---|---|---|---|---|---|---|---|---|---|---|---|---|---|---|---|
| | Crime | Misdemeanor amounting to a breach of the peace | Breach of the peace | Public offense | Offense other than an ordinance | Indictable offense | Presence | Immediate knowledge | View | Upon reasonable grounds that it is being committed | Felony | Larceny | Petit larceny | Crime involving physical injury to another | Crime | Crime involving theft or destruction of property | Committed in presence | Information a felony has been committed | View | Reasonable grounds to believe being committed | That felony has been committed in fact | Is escaping or attempting | Summoned by peace officer to assist in arrest | Is in the act of committing | Reasonable grounds to believe person arrested committed | Probable cause |
|---|---|---|---|---|---|---|---|---|---|---|---|---|---|---|---|---|---|---|---|---|---|---|---|---|---|---|
| Alabama | | | | X | | | X | | | | X | | | | | | | | | | X | | | | X | |
| Alaska | X | | | | | | X | | | | X | | | | | | | | | | X | | | | X | |
| Arizona | | X | | | | | X | | | | X | | | | | | | | | | X | | | | X | |
| Arkansas | | | | | | | | | | | X | | | | | | | | | X | | | | | X | |
| California | | | | X | | | X | | | | X | | | | | | | | | | X | | | | X | |
| Colorado | X | | | | | | X | | | | | | | | X | | X | | | | | | | | | |
| Georgia | | | | | | X | X | X | | | X | | | | | | X | | | | | X | | | X | |
| Hawaii | X | | | | | | X | | | | | | | | X | | X | | | | | | | X | | |
| Idaho | | | | X | | | X | | | | X | | | | | | | | | | X | | | | X | |
| Illinois | | | | | | X | | | | X | X | | | | | | | | | X | | | | | | |
| Iowa | | | | X | | | X | | | | X | | | | | | | | | | X | | | | X | |
| Kentucky | | | | | | | | | | | X | | | | | | | | | | X | | | | X | |
| Louisiana | | | | | | | | | | | X | | | | | | | | | | X | | | | | |
| Michigan | | | | | | | | | | | X | | | | | | | X | | | X | | X | | | |
| Minnesota | | | | X | | | X | | | | X | | | | | | | | | | X | | | | X | |
| Mississippi | | | X | | | X | X | | | | X | | | | | | | | | | X | | | | X | |
| Montana | | | | | X | | X | | | | X | | | | | | | | | | X | | | | X | |
| Nebraska | | | | | | | | | | | X | X | | | | | | | | | X | | | | X | |
| Nevada | | | | X | | | X | | | | X | | | | | | | | | | X | | | | X | |
| New York | | | | | X | | X | | | | X | | | | | | | | | | X | | | | | |
| N. Carolina** | | X | | | | | | | | | X | | | X | | X | | | | | | | | X | | X |
| N. Dakota | | | | X | | | X | | | | X | | | | | | | | | | X | | | | X | |
| Ohio | | | | | | | | | | | X | | | | | | | | | | X | X | | | X | |
| Oklahoma | | | | X | | | X | | | | X | | | | | | | | | | X | | | | X | |
| Oregon | X | | | | | | X | | | | | X | | | X | | X | | | | | | | | | X |
| S. Carolina | | | | | | | | | | | X | | | | | | | X | X | | | | | | | |
| S. Dakota | | | | X | | | X | | | | X | | | | | | | | | | X | | | | X | |
| Tennessee | | | | X | | | X | | | | X | | | | | | | | | | X | | | | X | |
| Texas | | | X | | | | X | | X | | X | | | | | | | X | X | | | | | | | |
| Utah | | | | X | | | X | | | | X | | | | | | | | | | X | | | | X | |
| Wyoming | | | | | | | | | | | X | X | | | | | | | | | X | | | | X | |

*For specific authority see referenced state code.
**Statute eliminates use of word "arrest" and replaces with "detention."

From Private Security, p. 397.

**CERTIFICATE AND DECLARATION OF ARREST BY PRIVATE PERSON
AND DELIVERY OF PERSON SO ARRESTED TO PEACE OFFICER**

DATE _____

TIME _____

PLACE _____

I, _____ , hereby declare and certify that I have arrested

(NAME) _____

(ADDRESS) _____

for the following reasons: _____

_____

_____

_____

_____

_____

and do hereby request and demand that you, _____ , a peace officer, take and conduct this person whom I have arrested to the nearest magistrate, to be dealt with according to law; and if no magistrate can be contacted before tomorrow morning, then to conduct this person to jail for safe keeping until the required appearance can be arranged before such magistrate, at which time I shall be present, and I will then and there sign, under oath, the appropriate complaint against this person for the offense which this person has committed, and for which I made this arrest; and I will then and there, or thereafter as soon as this criminal action or cause can be heard, testify under oath of and concerning the facts and circumstances involved herein. I will save said officer harmless from any and all claim for damage of any kind, nature, and description arising out of his or her acts at my direction.

Name of private person making this arrest

_____

Address _____

Peace Officer Witnesses to this statement

_____

_____

_____

**Figure 9-2 Sample citizen arrest form.**

Use of deadly force to prevent a crime is usually allowed only if the crime threatens life and no other means can prevent the crime. However, some jurisdictions do allow use of deadly force to prevent some felonies.

Force in *self-defense* is limited to that which is necessary to protect against a threatened injury. It is not reasonable to use force calculated to inflict death or serious bodily harm unless a person believes he or she is in similar danger and there is no other safe means of defense.

The question of use of deadly force most frequently arises in instances when security officers have used a gun to fulfill their responsibilities. Security officers who are required to carry a gun should be thoroughly trained in its use. Standard 2.6 of the Private Security Task Force Report (1976, pp. 107–8) stresses that "employees should not be allowed to carry firearms while performing private security duties unless they can demonstrate competency and proficiency in their use." Suggested training includes legal and policy restraints, firearms safety and care, and shooting ability.

## ☐ INVESTIGATING

According to the Private Security Task Force Report (1976, p. 24), investigative personnel are primarily concerned with obtaining information about any of the following:

➤ Crime or wrongs done or threatened.
➤ The identity, habits, conduct, movements, whereabouts, affiliations, associations, transactions, reputation, or character of any person, group of persons, association, organization, society, other groups or persons or partnership or corporation.
➤ Preemployment background check of personnel applicants.
➤ The conduct, honesty, efficiency, loyalty, or activities of employees, agents, contractors, and subcontractors.
➤ Incidents and illicit or illegal activities by persons against the employer or employer's property.
➤ Retail shoplifting.
➤ Internal theft by employees or other employee crime.
➤ The truth or falsity of any statement or representation.
➤ The location or recovery of lost or stolen property.
➤ The causes and origin of or responsibility for fires, libels or slanders, losses, accidents, damage, or injuries to real or personal property.
➤ The credibility of information, witnesses, or other persons.
➤ The securing of evidence to be used before investigating committees or boards of award or arbitration or in the trial of civil or criminal cases and the preparation thereof.

The Task Force Report (p. 9) notes that "investigative services may include preemployment investigation, surveillance, internal theft problems, undercover investigations, criminal investigations, polygraph examinations, and personal and property protection.

The EPPA stipulates that a lie detector can be used in the context of an ongoing investigation if the following conditions are met:

➤ The employer's business suffers the loss of injury and the wrongdoing was intentional.
➤ The employee must have had access to the property.
➤ There must be reasonable suspicion that the employee was involved.
➤ The employee must be given a statement explaining these facts before the test.

Investigations may involve searching as well as interviewing and interrogating.

## ☐ SEARCHING

The law clearly establishes the right of an arresting officer to search a person legally taken into custody to determine if the arrested person has a weapon that could cause harm to the officer or others. Any person who has been apprehended for committing a serious crime (a felony) should be searched. Some agencies advise their security officers to treat persons arrested for a felony as though they would kill the officer if given the chance.

---

Security officers usually have the authority to search a suspect's person and anything the person is carrying if the officers have a legitimate reason for detaining or arresting the suspect.

---

Most security searches do not involve arrests, however. They are conducted based on an established policy such as those discussed in Chapter 7 and involve cars, lunch boxes, lockers, purses, bags, and boxes. According to the Rand Report (Kakalik and Wildhorn, 1977, p. 324):

> The law of searches in the private sector has simply not been developed as it has in the public-police sector.
> The common-law right of self-defense might justify reasonable searches for weapons, but only where there is reasonable ground to fear imminent attack by use of a concealed weapon. Under the common law, the arresting individual is empowered to search a suspect who is *already under arrest.* . . . However, this power is limited to cases of formal arrest (i.e. where the person will be turned over to the authorities), not mere detention. . . . Additionally some states authorize private citizens in arresting a person to search for incriminating evidence about the person.

Even without an arrest, the common-law privilege of reclaiming stolen property would tend to support searching persons suspected of stealing. It is preferable if consent for the search can be obtained.

---

Any search must be conducted reasonably with the least possible use of force, intimidation, or embarrassment.

---

Searches should be conducted in private, except in emergencies. It is best to have the person conducting the search be of the same sex as the suspect, or, if this is not possible, to have a person of the same sex as the suspect be a witness to the search. Any weapons or evidence found during the search should be turned over to the local authorities if the person is arrested by security personnel. Stolen property found during such a search may be reclaimed by the rightful owner if no prosecution is to be undertaken.

In *United States v. Tartaglia* (1989), the Supreme Court ruled that a railroad investigator and Drug Enforcement Administration agents did not violate the defendant's Fourth Amendment rights when they acted on a tip about drugs being transported on an Amtrak train. The investgator and DEA agents located drugs in the defendant's suitcase with the assistance of drug-sniffing dogs.

# ☐ INTERVIEWING AND INTERROGATING

Security personnel are frequently responsible for questioning witnesses to or persons suspected of crime.

---

An *interview* is a controlled conversation with witnesses to or victims of a crime. An *interrogation* is a controlled conversation with persons suspected of direct or indirect involvement in a crime.

---

In actual practice, the difference between these two information-gathering processes is often blurred. What begins as an interview may end up as an interrogation. Security personnel should be instructed on how to make their questioning as efficient and effective as possible.

---

Interviewing and interrogating will be more effective if you:

➤ Prepare in advance.
➤ Obtain the information as soon as possible.
➤ Use a private setting and eliminate physical barriers.
➤ Establish rapport.
➤ Encourage conversation.
➤ Ask simple questions one at a time.
➤ Listen and observe.

---

## Preparation

If circumstances allow, the interviewer should learn as much as possible about the incident under investigation, including what information is needed and what relationship the person to be questioned has to the incident. Is the person friendly or hostile? Emotionally involved or an objective outsider?

Random questioning is seldom successful because it lacks direction and can indicate to the person being questioned that the interviewer is not prepared or does not know much about the incident.

## Timing

It is usually best to obtain information as soon as possible after an incident. People remember details better and also have less chance to fabricate a story or to think about the implications of becoming involved.

Sometimes, however, circumstances prevent immediate questioning. For example, it is best to delay questioning people who are emotionally upset. When emotions increase, memory decreases. Likewise, liquor, drugs, or physical discomfort may hinder effective communication. Someone who is cold, sleepy, hungry, or injured will usually be more concerned with his or her own condition than with answering questions.

## Setting

Whenever possible, interviews and interrogations should be conducted in private. People who fear their statements may be overheard are frequently reluctant to talk. Interruptions can also break a person's train of thought. Any outside interference, such as telephones ringing, noises from traffic passing, or office activity, detracts from the effectiveness of an inquiry.

Sometimes, however, the urgency of a situation requires that the questioning be done under adverse conditions. For example, private security officers may have to deal with a large crowd of people whose emotions are running high, with people shouting and contradicting one another. Obtaining accurate information under such circumstances is extremely difficult.

Physical barriers, such as a desk or counter, can also hinder effective communication and should be eliminated whenever possible.

## Rapport

The first few minutes of the conversation are important in establishing a friendly relationship, or rapport. This is accomplished by showing a sincere interest in the person being questioned, respecting the person's opinions and reactions, and trying to show the importance of cooperation. Frequently a person in a uniform with official credentials is seen as threatening. Some people fear or dislike authority and will not talk freely with officers of any kind. Others do not want to get involved. It takes skill to obtain information from such people.

## Possible Restrictions on Interrogations

*Public* law enforcement officers are required to inform suspects of their constitutional rights *before* any interrogation occurs. The well-known Miranda decision (*Miranda v. Arizona,* 1967) has specifically protected these rights since 1966. Many police officers carry a card containing the rights of citizens suspected of involvement in a crime (Figure 9–3).

Suspects can give up these rights (waive them), but if they do so, the waiver is usually obtained in writing to protect the officer.

Any statements or confessions resulting from police interrogation of a person in custody, under arrest, or accused of a crime are not admissible as evidence unless the appropriate warnings *precede* the interrogation.

The courts have not clearly established whether the same restrictions apply to private security officers. Lower courts addressing the issue have not yet required security officers to precede interrogations with a recital of the suspect's Miranda rights.

Calder (1980, p. 43) suggests that private security is often not bound by criminal justice system rules until the case enters the system at the charging stage. Some states have ruled that Miranda warnings do not apply to private security interviews because they are not done under the coercive threat of arrest by the police. In a California case (*Re Deborah C.*; 635 F.2d 446), a store detective placed a suspect under arrest without

```
┌──────────────────────────────────────────────────────────────────────┐
│                          MIRANDA WARNING                               │
│  1)  YOU HAVE THE RIGHT TO REMAIN SILENT.                              │
│  2)  IF YOU GIVE UP THE RIGHT TO REMAIN SILENT, ANYTHING YOU           │
│      SAY CAN AND WILL BE USED AGAINST YOU IN A COURT OF LAW.           │
│  3)  YOU HAVE THE RIGHT TO SPEAK WITH AN ATTORNEY AND TO               │
│      HAVE THE ATTORNEY PRESENT DURING QUESTIONING.                     │
│  4)  IF YOU SO DESIRE AND CANNOT AFFORD ONE, AN ATTORNEY               │
│      WILL BE APPOINTED FOR YOU WITHOUT CHARGE BEFORE QUES-             │
│      TIONING.                                                          │
│                             WAIVER                                     │
│  1)  DO YOU UNDERSTAND EACH OF THESE RIGHTS I HAVE READ TO             │
│      YOU?                                                              │
│  2)  HAVING THESE RIGHTS IN MIND, DO YOU WISH TO GIVE UP YOUR          │
│      RIGHTS AS I HAVE EXPLAINED TO YOU AND TALK TO ME NOW?             │
└──────────────────────────────────────────────────────────────────────┘
```

**Figure 9–3  Sample card listing suspect's rights—Miranda warning.**

out advising the suspect of his Miranda rights. The California Supreme Court held that Miranda warnings are not required because private security officers "don't enjoy the psychological advantage of official authority, which is a major tool of coercion." Employers, however, can use other forms of coercion, most notably the threat of terminating employment. On the other hand, businesses exist to make a profit and are not obligated to put the welfare of an employee above that of the company. Calder suggests that a correlation exists between the level of position, amount of power and socioeconomic standing of the employee in the company, and the subsequent amount of disciplinary action received. The higher a person's position in a company, the less disciplinary action is likely to be applied.

Despite the lack of an official ruling, many courts and judges require security officers to notify a suspect of these rights on the basis that they are, in reality, attempting to enforce the law, and in doing so must abide by public law enforcement standards. For example, in *People v. Haydel* (1973), the court ruled, in effect, that private store detectives used state law as authority and were, therefore, acting as agents of the state in the same manner as public police officers:

> The exclusionary rule is designed to deter illegal conduct by public officials, hence it is inoperative when the evidence is gained by a private citizen not acting as a public agent. The California Supreme Court has recognized, nevertheless, that the well trained and well financed private security forces of business establishments are heavily involved in law enforcement, that state laws such as Penal Code, Section 837, the citizen's arrest statute, blur the line between public and private law enforcement.

In *Wold v. State* (1989), a Minnesota court ruled that a confession given by a suspect under the influence of drugs or alcohol is admissible at trial.

Although this chapter has emphasized the role of the security officer in dealing with potential and actual crimes, remember that the majority of the security manager's time is spent dealing with noncriminal matters.

# SUMMARY

Security managers are responsible for preventing or reducing losses caused by criminal or civil offenses. A crime is an offense against the state for which punishment is sought. In contrast, a tort is an offense against an individual for which restitution is sought. A single action may be classified as both a crime and a tort.

The crimes of most concern to private security are larceny/theft, burglary, robbery, trespassing, vandalism, assault, arson; white-collar crime, including embezzlement, bad checks, and credit card fraud; and drugs in the workplace.

Losses from larceny/theft might be prevented or reduced by using the basic security equipment and procedures to deter employee pilferage and theft by nonemployees. Loss from burglary might be prevented or reduced by installing and using good locks, adequate indoor and outdoor lighting, and an alarm system, possibly supplemented with security patrols; keeping valuables in a burglar-resistant safe or vault; keeping a minimum amount of cash on hand; leaving cash registers open and empty at closing time; and being sure that all security equipment is functional before leaving.

Losses from robbery might be prevented or reduced by training employees how to react if a robbery occurs; by not building up cash; by using armed couriers to transport cash; by establishing strict opening and closing procedures; and by using extreme caution if someone seeks entrance to the facility after hours.

Larceny/theft, burglary, and robbery are often confused. Larceny/theft is the unlawful taking of the property of another without unlawful entrance or confrontation. Burglary includes unlawful taking and unlawful entry. Robbery includes unlawful taking and confrontation, that is, force or the threat of force.

Trespassing and vandalism can be prevented or reduced by strict access controls, security lighting, signs, and patrols. Assaults might be reduced by adequate lighting, patrols, communications systems, and/or escort services.

Security managers should suspect arson in fires that have more than one point of origin; deviate from normal burning patterns; show evidence of trailers; show evidence of having been accelerated; indicate an abnormal amount of air, fuel, or heat present; reveal evidence of incendiary igniters at the point of origin; or produce odors or smoke of a color associated with substances not normally present at the scene.

White-collar crime is business-related crime. One prevalent type of white-collar crime of special concern to private security managers is pilferage, or internal theft, a form of larceny. Bad checks and credit card fraud are also white-collar crimes.

Drugs commonly abused in the workplace include alcohol, marijuana, and cocaine—snorted or smoked as freebase or crack.

Not all crimes will be prevented. Security managers may be called on to enforce such rights as preventing trespassing, controlling the conduct of persons legally on the premises, defending lives or property, or preventing the commission of a crime. In many states, private security personnel can detain persons suspected of shoplifting and make citizen's arrests. Force can be used only when and to an extent that is reasonable and necessary. Deadly force can be used only to protect human life. Security officers also usually have the authority to search a suspect's person and anything the person is carrying if the officers have a legitimate reason for detaining or arresting the suspect. Any search must be conducted reasonably and with the least possible use of force, intimidation, or embarrassment to the suspect.

Security personnel may also be called upon to question witnesses and/or suspects. An interview is a controlled conversation with witnesses to or victims of crimes. An interrogation is a controlled conversation with persons suspected of direct or indirect involvement in a crime.

Interviewing and interrogating will be more effective if the person doing the questioning prepares in advance, obtains the information as soon as possible, uses a private setting and eliminates physical barriers, establishes rapport, encourages conversation, asks simple questions one at a time, listens, and observes.

## APPLICATION

1) While on patrol for the Smithtown Security Services, Kathy Ross pulls into the yard of a large warehouse where many semitrailer trucks are parked. As she patrols, her vehicle headlights shine on two juveniles hiding behind one of the tractor wheels. She also notices that the tire is going flat. As she orders the two juveniles to come out, she notices that one of them throws an instrument away. She has them retrieve it and, on inspection, sees it is an icepick. Further investigation reveals that two tires are flat, both having been punctured by what appears to be an icepick. Officer Ross arrests the juveniles and takes them to the police station. The youngsters, ages twelve and thirteen, have had extensive past contacts with police, all as the result of acts of vandalism.

   As manager of the Smithtown Security Services, how would you evaluate Officer Ross's actions?

2) The office manager of the Downtown Manufacturing Company states to the security manager that she has just apprehended Joe Myers, an employee, carrying an office typewriter out the side door of the building, and she is detaining him. The office manager demands that the security manager call the police and have Myers charged with robbery. If you were the security manager, how would you respond to this demand?

3) You are the security director called by the president of the Uptown Department Store to investigate the open, empty safe the president discovered when he went into his office. How would you begin the investigation? What information would you need to obtain?

4) As a member of the Housing Authority Security Police, you are confronted with numerous investigations concerning a rash of arson fires. You are requested to give a presentation as to what the statistics of the current FBI Uniform Crime Report reveal as to patterns, arrests, and types of arson most frequently committed. Obtain from the library the latest FBI Uniform Crime Report and give a presenta-

tion to the class as if you were talking to the residents of a public housing complex.

## DISCUSSION QUESTIONS

1) Private security officers are sometimes asked to arrest people. As a security director, what policies or guidelines would you adopt to cover these situations?
2) Discuss the advantages and disadvantages of private security officers carrying firearms.
3) What differences exist between interviewing a witness and interrogating a suspect?
4) Compare the statutory arrest authority of private citizens (p. 240) with those of public police officers in your state. How do the arrest powers of private security officers compare with those of public police officers in your state?
5) Why are some crimes divided into categories or degrees?

## REFERENCES

Bearman, David. The medical case against drug testing. *Security management*, June 1988, p. 67.

Bennett, W. and Hess, K. M. *Criminal investigation*, 3d ed. St. Paul, MN: West Publishing Company, 1991.

Braithwaite, John and Fisse, Brent. Self-regulation and the control of corporate crime. In *Private policing*, by Clifford D. Shearing and Philip C. Stenning, eds. Beverly Hills, CA: Sage Publications, 1987, pp. 221–46.

Bureau of Justice Statistics Special Report. *White collar crime*. Washington, DC: U.S. Department of Justice, September 1987, pp. 1–8.

Calder, J. D. The security-criminal justice connection: Toward the elimination of separate-but-equal status. *Journal of security administration*, Spring 1980, p. 43.

*Crime in the United States*. FBI Uniform Crime Reports, United States Department of Justice, Washington, DC: U.S. Government Printing Office, August 5, 1990.

Cunningham, W. C. and Taylor, T. H. *The Hallcrest report: Private security and police in America*. Portland, OR: Chancellor Press, 1985.

Gordon, Marsha. Employee theft. *Independent business*, July/August 1990, pp. 12–13.

Inciardi, J. A. and Binder, D. Arson. In *Encyclopedia of crime and justice*, by Sanford H. Kadish, ed. New York: The Free Press, 1983, pp. 76–82.

Kahler, Kathryn. Drug testing is no longer dreaded in the workplace. *Minneapolis star tribune*, January 20, 1991, p. 8D.

Kakalik, J. S. and Wildhorn, S. *The private police*. New York: Crane Russak, 1977 (The Rand Corporation).

*Private security*. Report of the Task Force on Private Security, National Advisory Committee on Criminal Justice Standards and Goals. Washington, DC: U.S. Government Printing Office, 1976.

Rea, Kelley V. EPPA: The fine print. *Security management*, May 1989, pp. 49–55.

Sutherland, E. H. and Cressey, D. R. *Criminology*, 10th ed. New York: J. B. Lippincott, 1978.

Wrich, Manes T. Beyond testing: Coping with drugs at work. *Security management*, June 1988, pp. 64–73.

Wrobleski, H. and Hess, K. M. *Introduction to law enforcement and criminal justice*, 3rd ed. St. Paul, MN: West Publishing Company, 1990.

## □ INTRODUCTION

Dickey (1985, p. 29), in "Is Getting in Getting out of Control?" cites the example of two programmers responsible for maintaining computer files of all purchases made by an oil company plant. The programmers created a dummy supply company and then manipulated their company's database to show the fictitious vendor as a regular supplier to the plant. As a result, the computer registered receiving both materials and invoices from the dummy company. Dickey notes that "for two years, the plant bought its own inventory twice— embezzlement to the tune of several million dollars. The programmers were eventually caught by a fluke audit. The company decided not to prosecute because it did not want to call attention to how easily its database was invaded or how long it took to discover that invasion. Ironically, the two programmers were promoted—and put in charge of computer security."

In another instance, a computer support consulting firm offered diagnostic packs to troubleshoot problems with specific computer programs. While they were troubleshooting a particular program, they also made copies of the client's records. They then tried to sell these records to the client's competitors. In fact, the selling of stolen information was the primary source of income for this consulting firm; the diagnostic service was simply a cover to gain access to the records.

The invention of the microchip in 1976, leading to the development of the personal computer, has revolutionized our lives. In 1989, about fifty million corporate personal computers were in use. By the year 2000, the total should exceed two hundred million computers. In addition there has been a tremendous proliferation of personal computers (PCs) and modems (telephone devices that can connect one computer to another). Computers control the airplanes flying overhead and the subways running underfoot. They have changed the way teachers instruct students, physicians practice medicine, architects design buildings, and corporations conduct business. They have made it possible for us to land astronauts on the moon and to begin exploration of outer space. *Computers and the Law* (1984) warns of another result of the growth in computer technology: "The power of the personal computer is awesome. The technology is transforming the world we live in. However, it is also spawning a new breed of criminal and a new type of crime."

Computer security is an important example of the new frontiers opening up in the loss prevention field in response to social and technological changes. Electronic data processing personnel have responsibility

## Chapter Ten

# Enhancing Computer Security

### DO YOU KNOW

➤ What constitutes computer crime?

➤ How serious computer crime is?

➤ What the greatest threats to computer centers are?

➤ What legislation pertains to computer crime?

➤ What security measures can be taken to reduce losses from computer crime?

➤ What factors to consider when investigating a computer crime?

➤ Who the typical "electronic criminal" is?

➤ What the probability of detection of computer crimes and the risk of prosecution are?

as coordinators, analysts, and security consultants. Coordinators work with conventional security departments and are responsible for implementing and maintaining computer security systems. An analyst usually is responsible for security inspections, surveys, and reviewing any threats to the security system.

## ☐ COMPUTER CRIME DEFINED

The definitions of computer crime are varied, but generally include common elements.

Computer crime includes accessing a computer's database without authorization or exceeding authorization for the purpose of sabotage or fraud. It includes theft or destruction of software and hardware as well.

In the nineteenth century, Thomas Carlyle observed "Man is an animal who uses tools. Without tools, he is nothing, with tools he is all." Computers might be thought of as the ultimate tool, processing, transmitting, printing, and storing information at lightning speeds. Likewise, crimes can be committed using computers—crimes that are simple to commit and extremely difficult to detect. Because computer crime exists, computer security becomes mandatory for businesses and corporations. According to computer security consultant Bruce Goldstein of Total Assets Protection, Arlington, Texas, computer security is the protection of all assets, especially informational, from both humanmade and natural disasters. Computer security includes protecting data, telecommunications, personnel, and physical environment. It also includes formulating, implementing, and testing a protection plan, and knowing when and how to seek additional expertise.

## ✗ THE SERIOUSNESS OF THE PROBLEM

"The number of crimes involving computers is increasing dramatically throughout the country," say Manning and White (1990, p. 46). "There are documented offenses of every type—theft, fraud, burglary, prostitution, murder, child pornography—in which a computer was used in some way. Drug dealers and others involved in organized crime are using computers both to keep records and to facilitate the commission of other offenses."

*Computers and the Law* (1984) cites the estimate made by computer security specialist Sanford Sheridan that computer thieves steal hundreds of millions of dollars each year. It notes the Wells Fargo case which it calls "a stickup bigger than either the Brinks Armored Car Job or Britain's Great Train Robbery. Yet the bandits used no guns or getaway cars. Instead they used a computer to help pull off a colossal $21 million embezzlement. In another case, seven workers at a state welfare office in Miami were convicted of stealing $300,000 worth of food stamps by feeding false data into the agency's computer. Similarly, a bank employee in Bridgeport, Connecticut, was arrested for using the bank's computer to transfer $37,000 to her own bank account."

Computer crimes cost hundreds of millions of dollars annually. In fact computer crime or failure might destroy a business.

Many businesses rely extensively on electronic data processing (EDP) and could not function effectively for very long without their computer(s). Computer failure can destroy a company. Robert Huber, computer security expert with National Cash Register Company, suggests that a business that relies on computers will close its doors in three to five days if the computers fail. Yet computers are neither infallible nor invulnerable. Therefore, establishments that rely on computers cannot ignore the inherent risks involved in their use.

The computer is no longer mysterious, accessible to and usable by only an elite few. Grade-school students are routinely taught to use computers. Computer use has become an accepted, integral part of our way of life, allowing tremendous advances in science, medicine, business, and education. Unfortunately, many people in management do not take the computer as seriously as they should. This can have devastating consequences. As suggested by Dickey (1985, p. 34), "If a firm's top managers do not understand computer technology or what it does, they have, in effect, given up control over corporate information."

James Black, Bunco-Forgery Division of the Los Angeles Police Department, (1986, p. 31) states that "unprecedented levels of sophistication are being advanced daily in ways to commit conventionally defined crimes through the use of computers. . . . These crimes are potentially more devastating in their effect, can be technically complex, and require a higher degree of preparedness."

Terminals in a large data-processing center consisting of computers, memory storage, and high-speed printers.

Gardner, likewise, stresses the magnitude of the problem. He recalls the well-known comment of Willie Sutton, reformed bank robber, to the question of why he robbed banks. Sutton's reply: "That's where the money is." Gardner (1985, p. 331) suggests that "today, computers is where the money is. It is estimated that over 400 billion dollars is transferred every day through commercial and governmental computers. Our society is becoming an increasingly cashless society through credit cards and a paperless society through computers. . . . Computer crime has been called the 'crime of the future' and home computers, the 'burglar tool of the electronic age.' These accusations may be exaggerations, but they do reflect the concern for the rising rate of computer crime in the U.S."

According to the Lipman Report (1988), the national direct cost to organizations of computer crime is estimated to be almost $560 million. However, the total direct and indirect costs of computer crime may be as much as $200 billion.

The National Center for Computer Crime Data has compiled data on the national costs of computer crime as summarized in Table 10–1.

According to the Hallcrest Report II (Cunningham et al., 1990, p. 75): "Management of computer security may be the greatest individual challenge facing private security managers over the next decade."

As noted in the Hallcrest Report II (p. 64):

> Many security directors have little personal knowledge about computers or computer security. It is likely, however, that in the coming years security managers will be expected—perhaps required—to become increasingly knowledgeable about computer security. Moreover, as computer systems proliferate within security departments—both as management information tools and as a part of electronic systems—their systems, too, may become targets.

The Hallcrest Report II (p. 64) suggests that security managers must consider the following key factors:

- ➤ Electronic intrusion is currently a minimal threat that has the potential of growing to significant risk levels in the next few years before it finally dissipates by the end of the decade.
- ➤ Most security managers are presently ill-equipped, personally and organizationally, to counter the computer security threat, particularly external, electronic intrusion.
- ➤ As security departments increasingly rely on computers, their vulnerability to electronic intrusion will commensurately increase.

**Table 10–1  Summary of national costs of computer crimes.**

| | |
|---|---|
| Total Annual Person-Years Lost | 930 |
| Total Annual Computer-Years Lost | 15.2 |
| Average Annual Loss per Organization | $109,000 |
| National Cost for Computer Crimes to Organizations | $555,000,000 |

SOURCE: *Commitment to Security*, Copyright National Center for Computer Crime Data, Santa Cruz, CA.

# □ TYPES OF THREATS TO COMPUTER SECURITY

Computer-related crimes can involve the input data, the output data, the program itself, or computer time. Adequate security requires not only physical security but at least a basic knowledge of how the computer works and how it can be used to commit crime. Input data can be altered (for example, a fictitious supplier can be entered into the billing system or figures can be changed or removed, leaving absolutely no trace). Output data can be obtained by unauthorized people through wiretapping, electromagnetic pickup, or theft of data sheets or punch cards. The computer program itself might be tampered with to add costs to purchased items or to create double payments for particular accounts. Computer time also is sometimes used for personal use and/or profit. There are no dishonest computers, only dishonest employees, competitors, and criminals.

A survey conducted by the Data Processing Management Association (DPMA), Park Ridge, Illinois, questioned one thousand data processing executives in *Fortune* 1000 companies. This survey found that the majority of computer abuses were rather mundane. Misuse of computer services made up nearly half of all incidents reported. Misuse included game-playing as well as using the computer for personal work to divert funds or alter records. The next most prevalent area was program abuse, i.e., copying or changing programs. Third was data abuse—diverting information to unauthorized individuals, and fourth was hardware abuse, i.e., damaging or stealing computer equipment.

According to Steinbrecher (1987, p. 41): "The unintentional, improper use of data remains the largest, most basic security issue. . . . Incorrect data causes far greater losses than the more dramatic security problem of computer fraud and theft." He notes that the person entering the data may not understand what the data means, leading to errors. In addition, accurate data may be transmitted by one computer and be inaccurately received by a personal computer (PC).

A somewhat different view is presented in the Hallcrest Report II (Cunningham et al., 1990, p. 60), which says: "Insider attacks by dishonest or disgruntled employees represent the greatest risk, accounting for up to 80% of incidents."

The National Center for Computer Crime Data (NCCCD) has categorized types of computer crimes and their incident rate, as summarized in Table 10–2.

This center also has summarized data on computer crime victims, as shown in Table 10–3.

Further, the center has summarized data on rates of computer crimes based on prosecution data, illustrated in Table 10–4.

---

The greatest security threats to computer centers are theft by fraud or embezzlement, hackers, sabotage, employee carelessness or error, and fire.

---

## Theft by Fraud or Embezzlement

Funds may be stolen by an outsider, using a telephone and the necessary passwords from a remote terminal to make an unauthorized transfer

**Table 10–2  Computer threat incident rates.**

| Category/Subcategory | Percent of Total/[Subtotal] |
|---|---|
| HUMAN INSIDER THREAT | 70% to 80% |
|   Human errors/accidents | 55% |
|   Dishonest employees | [15%] |
|   Disgruntled employees | [10%] |
| NONHUMAN PHYSICAL THREATS | 20% |
|   Fire | [15%] |
|   Water | [3%] |
|   Earthquake etc. | 2% |

SOURCE: *Commitment to Security,* Copyright National Cener for Computer Crime Data, Santa Cruz, CA.

**Table 10–3  Summary of computer crime victims.**

| Type of Organization | Percent of Attacks: 1986 | Percent of Attacks: 1989 |
|---|---|---|
| Commercial Organizations | 37% | 36% |
| Banks | 18% | 12% |
| Telecommunications Companies *sprint, AT&T* | 16% *up* *haven't really* | 17% |
| Governmental Agencies | *up* 14% *gone up that* | 17% |
| Individuals | *up* 11% *much* | 12% |
| Universities | 4% | 4% |

SOURCE: *Commitment to Security,* Copyright National Center for Computer Crime Data, Santa Cruz, CA.

**Table 10–4  Summary of rates of computer crimes (*Based on prosecution data*).**

| Type of Computer Crime | Probability of Occurrence: 1986 | Probability of Occurrence: 1989 |
|---|---|---|
| Money Theft | 45% | 36% |
| Information Theft | 16% | 12% |
| Damage to Software | 16% | 2% |
| Malicious Alteration | 6% | 6% |
| Deceptive Alteration | 6% | 2% |
| Theft of Service | *significant* 10% *has risen dramatically* | 34% |
| Harassment | 0% | 2% |
| Extortion | 0% | 4% |

SOURCE: *Commitment to Security,* Copyright National Center for Computer Crime Data, Santa Cruz, CA.

FINAL

of millions of dollars to a designated account. Instances of such fraud include the Equity Funding Fraud of the late 1970s that resulted in losses of over $100 million. In another such fraud, Jack Benny, Liza Minnelli, and another individual lost $925,000.

Computerized banks are frequently the victim of "check kiting," where a person makes simultaneous deposits and withdrawals using two or more banks to obtain credit before enough time has elapsed to clear the checks. Before the use of computers, bank personnel examined such transactions when they were made. Now, however, kiting can be detected only by using a special computer program to monitor unusually large transactions and continuous activity involving accounts with small running balances.

Funds can also be stolen by insiders, for example, employees who falsify claims in an insurance company, or the computer programmers with their fictitious supply company cited at the beginning of this chapter.

It is not always money that is stolen; sometimes the theft involves information or data. Computer data banks contain information worth billions of dollars, such as lists of customers, bank records, consumer records, trade secrets, business plans, and the like. In addition, secrets regarding the manufacturing of computers are also sometimes the target of computer thieves. For example, in 1983, during an FBI sting operation, agents arrested employees of the Japanese firm, Hitachi, Ltd., attempting to buy computer secrets from IBM. Gardner (1985, p. 133) notes that these employees "pleaded guilty to conspiracy to commit theft and Hitachi pleaded guilty and was fined $10,000 on federal charges of conspiring to transport secrets across state lines. The outcome was an out-of-court settlement of a civil suit against Hitachi reported to be $300 million plus attorney fees."

The thefts need not involve huge sums of money or information. Theft of services is also a problem. Employees may use company computers to play games, run their own programs, or, as in a few documented cases, even run their own businesses with their employers' computers and on their employers' time.

## Hackers

Another serious threat to computer security is the **hacker**—the computer enthusiast who engages in electronic snooping, software piracy, and other types of high-tech illegal activities. Sometimes the activities of such hackers is relatively harmless, as in the case of some computer students who electronically altered the Rose Bowl scoreboard to show Cal Tech playing MIT rather than UCLA playing Illinois. But it is not always harmless, as noted by Donn Parker: "There's an epidemic of malicious hacking going on across the country. Hackers consider breaking into computer systems an indoor sport, but there is a dark side."

This dark side is described by Folsom in *Security Management* (1986, pp. 92–93):

Consider the case of a group of hackers known as the 414s. One June morning, Chen Chui, systems manager for the Sloan-Kettering Cancer Hospital in

New York, made an alarming discovery. Sometime during the night the hospital's giant computer which monitors radiation treatments for the hospital's patients had failed. Chui discovered that someone had erased part of the computer's memory and that passwords had been issued to five unauthorized accounts. Hospital director Radhe Mohan was alarmed. He said, "If the files are altered, then a patient could get the wrong treatment."

Baffled officials called the FBI and the New York City Police, who placed a tap on the phone lines to the computer. The mystery was solved after the FBI tracked down a group of Milwaukee area computer buffs who called themselves the 414s after the city's area code. Using home computers connected to ordinary phone lines, the group had been breaking into computers across the United States and Canada.

In addition to accessing computers without authorization, hackers also frequently engage in software piracy, costing computer companies millions of dollars in lost sales. *Computers and the Law* (1984) notes that "selling software—the programs of instruction that tell computers what to do—is big business. Americans spend almost $20 billion a year on software. Companies have tried a variety of techniques to stop the pirates. For example, one video game maker employs fifteen full-time lawyers to bring copyright lawsuits against the pirates. Other companies use special codes designed to prevent copying, but Steve Jobs, former president of Apple Computer Company, says, 'I've never seen a code someone couldn't break.' "

Jackson (1987) says that criminal hackers are a very small percent of the overall computer security threat. Cunningham et al. (1990, p. 66) say criminal hackers are "minuscule in number" and engage in such activities as "theft of telephone service, vandalism of computer systems and records, alteration of vital medical records, credit card fraud and manipulation of credit records." They caution that simple "modem hunting" computer programs can dial thousands of telephone numbers searching for "vulnerable modems" and that "hackers are successful only against the undefended and the careless. They remotely prey on the easiest victims they can find."

## Sabotage

Another risk to protect against is sabotage. Competitors, activists, or dissatisfied employees might make the computer their target. Activists may see the computer room as the "vulnerable heart" of a business and make it the target of their attack. For example, one disgruntled programmer who thought he might be fired programmed the computer to destroy its database if it did not make up a salary check for him when the payroll was made up. Poor employee morale can greatly enhance the likelihood of computer sabotage.

Sabotage may be done by computer viruses. A virus is a "bug" entered into a computer program that can cause serious memory problems, destroying files or even entire programs. It can also spread from computer to computer. It can lay dormant for weeks or months until activated by someone with access to the computer. According to the *Washington Post* (1990, p. 7A), an advertisement such as the following might be placed by the U.S. Army:

Wanted: Experienced computer hackers capable of breaking into enemy software systems and destroying secret files. Knowledge of computer viruses a must.

The Army is actually exploring using computer viruses, "a type of unwanted software program that can propagate undetected from one computer to another, thwarting the computer's normal functions and sometimes garbling data." According to the *Post:* "Incidents of computer sabotage have swept the country in recent months as hackers become increasingly efficient at breaking into the systems of businesses, universities, and research centers."

In *State v. Burleson* (1988) a Texas court found a defendant guilty of harmful access to a computer to sabotage its operations. The defendant had boasted to a fellow employee of how he had installed a computer virus in his company's computer system. This is thought to be the first computer virus prosecution in the country.

## Other Threats

Employee carelessness and errors are also a significant risk. Improperly stored computer tapes can be damaged beyond use. Tapes wound too tightly can print through to the next layer. Excessive heat or humidity can destroy the tapes. A magnet closer than 12 cm might erase a computer tape. And one transposed figure or one omitted zero or decimal point can cost a company millions of dollars.

In addition, according to the Hallcrest Report II (Cunningham et al., 1990, p. 63): "Any communications or computer network connected to telephone lines, microwave links, modems, facsimile machines, or similar apparatus is hypothetically vulnerable to external, electronic intrusion."

The threat of fire is another serious risk. The large number of electric wires and connections involved in computer installations, often located under a raised floor, and the fact that computer rooms are fire-loaded with large quantities of combustible materials, make the risk of fire great. Even if a fire is detected early, the steam and humidity from extinguishing it may ruin the computer tapes.

Yet another problem is the controlled environment required for the computer to function correctly. Fluctuations in power can cause inaccuracies, so a continuous supply of unvarying power must be available. Air-conditioning must be maintained, or the computer can malfunction. Computers must also be protected against moisture; therefore, the location of water mains, air-conditioning pipes, sewer pipes, and the like should be checked to ensure that they do not pose a threat to the computer should they break. If such pipes do exist, a drain should be installed in the computer room's floor. The computer and tapes should be covered if construction or sandblasting is going on outside because the fine powder resulting from such activities can ruin a computer.

## ☐ LEGISLATION RELATED TO COMPUTER CRIME

As computer crime has grown, states have passed legislation to deal with it. According to Huber (1986), forty-eight states had passed some sort of legislation dealing with computer crimes by 1986. The laws aim at plugging loopholes in the criminal code, which prohibits traditional theft but does not include stealing electronic impulses from a computer. For example, in a 1976 case, *United States v. DiGilio*, DiGilio copied investigative records during office time, with a government machine, on government paper, and then sold them to the individuals who were the subjects of the investigation. The Third Circuit Court ruled that not only were government time and equipment illegally used, but also the contents of the documents themselves had been stolen.

Likewise, in a 1978 case, *United States v. Lambert*, the defendant was convicted of stealing computer-stored information listing names of informants and the status of government drug investigations.

California has enacted a model computer crime code that, according to Black (1986, p. 31), includes the following specific violations:

➤ Publishing access codes through the use of a computer.
➤ Theft of computer data.
➤ Unauthorized interruption of computer service.
➤ Computer tampering.
➤ Unauthorized access to a computer system.

Black makes this suggestion: "Direct application of computer crime statutes should apply only to those cases where a greater degree of technical expertise is required to commit the crime than is common among the general public. As an example, the use of a stolen credit card to obtain money from an automated teller machine should not be construed as a computer crime for investigative or complaint filing purposes."

## The Electronic Communications Privacy Act of 1986

On November 6, 1986, President Ronald Reagan signed into law the Electronic Communications Privacy Act, which amends Title 18, United States Code, by adding Chapter 121 — Stored Wire and Electronic Communications and Transactional Records Access:

2701. Unlawful access to stored communications

   **(a)** *Offense.* — Except as provided in subsection (c) of this section, whoever — (1) intentionally accesses without authorization a facility through which an electronic communication service is provided; or (2) intentionally exceeds an authorization to access that facility; and thereby obtains, alters, or prevents authorized access to a wire or electronic communication while it is in electronic storage in such system shall be punished as provided in subsection (b) of this section.

   **(b)** *Punishment.* — The punishment for an offense under subsection (a) of this section is — (1)If the offense is committed for purposes of commercial advantage, malicious destruction or damage, or private commercial gain —

   (A) a fine of not more than $250,000 or imprisonment for not more than one year, or both, in the case of a first offense under this subparagraph; and

(B) a fine under this title or imprisonment for not more than two years, or both, for any subsequent offense under this subparagraph; and

(C) a fine of not more than $5,000 or imprisonment for not more than six months, or both, in any other case.

---

The Electronic Communications Privacy Act of 1986 makes it illegal to intentionally access, without authorization, a facility providing electronic communication services, or to intentionally exceed the authorization of access to such a facility.

---

The bill is intended to protect the privacy of high-tech communications such as electronic mail, video conference calls, conversations on cellular car phones, and computer-to-computer transmissions.

The bill addresses the growing problem of unauthorized persons deliberately gaining access to, and often tampering with, electronic or wire communications that were intended to be private. If such access is for the purpose of commercial advantage, malicious destruction or damage, or private commercial gain, the penalties are much more severe than for "other" types of access, which would include that of hackers. Although hackers may feel their actions are harmless, hacking is now illegal. In the view of most computer experts, it has always been unethical. Susan Myeum, computer law specialist from Palo Alto, California, explains why: "Even if a hacker's actions are not malicious, they can have serious consequences. Just getting into the system and messing around may accidentally alter or destroy valuable, vital information. Computer joyriding is also an invasion of privacy, and it fosters disrespect for the property of others."

Huber suggests that frequently schools fail to include the moral responsibilities of the computer user in their courses on computer programming. Such "ethical education" should be an integral part of a computer literacy program.

## □ SECURITY MEASURES FOR COMPUTER SYSTEMS

The Hallcrest Report II (Cunningham et al., 1990, p. 61) suggests: "In a real-world sense, classified and restricted-access governmental and military computer systems are virtually impregnable, unless network operators have been negligent or there has been an 'insider' conspiracy."

According to the Hallcrest Report II (p. 62): "The technologies utilized to thwart electronic intrusion include: electromagnetic shielding and containment, optical disk storage, data encryption, local area network stations without local storage capabilities, computer-managed password software, audit trail software, increasingly sophisticated 'callback' modems, fiber-optic cabling, enhanced call-tracing capabilities by telephone companies, call-in telephone number identification signals, biometric identification access to terminal hardware and many others."

Protecting computers and the information they use is a vital function of security personnel.

Security measures for computer systems include logical controls, physical access controls, administrative controls, protecting against fire, and maintaining a backup system.

## Logical Controls

Logical controls are special programs written into the software. The most common are those that restrict access by requiring use of a password. That is, the user must type in a special password before the computer will follow any commands. The software might also determine what types of specific information a given user is allowed to access. Specific employees might be allowed into only certain parts of a file. Or they might be allowed to only read the data, but not make any changes in it.

Remote terminals must also be protected. When companies share time on a computer, care must be exercised to ensure that time-sharing customers are limited to their own database. Three ways to identify users wanting access to a computer by phone or terminal are a password (usually a word or phrase), a key or card, and physical characteristics. Use of a password is most common, but because passwords can be overheard or given to unauthorized persons, they should be changed often. Key- or card-controlled systems must, of course, be protected by rigid key/card control procedures, as described earlier. The safest system of authorization and user identification is one that relies on physical characteristics. However, such identification systems are expensive, and if voice identification is used, the system may deny access to authorized individuals whose voice characteristics have changed temporarily because of a cold or other illness.

Multilevel access capability makes a computer more flexible. Some access systems allow different operators to obtain different types of information, but only a limited number to have access to the total program.

Dickey (1985, p. 36) makes this suggestion: "For multiuser networked systems, most access-control software, which requires frequently changed passwords, guards against unauthorized access to systems and information resources. These programs log daily work activity, notify the system operator when unauthorized users attempt to access secured data and print reports of violations. Another security measure eliminates public telephone access to a network by implanting a block in the hardware architecture."

Another type of protection using logical controls is the call-back modem. Dickey describes it: "A user attempting to call into a system enters an identification code or password after dialing the computer; the modem scans its directory for the user's code and phone number and calls back. Only then is the user connected to the sysem."

One of the most effective types of logical controls is *data encryption,* in which an encryption device is placed between the host computer and a modem. The device puts the data into a code before it enters the transmission line. It is then decoded at the receiving end. The military uses sophisticated encryption systems that scramble messages to protect national security data.

Even with logical controls, no system is 100 percent safe. If hackers can break into a cancer hospital for a lark, what might serious criminals or terrorists do?

Programs can be built into the computer that will detect fraud and embezzlement. Currently, however, most computer crimes are discovered by chance, not by audit, because there is no visible evidence of tampering—no erasures or doctored numbers. The crimes are committed by removals and changes that are done in seconds and leave no trace.

## Physical Controls

Physical controls restrict access to computer terminals and other equipment and software.

Physical access control is critical to computer security. The practice of including computer centers in company tours to enhance public image has been discontinued by most establishments. Most computer centers are now in restricted areas with locked doors, alarm systems, and supervisory personnel on duty whenever the computer is operating. Potential for access through air vents, windows, and doors must be assessed. In computer centers where rigid access control is required, there is a single entrance/exit—ideally a riot door—then a corridor and a second (riot) door, both electrically controlled and guarded. Entrance may be obtained through use of an employee ID badge system, keys, key-cards, or identification systems using physical characteristics such as fingerprints, palmprints, or voice characteristics. In addition, various devices are available that lock computers to desktops.

The computer printouts and punch cards should also be safeguarded. When they are no longer needed, they should be run through a paper shredder. Company secrets can be obtained more easily through carelessly discarded printouts and punch cards than through "bugging." Nonetheless, "bugging" must also be guarded against. Equipment is available that can indicate when a "bug" is in operation.

Computer tapes and disks should be stored in locked files. The computer-tape library should be protected against unauthorized access and should make use of a rigidly enforced sign-out/sign-in procedure.

To minimize the threat of employee fraud or embezzlement and/or collusion, the functions of computer technicians, operators, and programmers should be clearly separated. Programmers should not operate the computers except to try out new programs, and then only under supervision. A programmer should not be in the computer room unsupervised. And only authorized persons should be allowed to change programs. Sometimes such separation is not practical, but where it can be accomplished, it should be. It is also a good policy to rotate personnel working on various programs.

## Administrative Controls

R. E. Johnston, director of data processing for Phoenix Mutual Life Insurance Company, makes this statement (Computer Security, 1986, p. 10):

Administrative controls establish the practice and procedures for anyone wishing to gain access to data. These procedures include:

➤ Having anyone who enters the building or a specified area sign an entry and exit log.

➤ Having employees submit written requests before they can access certain data.

➤ Reviewing the formal approval process periodically to ensure that it's being used properly.

Administrative controls essentially establish accountability. Accountability establishes that *someone* is responsible for an act. Those who try to access data are held accountable through a request form, roster, or report produced by the system listing those who tried to gain access at any time

Other administrative controls include making careful background checks on all employees and assuming responsibility for security, including stressing security during management meetings. Still other administrative security measures to protect against theft are periodic external audits as well as involving auditors in designing computer programs.

Administrative controls can also be used to reduce employee carelessness and ignorance. Employee carelessness and/or ignorance can result in tremendous losses for companies that rely on computers. All computer operators should be well qualified and should then be further trained on the specific hardware and software they will be using. Checklists and written instructions should be affixed to each machine and should delineate the procedures to be followed and any cautions to be taken. Detailed daily logs should be completed by each operator. Even the most skilled operators can make mistakes, however. Reporting of employee mistakes must be encouraged so that the mistakes can be corrected rather than covered up, thereby creating even more serious problems than the original mistake may have caused. A system of error analysis should be established to reduce further errors. Clearly established rules and procedures as well as regular reviews and inspections will help reduce losses that result from employee carelessness or ignorance.

## Recommendations for a Computer Security Program

In a report entitled "Computer Crime—Computer Security Techniques," the Bureau of Justice Statistics, U.S. Department of Justice, offers the following recommendations for a computer security program:

➤ Set up a system so that a user must get specific authorization to use it.
➤ Tightly control all after-hours processing.
➤ Carefully review and explain all computer shutdowns.
➤ Require that customer complaints about computer errors be investigated by a department other than the computer department.
➤ Control access to the computer operations center strictly.

- Commission independent consultants to audit the computer operations.
- Change passwords and security codes routinely as employees leave.
- Keep records of former employees' passwords and codes to trace the source of any subsequently discovered fraud.
- Staff and lock tape and disk libraries.
- Use scramblers and encryption devices for data transmission.
- Brief employees on security procedures frequently.
- Keep records of all unsuccessful attempts to access the computer system.
- Encourage employees to suggest security procedures that meet the company's specific needs.

## Preventing Computer Crime

An additional helpful listing of "crime-stoppers" is offered by William E. Perry (1985):*

1) *Evaluating computer security*

Is someone responsible for computer security in the central site?

Have standards been developed for designing controls into financial systems?

Has the confidentiality or sensitivity of each piece of information been identified?

Have procedures been developed to define who can access the computer facility, as well as how and when that access can occur?

Have procedures been developed to handle programs and data at remote sites?

Is someone accountable for security at each remote site?

Have security procedures been established for PCs?

Has the ownership of microcomputer programs and data been defined by the firm?

Is critical information that is transmitted over common-carrier lines protected (e.g., through cryptography)?

Have provisions been made to destroy sensitive information controlled by office systems?

2) *Evaluating personnel issues*

Are formal reports required for each reported instance of computer penetration?

Is one individual accountable for each data processing resource?

Does management understand the new threats posed by automated applications?

Is management evaluated on its ability to maintain a secure computer facility?

Are the activities of all non-employees in the computer center monitored?

Do procedures restrict non-employees from gaining access to computer program listings and documentation (e.g., shredding the program listings rather than throwing them out in the trash)?

Are employees instructed on how to deal with inquiries and requests originating from non-employees?

Are errors made by the computer department categorized by type and frequency?

---

* From William E. Perry, "Management Strategies for Computer Security," © Butterworth, 1985. Reprinted with permission.

Are records maintained on the frequency and type of errors incurred by users of data processing systems?

Steinbrecher (1987, p. 46) stresses: "A combination of controls and awareness of data integrity issues will help to safeguard your data—and possibly save your company from costly mistakes." He suggests the following error-reduction procedures:

➤ Use write/protect tabs on diskettes to prevent the accidental alteration of information.
➤ Erase files that are no longer needed.
➤ Establish logical file-naming rules.
➤ Label both the diskettes and the envelopes.
➤ Implement error-checking and correction procedures.

Individuals who deal with computer software should be familiar with the following guidelines:

➤ Avoid contact with recording surfaces of computer tapes and disks.
➤ Never write on labels on floppy disks with a ballpoint pen or pencil.
➤ Never use paper clips or rubber bands around computer disks.
➤ Store computer tapes and disks vertically at approximately 70 degrees Fahrenheit.
➤ Keep computer disks away from strong light, dust, and magnetic fields.
➤ Do not store computer disks in plastic bags.

## Preventing Losses by Fire

Although fire is a potential danger for any business, the hazard is greater for computer centers than for most other areas because of the higher probability of fire, the limitations on how such fires can be extinguished, and the tremendous losses of hardware, software, and data that could result.

Most computer centers have incorporated means to prevent fires—for example, not allowing smoking, using fire-resistant electric wiring and connectors, and removing printout sheets (frequently tons of them) as soon as practical. However, many managers fail to recognize that the greatest threat is that of a fire that begins outside the computer center. Other common causes are careless cigarette smoking and faulty electrical wiring. Therefore, an important preventive measure is to decrease fire-loading of all adjacent areas, including not only the rooms that have common walls with the computer center, but those above and below it as well.

The fire detection systems in computer rooms are most frequently ionization-type detectors that are installed inside each computer or console cabinet, under the floor, in the ceiling, and in the storage cabinets. Some detectors are also designed to shut off the electric power and all air-conditioning units. Many are connected to a visual display panel that shows the exact location of the fire.

Fire extinguishing systems are also important for adequate protection from fire losses. Three general alternatives are available. First is the automatic water sprinkler system, which is the least expensive, is reliable and generally trouble-free, and will continue to operate as long as the heat is above the designated temperature—usually 150 degrees Fahrenheit. This system also has important disadvantages, however. Recall that water and electricity do not mix and that water conducts electricity. Therefore, if such a system is used, it is imperative that it be connected so as to turn off all electrical power. Another important disadvantage is that water and heat cause steam and humidity, which can completely destroy the tapes and can also damage the computer itself. If the computer is not properly and thoroughly dried after a water sprinkler has been activated, it can rust and corrode. Further, if the fire originates in a computer cabinet, as is frequently the case, the water jets will not reach the fire.

The second type is the carbon dioxide extinguishing system. Although this system is more expensive than the water system, carbon dioxide does not conduct electricity or corrode the equipment, and the gas can penetrate computer cabinets. But this system, too, has serious disadvantages. It gives off a deadly gas, so all employees must be evacuated before it can be activated, thereby causing a delay that could result in greater losses. In addition, it is not continuous as is water, but rather shuts off when the gas has been expelled from the system. Carbon dioxide smothers rather than cooling like water does, so the chance of flareback is greater. Finally, carbon dioxide forms a cloud that can severely hinder fire-fighting efforts.

The third extinguishing system is Halon 1301 (freon). Like carbon dioxide, it is expensive, but unlike carbon dioxide, it is not lethal in the correct concentration and does not create a cloud. It is a nonconductor of electricity. However, it shares with carbon dioxide the disadvantages of expense and the possibility of a flare-back because it is not continuous like water. (Outdoor halon systems are always dangerous.)

Although experts disagree on which type of extinguishing system is best for computer rooms, many prefer halon. They oppose the water system because of the danger of electrocution and the damage caused by water and steam, and they oppose the carbon dioxide system because of the lethal gas it produces. Nonetheless, many insurance companies require a water sprinkler system in computer centers before they will issue fire coverage.

In addition to some type of automatic extinguishing system, computer rooms should also have portable carbon dioxide or halon extinguishers located throughout the area, and floor pullers (handles with rubber suction cups on each end), which should be easily accessible to remove floor tiles should a fire originate under a floor housing the electrical wiring for the hardware.

## Establishing a Backup System

Because establishments using EDP are so reliant upon computers, a backup system is usually mandatory. This includes backup power and air-conditioning, backup records, and access to backup hardware. Some companies keep duplicate tapes of almost every file, whereas others make duplicates of only very important files. The criticality of the information and budgetary considerations will help determine which tapes should be copied. The copies should be kept in a secure location away from the facility that houses the computer center.

It is usually not economically feasible to have an "extra" computer in the center to serve as a backup. The common practice is for two establishments to enter into a "mutual aid" agreement whereby one company can use the other's computer during a breakdown. Sensible preplanning can greatly reduce losses. The contingency plan must ensure that adequate time will be available for the computer runs critical to the company's operation. For example, if a company's computer breaks down just before it is to run payroll, it is important that the payroll be issued. If a fire should damage the computer to such an extent that it must be replaced, it is important that the payroll be able to be run on a different computer. For such a "mutual aid" system to work, each must be sure that the computer programs' software is compatible. This can most effectively be established through a trial run. Each should keep the other posted on any changes in hardware and/or scheduling requirements that occur. The initial trial run for compatibility should be periodically retested.

Computer centers should also be fully insured. The hardware and software represent a substantial investment and should accordingly be insured against all risks that may be present.

## ☐ INVESTIGATING COMPUTER CRIME

As noted by Coutourie (1989, p. 18) challenges presented by computer crime include the fact that "computer criminals leave no traditional crime scene for investigators to photograph and examine. The victim is very likely to be a corporation, and the perpetrators may never be physically at the 'scene of the crime,' making it difficult to establish the relationship between the attacker and the victim."

Black (1986, p. 32) discusses some difficulties of the computer crime investigation: "The detective in a computer crime case may find himself in a totally unfamiliar environment, dealing with persons who communicate in a language he doesn't understand. . . . The amount of cooperation he receives may vary greatly as a result of the investigative requirements outlined by the detective at the initial interview, possibility of subsequent public embarrassment, loss of workhours, press coverage, outraged stockholders, or other unknown reasons. . . . The investigation of a computer crime in a hostile environment requires a much different approach than the friendly environment investigation. The victim must be approached in the same manner as a suspect. . . ."

Factors to consider in investigating computer crime include the investigator's knowledge and whether outside expertise is required; the likelihood of the victim or an employee being involved; and the difficulty in detecting such crimes.

In the survey previously mentioned conducted by the DPMA, it was found that only 2 percent of discovered and reported computer abuses were perpetrated by people outside the firm. The vast majority were committed by the firm's own employees.

This survey also found that the motivation for the internal abuse included ignorance of proper professional conduct (27 percent), misguided playfulness (26 percent), personal gain (25 percent), and maliciousness or revenge (22 percent). According to the survey, technical people such as programmers, systems analysts, machine operators, data entry clerks, etc., were the most common perpetrators.

Folsom (1986, pp. 92–93) stresses that "pinpointing departments where computer crimes have a high probability of occurring is not difficult. The highest risks are found where the computer system generates negotiable instruments, transfers credit, processes loan applications, or stores credit ratings. The potential for abuse is also high when access to computer centers is not regulated, after-hours use is not monitored, computer personnel are not carefully screened, and unexplained lapses in computer operations go unexamined."

The typical computer "criminal" is a young, middle-class technical person, highly educated, with no prior criminal record, and employed by the firm reporting the crime.

Therefore, when investigating computer crimes, it is logical to start with a careful check of all employees having access to and knowledge of the computer and its programs. It will be necessary to know exactly how the security system was breached and what type of crime has been committed (altering of data, theft of data, etc.). Often it is necessary to know specifically what information was stolen in order to obtain a search warrant. Also, investigation of computer crimes often crosses several jurisdictional boundaries; consequently, security personnel usually do not handle investigation of such crimes alone. Often public enforcement agencies may also become involved. For example, the U.S. Secret Service is of great assistance in apprehending hackers.

## □ PROSECUTING PERPETRATORS OF COMPUTER CRIMES

According to Huber (1986), only 1 percent of all computer crimes are detected. Of these only 12 percent are reported to the authorities, and only 3 percent of offenders go to jail.

The chance of a computer criminal being caught and going to jail is approximately one in twenty-seven thousand.

For a variety of reasons, the majority of computer crimes are not reported. The suspect may be an employee with a long record of trusted service; the employer may fear a tie-up of the computer system, fear that others will see how easy it is to access the system, fear criticism by stockholders, or have numerous other reasons for not reporting the crime.

Even when computer crimes are reported, the majority are not prosecuted, often for the same reasons others do not even report them. In addition, prosecution is difficult because of lack of precedents and clear definitions. Frequently what has been stolen is information, which is intangible property and difficult to place a value on. In addition, as noted by Black (1986, p. 33), "the phrase, 'jury of your peers as trier of fact,' is probably a shade this side of impossible when applied to some of the more complex computer crimes . . . especially when the jury consists of people who believe that a floppy disk can be corrected by a good chiropractor." Nonetheless, to combat computer crime, a commitment to prosecution is vital in any security program.

## SUMMARY

Computer crime includes accessing a computer's database without authorization or exceeding authorization for the purpose of sabotage or fraud. It includes theft or destruction of software and hardware as well. Computer crimes cost hundreds of millions of dollars annually. In fact, computer crime or failure might destroy a business.

The greatest security threats to computer centers are theft by fraud or embezzlement, hackers, sabotage, employee carelessness or error, and fire. The Electronic Communications Privacy Act of 1986 makes it illegal to intentionally access, without authorization, a facility providing electronic communication services, or to intentionally exceed the authorization of access to such a facility.

Security measures for computer systems include logical controls, physical access controls, administrative controls, protecting against fire, and maintaining a backup system.

Factors to consider in investigating computer crime include the investigator's knowledge and whether outside expertise is required; the likelihood of the victim or an employee being involved; and the difficulty in detecting such crimes. The typical computer "criminal" is a young, middle-class technical person, highly educated, with no prior criminal record, and employed by the firm reporting the crime. The chance of such a criminal being caught and going to jail is approximately one in twenty-seven thousand.

## APPLICATION

1) In the movie *War Games*, David, a bright young high-school student, is an adept hacker. Computers are his entire life, except for his girlfriend. Outwardly shy, he's totally different when he's with his computer. At first his hacking involves tapping into his school's computer and changing grades. Later, however, he accidently plugs into a secret Defense Department computer and is faced with the ultimate computer game—diverting thermonuclear war.

a) How likely is it that David could actually break into his school's computer and change his grades? What crime would be involved?

b) How likely is it that he could break into the Defense Department's secret computer? What crime would be involved?

2) A man named George Nickolson (spelled with a "k"), former sales manager of a Honda distributor, used his former position to tap into the credit records and social security number of George Nicholson (spelled with an "h"), a schoolteacher. Using the information obtained from the illegitimate inquiry, Nickolson obtained a $5,000 loan from a local bank, obtained a $7,500 loan from another local bank, and charged purchases to American Express for over $6,750.

Shortly thereafter, the banks began hounding Nicholson for payment on the debts which he obviously knew nothing about. He and his wife then went through three years described as a nightmare, being hounded by creditors. Ultimately, Nickolson was arrested and charged with incurring $26,750 in debts over the past three years.

a) What would the formal charge probably be?

b) How would investigators probably locate the suspect? What evidence would be required?

c) Could Nicholson sue Nickolson for the nightmarish three years?

## DISCUSSION QUESTIONS

1) How familiar are you with computer systems? Which specific types?

2) Have there been recent computer crimes in your area? If so, what did they involve?

3) Do you know any computer hackers (or are you one yourself)? What types of activities are they most interested in? Do they perceive anything illegal about their activities?

4) How reliant is your local bank on a computer system?

5) Do you feel penalties for hackers should be as severe as they are under the Electronic Communications Privacy Act of 1986?

## REFERENCES

Black, J. K. Taking a byte out of crime. *Police chief*, May 1986, pp. 31–33.

Computer crime—computer security techniques. Bureau of Justice Statistics, U.S. Department of Justice.

Computer security: Protecting information from prying eyes. *Executive action series*, #321, November. Waterford, CT: Bureau of Business Practice, Division of Simon and Schuster, 1986, pp. 9–11.

*Computers and the law.* Random House; Filmfax Productions, Corp., n.p. 1984.

Coutourie, Larry. Preventing computer-related crimes. *FBI law enforcement bulletin*, September 1989, pp. 17–21.

Cunningham, William C.; Strauchs, John J.; and Van Meter, Clifford W. *Private security trends, 1970 to 2000: The Hallcrest report II.* Stoneham, MA: Butterworth-Heinemann, 1990.

Dickey, S. Is getting in getting out of control? *Today's office*, September 1985, pp. 29–36.

Folsom, W. B. A familiar theme—with variations. *Security management*, July 1986, pp. 91—93.

Gardner, T. J. *Criminal law: Principles and cases*, 3d ed. St. Paul, MN: West Publishing Company, 1985.

Huber, R. C. Becoming aware—dealing with computer crime. Speech at Normandale Community College, October 20, 1986.

Jackson, Carl. *The need for security, Datapro reports on information security.* Datapro Corporation, McGraw-Hill, 1987.

Lipman report. Safeguarding against computer crime. November 15, 1988.

Manning, Walt W. and White, Gary H. Data diddling, salami slicing, Trojan horses . . . Can your agency handle computer crimes? *Police chief*, April 1990, pp. 46—49.

Perry, W. E. *Management strategies for computer security.* Stoneham, MA: Butterworth Publishers, 1985.

Steinbrecher, David. Getting a lock on controlling corporate data. *Today's office*, May 1987, pp. 40—46.

*Washington post*, Army looking for a few good hackers to disable enemy software. *Star tribune*, Thursday, May 24, 1990, p. 7A.-

## ☐ INTRODUCTION

Security managers are also in the communications business. Of all the skills needed to be an effective manager, skill in communicating is the most vital. In addition, a large part of security work at all levels involves some form of communication.

Effective communication can produce several positive outcomes. It can be used to inform, guide, reassure, persuade, motivate, negotiate, or diffuse. In contrast, ineffective communication can result in confusion, false expectations, wrong conclusions, negative stereotypes, frustrations, anger, hostility, aggression, and even physical confrontations.

Security managers and on-line officers routinely communicate in every facet of their jobs, not only in their interactions with those for whom they work and their employees, but also in their interactions with the public and with professionals in other fields. Communication is all around us. We are continuously bombarded by spoken and written messages, yet most people give little thought to what the communication process consists of, nor are they trained in communicating effectively.

## Chapter Eleven

# Communicating

### DO YOU KNOW

➤ What the communication process involves?

➤ What the average speaking speed is? Listening or "word processing" speed?

➤ What nonverbal communication includes? Written nonverbal communication?

➤ What the lines of communication are?

➤ How to take notes?

➤ What the characteristics of effective notes are?

➤ What are the two basic types of reports security officers write?

➤ Why reports are so important?

➤ The characteristics of a well-written report?

➤ What is important in testifying in court?

➤ How a defense attorney might attempt to impeach a security officer's testimony?

## ☐ THE COMMUNICATION PROCESS

The communication process, on the surface, is rather simple, but when all the variations in each component of the process are considered, it is exceedingly complex.

Communications is the process through which information is transferred from one person to another through common symbols. It is sometimes explained as having a sender, a message, a channel, and a receiver. The message may be spoken or written, verbal or nonverbal. The channel can be a memo, letter, or report. It may be a phone call, a conversation, or a video. It may even be a shrug or a shove.

---

The communication process involves a sender, a message, a channel, and a receiver. It may also include feedback.

Successful communication occurs only if:

➤ The sender can correctly code the message.
➤ The channel is free of distortion.
➤ The receiver can correctly decode the message.

How messages can get lost in translation is apparent in going from one language to another. For example, a computer that translated Russian into English and vice versa translated the familiar phrase "Out of sight, out of mind" as "invisible idiot." In Mexico, an "H" on the water faucet means helado—cold. A "C" means caliente—hot. For the unsuspecting, the result can be surprising.

Messages do, indeed, often get lost in translation, be it from one language to another, or simply from one human mind to another. Effective communication, written or spoken, takes into consideration not only the message and channel but also the sender and receiver of that message.

## The Sender

Many variables must be considered when looking at the sender of the message, including age, sex, intelligence, education, biases, past experience, vocation, and purpose for communicating.

When security managers and on-line officers communicate, it is important to understand *why* they send the messages they do. They may be attempting to establish rapport, or they may be trying to calm a hysterical victim of a bloody accident. Other times they may be trying to extract information from a hostile person. The purpose behind the communication should be clearly understood if the communication is to be effective.

## The Message

The message can be written or spoken, verbal or nonverbal. Most messages consist of some form of words surrounded by other nonverbal factors. The message should be in simple, standard English, avoiding jargon and evasive or "impressive" language. All too often speakers and writers seek to *impress* rather than to *express*.

Security personnel must be aware of ethnic, cultural, and sexual differences in language and avoid using terms that might be viewed as derogatory, such as calling a woman "girl."

Messages must be clear and must avoid faulty thinking if they are to communicate well.

**Spoken messages** are common in security work. Security officers give directions, ask questions, and relay information over their radios. Sometimes these spoken messages are conveyed amid confusion and a multitude of distractions. Noise levels may be high, and distances may be involved.

**Written messages are** also common in security work. On-line officers take notes, primarily as reminders to themselves of information they obtain. They write reports based on these notes to communicate the facts of an incident to others. Security managers may also write letters, memos, and other types of messages for a variety of purposes. Effective written communication is discussed later in the chapter.

## The Channel

Having efficient channels to communicate is essential to security work both during routine functions as well as during emergencies. Specific methods of communication include telephone, paging and public address paging, two-way radio, closed-circuit television, conversations, reports, letters, and memos. Information conveyed using any of these methods should be brief, objective, courteous, and professional.

On-line officers are often expected to answer telephones, take messages, provide information, and page individuals if an emergency exists. Many businesses have a policy prohibiting use of the telephone for personal use. Some even have phones that record, measure, and count the calls made. Pagers allow immediate one-way contact with others as does a public paging system. Such systems can be invaluable in emergencies for getting information to all personnel immediately. Two-way radios also provide for immediate communication, but the message can be heard by anyone in the immediate area.

Written channels of communication include policies and procedures, letters, memos, proposals, and reports as well as many of the forms previously introduced in Chapter 7.

## The Receiver

The same variables surrounding the sender of messages surround those who receive the messages, including age, sex, intelligence, education, biases, past experience, vocation, and purpose for listening.

If the message is spoken, the receiver of the message must be a good listener. Yet this skill is lacking in many people, including security personnel. They hear, but they do not actively listen. Consequently, many messages are misinterpreted or not received at all.

## ☐ LISTENING

Says communications expert Elaine Thomas (1987, p. 99): "Of all the communication skills we use daily, we spend the most time listening." Research has shown that 45 percent of the total time devoted to communication is spent in listening, 30 percent in speaking, 16 percent in reading, and 9 percent in writing.

According to Montgomery (1981, p. 65): "We listen more than we do any other human activity except breathe." He goes on to note, however, that "listening is the most neglected and the least understood of the communications arts."

Too often people simply hear, but they do not listen. Why? A large part of the problem is the difference between the speed at which people speak and that at which they can mentally process information.

People can speak about 150 words per minute. People can listen to over 450 words per minute.

Further, people can probably think at least 1,000 words per minute. That lag time can be devastating to listening effectiveness. It allows the mind to wander, to daydream, to formulate arguments, and to attend to the person rather than the message being conveyed.

This hazard was recognized by listening expert Dr. Ralph Nichols (1957) over thirty years ago when he said: "Not capitalizing on thought speed is our greatest single handicap. The differential between thought speed and speech speed breeds false feelings of security and mental tangents. Yet, through listening training, this same differential can be readily converted into our greatest asset."

## Guidelines for Better Listening

The following guidelines can improve listening:

**Attitudinal**
➤ Be interested in the person and the message. Be empathetic. Show you care.
➤ Be less self-centered.
➤ Resist distractions.
➤ Do not let personal biases turn you off.
➤ Prepare to listen. Clear your mind of other things.

**Behavioral**
➤ Be responsive to demeanor, posture, and facial expressions.
➤ Offer encouragement.
➤ Look at the other person.
➤ Do not interrupt.
➤ Take notes. Adjust your note taking to the speaker.

**Mental**
➤ Ask questions (preferably open-ended ones).
➤ Do not change the subject.
➤ Listen for ideas, not just facts. Separate facts from opinions.
➤ Attend to content, not delivery. Look for main points.
➤ Listen optimistically.
➤ Avoid jumping to conclusions. Stay with the speaker; try not to jump ahead. Draw only tentative conclusions.
➤ Concentrate. Work at listening, especially when the material is difficult or complex.
➤ Use excess listening time to summarize the speaker's main ideas. But do *not* plan your response.
➤ Keep your mind open and your emotions in check. Do not judge.
➤ Exercise your mind.
➤ Periodically clarify what has been said.
➤ Pay attention to body language (nonverbal factors).

Listening is a skill, just as speaking, reading, and writing are. Listening can be improved by practicing. It should never be taken for granted.

Neither should it be taken for granted that what is heard will be remembered. If the information received is important, it should be written down.

## Understanding

Simply because a message has been sent, either written or spoken, does not mean that it has been understood. One way to illustrate this is to think of the sender of the message as having a "blue" outlook on the world and the receiver as having a "yellow" outlook on the world. The message is not likely to be either blue or yellow, but a shade of green. That is why one-way communication can be extremely dangerous.

## One-Way vs. Two-Way Communication

Most written messages are one way, that is, the sender writes the message, and it is relayed in some manner to the reader who reads it. If the reader of the message communicates back to the sender, this is two-way communication because **feedback** has taken place.

Feedback is critical to effective communication; it is an indication that a message is or is not understood. In a face-to-face conversation this can take the form of an affirmative nodding of the head (message understood) or a puzzled look (message not understood). Security managers and officers should watch for such feedback when they talk with people, and they should also provide such feedback to those with whom they talk. Much feedback is nonverbal. Indeed, much communication is nonverbal.

## ☐ NONVERBAL COMMUNICATION

A security manager's physical appearance—a suit and tie or an attractive dress—conveys a message of professionalism. Likewise, on-line officers' physical appearance—the uniform and badge, sometimes a gun— conveys a message of authority before they ever say a word. This can be intimidating to many people. A harsh look can add to the intimidation; a smile can weaken or even dispel it. Security officers should be aware of the nonverbal messages they send and use them to their advantage.

Likewise, effective communicators are alert to the nonverbal messages conveyed by those with whom they communicate.

Nonverbal communication includes the eyes, facial expressions, posture, gestures, clothing, tone of voice, proximity, and touch.

The **eyes** are very expressive. They can reveal if someone is happy, sad, excited, interested, tired, confused, sick, and perhaps lying. An entire science has sprung up around eye movements and what they can tell about individuals. People usually have very little control over the messages sent by their eyes.

**Facial expressions,** such as smiles, frowns, grimaces, scowls, pouts, or raised eyebrows, convey messages as do flushed cheeks and perspiration.

**Posture** also conveys messages. A person standing erectly with arms folded and feet apart conveys authority. A person slouching conveys a different message. **Hand gestures** can confirm or contradict what a person is saying, or they can even take the place of words, for example, a hand held out in protest or a finger to the lips can stop someone from speaking further. A hand behind the ear can cause a speaker to increase volume.

**Clothing** conveys messages, too, but must be very carefully interpreted. Millionaires have been known to dress as bums. Generally, however, it is accepted that clothes make a definite statement.

**Tone of voice** as well as pitch and rate can tell much about the person speaking. A high pitch and rapid rate can reveal nervousness or anxiety. **Proximity** can reveal if a person feels comfortable or threatened. In the United States we tend to stand eighteen inches to two feet away when talking. Standing closer is usually perceived as either intimate or threatening (perhaps both). Standing farther away than about four feet usually shows lack of interest or concern for the other person. In some cultures, however, the comfortable zone is much smaller, a fact security officers should be aware of when talking with individuals who are not Americans.

**Touch** in our culture also conveys messages, although not as much as in many other cultures. A handshake, a pat on the back, an arm around a shoulder can show personal care and concern. It can also lead to a sexual harassment lawsuit.

In *written communication* nonverbal messages are conveyed by the appearance and neatness (or lack of), the quality of the copy and paper, and the like. A poorly reproduced copy with a coffee stain on it conveys one message. A laser-printed original placed in a plastic carrier conveys quite another. Certainly a message written on a scrap of paper or on a page torn from a spiral notebook does not convey the image of professionalism desired by the security industry.

---

Written nonverbal communication includes neatness, paper quality, copy quality, binding, and the like.

---

## ☐ BARRIERS TO COMMUNICATION

Time is important to everyone, including security personnel. Communication systems have greatly enhanced the ability to pass information from one person or organization to another. On the other hand, computers, fax machines, copiers, and many other communications devices have deluged line staff and managers alike with information of many forms and types. The sheer volume of information can be overwhelming. Other barriers to communication include the following:

➤ Being preoccupied so the message is not heard.
➤ Being too emotionally involved to correctly interpret the message.
➤ Being defensive because of previous interchanges with a specific individual.
➤ Tending to hear what you want to hear.

- ➤ Noise—interference of any kind, physical or mental.
- ➤ Excessive repetition.
- ➤ Complex language.
- ➤ Lack of interest.
- ➤ Bad timing.

## ☐ LINES OF COMMUNICATION

Most businesses and organizations have established lines of communication.

Communication lines may be downward, upward (vertical), or lateral (horizontal). They may also be internal or external.

**Downward communication** includes directives, policies, and procedures from managers and supervisors, either spoken or written. When time is limited or an emergency exists, communication often must flow downward and be one way.

**Upward communication** includes incident reports as well as requests from subordinates to their superiors. It may also include a security survey being presented to the CEO or the board of directors. Security managers should ensure that all upward communications are in terms those unfamiliar with security will understand. Security risks can sometimes be better explained using photographs and charts. Probabilities of such risks and the potential loss in dollars might be best presented through graphs and charts, quite easily developed if the manager has access to a desktop publishing setup.

**Lateral communication** refers to communication between managers on the same level of the hierarchy and between subordinates on the same level. This would include on-line security officers talking to each other via two-way radios while making rounds.

**Informal channels of communication** also exist within most organizations. Sometimes referred to as the *grapevine* or the *rumor mill,* such channels tend to be unreliable but can cause great harm. Usually the grapevine is strongest in organizations in which information is not openly shared. Employees begin to guess and speculate about what they do not know—hence the rumors. Communicating with subordinates is an essential managerial responsibility because it is through these line officers that the security goals will be met. Officers who are told about their employer are more apt to be supportive. The more direct, personal communication that exists between management and employees, the greater the employee identification with management and the organization.

### Internal Communication

Security managers rely heavily on information provided by on-line officers. Much of this information may be relayed via radio or telephone rather than face-to-face, necessitating careful pronunciation and lots of feedback.

Accuracy is critical in security work, so officers should spell any words that might be misunderstood or spelled incorrectly, especially names and addresses. Such spelling is most effective if done in the phonetic alphabet adopted by most police departments.

| | | | |
|---|---|---|---|
| A | Adam | N | Nora |
| B | Boy | O | Ocean |
| C | Charles | P | Paul |
| D | David | Q | Queen |
| E | Edward | R | Robert |
| F | Frank | S | Sam |
| G | George | T | Tom |
| H | Henry | U | Union |
| I | Ida | V | Victor |
| J | John | W | William |
| K | King | X | X-ray |
| L | Lincoln | Y | Young |
| M | Mary | Z | Zebra |

If the spelling of a name is the "normal" spelling, this can be stated, for example, "Smith, normal spelling." But if the name is spelled *Smythe*, it should be spelled out.

Another way to enhance clarity of communication is to use the twenty-four hour clock rather than A.M. and P.M. This is also referred to as *military time*. It begins at midnight with 0000. The first two digits refer to the hour and the last two digits refer to the minutes. Usually the word *hours* follows the time designation. For example, ten minutes after midnight would be 0010 hours. Three fifteen in the morning would be 0315 hours. Noon is 1200 hours. From that point on 12 is added to each hour. One o'clock in the afternoon is 1300 hours. It continues full circle this way, with midnight also being called 2400 hours, depending on department policy.

**Twenty-Four Hour Clock**

| Morning | | Afternoon | |
|---|---|---|---|
| Midnight | = 0000 | 1 P.M. | = 1300 |
| 1 A.M. | = 0100 | 2 P.M. | = 1400 |
| 2 A.M. | = 0200 | 3 P.M. | = 1500 |
| 3 A.M. | = 0300 | 4 P.M. | = 1600 |
| 4 A.M. | = 0400 | 5 P.M. | = 1700 |
| 5 A.M. | = 0500 | 6 P.M. | = 1800 |
| 6 A.M. | = 0600 | 7 P.M. | = 1900 |
| 7 A.M. | = 0700 | 8 P.M. | = 2000 |
| 8 A.M. | = 0800 | 9 P.M. | = 2100 |
| 9 A.M. | = 0900 | 10 P.M. | = 2200 |
| 10 A.M. | = 1000 | 11 P.M. | = 2300 |
| 11 A.M. | = 1100 | Midnight | = 2400 |
| noon | = 1200 | | |

Portable radios are a vital link in the private security communications system.

Internal communication is also often in the form of activity logs and incident reports.

All incidents are to be reported in writing. Some facilities use an incident report log such as in Figure 11–1. This log contains a detailed, chronological description of everything the security officer saw and did during the shift. For example, opening or locking doors, minor water leaks, mechanical malfunctions, special requests, escorting individuals to specific locations, receiving phone messages, delivering packages, and any significant incidents that occur.

In addition, officers may complete incident reports for any potential, suspected, or actual security risks. A form such as in Figure 11–2 might be used. Most such reports will deal with a situation that requires a corrective action to be taken. When the corrective action has been taken, a follow-up report is written such as the one in Figure 11–3. If no follow-up or report is needed, that should be stated in the incident report.

Information in such reports should be kept confidential, and the reports themselves should be protected from access by unauthorized people. Before looking at how to write effective reports, consider the basis for most such reports—effective notes.

## □ TAKING NOTES

Notes are a permanent aid to memory. Good notes help security personnel remember conditions or incidents they observe, actions they take, and actions others take. They form the basis for official reports and may be of great assistance should a court appearance be required.

## Security Services Daily Activity Log

| Officer | | Badge # | Shift Time | Date |
|---|---|---|---|---|
| Assigned Area | | | | |

| Time | Detailed Activities |
|---|---|
| | |
| | |
| | |
| | |
| | |
| | |
| | |
| | |
| | |
| | |
| | |
| | |
| | |
| | |
| | |
| | |
| | |
| | |
| | |
| | |
| | |
| | |
| | |
| | |
| | |
| | |
| | |
| | |
| | |
| | |
| | |

Be  Sure All Information is Detailed and Accurate

This report has been read and approved by _____  Date _____

**Figure 11–1  Incident report log.**

---

Record all relevant information legibly, in ink, in a notebook.

---

Several procedures should be followed in taking notes. Common sense provides the reasons behind these procedures. First, information is recorded in a notebook, not on scraps of paper that can be easily lost. The notebook should be easy to carry ($3\frac{3}{4}$ by $6\frac{3}{4}$ is a good size). A loose-leaf notebook is best because it is easy to organize, pages can be removed or added, and it looks professional. It should be kept full of blank paper and well organized.

Index tabs are helpful to separate sections: observations, incidents, and the like. The notes should be removed and filed when they have

# Corporate Incident Report

File # _____

Today's date _____    Date incident occurred _____

Incident summary _____

_____

_____

Complete details of event (date, time, individuals, places, situations) _____

_____

_____

_____

_____

_____

_____

(continue on extra sheet of paper if required)

External involvement (describe location, individual statements, contacts, include law
enforcement contacts, etc.)_____

_____

_____

Estimated loss _____    Estimated recovery _____
                (dollars, assets, etc.)

Planned action to resolve incident _____

_____

_____

Individual responsible for follow-up _____

Reported by _____    Phone ( _____ ) _____

Name (s) of managers notified _____

Describe and attach any additional explanations and supporting documents.

*Incident Information Should Be Protected and Held in Strict Confidence*

**Figure 11–2  Incident report.**

served their purpose. Because notes frequently become part of the permanent record of a case, they should be recorded in ink rather than in
pencil, which can become blurred and smudged. Felt-tip or ballpoint
pens are acceptable.

The notes must be legible. Security staff do not want to waste time
later trying to decipher what they have written or, worse, to lose important information because it cannot be read.

Each page of notes should be identified with the officer's name, the
date, and the type of information contained on the page. Because officers work in several different areas on any given shift, it is important to
identify which notes belong to which incident.

# Corporate Incident Report Follow-up

Original Incident Report file # _____

Today's date _____ Date of original report _____

This incident was reported and investigated by (include dates) _____
_____
_____
_____

Have or will any discipinary actions take place as a result of this incident? _____
Explain: _____
_____
_____
_____

Describe any involvement by external organization/law enforcement agencies _____
_____
_____
_____

What resources, assets, or revenues were lost/recovered?_____
_____

Describe any personal injury, actual or threatened, relating to this incident _____
_____
_____

What lessons have been learned/or recommendations made as a result of this incident?___
_____
_____

List any other actions that have been or will be taken as a result of this incident. _____
_____
_____

Comments: _____
_____
_____

*Attach copies of investigations, supporting documentation, or other information pertinent to this incident.*

**Figure 11–3  Incident report follow-up.**

All relevant facts should be recorded as they are obtained, if possible. If an officer is called to deal with a personal injury, obviously, administering first aid would take precedence over taking notes. As soon as anything of an emergency nature is attended to, however, the information should be recorded. Officers should not wait until later to write down information because they may forget some important details. Not everything that is said is recorded, but officers should make note of anything that might be important. A good rule of thumb is: "When in doubt, write it down."

Officer recording information received from a concerned citizen.

All spellings, numbers, and dates should be verified as they are recorded. This can be done by simply repeating the information aloud as it is written and getting verification from the person providing the information.

---

Effective notes are:

➤ Accurate.
➤ Brief.
➤ Clear/complete.

---

The ABCs of effective notes are accuracy, brevity, clarity, and completeness. Accuracy is ensured by repeating information back, spelling names, and verifying numbers. Brevity is accomplished by omitting the articles *a, an,* and *the;* by omitting all other unnecessary words, and by using common abbreviations. Commonly used abbreviations in security notes are summarized in Table 11–1.

Good notes should be clear, complete, concise, accurate, and objective. They are the foundation for a good report.

## ☐ WRITING REPORTS

Most people enter private security for the activity and excitement. They often do not realize the amount of paperwork involved. For almost every action private security officers take, they must write a report. Security managers, too, write much.

**Table 11–1  Common abbreviations used in the security profession.**

| | | | |
|---|---|---|---|
| A&A | Assisted and advised | Off. | Officer |
| AKA | Also known as (alias) | Rec'd. | Received |
| Asst. | Assistant | R/F | Right front |
| Att. | Attempt | R/O | Reporting officer |
| Dept. | Department | R/R | Right rear |
| Dist. | District | S/B | Southbound |
| DOB | Date of birth | Subj. | Subject |
| DOT | Direction of travel | Sup. | Supervisor |
| E/B | Eastbound | Susp. | Suspect |
| GOA | Gone on arrival | S/w | Stationwagon |
| Hdqtrs. | Headquarters | UNK | Unknown |
| Hwy. | Highway | UTL | Unable to locate |
| I.D. | Identification | V. | Victim |
| L/F | Left front | Viol. | Violation |
| Lic. | License | W/B | Westbound |
| L/R | Left rear | Wit. | Witness |
| Memo | Memorandum | WFA* | White female adult |
| N/A | Not applicable | WFJ | White female juvenile |
| NFD | No further description | WMA* | White male adult |
| NMN | No middle name | WMJ | White male juvenile |
| N/B | Northbound | | |

*The "W" indicates the race. It is appropriate to substitute "B" for black, "O" for Oriental, "H"for Hispanic, and "I" for Indian.

Two major types of reports are administrative and operational.

**Administrative reports** deal with the routine functioning of the security department. They include such things as reports on proper uniform, reporting procedures, policies and procedures, security surveys, evaluation reports, and performance reports.

**Operational reports** deal with the actions taken by security officers. Most agencies have their own forms and procedures for completing operational reports, but many of the forms have common elements. For example, most have a series of boxes to be completed at the top, as in the form used at Canterbury Downs race track, illustrated in Figure 11–4. The specific information requested is not important in the illustration. What is noteworthy is that basic information is requested for every crime or incident involving a security officer.

If the department uses report forms that include boxes and blanks to be filled in, they should *all be filled in,* using N/A if information is not applicable or UNK if the information is unknown.

After the basic information is recorded, the officer must write a narrative account of the incident in the space following the boxes.

| CANTERBURY DOWNS SECURITY REPORT | | DATE | |
|---|---|---|---|
| | | ICR # | |

| CLASSIFICATION - TYPE of CRIME or INCIDENT | | | OFFICERS NAME | |
|---|---|---|---|---|

| TIME of INCIDENT | PERSON REPORTING | ADDRESS | PHONE # | TIME REPORTED |
|---|---|---|---|---|

**SUBJECT**

| NAME - LAST -FIRST - MIDDLE (AKA) | | | | | | | | M.R.C. # YEAR | |
|---|---|---|---|---|---|---|---|---|---|
| SEX | RACE | D.O.B. | AGE | HEIGHT | WEIGHT | HAIR | EYES | SOCIAL SECURITY # | |
| EMPLOYER | | | BARN # & TACK ROOM | | OCCUPATION | RES. PHONE | | BUS. PHONE | |
| RESIDENCE ADDRESS ———— CITY — STATE — ZIP | | | | | | | | | |

**SUSPECTS**

NAME & ADDRESS OF SUSPECT (S)
(1) _____
(2) _____

**WITNESSES**

NAME & ADDRESS OF WITNESSES
(1) _____
(2) _____

DETAILS: _____

PAGE_____of_____    OFFICERS SIGNATURE    BADGE NUMBER

**Figure 11–4 Canterbury Downs report form.**
*Courtesy of Canterbury Downs.*

A report is a permanent written record that communicates important facts to be used in the future.

Security officers' reports are *used*, not simply filed away. If they were not needed for the efficient operation of businesses' or agencies' activities, they would not be required. Reports are permanent records of all the important facts of an incident, a stockpile of information drawn on by several other individuals. They may be an aid to other security officers, supervisors, administrators, and, when necessary, the courts, law enforcement agencies, and other governmental agencies interested in safety and loss prevention.

# ☐ CHARACTERISTICS OF A WELL-WRITTEN REPORT

Because reports are so important in the security profession, it is vital that private security officers develop skill in writing effective reports. Such reports will not only communicate information better, but also reflect positively on the officer's education, competence, and professionalism.

A well-written report is factual, accurate, objective, complete, concise, clear, correct, in standard English, legible, and on time.

Each of the preceding characteristics is present in effective reports.

## Factual

The basic purpose of any operational report is to record the **facts.** A fact is a statement that can be proven. (It may be proven false, but the statement is still classified as a fact.) For example, the man is wearing a black leather jacket that has a bulge in the pocket. Facts need to be distinguished from two other types of statements: inferences and opinions. **Inferences** (sometimes called "judgments") are statements about the unknown based on the known—they use logic. For example, the bulge in the man's pocket is a gun. Notice that this inference will become a fact IF the matter is pursued, that is, if the person wearing the black leather jacket is frisked and a gun is, in fact, discovered—or not. Any inferences in official reports should be clearly identified as such.

The third type of statement is **opinion.** An opinion is a statement of personal belief. For example, people who wear black leather jackets are hoods. Opinions have no place in official reports.

Facts and inferences can be discussed and debated logically and reasonably and brought to some degree of agreement. Opinions, however, reflect personal beliefs on which there is seldom agreement. How do you resolve, for example, who has the best-looking spouse? You can't, as attested to by the adage "Beauty is in the eye of the beholder."

Incident reports must not contain assumptions or **conclusionary language.** Among the most common problems here are making statements about what someone can or cannot do. For example, it is a conclusion to write in an incident report, "The man *could not* answer my questions." The factual report would instead say "The man *did not* answer my questions." Even clear, however, would be to say, "The man shrugged and said nothing."

Another common problem is the phrase "signed by" as in "The camera pass authorization was signed by John Doe." Unless the report writer saw John Doe sign the authorization, the report should read "The camera pass authorization was signed John Doe." The little word *by* can get an officer into a lot of trouble on the witness stand.

Other problems arise when officers write about someone's state of mind, for example, saying a person is *nervous, frightened, uncooperative, belligerent.* These are all conclusions on the officer's part. The report should contain facts that lead to the conclusions. For example, rather than saying a person is nervous, describe the person's appearance and actions: "The man began to tremble, he began to perspire heavily, and his voice wavered. He repeatedly glanced over his shoulder at the door."

---

A well-written report is factual. It contains no opinions.

---

Inferences, on the other hand, are valuable in a report, provided they are identified as such and are based on sufficient evidence. Sometimes it is hard to distinguish between facts and inferences. One way to tell them apart is to ask the question: "Can the statement be simply proven true or false, or are other facts needed to prove it?"

For example, to verify the statement "The man is a good driver," you would need to supply several facts to support the inference. One such fact might be that he had never received a traffic ticket. But is that sufficient support to prove that he is a good driver? Perhaps he was simply lucky and never got caught driving carelessly. Or imagine you see a teenager staggering down an alley. You might infer she is drunk or high on drugs, but she might, in fact, be ill. An inference is not really "true" or "false"; it is "sound" or "unsound." And what makes an inference sound (believable) are facts to support it.

## Accurate

To be useful, facts must be accurate. A license number recorded wrong may result in the loss of a witness or suspect—or in a lawsuit for wrongful detention. Inaccurate measurements or recording of the time of an incident may cause problems in a later investigation of the incident. An effective report accurately records the correct time and date, correct names of all persons involved, correct phone numbers and addresses, and exact descriptions of property, vehicles, and suspects. Security officers should have people spell their names and should then repeat spellings and numbers for verification.

---

A well-written report is accurate; it is specific.

---

To be accurate, you must be specific. For example, it is better to say, "The female suspect had a pearl necklace, a gold watch, and a small diamond pin in her skirt pocket," than to say, "The shoplifter had several items of jewelry in her pocket." It is more accurate to describe a suspect as "approximately 5 feet tall" than as "short."

## Objective

Reports must be not only factual and accurate, but also objective. It is possible to include only factual statements in a report and still not be objective. Objective means non-opinionated, fair, and impartial. Lack of objectivity can result from two things: poor word choice and omission of specific facts.

A well-written report is objective, impartial.

Objectivity is attained by keeping to the facts, by using words with nonemotional overtones, and by including both sides of the account. The importance of sticking to the facts and leaving out personal opinions has already been discussed. The next means of achieving objectivity is through the words used. Word choice is extremely important in objective writing. A reader would react to the following three sentences very differently:

The man cried. The man wept. The man blubbered.

"The man cried" is an objective statement; "the man wept" is slanted positively; "the man blubbered" is slanted negatively. Although writers want to be specific, they must also be aware of the effect of the words chosen. Words that have little emotional effect, for example, "cried," are called *denotative* words. The denotative meaning of a word is its objective meaning. In contrast, words that have an emotional effect are called *connotative* words, for example, "wept" and "blubbered." The connotative meaning of a word includes its positive or negative overtones. The term *rent-a-cop* is a clear example of how word choice affects meaning.

Slanting can also make a report nonobjective. A good report includes both sides of an incident. Even when some facts tend to go against an officer's theory about what happened, the officer is obligated to include these facts. Omitting important facts is not being objective.

## Complete

Information kept in the reporting security officer's head is of no value to anyone else. An effective incident report contains answers to at least six basic questions:

WHO?   WHAT?   WHEN?   WHERE?   WHY?   HOW?

As noted, all applicable blanks at the top of a report form should be filled in. If a blank is not applicable, N/A is recorded in the blank so anyone reading the report will not erroneously conclude that information is missing. All relevant details should also be included in the narrative portion of the report. It is inconsiderate of the reader to begin a narrative: "On the above date, at the above-specified time, the above-named suspect. . . ." The narrative should be able to **STAND ALONE.** For example, the same narrative might begin like this: "On December 12, 1991, at 2200 hours, the suspect, Jack Jones, was. . . ."

The narrative will not include everything from the boxes at the top of the report form or from the notes taken regarding the incident. But the report as a whole, including both boxed information and narrative portion, must be complete.

A well-written report is complete.

Each specific incident requires different information. The "who," "what," "when," and "where" questions should be answered by factual statements. The "how" and "why" statements may require inferences. When this is the case, as already noted, the statements should be clearly labeled as inferences. This is especially true when answering the question of causes. To avoid slanting a report, officers must record all possible causes reported to them, no matter how implausible they may seem at the time.

## Concise

To be concise is to make every word count. No one wants to read a wordy report. Length does *not* necessarily indicate quality. Some reports can be written in half a page; others may require ten pages. No exact length can be specified. Reports will be effective if they include *all* relevant information in as few words as possible. This does not mean, however, omitting important details, or leaving out words such as *a, an,* and *the.*

A well-written report is concise.

Wordiness can be reduced in two basic ways: (1) leaving out unnecessary information, and (2) using as few words as possible to record the necessary facts. In the following (taken from an actual report), notice what information is not necessary: "I arrived within a minute of the call. I noticed upon my arrival numerous people standing around. I bent over to spit a bug out that flew into my mouth, and this male party came over and asked for help. . . . Once at the hospital I found myself assisting the doctors in emergency with this victim as two doctors and two nurses were not enough to get everything done and hold her at the same time. . . . I was thanked for my jumping in at the emergency room by both doctors and the family of the injured girl. I then cleared the hospital at 1800 hours."

It is not necessary to include the fact that a bug flew into the officer's mouth, that two doctors and two nurses were not enough personnel to care for the victim, or that the officer was thanked. Such details are superfluous.

Another way to be concise is to omit "empty words." For example, in the phrase "blue in color" the words "in color" are empty—blue IS a color.

Following are some wordy phrases and their more concise counterparts:

| Wordy | Concise |
|---|---|
| in view of the fact that | because |
| with reference to | about |
| made note of the fact that | noted |
| for the purpose of | for |
| subsequent to | after |
| along the lines of | like |
| for the reason that | because |
| comes into conflict with | conflicts with |
| square in shape | square |
| in the event that | if |
| despite the fact that | although |
| in the amount of | for |
| is of the opinion | thinks |
| attempt to ascertain | determine |
| month of April | April |
| state of California | California |

Make every word count.

## Clear

Statements in a report should have only one interpretation. There should be no chance of two people reading the report and coming up with a different picture. For example, "The man was tall," is open to interpretation, but the statement "The man was 6'11" is not. Or consider this statement: "The security officer saw the intruder on the elevator and he fired." WHO fired—the officer or the intruder? The sentence is not clear.

A well-written report is clear.

Sometimes unclear writing produces unintentional humor. Consider the following examples:

➤ She found a book of matches on the car seat that was not hers.
➤ Three cars were reported stolen by ABC Security yesterday.
➤ Here are some suggestions for handling obscene phone calls from the security manager.
➤ As the unauthorized person came toward me in the dark hallway, I hit him with my flashlight.
➤ Guilt, vengeance, and bitterness can be emotionally destructive to line staff. You must get rid of them.

➤ Changing the color of our shirts to navy blue will make the officers look more professional, less costly, and easier to launder.

To write clearly, keep descriptive words and phrases close to the words they describe. For example, lack of clarity is seen in this statement: "He placed the gun into the holster which he had just fired." It was not the holster he had just fired, it was the gun. It would be clearer to say, "He placed the gun which he had just fired into the holster."

Another way to achieve clarity is to avoid uncommon abbreviations. Confusion can result if two people have different interpretations of an abbreviation. For example, to most people, S.O.B. has negative connotations, but for people in health-related fields, it simply means "short of breath." In contrast, some abbreviations are so common, they can be used in reports, for example, Mr., Dr., Ave., St., Feb., N.W., and the like. Other abbreviations are commonly used in private security, but not by the general public, for example, A & A (assisted and advised), DOB (date of birth), DOT (direction of travel), L/F (left front), N/B (northbound), NFD (no further description), and NMN (no middle name). Such abbreviations can be used in notes (see page 286), but they should not be used in reports.

Yet another way to achieve clarity in writing is to use short sentences, organized into short paragraphs. Sentences that are not too long are easier to read. Likewise, paragraphs should be relatively short, usually five to ten sentences. The reports should be logically organized. Most reports commonly begin with "when" and "where" and then tell "who" and "what." The "what" should be in chronological order, that is, going from the beginning to the end without skipping back and forth. Each question to be answered in the report should be contained in its own paragraph. It is also "reader friendly" to skip a line between paragraphs.

## Mechanically Correct

Specific rules of English must be followed when notes (or the spoken word) are transferred into a written report. These include rules for spelling, capitalization, and punctuation.

A well-written report is mechanically correct.

If you were to hear the words, "Your chances of being promoted are good if you can write effective reports," you would not be aware of mistakes that could be contained in the written statement: "Yur chanses of bein promotid are gud if you kin rite effectiv riports." This sentence appears to have been written by a young child or by an illiterate adult. The mechanics involved in translating ideas and spoken words into written words are complex, but important, and must be mastered. Several good English grammar handbooks are available in this area.

If spelling is a problem, writers should use a dictionary or a speller/divider. Speller/dividers are easier to use in that they contain on one page what a dictionary would require ten to fifteen pages to include. No matter which resource is used, when you look up a word, make a tally mark in the margin (assuming the dictionary or speller/divider is your own). You will quickly see that you are looking up the same words over and over. Write these words in the back cover of your spelling reference—or *learn* to spell them.

Of special importance is correct use of *homonyms,* those troublesome words that sound alike but have different meanings and different spellings. They are usually taught in second grade. Writers who have not mastered their use will appear very uneducated. Table 11–2 contains some of the more common homonyms.

## In Standard English

People often disagree about what "standard English" is. And the standards between spoken and written English differ. For example, people often drop the "g" in the "-ing" ending when they talk. Listen for it. Even very well-educated people might say: "I'm goin' home." But they would NOT write it that way.

Just as there are rules for spelling, capitalization, and punctuation, there are rules for what words are used when. For example, it is "standard" to say "he doesn't" rather than "he don't," or "I saw it," rather than "I seen it."

A well-written report is written in standard English.

Experience with English is needed to know what is "standard" and what is not—especially for people raised in surroundings in which a standard English is not used. People who speak standard English, however, usually also write in standard English.

## Legible and on Time

It does little good to learn to write well if no one can read it or if the report is turned in after the need for it is gone.

A well-written report is legible. It must also be on time.

Ideally, reports are typed or done on a word processor. Often, however, this is not practical. And sometimes a poorly typed report is as difficult to read as an illegible one. Security officers who know they have

**Table 11-2 Common homonyms.**

| Word | Meaning | Use in a sentence |
|---|---|---|
| accept | to take, receive, agree to | I *accept* that alibi. |
| except | to exclude, leave out | It is sound *except* for one point. |
| affect | to influence (verb) | How will that *affect* me? |
| effect | result (noun) | The *effect* is devastating. |
| ascent | motion upward | His *ascent* to the top was swift. |
| assent | consent, agree | Do you *assent* to the conditions? |
| brake | device for stopping motion | Did the trolley *brake* fail? |
| break | fracture, interrupt | How did you *break* your arm? |
| capital | money, seat of government | How much *capital* is involved? |
| capitol | government building | Turn left at the *capitol.* |
| cite | quote, summon to appear in court | He *cited* the Fifth Amendment. |
| sight | act of seeing, perception | The *sight* was ghastly. |
| site | location | He reached the *site* at noon. |
| council | an assembly | The *council* was in agreement. |
| counsel | an attorney, advice | His *counsel* gave him *counsel.* |
| decent | proper, suitable, right | It's the *decent* thing to do. |
| descent | motion downward | The *descent* from the top was rapid. |
| dissent | disagreement | The *dissent* caused a strike. |
| desert | forsake, abandon | I will not *desert* my post. |
| dessert | course at end of meal | He had pie for *dessert.* |
| forth | onward or forward | He came *forth* on command. |
| fourth | numerically number 4 | He was *fourth* in line. |
| hear | perceive by ear, listen to | Did you *hear* him leave? |
| here | this place | We got *here* too late to save him. |
| its | owned by "it" | The car lost *its* wheel. |
| it's | contraction of *it is* | *It's* time for us to go. |
| knew | past tense of *to know* | Dan *knew* the suspect was guilty. |
| new | modern, fresh | The *new* car gets good mileage. |
| lead | a metal | He was hit by a *lead* pipe. |
| led | past tense of *to lead* | He *led* the procession. |
| meat | food | I eat *meat* once a day. |
| meet | encounter, come together | I will *meet* you on the corner. |
| principal | chief, money, head of a school | He is the *principal* witness. |
| principle | rule, a fundamental truth | It is a matter of *principle.* |
| precede | to come before | A *precedes* B in the alphabet. |
| proceed | to continue, to go on | The investigation will *proceed.* |
| right | correct, privilege | He was *right* to go first. |
| rite | ceremony | It was a religious *rite.* |
| write | to inscribe by hand | Can you *write* the note? |
| their | belonging to "they" | It is *their* car. |
| there | in that place | I went *there* yesterday. |
| they're | contraction of *they are* | *They're* late, as usual. |
| threw | past tense of *to throw* | He *threw* the brick through the door. |
| through | from end to end | He drove *through* the tunnel. |
| to | toward, in the direction of | He went *to* the store. |
| too | more than enough; also | I have *too* many, *too.* |
| two | number 2 | I have *two* cars. |
| vary | to change | His story did not *vary.* |
| very | extremely, much | He is *very* tired. |
| whose | belonging to "who" | *Whose* car is this? |
| who's | contraction of *who is* | *Who's* going to drive it home? |
| your | belonging to "you" | *Your* car has been stolen. |
| you're | contraction of *you are* | *You're* going to walk home. |

poor handwriting should print their reports. Although this is slower than writing in long-hand (cursive), it will be a benefit to the reader.

## Checklist

A checklist such as that in Figure 11–5 might be used to evaluate reports.

## ☐ EXTERNAL COMMUNICATION

External communications may occur with the general public, with the media, or with the courts. It includes all interactions with agencies and individuals outside the employing agency. These communications are critical to effectively conducting business as well as to a sound public relations program, discussed in the next chapter.

Most security managers have a policy that on-line officers are not to issue statements or opinions about any activities or conditions related to

---

**Evaluation Checklist for Reports**

➤ Is the report:
  ➤ factual?
  ➤ accurate?
  ➤ objective?
  ➤ complete?
  ➤ concise?
  ➤ clear?
  ➤ legible?
➤ Does the report use:
  ➤ first person?
  ➤ active voice?
  ➤ correct modification?
  ➤ correct pronoun reference?
  ➤ parallel sentence structure?
➤ Are the sentences effective with:
  ➤ no fragments?
  ➤ no run-on sentences?
  ➤ similar ideas combined into single sentences?
➤ Are the sentences mechanically correct in terms of:
  ➤ spelling?
  ➤ use of apostrophes?
  ➤ abbreviations?
  ➤ numbers?
  ➤ capitalization?
  ➤ punctuation?
➤ Are the sentences gramatically correct in terms of:
  ➤ correct use of pronouns?
  ➤ agreement of subject and verb?
  ➤ correct use of adjectives and adverbs?
  ➤ correct use of negation?
  ➤ correct use of articles?
➤ Does the report allow the reader to visualize what happened?

---

**Figure 11–5 Evaluation checklist for reports.**
From *For the Record: Report Writing in Private Security*. Kären M. Hess and Henry Wrobleski. Institute for Professional Development, 1991. Reprinted by permission.

their duties to any newspaper reporters or members of the press, radio, or television media. Such requests are to be referred to the security manager who may, in turn, refer them to the public relations department.

One form of external communication most security managers and on-line personnel dread is having to testify in court. It is not quite so difficult when security personnel is on the side of the prosecution, having important information about some crime that has been committed. It is much more difficult if the security manager or officer is the defendant, being sued for some action. The following discussion assumes that the security personnel involved are on the prosecution side. Keep in mind, however, that the opposite situation does occur.

## ☐ TESTIFYING IN COURT

Although the vast majority of information security personnel communicate to others will be through written reports, they may also be called on to testify in court. This can be a rather frightening experience, but it need not be if they know what to expect. Ideally, all security personnel should attend a few court trials in which they are NOT involved to get a feel for what happens.

To effectively testify in court, be prepared, look professional, and act professionally.

Thorough *preparation* is essential. It should begin with review of all notes and reports related to the case, going over the main facts and checking their accuracy. Be aware of anything that might discredit the testimony. If possible, discuss the case with the prosecutor beforehand and anticipate any problems that might arise with the testimony.

*Appearance* is also very important. In most instances security managers appear at trials in business clothes, whereas officers appear in their uniforms. These should be clean and well pressed. A careless appearance might suggest to a jury that an officer is also careless about his or her job. Security personnel should be well groomed and should not wear dark glasses. They should have good posture, carry themselves erect without being stiff, and maintain eye contact with the attorneys, the judge, and the jurors. They should not exhibit signs of nervousness, such as constantly shifting in the chair, staring at the ceiling or off into space, or drumming their fingers on the railing. They should not smoke, chew gum, or wear a hat in the courtroom.

*Behavior and attitude* are critical in effective testimony. Security personnel should not appear to "know it all" or take the process personally. They should speak clearly, without mumbling, and loudly enough so that everyone in the courtroom can hear the testimony. They should address individuals by the appropriate title, for example, "Your honor" and "sir."

The defense attorney will make every effort to discredit the testimony—that is the attorney's job. Discrediting testimony is technically known as "impeaching the witness."

Defense attorneys attempt to impeach security personnel's testimony by showing that they are biased or untruthful, by pointing out inconsistencies, by asking rapid-fire questions, by demanding "yes" or "no" answers to complex questions, or by questioning their ability.

Defense attorneys commonly attempt to show that security personnel have a vested interest in having the defendant found guilty. In many instances the defendant is on trial because of actions taken by a security officer. It is important that security personnel not view the process personally. Their job is to present the facts as they know them, not to determine the guilt or innocence of the defendant. To counter such tactics, security personnel should not discuss the case with anyone not officially involved, including the press. Such statements can easily be misinterpreted. In more than one case a defense attorney has learned of some uncomplimentary remark about a defendant made by a security officer to an acquaintance. This acquaintance may be called to the courtroom and asked to tell the judge and jury what the security officer has said.

Another common method of attempting to impeach witnesses is by pointing out inconsistencies in testimony. Any inconsistencies in security officers' testimony provide alert defense attorneys with a powerful weapon. In one case an astute defense attorney was able to show that measurements recorded in a sketch differed by inches from those contained in the notes. With this minor inconsistency as a starting point, the defense raised doubts as to the competency of the entire investigation. Such doubts can make the difference between conviction and acquittal. To avoid inconsistencies, officers should record all facts accurately, as stressed earlier. They should review the facts before appearing in court. And they should not be embarrassed to refer to these notes in court to refresh their memories. If inconsistencies are found in an officer's testimony, they should be explained, if possible.

The defense attorney tactic of asking rapid-fire questions can be countered by personnel taking their time before responding. Simply because the questions are asked in quick succession does not mean they must be responded to in a similar fashion.

Another defense attorney tactic is to ask that a "yes" or "no" answer be provided to a very complex question. To counter such tactics, security personnel should simply state that such a simplistic answer is not possible. They should ask the defense attorney to break the complex question into smaller questions.

Sometimes defense attorneys will attack the capabilities of security officers, playing on the stereotype of security officers as uneducated and ignorant. Security officers and managers should not allow such tactics to upset them, but maintain their professionalism.

One other tactic defense attorneys may use is to ask security personnel if they have rehearsed the case with the prosecutor, implying that such "rehearsals" are improper. If they have, in fact, discussed the case prior to the trial, this fact should be stated. It is one acceptable means of preparing to give testimony and should cause no feelings of guilt.

Some defense attorneys snarl, yell, and insult witnesses. Such actions should be ignored. They will make the defense attorney look ridiculous if he or she is unable to accomplish the desired result.

## ☐ COMMUNICATIONS AS PUBLIC RELATIONS

Every contact with employees and the public is a public relations contact. All members of the security force, especially those in positions of authority, must present a positive image and communicate effectively.

Effective communication—downward, upward, lateral, formal and informal, internal and external—is the lifeblood of the security department. Effective communication also establishes the image security will have as well as the amount of cooperation security will receive from those they work with. The public relations role of security is the focus of the next chapter.

## SUMMARY

Communication skills are essential both for managing and for accomplishing loss prevention goals. The communication process involves a sender, a message, a channel, and a receiver. It may also include feedback. The weakest communication skill for most people is listening. This is partly because people can speak about 150 words per minute but can listen to over 450 words per minute, leaving lag time that can be devastating.

Nonverbal communication includes the eyes, facial expressions, posture, gestures, clothing, tone of voice, proximity, and touch. Written nonverbal communication includes neatness, paper quality, copy quality, binding, and the like.

Communication lines may be downward, upward (vertical), or lateral (horizontal). They may also be internal or external.

Recording and communicating information is an important part of any security professional's job. Officers should record all relevant information legibly in ink, in a notebook. Effective notes are accurate, brief, clear, and complete. This information can then be used as the basis for reports.

Security reports are usually one of two types: administrative or operational. Such reports are important because they are permanent written records that communicate important facts to be used in the future. A well-written report is factual, accurate, objective, complete, concise, clear, mechanically correct, written in standard English, legible, and on time.

In addition to writing reports, security personnel may need to testify in court. To do so effectively they should be prepared, look professional, and act professionally. They should also be prepared for tactics commonly employed by defense attorneys to impeach their testimony, including attempting to show that they are biased or untruthful, pointing out inconsistencies, asking rapid-fire questions, demanding "yes" or "no" answers to complex questions, and questioning their ability.

## APPLICATION

Read and evaluate the following report written by a security guard at a racetrack. Determine if it is acceptable in the following ways:

_____ Factual
_____ Accurate
_____ Objective

____ Complete
____ Concise
____ Clear
____ Correct
____ In Standard English

Mark any instances of ineffective writing and, if you can, make needed corrections.

> While on stable patrol on 02/05/91, at 2120, right after coffee break, a Mexican-American approached me. He identified hisself as Jose Martinez, DOB 01/04/39. Mr. Martinez is a groom whose employed by a Mr. Andrew C. Wallace. Most Spikes can't get any better jobs at the track. Martinez complained of being robbed, which occurred between the hours of 1100 and 2100 hours, this day, 02-05-91. He was robbed from his tackroom, #C in Barn 3. Items taken was a insulated lite-wait jacket, cream in color, four pears of wool slacks, gray in color, and one pair of black shoes. Martinez stated the tackroom was unlocked cuz other grooms had to get in to get there gear. I seen that Martinez's bed was torn apart like someone searched the place real good. While swearing profusely about getting ripped off, I asked Martinez if he seen anyone hanging around the barn or the tackroom area, but he didn't. I suspect its an inside job done by someone who knows the area. No leads at this time. Case pending.

## DISCUSSION QUESTIONS

1) Which basic communication skill—speaking, listening, reading, writing—do you have most difficulty with? Why?
2) How can security managers encourage upward communication from their officers—an essential element of participatory management.
3) What are the most significant barriers to communication in security work?
4) How can you improve your skills at note taking? At writing reports?
5) How do internal and external lines of communication differ? What must be taken into account in each? Is one more important than the other?

## REFERENCES

Hess, K. M. and Wrobleski, H. M. *For the record: Report writing in private security. Eureka, CA: Innovative Publications Company, 1991.*

Montgomery, Robert L. Are you a good listener? *Nation's business,* October 1981, pp. 65–68.

Nichols, Ralph G. Listening is a 10-part skill. *Nation's business,* July 1957.

Thomas, Elaine. Listen well and profits will tell. *Successful meetings,* May 1987, pp. 99–100.

## ☐ INTRODUCTION

When you enter a business establishment and immediately encounter a uniformed security officer, how this officer acts toward you will greatly influence how you feel about the business itself. If the officer smiles, requests that you sign in with the receptionist, and indicates exactly where the receptionist is, you are likely to feel welcomed and as though you have been helped. If, in contrast, the security officer bars your way and demands to know your business, you will have a completely different reaction. The image projected by security officers is critical to a business's or organization's public relations efforts.

## ☐ PUBLIC RELATIONS DEFINED

**Public relations** is a planned program of policies and conduct designed to build confidence in and increase the understanding of a business's or organization's publics. These publics may include customers, suppliers, creditors, competitors, employees, stockholders, members of the community, or the government. Ferrell and Pride (1982, p. 520) define public relations as "a broad set of communication activities employed to create and maintain favorable relations between the organization and its publics—such as customers, employees, stockholders, government officials, and society in general."'

---

Public relations includes all activities undertaken to bolster image and create good will.

---

Think for a moment about what makes for good interpersonal relations. How should people act toward one another if they want to establish solid, lasting friendships? Obviously, they will be considerate, open, honest, caring, and the like. The same characteristics are important in building "public" relations. Most businesses and organizations are vitally concerned with how they are perceived by their many publics.

## Chapter Twelve

# Enhancing Public Relations

### DO YOU KNOW

➤ What public relations is?

➤ What role security personnel have in public relations?

➤ What factors are important to effective public relations?

➤ What special populations security personnel must learn to interact with?

➤ What medical or other conditions can be mistaken for intoxication or being high on drugs?

➤ What balance security managers should strive for when dealing with the press and the media?

➤ How effective public relations affects security?

# ☐ THE ROLE OF SECURITY PERSONNEL IN PUBLIC RELATIONS

Properly attired security officers who look professional and act professionally make a positive impression on those who come into contact with them. Such security officers, in fact, make a statement to employees and the public about how this particular company or organization does business, that is, that it takes itself, its business, and its customers seriously. The importance of this function is noted by Brennan (1985, p. 32):

> In many cases, a security guard is the first employee with whom customers come into contact, and the importance of first impressions cannot be overstated. The significance of a properly uniformed guard is obvious and well recognized in the case of banks and other facilities that have large amounts of cash on hand and where public trust is essential. Still, the benefits of highly visible professional security officers can be substantial for nearly any type of company.

Private security officers convey an image of their employer that can either promote or detract from public relations efforts. Promoting good public relations is a vital part of any security officer's job.

Brennan notes that before the Second World War most security was provided by night watchmen who made rounds with a flashlight. Because they worked when no one else was around, they dressed as they pleased, which was usually very casually. Unfortunately, this is the image many people still have of security officers: that of an untrained guard dressed like a bum, making rounds between snoozes. This image must be dispelled.

# ☐ FACTORS INVOLVED IN PUBLIC RELATIONS

To promote public relations, security personnel must be professional in every way.

Good public relations require that security personnel:

➤ Look professional.
➤ Act professionally.

## Appearance

One of the most important factors in a professional appearance is the uniform worn by the on-line officers. Brennan (1985, p. 32) warns: "Don't allow your guards to look like janitors and expect them to behave like professionals." He describes three types of uniforms currently in use: the military look, the security officer look, and the soft look. Each has advantages and disadvantages.

Military-type uniform.

*The military uniform* resembles that of police officers or officers in a branch of the military. It typically has a brimmed cap, a dark blue coat with matching pants, a white shirt and dark tie, and black shoes and socks. Such a uniform is often decorated with brass buttons, braids, stripes, and epaulets. The badge is likely to be metal. Advantages to the military look include the sense of authority it conveys, as well as its aura of professionalism. Such uniforms also have disadvantages, however, including the fact that they are frequently cumbersome and bulky and that they are relatively expensive—to buy and to maintain. In addition, care must be taken that they do not too closely resemble the community's public police officers' uniforms. Brennan suggests that the military look is perhaps best suited for "stationary security officer positions where a highly visible security presence is desired."

*The security officer uniform* is less "official"-looking. Many security companies have established their own identities and reflect these identities in the uniforms provided their officers. Such uniforms frequently are of a color different from the traditional "police blue," for example, brown, light blue, or forest green. Fabrics and styles are more functional, durable, and easy to keep up. The jackets are usually shorter than the military-type jackets, are lighter, and are water-repellent. They are not as heavily "decorated" as the military-style uniforms, and the badges are likely to be fabric rather than metal. Many do not have jackets. Such uniforms have the advantages of being clearly distinguishable from those of law enforcement officers, of being less bulky and cumbersome, and of

Security officer-type uniform.

being relatively less expensive—to buy and to maintain. Brennan cites the comments of Rick Massimei, vice president of Metro Security Systems, Inc., in Tampa, Florida, in support of the security officer-type uniforms:

> We want our guards to be distinguishable as legitimate security officers. . . . A properly uniformed guard who looks and acts professionally will deter would-be criminals just as effectively as a guard whose uniform closely mimics the police. . . . They can be even more effective, because their presence tells criminals they are assigned solely to the location they patrol, rather than being mistaken for police officers who just happen to be in the area.

*The soft look uniform* is much more casual than either the military or the security officer-type uniform. It usually consists of a blazer with a cloth badge and contrasting slacks, frequently gray or blue. These uniforms are most often used by officers who work exclusively indoors, usually in office buildings or institutions such as museums, libraries, and hospitals. The soft look is very low key and will blend in well with a corporate or office environment where an emphasis on security is deemed to be intimidating.

The style of uniform is not the only factor important in a security officer's appearance. Equally important is that it be clean and well pressed, and that the officer also be neatly groomed. Shirts should be clean, shoes should be shined, hair should be clean and combed, and a smile should be present, under normal circumstances.

For security officers who drive company vehicles, the appearance of the vehicle and its condition are important. Frequently it is all a citizen sees, so it makes a major impression. It should be washed regularly, and the interior should be kept free of debris. In addition, how officers drive their vehicles will reflect on their professionalism. Rudeness, impatience, and/or illegal driving should be scrupulously avoided.

Soft look uniform.

## Actions

Looking professional is not enough. Security officers must also act professionally. To do so, they must have a positive attitude toward their
work. Zaleski, (1986, p. 136), security supervisor at the corporate headquarters of Aetna Life Insurance Company, emphasizes this: "We should
make sure they have the proper attitude and what I consider to be the
three most important assets any security officer can have: a sense of
humor, a sense of compassion, and good, old-fashioned common sense."
Security officers should see themselves as providers of service and assistance, not as simply enforcers of company rules and policies. They
should be perceived of as friend rather than enemy. When they encounter situations where they must intervene in an "enforcing" way, their
actions should be objective, unemotional, and understandable. For
example, if a visitor is in an unauthorized area, the security officer
should calmly explain the situation and escort the visitor out of the
area. There is no need to be rude. A clear explanation and a firm
request for action of some sort is generally all that will be required.

If security officers are to act professionally, they must fully understand what they are protecting and why it must be secure. They need to
understand the company's policies as well as its goals and missions.
They must understand what is expected of them and be trained to do it.
And they must feel that they are supported. Zaleski (p. 135) notes the
importance of this support:

In many companies it is a firm policy that a direction given to an employee by a security officer carries the same force as a direction given by the employee's supervisor, as long as the security officer is acting within the bounds of his or her authority. Word of that type of support may spread quickly through your security department, and your officers will come to understand that if they act within the boundaries of their authority, they will always be supported, an especially important consideration when unpleasant situations occur on the job. . . . Security people like to feel their job is unique, and it does take a unique individual to be a good security officer. The fact of the matter is that security is not a nine-to-five job, and it is not for everyone. It takes a very special breed of person to be a security officer, to work seven days a week, rotating shifts in some cases, to work weekends and holidays, and to give up time with family and friends. There is a lot more than money at stake when a person decides to enter security as a career.

Security officers who have this positive self-image and are supported will do much to enhance their employer's image. In addition, although security officers are not usually thought of as part of management, they represent management when they enforce company rules. Hertig (1985, p. 85) suggests that, as a result of representing management, security officers "must be skilled in many of the same techniques required for management personnel, such as interviewing and assessment methods, written communication skills, and interpersonal communication techniques. In addition, security officers are frequently called on to instruct groups of people. . . . An officer's ability to communicate well is important to his or her job performance."

In addition to greeting people in a friendly manner and answering their questions politely, security personnel should know their facility so they can guide and direct people as requested. And they should be skilled at handling telephone conversations properly, an important way to build a positive image. The sound of a voice makes a profound impression on the caller. It should be firm yet friendly, and loud enough to be heard easily. If the officer is assigned to answer a phone, it should be done promptly—within three rings when possible. The officer should state his or her name and title, and ask what information or assistance is required. Seldom should a caller be asked to "hold." It is extremely exasperating to a caller to be put on hold.

## ☐ INTERACTION WITH INDIVIDUALS

The most significant interaction security personnel have is one-on-one, be it with employees, visitors, or clients/customers. As our society becomes more diverse, security personnel must understand the individual differences they are likely to encounter. Some differences such as age, sex, socioeconomic conditions, and educational levels have been recognized and dealt with in public relations programs.

One such difference becoming of increasing concern is the elderly population. Other differences are less commonly known and are often much more difficult for security personnel to deal with. These differences include people with disabilities, people newly arrived in the United States who speak little English, and the homeless.

---

Security personnel may need to interact with the elderly, the disabled, non-English-speaking individuals, and those who are homeless.

---

## The Elderly

In the past decade the number of Americans sixty-five years old and older has increased by approximately 23 percent (Exter, 1989). According to Manning and Proctor (1989, p. 1D) the first wave of "baby boomers" will turn fifty in 1996, beginning a "senior boom" in the United States. By 2010 one-fourth of our population will be fifty-five or older.

One problem often accompanying advancing years is Alzheimer's disease (A.D.). Some 2.5 million American citizens have Alzheimer's. According to the Alzheimer's Disease and Related Disorders Association (1987, p. 5) the symptoms of Alzheimer's disease include the following:

> Gradual memory loss, impairment of judgment, disorientation, personality change, decline in ability to perform routine tasks, behavior change, difficulty in learning, loss of language skills, and a decline in intellectual function.

Alzheimer's disease can cause several behavior problems that might bring the person into contact with security officers.

**Wandering** is common. A.D. victims may become hopelessly lost. They may not remember where they live or where they were going. They may become confused, uncooperative, or even combative when questioned.

**Indecent exposure** is sometimes the result of the tendency of Alzheimer victims to fidget and to repeat behaviors. As noted by the A.D. Association (1987): "The A.D. victim who zips and unzips his pants or unbuttons her blouse in public may simply be fidgeting." They also have limited impulse control, and if clothing is too warm or is uncomfortable, they may simply take it off.

**Shoplifting** may occur as the result of simply forgetting to pay for an item. In addition, A.D. victims may misplace their purses or billfolds while shopping and then accuse store personnel of stealing from them. They may forget how much money they have or how much they have spent.

**Poor driving** and **auto accidents** are also problems. A.D. victims may lose their cars, may forget that they drove somewhere and report their cars stolen, may have an accident and leave, actually forgetting that the accident happened, or they may simply keep driving.

**The appearance of intoxication** may bring A.D. sufferers to the attention of security personnel. Their wandering, confusion, inability to answer questions, or their driving behavior may be mistakenly interpreted as intoxication.

Individuals with Alzheimer's disease may appear to be intoxicated.

Security personnel should be familiar with the symptoms of A.D. and have strategies for dealing with A.D. victims whom they encounter. The following suggestions are offered by the A.D. Association:

➤ Look for an ID bracelet or other identification.
➤ Avoid lectures or confrontation. They will not work with these people, and they are likely to make things worse.
➤ Keep communication simple. Speak softly and slowly.
➤ Identify yourself and explain what you are or will be doing, even if it is obvious.
➤ Use distraction to end inappropriate behavior. Sometimes just your presence will accomplish that.
➤ Maintain eye contact when speaking.
➤ Try to maintain a calm atmosphere. A.D. patients are prone to "catastrophic reactions" which you want to avoid.
➤ During a catastrophic reaction, A.D. patients often lash out, verbally and/or physically, at people who try to help them.
➤ Avoid restraints if possible. Physical restraints are almost certain to cause a catastrophic reaction.

The elderly may also have vision or hearing problems, or both.

## Individuals with Disabilities or Impairing Diseases

Some physical disabilities are very obvious. Other disabilities, however, are not immediately apparent. Likewise, most impairing diseases are not immediately apparent and may be mistaken for intoxication, including Alzheimer's disease, as already discussed.

**The visually impaired** consist of over 11.5 million individuals according to the National Society to Prevent Blindness (Zehring, 1990, p. 33). When interacting with people who are blind, security officers should not only identify themselves, but also offer to let the person feel their badge or patch as a means of confirming their official capacity.

**The hearing impaired** are among those with "invisible" handicaps. Security personnel will interact more effectively with people who are hearing impaired if they understand that most deaf people are not good lip-readers.

In addition, the speech of individuals who have been deaf since birth may sound garbled and even unintelligible. It has been mistaken for intoxication.

King (1990, pp. 98–100), director of deaf education at the University of Southern Mississippi, states: "Deaf people communicate differ-

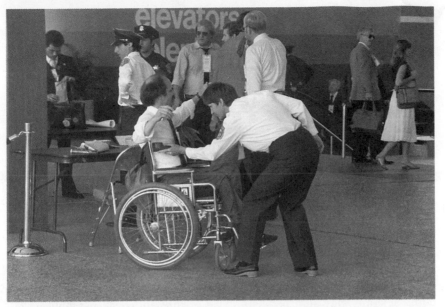

Going through security at a democratic national convention.

ently, depending on the age at which the person became deaf, the type of deafness, language skills, speech and speech-reading abilities, intelligence, personality and educational background.'' He notes that, for officers who find themselves in a situation in which they need to communicate with a deaf individual, the key is to determine how that particular person communicates and use whatever combination of techniques are needed to help communication. He offers the following suggestions:

1) Get the person's attention. Gently tap a shoulder, wave, or call out loudly yet respectfully.
2) Make sure the person understands the topic of discussion.
3) Speak slowly and clearly, but do not overenunciate or overexaggerate words. This makes lip-reading difficult, if not impossible. Speak in short sentences.
4) Look directly at the person.
5) Do not place anything in your mouth when speaking. Pencil chewing or smoking make lip-reading more difficult.
6) Maintain eye contact. This conveys the feeling of direct communication.
7) Avoid standing in front of a light source.
8) Do not hesitate to communicate by paper and pencil. Keep the message simple.
9) Use pantomime, body language, and facial expressions.
10) If possible, learn sign language. Even basic signing can overcome barriers.
11) Do not assume the message has been understood just because the person nods.

## People with Epilepsy

**Epilepsy** is a disorder that security officers should be familiar with. The Epilepsy Foundation of the University of Minnesota's educational program, "Epilepsy: A Positive ID," contains information all security personnel should know. The following discussion is based on information from that program.

Epilepsy is a disorder of the central nervous system in which a person tends to have recurrent seizures. It is:

➤ Chronic. (There is no cure. Medication or surgery is needed to control the seizures.)
➤ Episodic. (Seizures occur sometimes.)
➤ Sudden and unpredictable. (Seizures may occur at the most inopportune times—even when a person faithfully takes medication.)
➤ A disorder—*not* a disease. It is *not* contagious.

An important thing to know about seizures is that not all of them are convulsive. A seizure is not always a stiffening and jerking of the body. Seizures may alter behavior, level of consciousness, perception, and/or the senses of individuals with epilepsy (*not* epileptics).

**Absence seizures** (formerly called petit mal) are often mistaken for daydreaming or staring and can occur up to one hundred times a day or more.

**Simple partial seizures** consist of changes in motor function or sensations *without* accompanying alteration of consciousness. It may be characterized by stiffening or jerking in just one or more extremities, a strange feeling in the stomach, tingling, or an alteration of taste or smell.

**Complex partial seizures** involve impairment of consciousness and may last from a few seconds to several minutes. The following behaviors may occur:

➤ Incoherent speech.
➤ Glassy-eyed staring.
➤ Aimless wandering.
➤ Chewing/lip-smacking motions.
➤ Picking at clothing.

The individual may be confused or need to rest after a seizure. This type of seizure may be mistaken for a drug or alcohol-induced stupor. A person having a complex partial seizure will have a fairly prompt return (several minutes) of their faculties whereas a drunk or high person will not.

A epileptic seizure can look like street drugs or alcohol at work.

Figure 12–1 summarizes the differences between an epileptic seizure and drug/alcohol abuse symptoms.

| Complex partial seizure symptoms | Drug/alcohol abuse symptoms |
|---|---|
| Chewing, lip smacking motions | not likely |
| Picking at clothes | not likely |
| Should regain consciousness in 30 seconds to 3 minutes, except in the rare case of a complex partial status (when seizure continues) | a drunk/high person will not recover in 3 minutes or less |
| No breath odor | a drunk will smell like alcohol |
| Possibly wearing an epilepsy I.D. bracelet/tag | not likely |
| **Symptoms common to both**<br>• Impaired consciousness • Incoherent speech<br>• Glassy-eyed staring • Aimless wandering | |

**Figure 12–1 Epileptic seizure or drug/alcohol abuse?**
*Reprinted with permission of Epilepsy Education Program, University of Minnesota.*

Epilepsy Education of the University of Minnesota suggests the following *assistance* for someone having a complex partial seizure:

➤ If possible, guide the person to a safe place to sit and let the seizure run its course.
➤ Keep the person calm.
➤ Do not restrain the person in any fashion. He or she may resist.
➤ To determine level of consciousness, ask:
  ➤ What is your name?
  ➤ Where are you?
  ➤ What day is it?
➤ Check for medical alert bracelet or tag.
➤ Smell breath for alcohol.
➤ Do not leave a confused person alone.

**Generalized tonic** (stiffening) **clonic** (jerking) **seizures** (formerly called grand mal) are what most people commonly associate with epilepsy. These seizures may last a few seconds to several minutes and may result in the following behaviors:

➤ Loss of consciousness.
➤ Falling.
➤ Stiffening and jerking (hence, the name tonic clonic).
➤ Tongue biting—sometimes.
➤ Drooling.
➤ Loss of bowel and bladder control—sometimes.

Epilepsy Education suggests the following *assistance* for a person experiencing a generalized tonic clonic seizure:

➤ Cushion head.
➤ Remove glasses.

- ➤ Loosen tie, collar.
- ➤ Clear the area of any hard objects the person may hit.
- ➤ Look for medical alert bracelet or tag.
- ➤ Do not put anything in the person's mouth (e.g., finger, pencil, tongue blade). This may damage the teeth or jaw.
- ➤ When seizure has subsided, turn person on his or her side and allow saliva to flow from mouth and keep the airway open.
- ➤ To determine level of consciousness, ask:
  - ➤ What is your name?
  - ➤ Where are you?
  - ➤ What day is it?
- ➤ If you arrive after the seizure, ask onlookers what they witnessed.
- ➤ Call for an ambulance if:
  - ➤ The person has hit head.
  - ➤ You suspect injury.
  - ➤ The seizure lasts more than ten minutes.
  - ➤ The seizures occur one after another. This is a life-threatening situation requiring immediate action.

Epilepsy Education stresses that first responders need to be able to recognize seizures, administer the proper procedures, and be responsive to the sensitivities and pride of people with epilepsy. The incorrect handling of a seizure can be embarrassing for the person having the seizure and can make the first responder potentially liable.

## Non-English-Speaking Individuals

Thousands of immigrants and millions of foreign visitors arrive in our country annually. With such numbers, it is likely that security personnel will have encounters with individuals who speak no English or very limited English.

One obvious step toward effectively interacting with non-English-speaking individuals is to hire security personnel who speak other languages likely to be encountered within a given business or establishment.

Security personnel should recognize when a language barrier exists and be creative in finding ways to communicate. Often gestures are useful. If, for example, a security officer wants a non-English-speaking person to sign in, the officer could point to his or her name plate and imitate signing in. Many of the strategies useful with individuals having hearing impairments will work equally well with non-English-speaking individuals.

If management deems the language barrier to be a significant security/public relations problem, it might consider subscribing to the *language line*. This translation service offered by AT&T provides direct interpretations for police and other emergency service units that respond to calls. According to *Law Enforcement News* (1990, p. 3), the service is capable of providing translation for over 140 languages from Swahili to Sanskrit. Subscribers are given cards that list all the languages the service can translate, written so non-English speakers can read the name of their language in their native script and point to it so the subscriber can connect with the right translator. Subscribers who encounter communication problems can call a toll-free number from almost any type of telephone and request the language needed on a twenty-four-hour-a-day basis.

## The Homeless

Dealing with individuals who are homeless may be the responsibility of security personnel who are assigned to bus depots, airports, or any other type of structure where homeless people might seek temporary shelter.

According to Lamar (1988) more than two million people will be homeless sometime during the year, one-third of whom will be families with children and one-fourth of whom will have jobs—the working poor. Lamar also says that one-third of the homeless are mentally ill.

The change in public attitudes toward the homeless is illustrated in three major cities that have toughened regulations on panhandling, sleeping in public places, and other behavior associated with the homeless. As noted in *Insight* (1990, p. 22): "While the plight of the homeless remains at the top of the nation's urban agenda, the public's sense of guilt appears to be giving way to exasperation. Responding to an unmistakable shift in public attitudes, officials in San Francisco, New York, and Washington, three of the most staunchly liberal cities in the nation, have adopted policies that now are as much attuned to the concerns of the average voter as to the demands of the homeless advocacy groups."

In New York City police are enforcing new regulations prohibiting lying down on floors or benches in Pennsylvania Station or Grand Central Terminal, panhandling, fighting, or disrobing and urinating or defecating outside toilet facilities. In San Francisco new laws have displaced

Security officers may need to deal with homeless people during their rounds.

as many as 350 homeless who formerly camped in the Civic Center Plaza. In Washington, D.C., the city council overturned a 1984 "right-to-shelter-law" that was costing the city $40 million a year.

Security personnel should be aware of what kinds of assistance are available for the homeless and make this information known, including helping them to obtain services.

## Intoxicated or Drug-Impaired Individuals

Recognizing intoxicated or drug-impaired individuals was discussed in Chapter 9. Security personnel who encounter individuals who appear to be under the influence of drugs or alcohol should identify themselves as "security" and should determine whether the individual is an employee. If the person is an employee, in most instances, that person's manager should be notified immediately and asked to deal with the situation. If the person is not an employee and the person's behavior is disruptive, security personnel should politely but firmly ask the person to leave the premises. In either case, an incident report should be completed.

## Disorderly Individuals

Security personnel should usually follow the same procedures used for persons suspected to be under the influence of illegal drugs or alcohol. Report disorderly individuals to their managers. After identifying themselves as "security," they should politely but firmly inform disorderly nonemployees that their behavior is unacceptable and they must leave the premises. In either instance, an incident report should be written.

## ☐ UNDERSTANDING SELF AND THE IMAGE PROJECTED

In addition to being sensitive to the individual differences of those with whom they interact, security personnel should also be aware of their own beliefs, possible prejudices, insecurities in dealing with certain types of individuals, and the image they are presenting to coworkers and the public.

The following suggestions for improving the one-on-one citizen contact are adapted from suggestions given by the International Association of Chiefs of Police:

➤ Use a polite, unexcited, or calm reasoning approach whenever possible. Try to be impersonal from two points of view: (1) Remember the authority you wield is that of your employer, not yours personally, and (2) Try to remain detached and not take as a personal insult or affront people's reaction to your authority.
➤ Be businesslike and self-assured; do not show anger, impatience, contempt, dislike, sarcasm, and similar attitudes.
➤ Size things up as accurately as possible before making the contact. Be open-minded in evaluating the facts.

- Once you have the straight story, make your decision based on the policies and procedures under which you work and take decisive action.
- Offer explanations where advisable, but do not be trapped into arguing.
- Be civil and courteous.
- Show by your demeanor that you are not looking for and you do not expect any trouble.
- Try to avoid giving the impression that your presence constitutes a threat—either physical or psychological.

## □ INTERACTION AND COOPERATION WITH THE PRESS AND MEDIA

Garner (1989, p. 34) offers advice to police administrators that might be equally applicable to security administrators: "A police administrator can gain as much benefit from the media as they can from you. What they have to offer, in many instances, is publicity for your agency and to a lesser extent, yourself. With a little understanding, that publicity can be positive and make your organization look good. The secret to success is honesty and approachability."

Other keys to success in dealing with the media include the following:

- Have a clear policy on what information is to be released to the press and what is not.
- Treat all reporters fairly.
- Be as sensitive to the need for privacy of employees, victims, and witnesses as to the need of the public to know what is going on.

Some larger establishments have a public relations department which is the only one authorized to release information to the media.

Security managers should balance the public's "right to know" and the reporters' First Amendment right to publish what they know with their employer's need to withhold certain information and to protect their privacy.

## □ COOPERATION WITH PUBLIC POLICE

The importance of public police and private security personnel working together was discussed in Chapter 5. As noted by Bocklet (1990, p. 54): "The study [Hallcrest Report II] recommended that private security resources could contribute to cooperative, community-based crime prevention and security awareness programs. . . . The study recommended police and private security share crime prevention materials, specialized security equipment, expertise, and personnel."

How well public and private security agencies work together will depend in large part on how well they can communicate with each other and on how well the goals of each can be complementary rather than competing.

## ☐ PUBLIC RELATIONS AND THE PROMOTION OF SECURITY

Looking professional and acting professionally does much more than enhance public relations.

A security officer who looks and acts like a professional will have a greater likelihood of deterring crime, the primary purpose for being hired initially.

Brennan (p. 34) suggests that, as a rule, "Professionally equipped, properly attired guards deliver a higher level of security." He quotes James Dunbar, CPP, president of the Loughlin Security Agency in Baltimore:

> There's no doubt that proper equipment and professional uniforms play a part in maintaining guards' security awareness, so they *do* react properly when the need arises. But the greatest value comes from deterrence—the number of crimes *not* attempted because of the presence of a uniformed guard. This is where we [contract guard companies] provide our greatest service to our customers—crimes that never happen because one of our guards was on the scene, looking and acting in a professional way.

Good public relations can also promote the security program and its safety and protection objectives.

As noted by Shea (1987, p. 97):

> Every security department could benefit from using proven public relations methods to plan and develop its protection program.
> Your security program will be more successful if you can encourage employees to comply with security procedures voluntarily. . . . A velvet-glove approach—not an authoritarian one—is best suited to achieving security compliance.

Shea describes several principles emphasized by Bernard Posner, public relations specialist, that cannot guarantee success, but whose absence generally cause failure:

➤ Define the objectives of your program early.
➤ Research the nature of the audience you are attempting to reach.
➤ Identify specific groups in that audience.
➤ Identify the trendsetters in each of these groups.
➤ Select the proper medium for communicating with each group.
➤ Develop a theme or slogan for your campaign.

- Pace the campaign to suit the environment in which it will be presented.
- Time specific aspects of the campaign for moments when they will make the greatest impression.
- Cooperate with other groups.
- Collect feedback from the target audience.

Objectives should be specific, measurable, and in line with the overall philosophy and mission of the establishment. The audiences to be reached should also be very specific. In a retail establishment, for example, the audiences might include sales personnel, custodial staff, management, and the public. Identifying trendsetters from among internal audiences is important because they can be approached to lend their support to the security objectives being introduced.

The medium to be used can vary from audience to audience and objective to objective and might include posters, signs, newsletters, additions to policy manuals, memos, announcements, meetings, orientation programs, and in-service training sessions.

Timing and pacing can fit with state or national "drives" such as fire prevention week or accident prevention week. Cooperating with other groups would involve finding out what sort of personal, social, and professional groups employees might belong to. For example, in a university setting, instructors may belong to a faculty association which could serve as a means of promoting security objectives.

After specific security measures have been in place for a prespecified amount of time, their effectiveness should be evaluated by getting feedback from a representative random sample of those involved.

The importance to security programs of a good public relations program, going well beyond smiling and being friendly, is stressed by Shea (1987, p. 99):

> Friendly faces are pleasant to look at, but they don't communicate the need for specific security programs. Smiling security officers alone cannot persuade your target audience to comply with your security program. A successful security manager must know how to put a public relations program in gear. The successful application of proven public relations principles can increase a security department's ability to provide a safe and secure environment in which employees can work.

Although this chapter is brief, its message is extremely important. Every action a security officer takes, or does not take, will affect not only his or her own image but that of the employer/business/company/institution as well.

*Good public relations never stops. Look and act like a professional at all times.*

## SUMMARY

**P**ublic relations includes all activities undertaken to bolster image and create good will. Private security officers convey an image of their employer that can either promote or detract from public relations efforts.

Promoting good public relations is a vital part of any security officer's job. Good public relations requires that security personnel look professional and act professionally as they deal with groups and with individuals.

Security personnel may need to interact with the elderly, the disabled, non-English-speaking individuals, and those who are homeless. Individuals with Alzheimer's disease may appear to be intoxicated. Likewise, the speech of individuals who have been deaf since birth may sound garbled and even unintelligible and has been mistaken for intoxication. An epileptic seizure can look like street drugs or alcohol at work.

Security personnel may also interact with members of the media and the press. Security managers should balance the public's "right to know" and the reporters' First Amendment right to publish what they know with their employer's need to withhold certain information and to protect their privacy.

Security officers who look professional and act professionally will have a greater likelihood of deterring crime. Good public relations can also promote the security program and its safety and protection objectives.

## APPLICATION

Following is a list of public relations efforts a business or organization might engage in. Check those in which security personnel might play a role.

____ Open house
____ Reception
____ Tour of the establishment
____ Newsletter
____ Speaking to local schools

## DISCUSSION QUESTIONS

1) What type of uniform would you prefer to wear and why?
2) In what types of businesses is public relations most important?
3) Why is a sense of humor important for security personnel?
4) Why are communication skills important for security personnel?
5) What activities might a security officer volunteer to do to promote public relations?

## REFERENCES

Alzheimer's Disease and Related Disorders Association, Victim, not criminal: The Alzheimer sufferer, Chicago, IL, 1987.

Bocklet, Richard. Police-private security cooperation. *Law and order,* December 1990, pp. 54–59.

Brennan, J. Outfitting your guard force. *Security management,* June 1985, pp. 32–35.

Epilepsy Education. *Epilepsy: A positive ID.* Minneapolis, MN: University of Minnesota, 1990.

Exter, Thomas. Demographic forecasts—On to retirement. *American demographics,* April 1989.

Ferrell, O. C. and Pride, W. M. *Fundamentals of marketing.* Boston: Houghton Mifflin Co., 1982.

Garner, Gerald. Working with the media: Winning at the interview game, *Law and order,* May 1989, pp. 34—37.

Hertig, C. A. A holistic approach to security training. *Security management,* March 1985, pp. 84—86.

International Association of Chiefs of Police. Improving the officer/citizen contact. Training Key 94.

*Insight.* The new drift in homeless policy, August 6, 1990, pp. 22—24.

King, J. Freeman. The law officer and the deaf. *Police chief,* October 1990, pp. 98—100.

Lamar, Jacob V. The homeless: Brick by brick. *Time,* October 24, 1988, pp. 34—38.

*Law enforcement news.* Parlez-vous Miranda warnings? Language line gives police gift of gab. September 30, 1990, p. 3.

Manning, Anita and Proctor, David. Senior boom: The future's new wrinkle. *USA today,* January 31, 1989, p. 1D.

Shea, John B. More than a happy face. *Security management,* May 1987, pp. 97 — 99.

Zaleski, J. E., Jr. Should you remake your security image? *Security management,* August 1986, pp. 135—36.

Zehring, Timothy. New insights for the visually impaired, *Law and order.* December 1990, pp. 33—35.

# Section Three

# Security Systems to Prevent Losses

The basic security responsibilities discussed in Section Two can be adapted to fit specific security systems. The criteria for determining the amount of security needed are based primarily on the relative criticality and vulnerability of the establishment, as well as on management's perceived need for and commitment to achieving a reasonable degree of security.

Section Three presents some of the specific problems encountered and the security systems developed for industrial security (Chapter 13), retail security (Chapter 14), commercial security (Chapter 15), and institutional security (Chapter 16).

Security equipment, procedures, and personnel can be used singly or in combination to prevent losses.

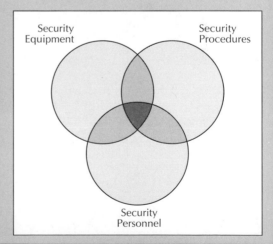

Where all three interact, the greatest security is provided.

Although security measures add costs, they can also result in considerable savings. The National Crime Prevention Institute cites several fundamental conditions that must exist before an effective security program can be implemented and more profits realized:*

- **M**anagement support of security from the top level.
- **O**rganizational structure allowing security access to top management.
- **R**ecognize and establish sound physical and procedural controls.
- **E**ducate employees to follow established procedures.
- **P**ost and impartially enforce all procedures.
- **R**ecord all incidents of procedural violations.
- **O**rganize operational procedures to avoid conflict of interest.
- **F**idelity bonds utilized and implications explained to employees.
- **I**nformation given to all employees regarding pure risk potential in job.
- **T**rain all employees to react properly to pure risk confrontation.
- **S**et example by refusing to violate rules at all management levels.

*"Understanding Crime Prevention" by the National Crime Prevention Institute.

## □ INTRODUCTION

Effective security can affect all aspects of industry, from selection of employees to distribution of finished products. Security is inseparable from good manage-ment and profits, and profits are vital to the national economy. As noted by the Task Force Report on *Private Security* (1976, p.51): "Manufacturing consis-tently accounts for nearly one-quarter of the gross national product." Manu-facturing includes a range of primary products, such as those related to food processing, textiles, transportation, met-als, machinery, electrical products, and heavy durable goods.

Security officers were first used in manufacturing plants on a large scale prior to World War I because of concern about sabotage and espionage. During World War II many manufacturing plants established proprietary security forces. Over two hundred thousand of these plant security officers were granted the status of auxiliary military police because their primary duties were to protect war goods and products, supplies, equipment, and personnel. After the war, many larger manufacturers continued to maintain propri-etary security forces, but more recently, as such programs have become more expensive, many plants have begun using contractual security officers. Sometimes the contract security officers are supervised by a small proprietary security force.

As in any other type of establishment, the criteria for determining the expense and effort to be expended to protect a particular plant are based largely on the plant's importance and vulnerability. Especially vul-nerable are plants whose products are small, valuable, or particularly desirable, such as watches, calculators, small transistor radios, television sets, and jewelry. The incidence of theft is usually high in general mer-chandising warehouses and factories that manufacture such valuable articles. The incidence of theft is usually lower in heavy industrial plants, such as steel mills or furniture factories.

In addition, security needs generally increase as the size of the plant increases. Some plants cover many acres and have many buildings, such as Minnesota Mining and Manufacturing (3M) which, during the day, has more employees present than the population of many cities. When employees number in the thousands, it is extremely difficult to deter those who steal company property or break company rules.

## Chapter Thirteen

# Industrial Security

### DO YOU KNOW

➤ What types of losses are usually specific to industry?

➤ How to protect against loss of tools?

➤ What special problems must be considered in industrial security?

➤ What sabotage and espionage are?

➤ How to protect against industrial espionage?

➤ What areas are most vulnerable to theft?

➤ What cargoes are most frequently stolen from trucks?

➤ What security measures have been used by the trucking industry?

➤ What the primary security problems of the railroad industry are?

➤ What security measures have been taken by railroads?

➤ What security problems exist at utility companies?

➤ How to protect against a utility company's losses?

# ☐ INDUSTRIAL SECURITY RESPONSIBILITIES*

Industrial security personnel may use any of the physical or procedural controls discussed in Section Two. Fences, locks, lighting, alarms, access control through passes or badges, inspections, package pass systems, and vehicle control are all very appropriate for industrial security. The Task Force Report explains some industrial security responsibilities:

> The responsibilities of security [officers] in manufacturing plants often include the monitoring of electrical utility systems for failure or malfunction of automated machinery, fire prevention, and inspections for Occupational Health and Safety Act (OSHA) violations. These responsibilities, coupled with crime prevention and detection functions, essentially comprise manufacturing security, which is often referred to as "plant protection."
>
> A major emphasis of plant security programs is the regulation and screening of visitors; service, repair, delivery, and maintenance personnel; vendors; truck drivers; and employees (p. 52).

Plant security personnel coordinate their efforts with local, county, and state law enforcement agencies in investigating internal theft and criminal incidents that occur on the premises. Defense-industry security personnel maintain liaison with the FBI and the Defense Investigative Service, Office of Industrial Security, and must report all security violations theft of classified materials and/or products to the Defense Supply Agency.

The security linkage between the Department of Defense (D.O.D.) and the industrial sector in the United States is not only massive, but also complex. Strict regulations are spelled out in the D.O.D.'s *Industrial Security Manual* as well as in other security requirements specified by the military branches, NASA, the Atomic Energy Commission, and the like. As noted by Gallati (1983, pp. 201–202):

> The Department of Defense supplies governmental security employees and nongovernmental security personnel with rules and regulations that must be carried out to the letter.
>
> Security personnel, both military and civilian, must have clearances for access to classified documents and materials as well as buildings, parts of buildings, and spaces and locations. . . .
>
> D.O.D. regulations are very specific about the types of storage for classified materials. Some of these files, locking devices, safes, and vaults are extremely expensive and would not normally be used in most security operations. Likewise, classified areas are protected by specific physical electronic and guard protections, usually far in excess of the installations found in non-D.O.D. security systems. Most security directors envy their colleagues in D.O.D. facilities for the ease with which they can obtain budget support for the ultimate in security resources. On the other hand, there are threats involved that are more acute, and hazards that are of international consequence—sabotage, espionage, theft of top-secret documents, and so on that justify these security expenditures.

---

*Further information on specific kinds of industrial security problems may be obtained by contacting the American Society for Industrial Security, 1655 North Fort Myer Drive, Suite 1200, Arlington, VA 22209. (703)522-5800 FAX 703/243-4954

$15.4 million National Military Command Center at the Pentagon.

A new industrial security responsibility is that arising from the introduction of robots into the workplace. Dr. Ted S. Ferry, author of "Safety Management Planning," cites four high-tech developments in industry that will cause new protection and insurance needs:

➤ CAD computer-assisted design
➤ CAM computer-assisted manufacturing
➤ CIM computer-integrated manufacturing
➤ CAE computer-aided engineering

The increasing interaction between robots and people will cause accidents more costly than those in the past. Ferry suggests that "the exorbitant costs will put an increased burden on security professionals responsible for loss control and planning."

## ☐ TYPES OF INDUSTRIAL LOSSES

Although industry is susceptible to the same types of internal theft as any business, as well as to burglary and/or robbery, certain types of losses are more frequently encountered in industry than in other businesses.

Industrial losses frequently include tools, materials, supplies, products, pallets, hand trucks, valuable scrap, uniforms, side-products, time, and vital information.

The Task Force Report (*Private Security*, 1976, p. 52) elaborates on this:

> Internal theft by employees is a major contributor to manufacturing crime losses. The items most frequently stolen include tools; electronic components; assembly parts; consumable items such as cleaning supplies, oils and greases, paints, wire, and the like; plumbing and electrical supplies; and manufactured products, including consumer products that can be readily used by employees. External theft losses include not only cartons and containers of finished products but also raw materials in usable form, silver, gold, and other precious metals, small machinery and power tools, and office equipment from administrative offices located at production facilities.

Reported instances of internal theft from employees within the manufacturing sector include:

➤ Taking raw materials
➤ Taking company tools and equipment
➤ Getting paid for more hours than worked
➤ Getting excess expense reimbursement
➤ Taking finished products
➤ Taking precious metals

Some employees engage in three or four of these types of internal theft. The categories are *not* mutually exclusive.

In many types of industry, side-product control is important. Such items as metal shavings, wood scraps, and reclaimable oil may be recovered and sold as salvage. Food scraps may be sold as hog feed. Employees, however, may mistakenly believe that such side-products are of little value to their employer and may take them for their own use. Employees should be told of any side-products having potential value. Then, the weighing, loading, and disposing of valuable salvage should be carefully supervised.

A manufacturing company that provides uniforms should caution employees that personnel are expected to care for their uniforms and not take them for personal use. Pallets and hand trucks are also sometimes taken for personal use and never returned. In addition, these should be kept secured because burglars can transport stolen goods on pallets and hand trucks. Security officers should also be aware that intruders might use the company's own acetylene torches to open safes and that prybars, cutting tools, ladders, and forklifts should be secured so as not to make the task of a would-be thief easier.

Maintenance supplies such as cleaning liquids, paper towels, soap, and even toilet paper are often stolen by employees and, consequently, should be kept secure. Proprietary gas pumps, too, may be used for personal vehicles and must be kept secured. Records should be kept of company vehicles' gas and oil use and mileage to further ensure that such supplies are not being transferred to personal vehicles.

Finally, employees who are allowed to use company products or who are given discounts when purchasing products may abuse this privilege by making purchases for friends or for selling such products at a profit, resulting in considerable loss to the employer.

Security problems faced by industry are typified by those encountered in the building and timber industry. Burton (1983, p. 65) discusses losses in this industry: "By conservative estimate, two-thirds of losses in the building and timber industry were sustained as a result of internal theft by employees conniving with visiting customers. The remaining third was made up of goods that never made it from the distributors to the lumber or brick yards and goods stolen by customers who were able to help themselves because of the firm's lax security systems." Burton (p. 66) outlines the types of theft common in a lumber yard:

> The most common theft in lumber yards is giving customers extra goods at the loading dock in hopes of receiving a tip. Other tricks include:
>
> ➤ Keeping a supply of damaged and broken goods—plasterboard, cement, damaged timber—hidden from the foreman (unless he's in the shareout). If no legitimately damaged goods are available, the thieves damage the goods themselves and are then able to acquire them at a reduced price.
> ➤ Stealing tickets, used and unused, so the thieves can write out bogus customer receipts.
> ➤ Hiding produce in dustbins or garbage cans and leaving them outside to be taken away by the "trash collectors."
> ➤ Signing nonexistent goods in for truck drivers and turning the delivery tickets in to management for payment.
> ➤ Befriending the security officer by offering him bathroom facilities at certain times of the day so illegal customers can go in and out. Talking to the security officer to find out whether he has product knowledge before smuggling merchandise past him.
>
> If an employee wanted to steal from the company, he would work exceptionally hard, smiling on those above him and frowning on those below. He would be polite to management, want to work lots of overtime, and not want to take holidays. Someone in this position could hide copper tube inside plastic piping, conceal extra fittings inside baths, or put extra goods in boxes sealed with security tape. Eventually he would try to get the best job of all—that of local delivery driver. This position can be a license to print money in some of the following ways:
>
> ➤ Under-delivering. Stealing damaged goods from the lumber yard and re-delivering them so corrupt customers can get credit.
> ➤ Trying to persuade management to let him take the vehicle home at night so he can use it for theft and other jobs.
> ➤ Submitting fraudulent bills for diesel petrol fuel, antifreeze, tires, wipers, etc.

Burton continues (p. 66): "To attack the theft situation in the building and timber trades successfully, an investigator or security consultant must have product knowledge. . . . Different grades of timber, importation marks, and the colored ends of timber, which indicate the origin of soft and hard woods, are a recognized part of training for investigators in the building trades. The different types of bricks, materials, and trade jargon must also be understood if the investigator is to break into the magic circle of theft."

## Tools

Tools constitute one of the most serious areas of industrial loss. Losses can result either from the improper use of tools or from actual theft. Proper maintenance not only lengthens a tool's life, but also avoids merchandise damage and production slowdowns.

Hand power tools, drills, wrenches, hammers, and pliers are highly susceptible to theft, especially if employees use their own tools as well as those belonging to the plant. All company tools should be checked into a tool room or a tool crib at the end of each shift.

---

Reduce tool loss by having a tool room or tool crib with an attendant, a check-in/out procedure, distinctive markings on the tools, periodic inspections and inventories, metal detectors at gates, and possibly a system for lending tools for personal use after hours.

---

Tools should be locked up when not in use. If possible and practical, a single check-out and service point should be used. The tool rooms should be kept neat and attractive to impress on employees that tools are important. Tool room attendants should know about tools and be able to keep them in good condition. They should have the necessary equipment to maintain the tools, for example, equipment for sharpening cutting tools, and they should be able to make minor repairs.

A check-in/out procedure should be established and followed. In addition, a procedure for lost, broken, or damaged tools should be clearly specified. Any broken or damaged tool should be turned in and the employee required to complete a brief report describing how the loss occurred. If such procedures are not followed and the tool does not have to be turned in, the employee might report a tool broken when it was actually taken for personal use.

Expensive tools are often identified with a serial number. Some companies paint the handles of their tools a bright color such as red or orange to make identification easy. Some companies, having experienced severe tool loss, have combated the problem by installing a metal detector at the gate.

## ☐ SABOTAGE AND ESPIONAGE

Although security measures were originally introduced into manufacturing companies to protect against sabotage and espionage during wartime, these two threats remain very real even during peacetime. They can be committed by competitors or by dissatisfied employees.

---

Two special concerns of industry are sabotage and espionage.

---

### Sabotage

The word **sabotage** originated in France during the Industrial Revolution when disgruntled factory workers threw their wooden shoes (sabots) into the machinery, thereby halting production.

$S$abotage is the intentional destruction of machinery or goods, or the intentional obstruction of production.

In April 1985, almost 80 percent of the United Auto Workers (UAW) at the American Motors Corporation (AMC) Jeep plant in Toledo, Ohio, were sent home without pay because of extensive vandalism occurring on the assembly line. The UAW's Jeep unit chairman, Danny Wilson, reported "major damage to at least 65% of the unfinished Jeeps in early April." The destruction began when AMC cut the employees' investment plan payments to a few hundred dollars rather than the several thousand the workers were expecting. The most serious damage was done in the body and paint departments. As noted by a UAW spokesperson, "In the body shop people have hammers in their hands. They took pick hammers and literally caved in quarter panels on cars and welded car doors shut."

Chamberlain (1985, p. 19) stresses that "preventing internal destruction of company property is always more difficult than protection against outsiders. Fences, guard stations, alarms and other protective devices are almost useless against deliberate internal attacks. More importantly, this type of crime cannot be prevented by the security department alone. It requires a concerted effort from all levels of management." Chamberlain goes on to make this suggestion:

> Response to internal vandalism should include plans for closing the operation on a moment's notice because even an hour's delay can result in thousands of dollars in damage. Alternate delivery and maintenance operations also should be developed. Employees are often aware of which suppliers and deliveries are most vital to production. In low-tech machinery operations alternate facilities or sub-contracting should be considered.
>
> Most importantly, other methods to control internal sabotage should be discussed. Like the instances at GMC, most vandalism is caused by employees with a real or perceived grievance against the employer. Strong company policies, well publicized and uniformly enforced, are usually the best prevention. . . .
>
> Modern technology has sped up production faster than ever before. But the human factor is the backbone of every plant, no matter how automated. The satisfied employee increases production. The angry, vengeful employee throws a "sabot" in the works.

Methods of sabotage may be chemical, electrical, explosive, mechanical, or psychological (strikes, riots, and boycotts). Psychological sabotage has become more frequent in the last decade. For example, in Minnesota, protestors against electrical power lines running through privately owned fields have toppled several of the huge powerline towers, each at a cost of hundreds of thousands of dollars. These costs were passed on to the consumer in higher energy rates. Access control and inspections are two means to prevent sabotage.

## Espionage

Traditionally **espionage** is associated with spying, especially spying to obtain military secrets. More recently the term has broadened considerably in meaning.

Industrial espionage is the theft of trade secrets or confidential information.

Some well-intentioned executives may claim they are not concerned with espionage, that they have no secrets to hide. However, Hemphill (1971, pp. 180–81) suggests that "the company that has no secrets to protect is not really in the business of competing. And it is well known that this competition is the 'fuel' of the American economy. Nowhere is this manifested more clearly than in industries that are trying to reach the market with improvements on an established item. All too often there are some executives who delay until competition has driven them to near bankruptcy before they will acknowledge the need for protecting secrets."

Hemphill cautions that this does not imply that industries are surrounded by spies or that they need to immediately adopt radical new security procedures. It does imply, however, that executives need to be aware of the threat of internal and external espionage. Espionage has, in fact, been in existence just as long as sabotage. Hemphill gives as an example an incident occurring in 1790:

> A drunken pattern maker in the hire of the celebrated Scottish inventor James Watt bragged that Watt had discovered a way to obtain circular motion from a reciprocating piston. Other engineers and machinists who overheard this conversation in a pub expressed disbelief that this was possible, and the pattern maker chalked a sketch of Watt's mechanical contrivance on the bar. One of the bystanders was James Pickard, a Birmingham button manufacturer who realized the mechanical possibilities of Watt's contrivance. Wasting no time thereafter, Pickard went to the patent office in London and obtained a patent for this device as the "crank and connecting rod." Although there was little question that Watt had been the inventor, the courts upheld the patent rights of Pickard.

Hemphill equates this to modern businesses with a warning: "A business today that fails to provide engineering and scientific personnel with guidelines for security must assume the risk that these employees may disclose proprietary information, the real worth of which they may never realize."

Competition is the heart of the free enterprise system. As noted, most manufacturers have information they want to conceal from their competitors because "lead time" is so critical. Confidentiality of information buys time to "get a jump" on the market. In other instances, secret formulas are a company's primary source of profits. Although many products can be protected by patents, some cannot. Trade secrets such as formulas are much harder to protect than real property because, if they are stolen, the rightful owner still has possession, but not exclusive possession, thereby greatly diminishing the value of the formula. Sometimes, in fact, the rightful owner may never realize the formula has been stolen.

Other types of information that may be stolen include new product research, production costs, sales figures, profit breakdowns, markups, salaries, reports on problems, merger plans, blueprints, and the like. The minutes of executive committee meetings often contain such information and should be carefully guarded.

Trade secrets should be identified as such, be secured, and be made known to the fewest people possible.

Confidential information should be stamped "Confidential" or "Secret." Some companies place a warning on the front of confidential material which states: "This document is the sole property of Company X and may not be reproduced or duplicated." Each classified document should be numbered. If more than one copy exists, it should be identified by copy number, for example, Document 187, Copy 3 of 4. The original and all copies should be kept in a locked file or vault and should be signed in and out, with precautions taken to ensure that copies or photographs are not made while the materials are check out. Some highly confidential material may be marked "Eyes Only," meaning that the originator of the document must hand-carry it to the individuals who are to read it and must wait while they do so. Therefore, the document never leaves the sight of the originator.

Confidential information should be known by as few people as possible. The adage, "Once you share a secret with a friend it is no longer a secret," holds true of trade secrets; the fewer people knowing a trade secret, the better. A good example is the formula for Worcestershire sauce. It has been kept secret for over one hundred years because only two company officials know it at any one time.

Business secrets can fall into the wrong hands either through carelessness or through theft. Leaks can result from scientists who boast or who share ideas with other professionals, from spouses who know trade secrets and inadvertently let information slip, from mailroom personnel or secretaries who read confidential information, from janitors who see confidential information lying around, from consultants who obtain information while working for a firm, or from ex-employees.

Prevent espionage by careful screening of personnel, document control, and clear guidelines for personnel.

Thorough background checks should be made of employees who will be working with confidential materials. Sometimes security clearances are required before a person can work in a given area, especially in government production plants. Employees should know what things are not to be discussed with anyone, including spouses. Some companies require new employees who will be working with confidential material to sign an agreement against unauthorized disclosure of trade secrets. Courts will usually uphold such agreements.

Engineering and scientific personnel should be provided with clear guidelines for security and should know what they "own" of what they invent. Of great concern is the scientist or inventor who leaves one company to join another. When scientific or engineering personnel are terminated, they should have a termination interview and sign an agreement that specifies precisely what information is not to be disclosed to the new employer. They should also turn in all confidential files, records, and keys. An even greater threat is an employee who moonlights for a competitor and shares the secrets of the full-time employer with this competitor.

Employers should be suspicious of a break in security if competitors are consistently ahead of them, if they lose bids more often than usual, or if their competition is hiring away key people.

Manufacturing firms working under Department of Defense contracts must protect classified information and materials and follow prescribed governmental regulations for safeguarding classified defense information, documents, materials, end products, and storage and work areas. The security programs and policies at these manufacturing plants are mandated by Department of Defense regulations, and the plants can be inspected at any time by the Office of Industrial Security of the U. S. Defense Supply Agency.

## ☐ VULNERABLE AREAS

A study conducted by the Office of Transportation Security, U. S. Department of Transportation, showed that most cargo thefts occurred in warehouses, loading docks, shipping and receiving areas, and distribution centers during normal operating hours. Most of these thefts were accomplished by people and with vehicles that were authorized to be in the area, indicating a considerable degree of collusion between employees and outside individuals.

---

The areas most vulnerable to theft are tool rooms or tool cribs, warehouses, loading docks, shipping and receiving areas, and distribution centers.

---

Warehouses and stockrooms should be kept orderly and should have an attendant on duty. Appropriate lighting and locks should be used, along with alarms, if necessary. Rotating the stock and keeping a perpetual inventory will also help to reduce losses. Packing crates should be randomly opened and checked. In one instance, the person taking inventory of refrigerators in a warehouse simply pushed against the cartons to ensure that they were as heavy as they should be. It was later discovered that several of the cartons were empty and had been nailed to the floor.

Dumps should be fenced and kept locked. Trash containers and/or dumpsters should be inspected periodically. If possible, trash should be compacted so that discarded, defective merchandise is not recovered by employees and turned in for a refund.

Losses also occur frequently during shipping. To avoid this type of shrinkage, instruct transporters to carefully count merchandise, use factory-sealed cartons, seal the truck trailer doors, make sure the delivery trucks are kept secure, make nonstop hauls, and send trucks in convoys when possible.

It is best not to pre-load trucks,* but if this cannot be avoided, the loaded trucks should be parked back to back.

Railroad spur lines are also highly vulnerable. Ideally, the area around railroad spurs should be fenced, locked, and kept lit at night. Railroad cars should be unloaded immediately. If this is not possible, they should be sealed until they can be unloaded.

## ☐ TRANSPORTING GOODS BY TRUCK AND RAIL**

Our national economy depends on the movement of goods and merchandise by our transportation system, one of the largest industries in the United States. Manufacturing and industrial enterprises depend on the transportation system to supply them with raw materials for production and to then distribute the finished merchandise to customers. Most materials and goods are transported by common carrier, rather than by company-owned transportation fleets.

For this discussion *cargo* refers to anything that enters and is moved by the nation's transportation system, beginning at the shipper's loading platform and ending at a consignee's receiving dock. *Cargo theft* may involve entire shipments, containers, and cartons, or pilferage of smaller amounts of merchandise.

Commodities such as clothing, electrical appliances, automotive parts, food products, hardware, jewelry, tobacco products, scientific instruments, and alcoholic beverages make up about 80 percent of the total national losses.

Most security staffs have developed effective countermeasures against cargo theft, but common denominators can be seen. Measures that can be equally effective in all types of transportation to protect both shippers and carriers from losses due to theft and vandalism include personnel security, physical security, procedures for accepting cargo, secure packaging, documenting movement and delivery, periodic review of security procedures, and prosecution of offenses.

Agencies that may assist with investigating cargo crime include the local police department, the United States Custom Service, and the FBI. Liaison with other carriers should be maintained to insure mutual cooperation in all areas related to cargo security. Prosecution is of vital importance in deterring future thefts.

### The Trucking Industry***

Virtually all cargo moves by truck at least once during shipment. Cargo theft can occur at any point in the distribution system: warehouses, receiving and shipping platforms, storage areas, depots, distribution centers, ter-

---

*Loading several hours prior to the scheduled departure time.
**Transportation Security—See *Private Security,* pp. 58–59.
***Cargo Theft—See *Private Security,* pp. 58–60.

minals, and piers. Direct financial loss to the transportation industry due to cargo theft is estimated at from $1 to $2 billion annually.

The Office of Transportation Security, United States Department of Transportation, estimates that cargo theft losses were the result of hijacking (5 percent), breaking and entering and external theft (10 percent), and internal theft, collusive theft, and unexplained shortages (85 percent). Although hijackings receive national publicity, they account for only a small portion of losses. As noted by the Department of Transportation, 85 percent of the goods and materials stolen go out the front gate, and those transporting these items have authorization to be in the cargo handling area.

The cargoes most frequently stolen from trucks include clothing and textiles, electrical and electronic supplies and components, foods, tobacco and liquor, appliances, automotive and other vehicle parts, and paper, plastic, and rubber products.

Organized crime activities account for 15 to 20 percent of the *value* of all cargo thefts, with the remainder resulting from employee collusion either among themselves or with people outside the transportation system and fences, organized along geographic areas and/or product lines.

Security measures in the trucking industry include use of proprietary and/or contract guards in shipping, receiving, and storage areas; access control systems and perimeter fencing and lighting; CCTV systems and alarms; and special security seals and alarms on trucks.

The seal system is adapted from that initiated by the railroads several years ago. Under this system a numbered metal band is used to seal the door. Careful records should be kept of all seals. It is a federal crime for a nonauthorized person to break the seal on any interstate shipment. Therefore, if a seal is broken, the FBI and local police should be called to investigate.

Some high-value shipments are monitored by transmitters on the vehicle or by a directional monitoring receiver in a helicopter. In addition, most of the security measures discussed in Chapter 7 regarding safeguarding shipments are also applicable to common carriers.

Because employee theft accounts for such a large percentage of loss, a system of accountability with proper documentation from the purchase order to invoice and receiving slip is necessary. Although truckers have no control over the issuing of such documentation, drivers are responsible for carefully checking shipments as they are loaded and unloaded.

## Railroad Security*

Railroad security is provided by the oldest, perhaps most highly organized segment of the private security industry, the railroad police. The

---

*Railroad Security—See *Private Security,* pp. 54–55.

country's thirty-five hundred railroad police work closely with local, state, and federal law enforcement agencies. Although the railroad police are paid with corporate funds, at least forty states have given them broad police powers. In these states, the railroad police have a dual responsibility to the rail industry and the public.

The Police and Security Section of the Association of American Railroads describes the basic objectives of the railroad police as protecting life and property; preventing and suppressing crime; investigating criminal acts committed on or against the railroad, patrons, or employees; arresting criminal offenders; supervising conduct on railroad property; and performing certain nonpolice services such as accident and claims investigation and safety management.

Theft of railroad cargo may occur on any point along a quarter million miles of track. It is one of the most important concerns of the railroad police.

The primary security problems of the railroad industry are cargo theft, vandalism, and theft of metals.

Total losses incurred by these crimes cost railroad carriers millions of dollars every year. The security problems faced by railroads are immense (p. 54):

> ➤ A freight car loaded at one part of the country may move over several different railroads to its final destination in another part of the nation. The cargo is not examined unless an exception to a seal is noted during the movement or the car is listed on a special bulletin as a high-value load.
> ➤ Many railroads pass through the most crime-ridden areas of our largest cities.
> ➤ It is impossible to fence or adequately patrol the approximately 400,000 miles of railroad right-of-ways.
> ➤ Most criminals causing major problems are not railroad employees; therefore, internal controls do not suffice.
> ➤ Many thefts occur in large rail yards which are difficult to monitor with conventional hardware.
> ➤ The number and size of rail yards also make them difficult to cover by saturation of manpower.
> ➤ Metals belonging to the railroads are easily stolen and fenced. Examples are copper communication wire, brass rail car bearings, and steel track material.
> ➤ The physical nature of railroads makes them vulnerable to acts of vandalism by trespassers, especially by juveniles.

Security measures used by railroads include patrol, surveillance, undercover operations, CCTV monitoring, locking devices and gate controls, and seals.

Railroad police prevent and control crime and enhance security by using such security measures as radio-equipped foot and vehicle patrol, canine patrol, and fixed-wing aircraft and helicopter patrol; fixed-surveillance stakeouts; undercover operations; exchange of intelligence information with public law enforcement agencies; employee security-consciousness programs; criminal investigations aimed at prosecuting persons found responsible for crimes against the railroads; task forces moving many railroad police officers into a specific problem area to perform a tactical mission; public relations and eduction programs aimed at community awareness and support of railroad police activities; and installation protection, including CCTV, electronic security, and sophisticated locking devices and gate controls.

Most railroad security administrators believe engineering improvements to cars and trailers would help prevent cargo theft and vandalism, including improved door construction of boxcars and trailers, container locking mechanisms, boxcar and trailer locking devices, and cable seals. They also suggest that further research is needed in other areas such as night lighting (portable and permanent) for operational surveillance; helicopter patrol for theft and vandalism surveillance; canine units for trailer terminals and rail yard patrol; CCTV in trailer terminal operations; photographic methods for trailer terminal operations; sensor devices used on rail car and trailer shipments; use of computers for determining claim and theft patterns; and use of screened rail cars to protect auto shipments from vandalism and theft.

## Seaport Security

Confusion and masses of materials make cargo security at seaports especially difficult, as unauthorized vehicles may carry out thousands of dollars of cargo at a time. Imported cars are especially a problem at seaports. Most cars are stored in areas with no perimeter fencing, with inadequate lighting facilities, and without proper guard protection. The result is that many vehicles are stolen and vandalized.

Airline and airport security are discussed in Chapter 15.

## ☐ SPECIAL PROBLEMS IN THE UTILITIES INDUSTRY

Everyone has contact with utility companies—water, gas, electric companies. We are heavily dependent on them daily. Higgins (1985, p. 79) notes that the accessibility of utilities makes them "subject to a variety of crimes, from trespassing to vandalism, from robberies to terrorism, and leaves them vulnerable at many points." He goes on to note the primary problems facing the security director for a utility company.

Primary problems at utility companies include loss of tools, loss of stored items, trespassers and vandals at substations and distribution centers, security at construction sites, access control for office buildings, protection of collection centers from theft and robbery, plans for emergencies, and detection of resource diversion.

Utility service trucks are heavily equipped with supplies and tools that remain in the vehicles even when they are not in use. These are highly vulnerable to theft. To counter this problem, inventory control and strict check-in/out procedures are needed. In addition, when the vehicles are at a service location, crew members often must leave the vehicle unattended—and, again, vulnerable.

Another problem is encountered in utility companies' numerous unstaffed substations, frequently secured with chain-link fences and security lighting. Despite these measures, trespassers and vandals may pose serious problems. Higgins cites additional problems with crews using the substations for beer parties, gambling, and an "occasional prostitution fling"; homeless individuals taking over the buildings; and contractors moving mobile homes onto a site and hooking up to the substation's electricity and water. Solutions to such problems might include alarms, guard dogs, or roving patrols.

Construction of major generating facilities presents additional security problems. According to Higgins, such sites can be valued at over $1 billion and can incur losses of 10 to 30 percent of this total value. He suggests that the major key to solving construction site theft is "not allowing tools and materials to leave the site" and continues, "All personal vehicles should be parked off site and all employees or contractors must wear badges and enter the site at controlled points."

Like any other business, utility companies also have valuable records: subscriber credit histories, financial data, and the like, often stored on computer. Controlling access to this information is the same as for any other business and might include locks, alarms, sign-in/out procedures, and guards.

In addition to records and information, utility companies also handle large amounts of cash. Money at collection sites must be protected from internal theft as well as from robbery. For cash-handling problems, Higgins suggests that "utilities would be wise to adopt the proven methods used by banks and even retail stores in the periodic removal of excess cash from the teller booths." They might also consider having panic alarms and CCTV cameras installed and training employees who handle cash in responding to a robbery.

Yet another area of concern is that of emergencies. Although utility companies are particularly accustomed to dealing with emergencies, emergencies must still be built into the overall security plan. Included are fires, bombs, and bomb threats. As for any other type of establishment, procedures for evacuation should be determined and practiced.

Yet another area of concern, which lacks the high visibility of emergencies, is that of diversion of the resource provided by the utility, whether gas, electricity, or water. The most usual means of diverting the resource is bypassing the meter that measures its use. Higgins cites the example of a large restaurant with an all-electric kitchen whose owner "allegedly paid a utility employee to bypass the electric meter. One light bulb was connected to the meter to show some usage. This ploy was discovered when a new employee of the restaurant had an electrical problem and called the utility. A utility repairman not included discovered the diversion." Such losses might be reduced by monitoring monthly usage and comparing it with predetermined norms.

A utility company's losses can be reduced by careful access controls to tools and supplies, careful check-in/out procedures, alarms and surveillance cameras at substations, attention to cash-handling procedures, and establishment of emergency plans.

Other measures that might be employed will vary from utility to utility. The following list of risks and responsibilities facing utility security professionals, compiled by Higgins (p. 80), should indicate what other types of security measures might be appropriate.

- No corporate security policy oriented toward utilities
- Executive protection
- Terrorism—bomb threats, etc.
- Physical security
- Emergency operations/procedures
- Access controls
- Employee entry controls/visitor badging and controls
- Operations center security
- Warehouse security
- Distribution center security
- Substation security
- Transmission line security
- Diversion of assets and electric power diversion
- Guard dogs and incident reports
- Records maintenance
- Position descriptions for security personnel
- Lost/found procedures
- Security meetings
- Key and lock control procedures
- Construction site security
- Fire safety
- Patrols and surveillance
- Trespass procedures
- Cash-handling—holdup procedures
- Parcel pass procedures
- Screening and investigation of applicants
- Guard contracts
- Alarm station contracts
- Alarm equipment evaluations
- Communications
- Employee theft
- Computer security
- Office building security
- Plant security
- Parking lots
- Lighting standards
- And others

## SUMMARY

Industrial losses frequently include tools, materials, supplies, products, pallets, hand trucks, valuable scrap, uniforms, side-products, time, and vital information. Of special concern is tool loss, which can be minimized by having a tool room or tool crib with an attendant, a check-in/out procedure, distinctive markings on the tools, periodic inspections and inventories, metal detectors at gates, and possibly a system for lending tools for personal use after hours.

Two special concerns of industry are sabotage and espionage. Sabotage is the intentional destruction of machinery or goods, or the intentional obstruction of production. Industrial espionage is the theft of trade secrets or confidential information. Trade secrets should be identified as such, be secured, and be made known to the fewest people possible. In addition, espionage can be prevented by careful screening of personnel, document control, and clear guidelines for personnel.

The areas most vulnerable to theft are tool rooms or tool cribs, warehouses, loading docks, shipping and receiving areas, and distribution centers.

The transportation industry also relies heavily on security for carriers such as trucks and railroads.

The cargoes most frequently stolen from trucks include clothing and textiles, electrical and electronic supplies and components, foods, tobacco and liquor, appliances, automotive and other vehicle parts, and paper, plastic, and rubber products. Security measures in the trucking industry include use of proprietary and/or contract guards in shipping, receiving, and storage areas; access control systems and perimeter fencing and lighting; CCTV systems and alarms; and special security seals and alarms on trucks.

The primary security problems of the railroad industry are cargo theft, vandalism, and theft of metals. Security measures used by railroads include patrol, surveillance, undercover operations, CCTV monitoring, locking devices and gate controls, and seals.

Primary problems at utility companies include loss of tools, loss of stored items, trespassers and vandals at substations and distribution centers, security at construction sites, access control for office buildings, protection of collection centers from theft and robbery, plans for emergencies, and detection of resource diversion. A utility company's losses can be reduced by careful access controls to tools and supplies, careful check-in/out procedures, alarms and surveillance cameras at substations, attention to cash-handling procedures, and establishment of emergency plans.

## APPLICATION

As security director of a manufacturing company, if you were informed that an employee was engaging in the theft of company trade secrets, what steps would you take to investigate the charge? If the charge was well founded, what steps would you take? What resources would you use?

## DISCUSSION QUESTIONS

1) What are some preventive measures a security director might apply to guard against espionage in a computer manufacturing company?

2) Name several effective ways to protect vital documents and records from destruction or theft.

3) What methods might espionage agents use to undermine a competitor?

4) What are some reasons employees engage in sabotage?

5) What security measures are effective in minimizing the possibility of cargo theft from trucks? Railroad cars?

# REFERENCES

Burton, P. J. Theft in the lumber industry. *Security management,* August 1983, pp. 65–67.

Chamberlain, C. S. Internal vandalism presents a problem that demands both prevention and response. *Security world,* June 1985, p. 19.

Gallati, Robert J. *Introduction to private security,* Englewood Cliffs, NJ: Prentice-Hall, 1983.

Hemphill, C. F., Jr. *Security for business and industry.* Homewood, IL: Dow-Jones Irwin, Inc., 1971.

Higgins, C.E. Shedding light on utility security. *Security management,* May 1985, pp. 79–82.

*Private security.* Report of the Task Force on Private Security, National Advisory Committee on Criminal Justice Standards and Goals. Washington, DC: U. S. Government Printing Office, 1976.

## Chapter Fourteen

## □ INTRODUCTION

It is a Friday evening. In the X Supermarket, a woman buys a dozen rolls from the bakery department. The rolls are placed in a white sack with the price marked on the outside. To this sack, the woman adds a pen and three cigarette lighters. She hurriedly pays the cashier the correct amount for the rolls in change and leaves without waiting for a receipt. The cashier pockets the money. At the next counter a man is cashing a stolen government check. Across the street, the corner gas station is being held up. Farther down the street, in a large department store, some teenagers are palming small objects as an initiation into the local gang, a woman is in a fitting booth putting her street clothes on over an expensive bathing suit, another woman is switching prices on jewelry, and an employee is marking down prices on items she is purchasing for herself.

Hourly, across the country, such actions result in tremendous losses to retailers. Retail establishments include general merchandise department stores, specialty and clothing stores, food and drug stores, appliance and furniture stores, radio and television stores, hardware stores, lumberyards, restaurants, fast-food shops, automobile dealers, and gasoline service stations. Retail businesses that absorb the greatest losses are general merchandise and clothing stores, food stores, and drug stores, in that order.

### DO YOU KNOW

➤ What crimes are most frequently committed against retail establishments?

➤ What legally constitutes shoplifting?

➤ How shoplifters are classified?

➤ What methods are commonly used to shoplift?

➤ What preventive methods can be taken to curtail shoplifting?

➤ What basic difference exists between security officers and floorwalkers?

➤ What merchandising techniques, procedures, and physical controls can be used to deter shoplifting?

➤ When and how to apprehend individuals suspected of shoplifting?

➤ What factors influence when prosecution is advisable?

➤ How to deter losses from bad checks?

➤ Which types of checks are considered high-risk checks?

➤ What the most common types of bad checks are?

➤ How checks should be examined?

➤ What identification to require?

➤ How to deter losses from credit cards?

➤ What types of employee theft frequently occur in retail establishments and what preventive measures can be taken?

➤ What honesty shopping is?

➤ What the two primary objectives of shopping center security are?

A modern phenomenon is the large shopping mall, centralizing a large number of retail, entertainment, professional, and business operations into one location that provides ample parking and easy access for thousands of customers. Shopping center management has become such a specialized field that the International Council of Shopping Centers (ICSC) has begun to certify the qualifications of managers for shopping centers. Different combinations of local law enforcement personnel and proprietary and/or contractual guard forces provide security for these shopping centers. Some of the larger centers are assigned local law

**341**

enforcement officers. In others, shopping center security personnel are given limited police powers through local ordinances. Most larger shopping centers have a director of security, a proprietary security force, CCTV, a communications system, and mobile patrols for parking lots.

Whether located in a shopping mall, in a downtown business district, or in isolation from other businesses, retailers face many common problems. Managers of such establishments often use security measures to protect their assets.*

The highest-loss items in department stores are junior sportswear and high-fashion clothing, jewelry, leathers, furs, cosmetics, compact discs and tapes, and small electronic items. Losses from drug stores include cosmetics, costume jewelry, candy, toys, drugs, and tapes. Careful records on high-loss items are necessary to plan appropriate security measures.

Reported crimes committed against all types of retail establishments in order of frequency are shoplifting, burglary, vandalism, bad checks, fraudulent credit cards, employee theft, and robbery.

Some suggest, however, that employee theft is much greater than indicated because much of it is undetected and is assumed to be the result of shoplifting. Emphasis on theft by employees and customers is noted in ''The Siege on Supermarkets'' (p. 7):

> Enough food is stolen annually from supermarkets across the U.S. to feed every man, woman, and child in both San Francisco and Boston for a full year. Adding insult to injury, the store's own shopping carts often serve as the get-away vehicles.
>
> The problem of losses in supermarkets approaches monumental proportions. Industry sources report that 48 percent of all customers shoplift at one time or another, while 58 percent of all employees help themselves to an occasional apple or pack of cigarettes. Employee theft of all kinds, including shoplifting, cash shortages, and inventory losses, accounts for 66 percent of a supermarket's total shrinkage.

The physical and procedural controls discussed in Section Two are the most effective means of deterring robbery, burglary, and vandalism in retail establishments. Proper lighting, locks, alarm systems, and other measures are also appropriate in retail establishments. Of equal or greater importance, however, is safeguarding against losses from shoplifting, bad checks, fraudulently used credit cards, and employee theft, the focus of this chapter.

## ☐ SHOPLIFTING

**Shoplifting** is generally considered to be the most widespread crime affecting retail stores. It is also generally considered to be a security problem rather than a law enforcement problem.

---

*Retail Security—See *Private Security,* pp. 55—58. Shopping Center Security—See *Private Security,* p. 44.

Shoplifting* is the theft of retail merchandise while lawfully on the premises. Concealment of merchandise is prima facie evidence† of intent to shoplift. In many states price changing is also considered shoplifting.

Shoplifting is a form of larceny costing billions of dollars annually. Compounding the problem is public apathy. Most people have shoplifted at one time in their lives, and many have very little sympathy for big business. Thus, the responsibility for preventing shoplifting losses falls almost entirely on retail management.

The problem has many facets. Sales and security personnel must be familiar with the various types of shoplifters, methods they commonly use, signs indicative of shoplifting activity, and means to prevent the crime. They must also be knowledgeable of the establishment's policies and procedures for apprehending, arresting, interrogating, and deciding whether to prosecute offenders.

## Types of Shoplifters

Although anyone can be a shoplifter, it is helpful to recognize the most common types of shoplifters.

Shoplifters can be classified as amateurs—students, housewives, vagrants, alcoholics, drug addicts, and kleptomaniacs—or as professionals: those who steal for resale of merchandise.

The great majority of shoplifting is done by amateurs—ordinary customers who give in to temptation. Most shoplifting incidences are impulsive. Shoplifting is often called a "crime of the young." Many studies indicate that juveniles are involved in at least half of shoplifting incidents. Juveniles seldom steal from true need, but rather for "kicks," as a dare, or to be initiated into a club. They often enter stores in gangs and "rip off" the merchant. Some steal items they have been given money to purchase and then use the money to purchase drugs or alcohol.

Housewives are the next most common category of shoplifters. This may be partly because they frequently do most of the family's shopping and, therefore, are exposed to temptation more often than other individuals. They may also be trying to stretch their budget. Vagrants and alcoholics frequently are truly in need of food or liquor and steal to meet these needs. They are often easy to detect as they are clumsy and obvious in their actions. Drug addicts, because of their desperation, pose a very direct threat to the safety of store personnel and should always be approached cautiously. **Kleptomaniacs** (compulsive thieves) seldom need the items they steal, but simply cannot help themselves. There are very few true kleptomaniacs.

---

*Some states call shoplifting "retail theft."
†Evidence established by law. Also called "direct evidence," e.g., 0.1 percent ethanol in the blood is prima facie evidence of intoxication in some states.

Professional shoplifters are much more difficult to detect. For them shoplifting is a way of life, often their sole source of income. They usually steal to resell the items, either to a fence or on the black market. This not only results in a direct loss to the store, but also sets up competition for the victim—with the victim's own merchandise. Many professional shoplifters steal "on order."

## Common Methods of Shoplifting

Shoplifters usually prefer crowded first floors, large sales, and self-service establishments where they are less apt to be detected. Most shoplifting thefts are simple and direct. Items are simply picked up and put into a pocket or purse. Professional shoplifters, on the other hand, may use sophisticated methods and devices. Adults may have children unknowingly carry out merchandise that has not been paid for. Some professional shoplifters have claimed items in the layaway areas having only a small amount left due, paid the small balance and taken the item. Some are even bold enough to stand behind an unattended register and sell merchandise to customers, pocketing the money.

Shoplifting methods include palming objects, dropping articles into a receptacle, placing items inside clothing, wearing items out of the store, and switching price tags.

Palming articles is a frequent method. This practice is often aided by using packages, newspapers, coats, gloves, and the like. Items may be knocked off counters into packages, knitting bags, shopping bags, or umbrellas.

Some shoplifters have specially tailored clothing that aids in their thefts. They may have coats and capes with hidden pockets and slits or zippered hiding places. Some coats have special hooks or belts inside on which to hang articles. Aprons and undergarments may be designed to hold articles; for example, "shoplifter bloomers" have elastic waistbands so the thief can stuff all manner of articles into them and they will not fall out. Others may wear bulky clothing and place articles between their legs, walking in the "shoplifter's shuffle" from the store.

A favorite device of professional shoplifters is the "booster box," a box whose top, bottom, or end is hinged so that articles can be placed inside without actually opening the box.

Articles may also be worn out of the store, either under street clothing, or in place of clothing that was worn upon entering. Jewelry, hats, purses, cameras, and sunglasses may all be worn so as to imply that they are the personal possessions of the shoplifter.

Items may also be dropped down the neck of clothing or placed into socks. A customer who frequently adjusts her hair may be concealing articles either in her hair or by dropping them down the back of her dress.

Frequently, professional shoplifters work in teams, with one diverting the clerk while the other, who is "just waiting," steals merchandise.

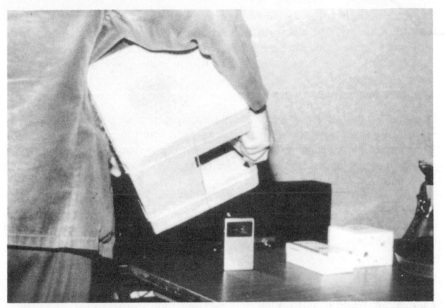

Booster box.

Another common ploy is to send the clerk away for another size or color and then to shoplift while the clerk is gone.

## Indicators of Possible Shoplifting

Knowing how shoplifters operate can be of great value in spotting the potential or actual shoplifter. Personnel can be trained to watch for certain characteristics and actions commonly associated with shoplifting.

**ACTIONS**  Actions that might be indicative of shoplifting include picking up and putting down items; comparing two identical items; frequently opening and closing a purse; adjusting hair and clothing; continuously looking around; walking in an unusual way; reaching into display counters; walking behind sales counters; showing disinterest in articles asked about; roaming while waiting for someone else to shop; walking aimlessly around the store; appearing nervous, flush-faced, or dry-lipped, or perspiring heavily; keeping one hand constantly in an outer pocket; frequently using elevators and/or rest rooms; sending clerks to get merchandise from back rooms; making rapid purchases and leaving the area hastily; and changing packages with someone else.

**CLOTHING**  Clothing, too, might be indicative of shoplifting, including bulky clothing in warm weather, a coat over an arm, a full skirt, or a large hat.

**RECEPTACLES**  Individuals who carry many bags or boxes; carry briefcases, newspapers, or umbrellas; or have an arm in a sling might be using these items to conceal shoplifted merchandise.

Although any one or two of the preceding could be very normal, for example, having a briefcase and carrying a topcoat over the arm, a combination of several of the preceding may be regarded as suspicious.

## Deterring Shoplifting

Numerous approaches to deter shoplifting are open to management. Commonly used preventive measures include training personnel, implementing antishoplifting merchandising techniques, and using physical and procedural controls. Such deterrents discourage borderline thieves and help trap bold ones.

The single most effective deterrent to shoplifting is surveillance by an alert, trained sales force. This may be supplemented by security officers or floorwalkers.

Clerical attention to customers may be the single most important factor in deterring shoplifting. Self-service establishments that save in personnel costs may simply be trading such savings for increased losses from shoplifting.

Sales personnel should be trained in the characteristics that may indicate shoplifting as well as in the common methods of shoplifting. This can be done by films, demonstrations, talks, pamphlets, posters, and conferences. It is important, however, not to teach personnel how to shoplift themselves. In some instances, employees have become intrigued with the ingenuity of various shoplifting methods and have attempted the same methods themselves.

In addition to being alert and observant, sales personnel should be trained to serve all customers promptly. Fast, efficient service will usually deter shoplifting, especially that committed by youths. True customers will appreciate this promptness; shoplifters will be aware that they are noticed. If the salesperson is busy with one customer when another enters, the salesperson should tell the other customer, "I'll be with you in a minute." Salespeople should not turn their backs on customers, if possible. They should keep an eye on people who are "just looking" or wandering aimlessly around the store and should never leave the assigned area unattended.

Sales personnel may be supplemented by security officers or floorwalkers, at least during peak sales periods.

Security officers are prevention oriented, seeking to deter crime by their presence. In contrast, floorwalkers are apprehension oriented, seeking to arrest and prosecute shoplifters.

Security officers, usually in uniform, may be positioned at entrances and/or exits and may also "float" around in a retail establishment, making their presence very obvious. Floorwalkers, on the other hand,

Retail security officer.

pose as customers and seek to remain unnoticed so that they can catch shoplifters "in the act." Thus, the goals of trained salespeople and those of floorwalkers are often in direct conflict. Salespeople who approach customers, believing they may be about to shoplift, thwart the objectives of the floorwalker. Whether the focus should be on prevention or on apprehension is a critical management decision. Whatever approach is selected, working hours of personnel should be scheduled with floor coverage in mind.

Other deterrents to shoplifting that require little expense but that can result in great savings include merchandising techniques that thwart the would-be thief. Although modern merchandising rests on the premise that customers should be able to examine items, this also makes these items more susceptible to theft.

Merchandising techniques to deter shoplifting include keeping displays orderly and not stacking merchandise too high; returning to the display any item looked at and not bought; keeping small, valuable items locked in display cases; placing identifying tags on all merchandise; displaying only one of a pair; not displaying expensive merchandise near exits; and having small, easily stolen items located by the checkout.

Merchandise should be displayed in an orderly way so that any losses are very obvious. Counters piled high with merchandise or counters arranged in a haphazard fashion make it easier for the shoplifter to operate undetected.

Coat racks with expensive clothing should not be near a door because a thief may simply reach in and grab an armload of clothing. To discourage such acts, some stores alternate coat hangers, with every other one facing the opposite direction, making snatching an armload of clothing virtually impossible.

Small, easily stolen items such as razor blades, pens, film, gum, candy, and the like are frequently displayed close to the checkout. Additionally, all merchandise should be clearly identified as store property.

Procedural controls are another inexpensive way to counter shoplifting losses.

---

Procedures such as keeping unused checkout lanes closed, locking the back door, having package checks, carefully checking price tags, maintaining tight controls on fitting rooms and rest rooms, issuing receipts, controlling refunds, and establishing a communication system are important in deterring shoplifting.

---

**CHECKOUT LANES**   Requiring that customers pass by a checkout before leaving a store is a good deterrent to shoplifting. Unused checkout lanes should be chained or blocked off.

**PACKAGE INSPECTIONS**   All packages brought into a store should be inspected and stapled closed or checked. If a package inspection policy is clearly posted, customers should have no objection to having packages examined. Some stores require all packages to be checked before customers are allowed to enter the merchandise areas.

**PRICE TAG CHECKS**   Salesclerks should be alert to price tags that look as though they have been altered or to prices that seem too low for the article. Prices that are stapled to items may use a specific staple pattern recognizable to the clerk. Prices marked in ink will deter price changing, and prices fastened with strong plastic string will deter price switching. Other price tags are available that fall apart when they are removed. These are commonly used in liquor stores. Extreme care must be exercised if a clerk suspects price changing or switching, as such charges are almost impossible to prove unless the acts are actually observed. In fact, the price may have been changed by a customer who intended to shoplift the article and who then thought better of it. An innocent person may then have recognized the bargain and selected the item, with no intent to steal from the merchant.

Clerks should also be alert to possible instances of carton switching or instances of smaller items being concealed within larger items being purchased.

**FITTING ROOMS**   Fitting rooms pose a particular problem for security. One simple procedure to deter shoplifting while in a fitting room is to limit the number of people allowed in the rooms and the number of items a person may take in. Many clothing stores have sales personnel stationed at the fitting room entrance to issue a color-coded marker or a number indicating the number of garments taken into the fitting room and to then check the number of items brought back out. Frequently fitting rooms are kept locked when not in use, requiring customers to ask a salesperson for the key to enter. Sales personnel should watch to see that old clothes are not replaced by new clothes and that price tags have not been altered. They should check fitting rooms for discarded price tags (sometimes stuck behind mirrors) or for empty hangers, indicators that shoplifting has occurred. Packages should never be allowed into fitting rooms.

**RECEIPTS** All purchases made should be accompanied by a receipt. If this policy is followed without exception, a person having an article from the store and no receipt can be assumed not to have paid for it. Closely related to this policy, however, is the potential problem presented by receipts lying around that another customer can pick up and use as proof of purchase. If the customer does not take the receipt, as is often the case with cash register tapes, the salesclerk should immediately discard the receipt. Some establishments counter this problem by stapling the receipt to the bag or by placing it inside the bag rather than handing it to the customer or placing it on the checkout counter.

**REFUND PROCEDURES** A refund procedure should be established and followed to prevent shoplifters from stealing merchandise and then returning it for cash. Many establishments require the original sales slip before a refund will be given. Others give no refunds, but will allow credit toward other purchases. In any event, the refund system should require written documentation of the name, address, and telephone number of the person receiving the refund, the reason for the return, and the amount refunded. The identification of the returner should also be verified. Periodic audits of the refund vouchers will indicate if one person is making a suspiciously large number of returns.

**COMMUNICATIONS SYSTEM** A communication system is also important in deterring shoplifting, especially in larger stores having many departments. Sales personnel who notice someone acting suspiciously can alert a security officer or floorwalker to take up surveillance or can warn other sales personnel if the person is heading for their department. Close cooperation is needed. A warning system should exist to alert all sales personnel when the presence of a shoplifter is suspected. In smaller stores, this might be simply a code word.

Although they require some capital outlay, physical controls often pay for themselves in preventing shoplifting losses.

---

Physical controls to deter shoplifting include changing the actual store layout, posting signs, installing locks and alarms, and installing surveillance equipment such as convex mirrors and/or CCTV.

---

**PHYSICAL LAYOUT** The physical arrangement of a store can aid or hamper the would-be thief. The physical layout can be changed to eliminate too many entrances and exits, merchandise too close to doors, crowded aisles, display counters that obstruct the salesperson's view, and incorrect placement of the cash register. Low counters in orderly rows are a good deterrent to shoplifters, as is adequate lighting. The checkout counter should be positioned so that sales personnel can view the display area. The cash register and phone should be located so that the checkout person does not need to turn away from the display area while ringing up sales or taking phone calls.

Some stores have the office and accounting department located on a balcony that offers a view of the entire floor below. All back exits should be locked if fire regulations permit. Otherwise they should be alarmed.

**SIGNS** Signs stating "Shoplifters will be prosecuted" may deter shoplifting, but as indicated in at least one study, such signs may plant the idea in the mind of someone who had not thought of it before. The signs may also cause the store to be selected as a target by juvenile shoplifters because they see it as posing a greater risk and challenge.

**LOCKS** Locks are also effective. Display cabinets can be locked, as can valuable items such as stereos and televisions. Furs may be locked to hangers that are not removable. Such locks are often supplemented by alarms. For example, a rack alarm may be activated if someone attempts to remove permanent hangers. Display case lock alarms may go off if the case is not locked. The weight of the salesperson on the mat by the lock overrides the alarms.

**ALARMS** Loop alarms, coaxial cables that form a closed electric circuit, may be looped through handles of expensive items such as televisions and photographic equipment; if the cable is cut or broken, the alarm sounds. Cable alarms, coaxial cables with a pad that is attached to merchandise, may be used with merchandise that has no holes or handles, such as typewriters and adding machines.

Other alarms are operated by pressure. For example, a wafer switch alarm can be set under an object; if the object is lifted, the alarm goes off. The removal of as little as one ounce of pressure may activate the alarm. In contrast, the ribbon switch alarm is activated when pressure is applied. Such alarms are often used on furniture or large appliances. Anyone attempting to lift such items will set off the alarm. Plug alarms are simple devices used for calculators, typewriters, stereo equipment, and televisions. When such merchandise is unplugged, the alarm sounds. Art dealers often use a special type of canvas painting alarm that is sensitive to any vibration, such as that caused by a thief attempting to remove the painting from its frame.

Electronically activated price tags are being used more and more. Such tags set off an alarm if the item is taken from the store with the price tag still on. These tags may be wafers, pellets, or long plastic strips which are removed with a special instrument by sales personnel. Anyone attempting to remove the tags without the instrument will damage the article. There is a real danger, however, if sales personnel are not meticulous about removing the tags. Should a tag be left on carelessly, an innocent customer will set off the alarm. Lawsuits may result. For example, in *Dent v. May Department Stores Company (1982)*, a customer at one of the defendant's stores was stopped by a security guard as she was about to leave the store. A skirt she had purchased at the store had activated a buzzer because the cashier had failed to remove a magnetized

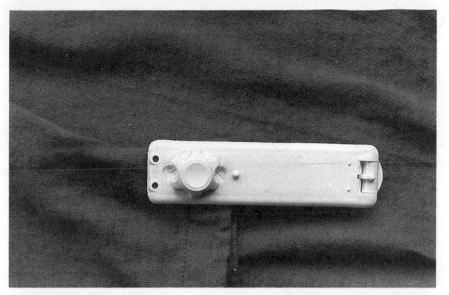

Electronic price tag.

surveillance device designed to detect shoplifters. The customer filed an action for false arrest and imprisonment, and the case made its way to the District of Columbia Court of Appeals. The court ruled in favor of the store, observing that the guard had probable cause to detain the customer when the alarm sounded. Also, because the guard allowed the customer to leave once the tag was removed, the customer was *not* illegally detained.

**SURVEILLANCE DEVICES**  Surveillance devices are also commonly used in retail establishments. Wide-angle (convex) mirrors are one inexpensive, effective surveillance device. Sometimes called detection mirrors, they are often used in fitting room aisles, in difficult-to-see areas of an establishment, and above book racks and displays of merchandise likely to be stolen. Some security experts, however, feel that such mirrors enhance safety more than they deter shoplifting because they distort the image. It is critical that salespersons, guards, or floorwalkers see the stolen object clearly. Flat mirrors in hard-to-see areas are perhaps more satisfactory in this respect because they do not distort the image.

Many stores use CCTV, with the cameras very obviously mounted to act as a deterrent. Some even have signs such as "Smile, You're on Camera," and phony cameras interspersed with functional cameras, giving the impression of greater coverage. CCTV cameras can pan the entire display area, but they must be continuously monitored to be effective. Videotape recording (VTR) equipment is sometimes preferred because it is a permanent record, can "replay" an incident, and does not have to be watched continually. Some stores use a combination of CCTV and VTR equipment.

As noted by Tyska and Fennelly (1987, pp. 262–63), by the year 2000:

In-house protection of stock will continue to use the principles of electronic article surveillance, closed circuit television and two-way radio communication. But a strong likelihood exists that physical protection in the form of locks, bolts and bars, etc., will be far more dominant than it is in the 1980's.

Article surveillance tags will serve a dual purpose to their present primary function. They will also bear pure merchandising information such as stock codes and selling prices.

By the year 2000, closed circuit television within retail outlets, probably linked with a two-way sound facility, will be far more widespread and flexible, in color and accepted as being an effective tool of management in fields other than pure security. Fiber optics will be considered as the normal means of picture communication.

Peepholes, two-way mirrors, and CCTV in dressing rooms may present legal problems for merchants. State statutes regarding such surveillance should be checked carefully before such procedures are used.

Many other deterrents to shoplifting have been implemented in retail establishments. Some stores have an employee incentive program that rewards personnel who assist in deterring or apprehending shoplifters. Others have encouraged customers to help in the detection of shoplifting. For example, the General Mills Honesty Patrol encourages supermarket customers to report retail theft. Customers are given "Honesty Patrol" buttons and can report any retail thefts anonymously. They do not have to confront the suspect. Educational programs in the schools can also help deter shoplifting.

In addition, a careful system of inventory control so that the magnitude of the problem can be recognized and a careful record of shoplifters detained (whether prosecuted or not) can help combat shoplifting. Such a list can be circulated to other merchants, provided it is marked "Confidential." Many cities have established a merchants' protective association to assist in maintaining and circulating a central list of shoplifters and bad-check passers.

Keep in mind, however, that all the preceding procedures and devices are supplemental to an alert, trained sales force—the first line of defense against shoplifting.

## Apprehension of Shoplifters

It is critical to distinguish the thief from the absent minded shopper who simply walks out of a department or store carelessly, but not fraudulently, without paying for an article. Recall the earlier discussion of individuals with Altzheimer's disease. Shoplifters should be apprehended so stolen merchandise can be recovered; this is a basic purpose of private security—to protect assets.

To apprehend a suspect for shoplifting, someone must actually see the item being taken and concealed or be reasonably certain an item has been taken; and the suspect must be kept under *continuous* observation until apprehension is made. This may occur on the premises or outside the premises, depending on state statute.

Mere suspicion is not enough. There must be evidence of an intent to steal, including such actions as leaving the department or floor without paying, concealing the property, taking off price tags, or having no money to pay for items.

Watch for all actions that make you suspicious, such as a person entering a fitting room with six dresses and coming out with only one, a fitting room with empty hangers and price tags lying all over, a person who goes into a fitting room with a relatively empty shopping bag and comes out with it bulging, and the like. In such instances, a merchant or the merchant's employee can detain the person *if* reasonable grounds exist for believing shoplifting has occurred.

In Minnesota, for example, state statute 629.366 states this: "A merchant or merchant's employee who has reasonable cause for believing that a person has taken, or is in the act of taking, any article of value without paying therefor, from the possession of the merchant in his place of business or from any vehicle or premises under his control, with the intent wrongfully to deprive the merchant of his property or the use and benefit thereof or to appropriate the same to the use of the taker or any other person, may detain such person for the sole purpose of delivering him to a peace officer without unnecessary delay and then and there making a charge against such person to the peace officer. The person detained shall be informed promptly of the purpose of the detention and shall not be subject to unnecessary or unreasonable force, nor to interrogation against his will."

The key phrase in the preceding statute is **reasonable cause**. This is interpreted in the same way as **probable cause** by the courts. The United States Supreme Court has defined probable cause as "facts and circumstances within their knowledge and of which they had reasonable trustworthy information [that] were sufficient in themselves to warrant a man of reasonable caution in the belief that the suspect had committed a crime" (*Carroll v. United States*, 1925).

In many states, concealment is prima facie evidence of the intent to permanently deprive. In addition to seeing the item being taken, salespeople must provide continuous surveillance; otherwise, the suspect may pass the stolen merchandise to a confederate or simply get rid of it. The result would be "no case" and the risk of a false imprisonment suit.

A set procedure should be established for apprehending shoplifters. In most states it is no longer necessary for the shoplifter to leave the store, although prosecution is easier if the person has left the premises. In addition, an apprehension outside the store causes less commotion and interference with the store's operation. However, if the merchandise is valuable and the thief may get away if allowed to leave the premises, the suspect should be apprehended inside the store.

Usually salespeople do *not* apprehend shoplifters; rather, they notify the manager, security officer, or floorwalker. It takes courage and confidence to confront a shoplifter and a strong personality able to withstand verbal and sometimes even physical abuse. The person who does the apprehending should first seek assistance because the suspect may have an accomplice to come to the rescue. The apprehending employees should never call the suspect a "thief" or use the word "steal," nor should they touch the suspect unless absolutely necessary.

The usual procedure is for the person making the apprehension to identify himself, to instruct the person to give up the merchandise, to describe it specifically and state where it was taken from, and to then

Security officer at jewelry store on Rodeo Drive in Beverly Hills, Los Angeles.

ask for the sales slip. If the suspect cannot produce a receipt, he or she is taken to the office. Force can be used if necessary. Courts have repeatedly ruled that requiring a suspected shoplifter to return to a store once outside constitutes an arrest, even if no physical force is used.

Managers, security officers, floorwalkers, or sales personnel may make a citizen's arrest, but must use extreme caution. It is usually better not to arrest until after questioning is completed.

Case law has upheld the right of management to search suspected shoplifters and to recover stolen property by force, if necessary. However, recent California Supreme Court rulings may preclude such practices in the future. In *People v. Zelinski* (155 California Reporter 575), the California Supreme Court ruled that the Exclusionary Rule applies to private security officials when acting in a "public" capacity. In this case two detectives in Zody's Department Store observed a suspect put a blouse in her purse. They stopped Virginia Zelinski outside the store and returned her to the security office, where they opened her purse and retrieved the blouse as well as a vial later determined to contain heroin. She was subsequently charged with heroin possession. The trial judge allowed the evidence to be presented, stating that store detectives were not governed by the prohibition against unreasonable searches. On appeal, the California Supreme Court reversed this decision.

Historically, courts have allowed such evidence to be presented. In the Zelinski case, however, the judges viewed the actions differently, an important precedent.

A witness should be present when questioning a shoplifting suspect to avoid the charge that undue pressure was applied. Any involuntary confession is inadmissible, as is any confession given after prolonged questioning. The suspect should be treated courteously. If the suspect confesses, obtain a written confession to avoid civil lawsuits.

Persons detained on suspicion of shoplifting are often asked to sign a standard release form such as the following:

I hereby release the person(s) who detained me in connection with this incident and his or her employees, superiors, principals, and customers from any claim or demand arising out of or in connection with the incident.

Such waivers often are not upheld in court, however. If items are taken from the suspect, they should be marked with the initials of the person obtaining the evidence, as well as the place and date. Careful records should be kept of all persons apprehended, whether prosecuted or not.

## Prosecution

Existing state statutes and the severity of punishment may be factors in whether prosecution is undertaken. In some states, punishment depends on the value of the item and how many times the person has been caught for a similar offense. Shoplifters may receive a fine and/or a jail sentence. In some states a civil suit can also be brought. Procedures for prosecuting juveniles must be especially well defined; in some states, such as California and Illinois, parents of minors are held civilly responsible for shoplifting offenses of their children.

Some managers feel all shoplifters should be prosecuted and that failure to prosecute even "first offenders" encourages shoplifting. They hold that the person who steals will also lie and may very well have shoplifted before, but have gotten away with it. Prosecution will serve as a deterrent to others, these managers argue; it will also help avoid false arrest suits and will improve security staff morale. Other managers, however, feel that criminal prosecution is a law enforcement objective that does not meet security (prevention) objectives.

Even if a person has admitted guilt, the store does not always prosecute. There are many reasons for nonprosecution, including the fear of losing a good customer; the fear of damaging the store's reputation; the loss of time and the expense of testifying; and the leniency of the courts to first offenders. Additionally, while security or sales personnel are in court testifying, the establishment is more vulnerable to other losses from shoplifting. Obviously, not all shoplifters will be prosecuted. Again, management must decide on goals and establish guidelines.

Establish reasonable guidelines for prosecuting shoplifters. Consider the value of the article, along with the person's age, number of offenses, and attitude. Guard against illegal detention, malicious prosecution, and slander suits.

Factors to consider in establishing a policy on prosecuting shoplifters include the following:

➤ *Age*—Those twelve and under usually have their parents called and then are released to them. Those thirteen to sixteen are treated as juvenile offenders.
➤ *Monetary value*—Taking a 50¢ package of gum (a misdemeanor) differs from taking an $850 camera (a felony).

> *Past history*—A person with a past record of shoplifting is more likely to be prosecuted.
> *Attitude*—Is the suspect repentant and sorry or belligerent and hostile?
> *Strength of the case*—Are there witnesses, a confession, recovered property?

One primary reason for not prosecuting shoplifters is the time involved in going to court. Experiments in shoplifting courts may be a solution to this problem. In 1973 Cook County, Illinois, initiated the first shoplifting court system. This system used existing municipal courts to hear one hundred or more cases each afternoon. Illinois also has the stiffest penalties for shoplifting convictions. Yet there is no evidence that the special courts or the stiff penalties have deterred shoplifting.

## □ BAD CHECKS

Most checks are cashed not in banks, but in retail stores. Some estimate that as many as 80 percent of all checks are cashed in retail stores. In essence, as a service to customers, retailers substitute for banks as the major supplier of cash. Providing this service, however, creates the risk of loss through bad checks. One-third of check losses are sustained by supermarkets, 30 percent by department stores, and the next greatest amount by liquor stores and gas stations.

---

To reduce losses from bad checks, retailers should do the following:

➤ Teach personnel to recognize the different types of checks and the common types of bad checks.
➤ Establish a check-cashing policy and adhere to it.
➤ Train personnel to examine checks and identification.
➤ Record relevant information on the backs of all checks cashed.
➤ Reconcile identity documents with check passers' characteristics.

---

### Types of Checks

Retail sales personnel are likely to encounter seven types of checks.

1) A *personal check* is written and signed by the individual offering it made out to the firm. This is the most commonly encountered check in retail establishments.
2) A *two-party check* is issued by one person to a second person who endorses it so that it may be cashed by a third person. This type of check is most susceptible to fraud because, for one thing, the maker can stop payment at the bank.
3) A *payroll check* is issued to an employee for services performed. Usually the name of the employer is printed on it, and it has a number and is signed. In most instances, "payroll" is also printed on the check. The employee's name is printed by a check-writing machine

or typed. In metropolitan areas, you should not cash a payroll check that is handprinted, rubber stamped, or typewritten as a payroll check, even if it appears to be issued by a local business and drawn on a local bank. It may be a different story in a small community where you know the company officials and the employee personally.

4) A *government check* can be issued by the federal government, a state, a county, or a local government. Such checks cover salaries, tax refunds, pensions, welfare allotments, and veterans' benefits, to mention a few examples. You should be particularly cautious with government checks. Often they are stolen, and the endorsement has been forged. In some areas, such thievery is so great that some banks refuse to cash Social Security, welfare, relief, or income tax checks, unless the customer is known by or has an account with the bank. You should follow this procedure also. In short, know your endorser.

5) A *blank check* or sometimes known as a *universal check* is no longer acceptable to most banks due to the Federal Reserve Board regulations that prohibit standard processing without the encoded characters. This check may be used, but it requires a special collection process on the part of the bank and, therefore, they incur a special cost.

6) A *counter check* is still used by a few banks and is issued to depositors when they are withdrawing funds from their accounts. It is not good anywhere else. Sometimes a store has its own counter checks for the convenience of its customers. A counter check is *not* negotiable and is so marked. You should check local bank practices on blank checks and counter checks because of the coded magnetic tape imprints which many banks use for computer processing. Personal printed checks often have the individual's bank account number in magnetic code.

7) A *traveler's check* is a check sold with a preprinted amount (usually in round figures) to travelers who do not want to carry large amounts of cash. The traveler signs the checks at the time of purchase and should countersign them only in the presence of the person who cashes them.

In addition, a *money order* can be passed as a check. However, a money order is usually bought to send in the mail. Most stores should not accept money orders in face-to-face transactions. Some small stores sell money orders. If yours does, never accept a personal check in payment for money orders. Purchasers having a valid checking account, do not need money orders. They can send a check in the mail.

---

High-risk checks include second-party checks, counter checks, illegible checks, post-dated checks, and out-of-town checks.

---

## Types of Bad Checks

Writing a "bad" check is a crime. It may be either forgery or fraud, depending on the type of check written. In either event, bad checks are of major concern to businesses. Often forged traveler's checks and other such drafts that on their face are valid will not be paid to the company if they have been fraudulently passed. That is, traveler's checks are as good as cash for the purchaser, but many issuing banks treat a forged traveler's check just like any other forged check and will refuse to pay the party who cashes it.

---

The most common types of bad checks are forged or altered checks, no-account checks, and non-sufficient funds checks.

---

*Forged checks* include stolen checks bearing a forged endorsement on the back, deliberately altered third-party checks such as Social Security or government checks, or payroll checks endorsed to a retail merchant. The amount of the check may also be raised or the name of the payee changed. Counterfeit checks may be printed to resemble payroll or government checks.

*No Such Account* (NSA) checks are those drawn on an account that never existed or that has since been closed. Although sometimes such checks are honest mistakes, they often are written by a person who deposits money to obtain checks and then closes the account, writing several checks over a weekend before the fraud can be detected.

*Nonsufficient Funds* (NSF) checks are drawn against an account that exists, but does not contain enough money to cover the check. The majority of such checks are honest mistakes caused by such things as mathematical errors in the check ledger, failure to record checks written, or two people having checkbooks for the same account and not keeping careful records. Most NSF checks will be cashed when they are deposited a second time, but often with a hefty fee attached.

*Incorrectly written* checks are also often returned by the bank unpaid. Mistakes can include an incorrect date, a discrepancy between the amount in figures and that written in words, or a questionable signature.

Only a small percentage of money lost through bad checks is recovered, so *prevention* is the key to reducing losses from bad checks.

## Establishing Check-Cashing Policies

Every retail establishment should establish a check-cashing policy and post it. Customers will therefore not feel they are being treated unfairly, and employees will be constantly reminded to enforce the policies. The following check-cashing policies are among those often established by retailers:

➤ No checks cashed.
➤ No checks cashed above the amount of purchase.
➤ Checks cashed for only $X over the amount of purchase.
➤ No out-of-town checks.
➤ No two-party checks.
➤ No government checks.

➤ No checks cashed unless registered with the store.
➤ No checks cashed unless registered with a check verification system.
➤ No checks cashed without proper identification.
➤ No checks cashed without two pieces of identification.
➤ All checks over $X must be authorized by the supervisor.
➤ All checks over $X must be verified by the bank.
➤ No checks cashed that are numbered lower than 300.

Although the first policy is the simplest and safest, it also may result in losing many customers who do all their purchasing by check and do not carry much cash.

## Examining Checks

Personnel who cash checks should be taught how to examine all checks presented to them.

---

Checks should be carefully examined. Look at the printed name and address, check number, date, payee, numerical and written amount, bank and address, and signature (or endorsement). Accept no checks that are illegible, that are not written in ink, or that contain erasures or written-over dates or amounts.

---

The name of the person holding the account, the address, and often the phone number are usually printed in the upper left corner of the check. These should be compared with identification presented. The address and/or phone number can also be verified in a local phone directory. The number on a personal check should be examined. Most banks begin their numbering sequence with 101 and continue in sequence. Experience shows that more personal checks under 300 are returned than are those over this number. Bad-check passers, however, may be aware of this and request that their numbering begin with a number over 300.

The date should be correct. A check with no date, a date later than the actual date (post-dated), or a date more than thirty days ago should not be accepted.

The dollar amount in digits and words should be identical. If the amount of the check is over the amount of the purchase, many establishments record the actual amount of purchase at the top of the check. Personnel authorized to cash checks should be aware that most bad-check passers write checks for between twenty-five and thirty dollars, assuming that retailers will be less suspicious than if they wrote the check for a greater amount. Checks over a certain amount frequently require authorization by a supervisor.

The check should also indicate the name of the bank and its address. Extra care should be used in examining a check drawn on a nonlocal bank.

Finally, the signature or endorsement should be checked and compared with the identification required. Be wary of checks in which the maker's name is preceded by a title (Mr., Mrs., Ms, Dr., etc.) or extends past the allotted space.

## Examining Identification

Many establishments require at least two pieces of identification before a check may be cashed. However, a person who steals checks may also steal identification.

Persons presenting checks to cash should be required to produce identification containing a physical description (preferably a photograph) and a signature. The description should be compared with the person; the signature should be compared with the signature on the check.

Owens (1990, p. 18) suggests these measures to reduce losses from bad checks:

➤ Collect as much information as possible: driver's license number, bank check guarantee card, place of employment, and employer's phone number.
➤ Examine the check and customer's ID carefully for signs of alteration. Checks without perforation marks, for example, may be forged duplicates. Also check the signature against another piece of signed identification, and be sure the photo on a photo ID matches the person presenting the check. If the check is large—and you have the time—call the bank or the employer for verification.

Acceptable forms of identification include driver's licenses, military or government IDs, and national credit cards. Always check the date on the identification to be sure it is current.

The following should *not* be used as identification:

| | |
|---|---|
| bank books | learner's permits |
| birth certificates | letters |
| business cards | library cards |
| club or organization cards | Social Security cards |
| customer's duplicate cards | unsigned credit cards |
| initial jewelry | voter's registration cards |
| insurance cards | work permits |

In addition, some stores use photo-identity cameras that take a picture of the person writing the check, the check itself, and the identification presented. If a check is returned, the specific section of film bearing that check number can be developed and used in attempting to identify the bad-check passer.

Some establishments also make use of a thumbprint made without ink on the back of the check as a means of identification.

## Recording Information

The identification presented should be recorded on the back of the check. Many establishments use a stamp such as the one shown in Figure 14–1. In addition, the person who accepts the check should initial it, in the event that later identification of the person writing the check is required. If a supervisor is called to authorize the check, the supervisor should also initial the check.

A list of all returned checks should be kept at each checkout, and sales personnel should compare checks presented against this list. Some merchants tape bad checks to the register, an embarrassing situation for a local bad-check passer. The list of bad checks can also be circulated among retailers in a city.* Such cooperation can help to minimize bad-check losses. All check law violators should be reported to the local authorities. Merchants should know their state laws regarding bad checks and should prosecute when possible.

## Refusing Checks

Retailers do *not* have to accept checks if they are suspicious of the person presenting the check, even if the person presents the required identification. Checks should not be accepted if they have the word *hold* written on them or if the person presenting the check is intoxicated or acting suspiciously. Sometimes bad-check passers will wave to someone in the store, often another employee; will drop names of people who work there; or will

```
                              PRINT
    _____
    Salesperson—Name and No.
    _____
    Auth. Signature
    _____
    Customer's Address
    _____
    Home Phone                              Business Phone
    _____
    Ident. No. 1
    _____
    Ident. No. 2
    _____
    Dept. No.                               Amount of Sale
    _____
    Take            Send            COD            Will Call
```

**Figure 14–1  Check-cashing information stamp.**

---

*Posting/circulation practices may be illegal in some locations.

claim to be "old customers." Such actions should never cause the sales personnel to ignore established check-cashing policies.

## ☐ FRAUDULENT CREDIT CARDS

Use of credit cards is a way of life for many Americans. Gardner (1985, p. 327) states that the average adult in our country carries five to six credit cards, with almost 550 million such cards in use: "With the increased use of credit cards as part of everyday life, the possibilities for fraud will continue to exist." He describes precautions being taken to deter such fraud, including hiring more investigators, making careful checks before credit is extended, verifying shipments of cards that are sent out to make sure the true cardholder has placed the order, and the like. Even though fraud constitutes a small fraction of total credit card sales, Gardner contends that "yearly losses in the United States are estimated between $100 and $300 million in credit card fraud."

Gardner suggests that burglars, robbers, and thieves have many and varied methods of obtaining credit cards for fraudulent use, including picking pockets and snatching purses. Or, a prostitute might decide that stealing credit cards is more profitable than "turning tricks." Restaurant, retail store, or gas station employees might simply keep a card after completing a transaction. Or the cards might be stolen from the mail or during a burglary. They can also be counterfeited or altered, or obtained through corrupting credit card manufacturer employees or postal employees.

According to Gardner, it is also easy to obtain credit card numbers. He cites as an example a woman who asked a drugstore to save the used carbons from credit card purchases for her child to do a school project. The store complied, setting aside bundles of carbons for her. The woman then used these numbers to make unauthorized charges at other stores. The same care that is exercised in accepting checks should be used in accepting credit cards. The signature should be compared with that on the sales charge slip. The expiration date should be examined. Frequently, stores have a **floor release limit,** meaning that any charge above a certain amount must be cleared through the credit card company. Some stores have a **zero floor release limit,** meaning that all charges are cleared with the credit card issuer.

---

Protect against losses from fraudulent use of credit cards by comparing the signature on the card with that on the sales slip, checking the card's expiration date, and establishing a reasonable floor release limit.

---

In addition to the various types of theft of credit cards or numbers, other fraudulent uses of credit cards include the following (Gardner, 1985, p. 328):

➤ Knowingly receiving stolen credit cards.
➤ Use of a credit card without the cardholder's consent.

- Use of a revoked or canceled credit card.
- Knowing use of a counterfeit or altered card.
- Illegal use of a credit card number (or use of the pretended number of a fictitious card).
- Use of an illegally possessed card to negotiate a check.
- Receiving or possession of an illegally obtained card with intent to defraud.
- Delivery or sale of an illegally obtained credit card.

Illegal use of credit card numbers to make long distance phone calls is a major concern. Gardner gives as an example a Michigan labor union that received a phone bill for approximately $321,000, and a New York woman who received a bill for $109,500. He suggests, because the calls are often global and the practice is persistent, that much of the fraud is committed by organized narcotic and other criminal groups wanting to avoid detection by law enforcement officials or the IRS.

The illegal use of a credit card number (rather than the card itself) *is* fraud, as established in the case of *United States v. Bice-Bey* (1983), in which the Fourth Circuit Court of Appeals held that "the core element of a credit card is the account number, not the piece of plastic."

## ☐ RETAIL EMPLOYEE THEFT

Although statistics indicate that shoplifting accounts for the greatest retail losses, some experts claim that dishonest employees account for two-thirds of retail theft. Many losses assumed to be the result of customer shoplifting may actually have been caused by employees. Employees have an easier time shoplifting because they know what security measures exist, and they may frequently be in a department alone. In addition, turnover in personnel may be high, and extra personnel may be added during peak seasons when the risk of theft is known to be higher than usual.

Security measures previously discussed have special relevance to curbing retail losses. First, have effective preemployment screening so that honest employees are hired. Next, establish the proper climate for honesty. Employees who are treated fairly and paid fairly are less likely to steal from their employers. A "zero shortage" attitude should be adopted, maintained, and rewarded. Incentives to reduce employee theft include the following:

- Make certain each person is matched to his or her job.
- Set reasonable rules and enforce them rigidly.
- Set clear lines of authority and responsibility.
- Give employees the resources they need to achieve success.
- Be fair in rewarding outstanding performance.
- Remove the temptation to steal.

In addition, physical and procedural controls are essential. Limiting the number of employee exits, keeping storerooms locked and allowing entrance only by authorized personnel, checking lockers and packages, flattening trash, and restricting access to assets, as feasible, should all be part of the retail security plan.

Special employee security problems in retail establishments include access to merchandise and cash. Specific pricing procedures, cash-handling procedures, and refund procedures are essential. Personnel should be rotated periodically, and responsibilities should be separated.

## Pricing

One major cause of inventory shrinkage is loosely controlled pricing procedures. Price switching or price altering can be done either by employees or by customers. The pricing procedures suggested earlier should thwart such actions.

To deter employee theft by price alterations:

➤ Allow only authorized employees to set prices and mark merchandise.
➤ Mark merchandise by machine or rubber stamp, never pencil.
➤ Conduct periodic audits of prices recorded and prices charged.
➤ Check on the "popular" salesperson.

A special risk is the salesperson who adds extra items to a customer's purchases to win the favor of that customer or who undercharges friends or relatives. Clerks who sell articles to friends and/or relatives at lower cost (called *sliding*) will find that once they start, they cannot stop without losing friends. Although the "popular" salesperson is certainly an asset to an establishment, his or her popularity should be for the right reasons. In one instance customers stood in line to wait for one saleswoman, refusing to be served by anyone else. Investigation revealed that she switched tickets for many "special" customers, giving them substantial markdowns. Store losses amounted to about three hundred dollars a week, not including the twenty-five dollars a week in increased commissions for the dishonest saleswoman. Pay special attention to salespeople who are visited by too many personal friends. To discourage such socialization, some retailers hire employees who live outside the store's vicinity.

Employees who are allowed to make purchases at a discount may abuse the privilege and buy for friends and relatives, or sometimes even for resale at a profit, setting themselves up in direct competition with their employer. To thwart such actions, a manager or supervisor should make all employee sales and should keep a record to see that the cumulative amount is reasonable. In addition, employees should not shop until the end of the day and should leave the premises after their shopping is completed.

Other methods of cheating employers include picking out expensive clothes and putting them on layby* under a fictitious name. Then, when

---

*Putting money "down" on an item so that the store will save it for the customer until the full payment has been made.

the clothes are out of season and are put on sale, the employee purchases them at a considerable savings.

In restaurants, unauthorized consumption of food and drink can result in tremendous losses. Policies establishing what employees can and cannot eat or drink while on the job should be clearly established.

## Cash Handling

Cash is particularly vulnerable to theft. The customer who hurriedly lays the correct change on the counter and leaves without waiting for a receipt presents an especially tempting situation for cash-handling personnel. All cash-handling personnel should be properly trained, supervised, and rewarded for efficiency and honesty.

To reduce losses of cash:

➤ Establish strict cash-handling procedures.
➤ Use a tamper-proof recording system.
➤ Have each clerk responsible for his or her own receipts.
➤ Have cash receipts balanced by someone else.
➤ Perform unannounced audits.
➤ Use honesty shoppers.

Cash receipts can be handled in many ways. One of the most common is the *cash register system* in which each transaction is recorded on a tape. When this system is used, each clerk should have his or her own register and be responsible for the receipts, but someone other than the clerk should balance it. When the sale is made, the clerk should call back the price of each item, the total amount of the sale, and the amount of money tendered, and then count back the change. The customer should always be given a receipt. Failure to do so is usually indicative of poor supervision. The cash drawer should be closed after each transaction.

Several methods may be used to steal money from the cash register, often called "till tapping." Clerks may fail to ring up a sale and simply pocket the money. They may purposely shortchange people. They may deliberately under-ring a purchase and then "catch" the error, adding the charge manually to the customer's receipt and receiving the full price from the customer; the added amount would not show on the tape, and the clerk would be free to pocket the money. Clerks may also enter an over-ring, as though to correct an error, when they are actually pocketing the money. Supervisors should make periodic checks of the registers to ensure that they balance. A clerk who is consistently over or under the correct amount should probably be given a job that does not involve handling money.

Griffin (1980, pp. 60–63) describes an instance involving a clerk in a pharmacy who stole five thousand dollars from her employer during the course of the year. It was a policy of the store that all customers receive a written receipt to be used for income tax purposes. The clerk used this receipt as the means to cover her dishonest actions. She gave the customer the receipt and simply kept the payment. If the payment was by check, she put the check in the drawer and took out a comparable amount of cash. An audit eventually revealed five checks totaling $96.41 that were not recorded on the register tape.

In addition to audits, other ways to prevent such thefts are available; for example, a *validating* cash register uses a process in which each check is inserted into the register with the amount rung up printed on the check. Another safeguard is to have registers that display a readout of the transaction on the customer's side, so that the customer and store supervisory personnel can observe the amount easily.

A second frequently used system is the *written sales slip* system, in which each salesclerk has a sales book. In such a system, all sales slips should be numbered in sequence and duplicate sales slips kept in the book. Periodic audits of cash in the register and amounts shown in the sales book should be made.

A third commonly used system of handling cash is the *autographic register system*, which uses a locked box into which the audit copy of the sales ticket is cranked when the customer's copy is removed. Again, such forms should be prenumbered. Key control is also essential when such a system is used.

Figure 14–2 illustrates one way to separate the functions of employees who deal with cash and how to trace transactions.

---

Honesty shopping, or a shopping service, tests the honesty of sales personnel who handle cash.

---

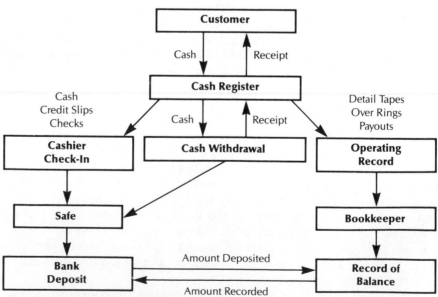

**Figure 14–2 Retail cash and cash records flow.**
*From the National Crime Prevention Institute.*

Retailers frequently hire personnel from security firms who offer shopping services, that is, professional shoppers who pose as customers and who then check for violations of cash-handling procedures. Such services are often used in retail stores, bars, restaurants, and other sales establishments.

Typically, the honesty shopper makes a purchase using the correct change and leaves hurriedly (called a *put down*), the ideal situation for the till-tapping clerk. A second honesty shopper may observe whether the clerk rings up the sale, or the register tape may later be examined to see if that sale was recorded. Some honesty shoppers also use marked money. Remember, however, that employees may make an honest mistake, get busy, and forget to ring up a sale. However, if it *is* an honest mistake, there will be an overage for that amount at the end of the day.

Honesty shopping is an effective means of discovering salespeople who are stealing cash. It can be used on a large scale and be repeated often. When employees are informed that such a system is used, it will also act as a psychological deterrent to potentially dishonest employees.

Honesty shopping may also be used to check on the sales personnel's efficiency and courtesy, information that is helpful for management. Some security experts feel that one person cannot effectively perform both types of evaluation at the same time and recommend that the store have two separate operations, an honesty shopper and a service shopper.

## Refunds

It is easier for employees to abuse the return/refund system than it is for customers. Therefore, the same policies regarding refunds discussed previously should be rigidly applied to employees as well.

---

Require all employees to comply with the return/refund policy. Keep tight control of all credit documents, and match items to the return vouchers. Conduct periodic audits of return vouchers.

---

Employees are often given first chance to buy damaged merchandise. Some may even intentionally damage merchandise to get the markdown. Often, however, an employee will purchase "as is" merchandise and then attempt to return it for a full refund. The merchandise should be inspected by someone other than the person who made the sale. Returned items should be carefully matched to the return vouchers and then returned to stock as quickly as possible.

Other times employees may report phony customer returns and refunds, simply pocketing the money. They may keep receipts that are left by customers and use the receipts to cover shortages. Periodic audits of refund vouchers should be made; several people who presumably have received refunds should be called to verify that they actually did receive a refund and that the amount recorded was correct.

## ☐ ASSISTANCE IN RETAIL SECURITY

Retail security requires that merchandise and cash be protected from internal (employee) and external (customer, burglar, or robber) theft. Advice, assistance, and information on retail security can be obtained from merchant's protection associations, retail credit bureaus, better business bureaus, police departments, and/or district attorneys' offices.

## ☐ SHOPPING CENTER SECURITY

Shopping centers and malls are found throughout the country and pose special problems for security officers. The goal of these centers, like that of the individual establishments located within them, is profit. Because security represents a cost rather than a profit, it must make its contribution felt in other ways.

The primary objectives of shopping center security are loss prevention and public relations.

The predominant area of loss prevention is that of losses resulting from criminal activity—primarily theft. Potter (1984, p. 34) suggests that "effective shopping center security programs prevent criminal activity in three ways:

*Deterrence.* Security must provide a highly visible, effective deterrent to criminal activity. Adequate lighting, alert and aggressive patrols, and appropriate physical security measures such as controlling access to nonpublic areas are all effective deterrents in a shopping center environment.
*Detection.* No retail facility can deter all criminal activity and remain in business. However, an effective security program must be able to detect criminal activity, through the use of closed circuit television and intrusion alarm systems, for example, and then generate an appropriate response.
*Limitation of loss.* The response to any threatened or actual criminal activity must be designed to prevent loss of life and limit or eliminate property losses and potential liability.

Losses from criminal actions are not the only type of losses for which security personnel are responsible. They should be observant and watch for any fire or safety hazards that could ultimately result in a loss.

The second primary objective of shopping center security is to promote good public relations. Potter emphasizes this (1984, p. 35): "To the shopping public, the uniformed security officer is shopping center management, and a sharply uniformed, courteous officer is a tremendous asset. Many shopping centers enhance this image by allowing officers on patrol in parking areas to assist customers by jump-starting cars with dead batteries, opening cars locked with the keys inside, and even changing flat tires. Such tasks detract little or nothing from the officer's visibility and generate invaluable customer loyalty to the mall."

Some shopping centers have experimented with having their officers wear blazers and slacks rather than the more traditional, military-type uniforms. This does foster public relations, but research also shows that much of the deterrent effect of the highly visible, uniformed officer is lost.

## ☐ RETAIL SECURITY IN THE FUTURE

Tyska and Fennelly (1987, p. 260) suggest: "The older type of multi-floored department or chain store will be a thing of the past. . . . Overall technological progress will be principally electronic with the micro-chip and micro-processor playing an even greater role than it does at present." They further suggest (1987, p. 261):

> The application of security or loss control measures will have to be very clearly defined and positively enforced.
>     Although the general level of security staffing in retail establishments will be similar to today, the calibre of personnel involved will be much higher, far more retail management orientated. The actual job descriptions will be substantially upgraded. The days of second career security operatives will be long gone and career prospects will have to be offered to direct entry special-ist security employees. Professional security associations and institutions will play a far greater and wider role in personal and general security education in retail communities.

Tyska and Fennelly (1987, p. 263) stress: "One thing stands out. Full cognizance will have to be taken by management of loss control on a basis of the widest possible meaning of the expression. Those who fail to assess fully and react appropriately will stand every chance of not sur-viving."

## SUMMARY

Reported crimes committed against all types of retail establishments in order of frequency are shoplifting, burglary, vandalism, bad checks, fraudulent use of credit cards, employee theft, and robbery. The focus of this chapter is on shoplifting, bad checks, and employee theft.

Shoplifting is the theft of retail merchandise while lawfully on the premises. Concealment of merchandise is prima facie evidence of intent to shoplift. In many states price changing is also considered shoplifting.

Shoplifters can be classified as amateurs—students, housewives, vagrants, alcoholics, drug addicts, and kleptomaniacs—or as profession-als: those who steal for resale of merchandise. Shoplifting methods include palming objects, dropping articles into a receptacle, placing items inside clothing, wearing items out of the store, and switching price tags.

The single most effective deterrent to shoplifting is surveillance by an alert, trained sales force. This may be supplemented by security officers or floorwalkers. Security officers are prevention oriented, seeking to deter crime by their presence. In contrast, floorwalkers are apprehension oriented, seeking to arrest and prosecute shoplifters.

Merchandising techniques to deter shoplifting include keeping dis-plays orderly and not stacking merchandise too high; returning to the display any item looked at and not bought; keeping small, valuable items locked in display cases; placing identifying tags on all merchandise; displaying only one of a pair; not displaying expensive merchandise near exits; and having small, easily stolen items located by the checkout.

Procedures to deter shoplifting include having unused checkout lanes closed, locking the back door, having package checks, carefully checking price tags, maintaining tight controls on fitting rooms and rest rooms, issuing receipts, controlling refunds, and establishing a communication system.

Physical controls to deter shoplifting include changing the actual store layout, posting signs, installing locks and alarms, and installing surveillance equipment such as convex mirrors and/or CCTV.

To apprehend a suspect for shoplifting, someone must actually see the item being taken and concealed or be reasonably certain an item has been taken; and the suspect must be kept under *continuous* observation until apprehension is made. This may occur on the premises or outside, depending on state statutes. Reasonable guidelines for when to prosecute shoplifters should be established, taking into consideration the value of the article as well as the suspect's ge, number of offenses, and attitude. Illegal detention, malicious prosecution, and slander suits must be guarded against.

Losses from bad checks are a second major concern of retail establishments. To reduce losses from bad checks, retailers should teach personnel to recognize the different types of checks and the common types of bad checks, establish a check-cashing policy and adhere to it, train personnel to examine checks and identification, record relevant information on the back of all checks cashed, and reconcile identity documents with check passers' characteristics. High-risk checks include second-party checks, counter checks, illegible checks, post-dated checks, and out-of-town checks. The most common types of bad checks are forged or altered checks, no-account checks, and nonsufficient funds checks.

All checks should be carefully examined, including the printed name and address, check number, date, payee, numerical and written amount, bank and address, and signature (or endorsement). No checks should be accepted that are illegible, that are not written in ink, or that contain erasures or written-over dates or amounts.

Persons presenting checks to cash should be required to produce identification containing a physical description (preferably a photograph) and a signature. The description should be compared with the person; the signature should be compared with the signature on the check.

Protect against losses from fraudulent use of credit cards by comparing the signature on the card with that on the sales slip, checking the card's expiration date, and establishing a reasonable floor release limit.

Another retail security problem is employee theft. Special risks in retail establishments include easy employee access to merchandise and cash. Specific pricing procedures, cash-handling procedures, and refund procedures are essential. Personnel should be rotated periodically, and responsibilities should be separated.

To deter employee theft by price alterations, allow only authorized employees to set prices and mark merchandise, mark merchandise by machine or rubber stamp, conduct periodic audits of prices recorded and prices charged, and check on "popular" salesperson. To reduce losses of cash, establish strict cash-handling procedures, use a tamper-proof recording system, have each clerk responsible for his or her own cash receipts, have cash receipts balanced by someone else, perform unannounced audits, and use honesty shoppers. Honesty shopping, or a shopping service, tests the honesty of sales personnel who handle cash.

In addition, require all employees to comply with the return/refund policy. Keep tight control of all credit documents, and match items to the return vouchers. Conduct periodic audits of return vouchers.

The primary objectives of shopping center security are loss prevention and public relations.

## APPLICATION

1) Terry Benson, a private security officer, is working in a liquor store to prevent armed robberies and the purchase of liquor by juveniles. The manager of the store has taken into custody a man who presented a check for payment of liquor; on being asked for identification, he ran out of the store with his purchase. The manager has caught him and brought him back to Officer Benson. What actions should Officer Benson now take?

2) The Riteway Department Store is being sued by a shoplifting suspect for destruction of his property. The suit is the result of the actions of a private security officer, Donald Clough, who saw a white male about twenty-four years old palm a watch and put it in his jacket pocket. When Officer Clough approached the suspect to make inquiry, the suspect ran from the store to the parking lot, where he entered his car and then closed and locked the doors. Officer Clough ordered the suspect to open the car door. When he refused, Officer Clough broke the window and arrested the suspect. A search of the car revealed the stolen watch under the car's front seat.

   As security director for Riteway, would you recommend that management try to settle out of court or that it fight the charges? Why?

3) Evaluate the completeness of the retail security checklist in Figure 14–3. Are any important areas missing? If so, which ones?

4) As the security manager for the Mytown Retail Sales Company, you are asked to develop a form to use when dismissing dishonest employees and attempting to recover any losses. What would you add to the form in Figure 14–4 to further protect the company from any civil litigation?

## DISCUSSION QUESTIONS

1) What are the advantages and disadvantages of prosecuting juvenile shoplifters? Adult shoplifters?

2) What type of system would aid retail stores in combatting worthless check artists?

3) How can retail stores aid one another in preventing shoplifting? What is done in your area?

Page 1
REQUEST ——— 
ROUTINE ———

CRIME PREVENTION SURVEY
RETAIL BUSINESS ———
RESIDENTIAL ———

COMPLAINT NUMBER
—————————

Business Name ———————————— Address ————————————

Manager's Name ———————————— Business Phone ——— Home Phone ———

Survey Date(s) ———————————— Officer(s) ————————————

Type of Goods ———————————— Survey Based On ————————————

| | | 1 2 3 | | | 1 2 3 |
|---|---|---|---|---|---|
| I. SAFE | a. Anchored<br>b. Visible<br>c. Lighted<br>d. Decals<br>e. Locks operable | — — —<br>— — —<br>— — —<br>— — —<br>— — — | VI. BLDG (front) | a. Doors<br>b. Locks<br>c. Windows<br>d. Vents<br>e. Lighting | — — —<br>— — —<br>— — —<br>— — —<br>— — — |
| II. CASH DEPOSIT | a. Excess in safe<br>b. Excess in register<br>c. Other locations<br>d. Armored car<br>e. Employee(s) | — — —<br>— — —<br>— — —<br>— — —<br>— — — | VII. BLDG (left side) | a. Doors<br>b. Locks<br>c. Windows<br>d. Vents<br>e. Lighting | — — —<br>— — —<br>— — —<br>— — —<br>— — — |
| III. EMPLOY-EE TRAIN-ING | a. Shoplifting<br>b. Robbery<br>c. Till tap<br>d. Short change<br>e. Checks | — — —<br>— — —<br>— — —<br>— — —<br>— — — | VIII. BLDG (rear) | a. Doors<br>b. Locks<br>c. Windows<br>d. Vents<br>e. Lighting | — — —<br>— — —<br>— — —<br>— — —<br>— — — |
| IV. EMPLOY-EE SCREEN-ING | a. Previous employers<br>b. Neighbors<br>c. Fingerprints<br>d. Police record<br>e. Polygraph | — — —<br>— — —<br>— — —<br>— — —<br>— — — | IX. BLDG (right side) | a. Doors<br>b. Locks<br>c. Windows<br>d. Vents<br>e. Lighting | — — —<br>— — —<br>— — —<br>— — —<br>— — — |
| V. EMPLOY-EE AC-CESS CNTRL | a. No. exterior keys<br>b. No. ex-emp. w/keys<br>c. Date comb. changed<br>d. Date locks changed<br>e. No. emp. opening<br>and closing | — — —<br>— — —<br>— — —<br>— — —<br>— — — | X. BLDG (roof) | a. Doors<br>b. Locks<br>c. Skylights<br>d. Vents & ducts<br>e. Lighting | — — —<br>— — —<br>— — —<br>— — —<br>— — — |

ADDITIONAL COMMENTS ————————————————————————
————————————————————————————
————————————————————————————

NOTE:    1–Adequate    2–Inadequate    3–Comments

**Figure 14–3 Retail security checklist.**
*Courtesy of Chattanooga Police Department.*

4) What considerations should be evaluated when a private security officer notices that an employee is stealing?
5) What training devices might be used in conducting a shoplifting reduction seminar?

# REFERENCES

Gardner, T. J. *Criminal law: Principles and cases*, 3d ed. St. Paul, MN: West Publishing Company, 1985.

Griffin, R. K. Case history: Profile of a typical retail theft. *Security management*, March 1980, pp. 60–63.

COMPLAINT NUMBER
_____

Emergency Call List:

| NAME | POSITION | ADDRESS | PHONE |
|---|---|---|---|
| _____ | _____ | _____ | _____ |
| _____ | _____ | _____ | _____ |
| _____ | _____ | _____ | _____ |

## BURGLAR ALARM

| | Yes | No | Comments: |
|---|---|---|---|
| A. Intrusion | | | |
| 1. front | ___ | ___ | _____ |
| 2. left side | ___ | ___ | _____ |
| 3. rear | ___ | ___ | _____ |
| 4. right side | ___ | ___ | _____ |
| 5. roof | ___ | ___ | _____ |
| 6. traps | ___ | ___ | _____ |
| 7. safe | ___ | ___ | _____ |
| B. Robbery | ___ | ___ | _____ |
| C. Fire | ___ | ___ | _____ |
| D. Audible | ___ | ___ | _____ |
| E. Central Station | ___ | ___ | _____ |
| F. Police Dept. | ___ | ___ | _____ |
| G. Other (describe) | ___ | ___ | _____ |
| H. System last treated on: | | | _____ |

Name and address of installing and maintenance alarm company:

NAME _____ ADDRESS _____

PHONE NUMBER _____

| ITEM NO. | | ITEM NO. | |
|---|---|---|---|
| | | | |
| | | | |
| | | | |
| | | | |
| | | | |
| | | | |
| | | | |
| | | | |
| | | | |
| | | | |
| | | | |
| | | | |

**Figure 14–3 Retail security checklist** (*continued*).

Owens, Thomas. Bum checks. *Independent business*, July/August 1990, pp. 14–18.

Potter, A. N. Shopping center security. *Security management*, December 1984, pp. 34–35.

*Private security*. Report of the Task Force on Private Security, National Advisory Committee on Criminal Justice Standards and Goals. Washington, DC: U.S. Government Printing Office, 1976.

The siege on supermarkets. *Security management*, March 1980, pp. 7–8, 56–59.

**MYTOWN RETAIL SALES CO.**

**STATEMENT**

Date: _____ Time: _____ Page: _____

I, _____ Age, _____ Date of birth, _____

Marital status, _____ Address, _____

Phone, _____ Department, _____

have been advised of my rights according to the company personnel rules and regulations, and
herewith give this statement of my own free will and voluntarily to _____
whom I know to be a security officer of the Mytown Retail Sales Co. No threats or acts of force
have been made against me, nor have any promises of any kind been made to me. I understand
that this statement will contain only facts for which I am responsible, and I wish to clear myself
of other suspicions and do admit to the following:

_____

_____

_____

_____

_____

_____

_____

_____

_____

_____

_____

_____

_____

_____

_____

Witness:                                    Signature _____

                                             This is a true statement to the best of my knowledge.

_____

_____

**Receipt**

I have written and/or read the above statement consisting of _____ pages and have signed
each page of _____ copies and have received one copy of this statement from _____ at
_____ a.m./p.m.

Date: _____ Signature for receipt _____

**Figure 14–4 Sample employee statement.**

Tyska, Louis A. and Fennelly, Lawrence J. Retail security in the year 2000. In *Security
in the year 2000 and beyond,* by Louis A. Tyska and Lawrence J. Fennelly, eds.
Palm Springs, CA: ETC Publications, 1987, pp. 259–64.

# ☐ INTRODUCTION

Several types of security systems besides those already examined are important. These systems are in place in businesses most people consider to be public. Because of this, they pose special problems.

These public places should, of course, follow the basic lines of defense against internal and external crime and against threats to safety which apply to the types of facilities already discussed. It is assumed that a facility's physical vulnerability has been minimized by adequate lighting, fencing, locks, and alarms as appropriate and that basic procedural security controls have been established to minimize risk.

## Chapter Fifteen

# Commercial Security

## DO YOU KNOW

> What commercial enterprises rely heavily on private security?
> What specific security problems are encountered in each type of enterprise?
> What targets are most common in each?
> What special security precautions are implemented to protect the assets of each?
> What is required by the Bank Protection Act?
> What agency regulates security of airports and airlines?

---

Financial institutions, office buildings, public and private housing, hotels and motels, facilities housing large public gatherings, racetracks, recreational parks, airports and airlines, and mass transit are now making use of private security concepts, equipment, procedures, and personnel on an ever-increasing scale.

---

# ☐ FINANCIAL INSTITUTION SECURITY*

According to the Private Security Task Force Report (1976, p. 46): "The security and stability of the Nation's financial institutions (commercial banks, savings and loan associations, credit unions, loan companies, and brokerage houses) are critical to a lasting and healthy economy. In contrast to the many indirect losses sustained by other businesses, most losses in the financial community are direct financial losses. . . ."

Financial institutions are highly attractive to robbers, burglars, embezzlers, and other types of thieves. In addition, enormous losses are incurred yearly through fraudulent use of credit cards and checks. Added to these losses are an estimated $40 million in stock certificates and $25 million in government bonds that are lost or stolen annually.

## Security Problems in Financial Institutions

Newer marketing techniques such as electronic fund transfer systems, remote tellers, automatic bank machines, and telephone transferring have had a major impact on security problems of financial institutions.

---

*Financial Institutions—See *Private Security,* pp. 46–48.

Security officer stands guard as regulators seize Florida's largest thrift.

The movement to make banking activities more accessible to citizens makes security more difficult. In addition, the large amounts of financial assets centralized in one location are extremely attractive to thieves. The most frequent losses involve theft of cash or stocks and bonds, check and credit card fraud, and embezzlement of funds.

A bank's security program is not limited to areas where money and valuables are exchanged or stored, but rather is closely related to all aspects of the business operation. For example, embezzlement may account for more losses than burglary and robbery combined.

Of special concern is the problem of automatic teller machines (ATM). A special report prepared by the Bureau of Justice Statistics in March 1985, "Electronic Fund Transfer Fraud," summarized data from a survey of sixteen American banks, fifteen of which had deposits over one billion dollars:

➤ In 1983, 2.7 billion transactions involving $262 billion were processed through automated teller machines.
➤ Of a sample of 2,707 ATM-related incidents (transactions resulting in account holder complaints), 45 percent were found to be potentially fraudulent, involving, for example, unauthorized use of lost or stolen cards, overdrafts, and "bad" deposits.
➤ Nationwide, ATM bank loss from fraud during 1983 is estimated to have been between $70 million and $100 million, with a median bank loss of approximately $84 million.

The ASIS Standing Committee on Banking & Finance, in "Keeping the Lid on the Cookie Jar," describes the six categories of criminal activity involving ATMs: unauthorized card use, fraudulent card use, insider manipulation, embezzlement, robbery and mugging, and physical attack on the ATM itself.

**UNAUTHORIZED CARD USE** The Electronic Funds Transfer Act (the Federal Reserve Board's Regulation E) defines an unauthorized electronic funds transfer as ". . . a transfer from a consumer's account initiated by a person other than the consumer without actual authority to initiate such transfer and from which the consumer receives no benefit." These unauthorized transfers can be initiated through ATM access cards. Typically unscrupulous users obtain these cards by stealing the holder's purse or wallet. Because many customers keep a written record of their personal identification number (PIN) with their card (although all financial institutions advise against it), access to the customer's account becomes all too simple.

**FRAUDULENT CARD USE** Fraudulent card use can occur in many ways. Customers can defraud financial institutions by withdrawing more money than is actually in their accounts, or by depositing worthless checks and then withdrawing the money before the scam can be stopped. Collusion is still another way in which a customer can defraud a financial institution. In this case, ATM cardholders dispute a transaction after knowingly giving their card and PIN to someone else and allowing that person to make a withdrawal from the account.

**INSIDER MANIPULATION** Bank employees can also be involved in fraudulent card use. Employees may establish fictitious accounts and order ATM cards for these accounts, or they may have access to legitimate cards and PINs through undelivered mail that is returned to the bank. An employee could also order a duplicate card for a customer and then have the card and the PIN sent to an address other than the one supplied by the customer. A similar problem can exist when the financial institution uses customer-generated PINs. Employees can watch a customer select a PIN and then order a duplicate card for themselves, thereby gaining access to the customer's account.

**EMBEZZLEMENT** Employees are also responsible for this category of ATM crime. Although the misappropriation of funds by an employee is nothing new to financial institutions, the advent of the ATM has provided another source of funds for dishonest workers. The money in the machine itself can be taken either by bank employees or by personnel who service the machines. Also, funds deposited through the ATM are vulnerable to embezzlement and manipulation by employees who process these deposits.

**ROBBERY AND MUGGING** Service personnel who replenish the ATM cash supply or repair breakdowns are susceptible to robbery at ATM sites, particularly after normal banking hours. In addition, customers not only have been robbed while making withdrawals, but also have been forced by thieves to return to the ATM and withdraw additional funds. A recent staff commentary by the Federal Reserve Board held that such robberies of customers at ATMs constitute an unauthorized transfer as defined under Regulation E; consequently the customer's liability in these situations is limited.

**PHYSICAL ATTACK**  Finally, the ATM itself is subject to attack. In some cases, vandalism is the problem. But in others, professional burglars attempt to break into the machine and obtain the cash supply. Thieves have been known to drill into the machines, burn through them, pull the cash dispenser out of the wall, and even blow them apart with dynamite.

## Security Measures in Financial Institutions

Great vulnerability existed in the amount and type of security measures used in financial institutions before 1968. This variability was of concern to the government agencies that regulated federally insured financial institutions. FBI investigations of bank robberies revealed that many banks had totally inadequate protective and preventive measures against robbery. These findings were confirmed in a survey conducted between 1967 and 1969 by the Federal Home Loan Bank Board, whose survey of 194 banks showed fewer than 50 percent having alarm systems, only 17 percent using cameras, and just over 10 percent having security guards.

Significant increases in bank robberies, larcenies, and burglaries, and the obvious absence of adequate protective measures, moved Congress to enact the Bank Protection Act in 1968.

---

The *Bank Protection Act (1968)* requires all federally insured banks, savings and loan institutions, and credit unions to:

➤ Designate a security officer.
➤ Cooperate with and seek security advice from the FBI and other law enforcement agencies.
➤ Develop comprehensive security programs and implement protective measures to meet or exceed federal standards.
➤ Maintain "bait" money.*
➤ Periodically remove excess cash from tellers' windows and bank premises.
➤ Develop security-conscious opening and closing procedures and stringent security inspections.

---

By February of 1970 each federally insured financial institution was to develop a written security plan that met federal standards, appoint a security officer, file a formal report on current security measures at the facility, and install and maintain required security equipment.

---

*Bait money is currency whose serial numbers have been recorded. Sometimes this money is placed so that picking it up sets off a silent alarm.

> In addition to developing and implementing a formal, written security plan and appointing a security officer, federally insured financial institutions must install and maintain vault area lighting systems, tamper-resistant exterior doors and window locks, cameras, and alarm systems.

Unfortunately, many small-town banks installed poor-quality cameras that use fast film and have poor resolution. Consequently, the resulting pictures are often worthless. In addition, the cameras are sometimes installed at a six-foot level, making them susceptible to being blacked out with spray paint or shaving foam.

According to Green (1987, p. 30), banks have "a heavy reliance upon electronic technology and physical security rather than large numbers of personnel."

## ☐ OFFICE BUILDING SECURITY*

The United States once had more blue-collar (production) workers than white-collar workers, but this situation has reversed. Increasing mechanization in manufacturing has caused a decrease in the number of blue-collar workers needed. As the number of white-collar employees increases, so does the incidence of white-collar crime. Additionally, offices are more often the targets of thieves.

Many contractual and proprietary security forces perform guard, alarm, and armored car/courier services at thousands of office buildings throughout the country as corporations seek to protect company assets as well as the lives and personal property of their employees.

Some companies establish specific levels of security in their offices or buildings to meet requirements stipulated in government contracts. Others feel their corporation's work is highly sensitive, involving, for example, trade secrets, and thus view security as essential. In yet other instances, private developers build, own, and manage inner-city office buildings and/or commercial industrial parks (frequently suburban office complexes that include nonmanufacturing businesses such as research laboratories, sales facilities, medical buildings, and other professional offices situated along the front of the building with warehouses behind). These private developers may either provide security for the buildings and tenants in the complex or assign this responsibility to the prime tenant, the tenant who is leasing the most space in a particular building. Most private developers use the services of contract security firms to protect the entire complex.

### Security Problems of Office Buildings

"Open for Business" means open to the public. Most offices have a steady stream of outsiders. Among them may be persons intent on committing such open-hour crimes as robbery or larceny. In addition, a

---

*Office Building Security—See *Private Security,* pp. 43–44.

would-be thief may "case" a particular office during business hours with the intent of returning for an after-hours burglary. Custodial personnel and tenants having keys to the building pose another after-hours threat. Further, employees' pilfering of office supplies and/or petty cash can occur during or after business hours.

➤ *The major security problems* in office buildings include after-hours burglaries and theft; theft from a tenant by another tenant's employees; theft by service, maintenance, and custodial employees; assaults, rapes, and other crimes against persons; regulation and control of visitor traffic; bomb threats; protection of executive offices and personnel; and fire watch.

➤ *The items most frequently stolen* from office buildings include small office equipment such as typewriters, calculators, duplicating and photocopying machines, and computers and peripherals; office furnishings; securities and valuable documents; blank payroll checks; and check-writing machines.

Other corporate valuables that are often burglary targets include blank (unissued) stock certificates, the corporate seal, corporate minutes, office art and decorations, and books. Many larger corporations maintain extensive professional libraries containing thousands of dollars worth of books, yet they often provide little or no control over access to them. And, as in any other type of business, office supplies and petty cash present another potential area for loss.

An additional problem in office security is that frequently some tenants do not perceive a need for security, thereby increasing the risk for other tenants in the same building who have security needs. As noted earlier, a nonsecure area adjacent to an area seeking security provides a vulnerable area for the "secure" office. Further, fire loading one office may pose a direct threat to other tenants, who may be completely unaware of such a threat. Compounding the problem is the fact that in office buildings having many different tenants, it is usually impossible to conduct fire or bomb evacuation drills.

## Security Measures in Office Buildings

The amount of security devices and personnel required in an office building depends on the size and location of the building, the number and nature of tenant businesses, and the crime rate of the area.

Primary security measures in office buildings are access control, proper authorization and documentation of the use of corporate assets by employees, and periodic fire inspections.

Usually office or tenant space is protected primarily through access control: master key systems, card-key readers, closed-circuit television

(CCTV), and security officers. Many new office buildings are constructed using the **core concept,** which has all elevators, rest rooms, lobbies, and service facilities located at the building's center, thus allowing more effective control of "public" areas while also permitting more flexible use of office space. Extra security measures to protect these public areas include CCTV, receptionists to monitor a visitor pass system, and security officers. Some security firms have successfully controlled access by training their security guards to recognize potential thieves.

Elevators can be programmed to allow only authorized personnel to operate the elevators or to obtain access to specified floors after hours. Fire stairwells are often a key security concern for many high-rise office buildings because local fire codes may require that the stairwell doors be left unlocked. Installing crash-bars with alarms may overcome this security problem.

In addition to access control, many offices use security officers for patrol, generally following programmed watchclock stations. Many newer, larger office buildings have central consoles to monitor access along with heating, ventilating, and air-conditioning systems. These central consoles reduce personnel requirements, increase monitoring and detecting efficiency, and allow faster response by security personnel.

Corporate assets such as records, stocks, securities, and cash are usually stored in vaults, which are frequently equipped with CCTV or time-lapse cameras. Additionally, many companies keep vital information on computers, which poses another security problem. Protecting a computer processing center's remote terminals and the information contained in the machine is discussed in Chapter 10.

Recording the serial numbers on office machines is an important security procedure. If these machines are stolen, the numbers can be reported to police, greatly increasing the chances of recovering the stolen property. For example, California has established a successful recov-

Using multi-image closed-circuit TV sets, a guard monitors security for a large high-tech plant in Irvine, CA.

ery program to trace stolen electric typewriters through the joint efforts of the Department of Justice and International Business Machines Corporation (IBM). State law requires dealers to report by serial number all used business machines bought, traded, repaired, and received. Investigators can then match the serial numbers with their list of stolen items and relay the information to local police for recovery of the stolen item.

Internal losses can be minimized by requiring authorization and proper documentation of the use of company assets. For example, supplies should be obtainable only by requisition. The requisition forms should be checked periodically to ensure that the usage is reasonable. Petty cash is an easy target for internal loss unless a system of authorization and documentation is established. Vouchers should be required for all petty cash disbursed (see Figure 15–1). The person responsible for disbursing petty cash might alter the amount on a voucher; for example, a voucher for five dollars might be changed to read thirty-five dollars, with the person in charge pocketing thirty dollars. Therefore, vouchers should be periodically routed to the person signing for the cash to ensure that such changes have not occurred. Vouchers should be canceled after they are recorded to prevent their reuse. In addition, unannounced audits of vouchers and petty cash ledgers should be made.

Libraries should have a book checkout system similar to that used in public libraries. All books in the library should be clearly marked as company property.

The mail room is another target for loss. Losses may occur because stamps are stolen or because mailroom personnel are not taught to weigh packages correctly or to determine the best postal rate and may be sending everything first class when third class or book rate might be more appropriate. Such practices, over time, can involve considerable financial loss for a business.

## ☐ HOUSING*

Although private security is usually thought to be solely involved with business and industry, it is becoming more important in residential units, where it is also needed. Burglaries of residential dwellings now

DATE: _____

AMOUNT: _____

FOR: _____

_____

BY: _____

RECEIVED PAYMENT: _____ (Signature)

DISBURSED PAYMENT: _____ (Signature)

Figure 15–1 Sample petty cash voucher.

---

*Housing—See *Private Security,* pp. 50–51.

account for hundreds of millions in property losses annually, and this figure is probably underreported. In addition, muggings and vandalism create problems for homeowners and renters.

---

Security problems of residential units include theft, vandalism, and assaults, particularly muggings. Security consultants address these problems.

---

Although it would seem logical that expensive homes in exclusive neighborhoods would be the targets of thieves, often such is not the case. Studies by the U.S. Department of Housing and Urban Development indicate that crime is considerably higher in public housing with low- and medium-income residents and with senior citizen residents than in other residential areas. In fact, crime rates in some public housing projects are two to four times higher, with higher rates of victimization per household or dwelling unit and substantially higher rates of multiple victimization of the same dwelling—that is, a large number of residences experiencing more than one burglary.

Anyone who has come home to find their house or apartment has been burglarized may feel indignation, anger, rage, and desire for revenge. It is, indeed, one of the most traumatic experiences a person can have. Knowing some stranger has gone through your most private possessions has an impact surpassed only by a personal assault or rape.

Some steps individuals can take to deter burglars are given in a security checklist with the acronym STOP THIEF, shown in Figure 15–2.

Security consultants and firms advise homeowners on security measures they might take (see Figure 15–3). Many also offer around-the-clock monitoring of security systems installed within private homes. Such systems may include fire alarms connected directly with the fire department as well as sensors that will detect if the temperature drops below freezing.

Contractual security services may be hired to patrol neighborhoods and to protect public housing units, high-rise apartments, and exclusive residential developments.

---

Access control, patrol by security officers, and the provision of youth programs help to reduce residential losses.

---

Increasing numbers of homeowners are installing special locks, floodlights, and less expensive burglar alarms, and/or buying safes and large dogs to protect their homes, valuables, and families. Some homeowners' associations and exclusive residential developers hire security personnel to perform patrol services and to monitor central-gate entrances.

The rapid increase in the rate of burglaries and muggings has also resulted in increased security measures in private high-rise apartment

**S** ecure your home with good locks on doors and windows. Don't give the thief any help in his break-in effort.

**T** ake care of your keys; don't give others a chance to duplicate them.

**O** utside, don't let your house look unoccupied. Keep things from piling up . . . have your lawn mowed and snow shoveled while you're gone.

**P** ut a light on while you're away . . . preferably one with an automatic timing device.

**T** hink twice before letting strangers know when you'll be away from home, or before letting one in.

**H** ave police and a trusted neighbor check your home while you're away for more than a few days.

**I** nsure your possessions and keep an up-to-date inventory of them.

**E** tch an identifying number on items a thief might steal. Keep valuables in a safe deposit box.

**F** ind out about burglar alarm systems and install one.

**Figure 15–2 Stop thief.**
*Courtesy of State Farm Fire and Casualty Co.*

Many private homes have installed electronic security systems monitored by a central station.

# Home Security Is Good Housekeeping

**Crime Prevention can be best achieved by:**
1. Recognition of Security Risks
2. Initiation of corrective action to remove them

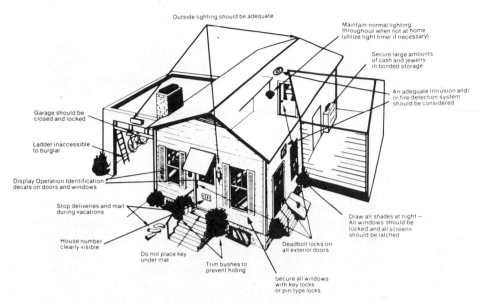

Outside lighting should be adequate

Maintain normal lighting throughout when not at home (utilize light timer if necessary)

Secure large amounts of cash and jewelry in bonded storage

An adequate intrusion and/or fire detection system should be considered

Garage should be closed and locked

Ladder inaccessible to burglar

Display Operation Identification decals on doors and windows

Stop deliveries and mail during vacations

House number clearly visible

Do not place key under mat

Trim bushes to prevent hiding

Deadbolt locks on all exterior doors

Draw all shades at night — All windows should be locked and all screens should be latched

Secure all windows with key locks or pin-type locks

These are a few of the security measures that you can institute to help reduce criminal opportunity.

Remember, Your home should always give the appearance that it's occupied.

## Home Security Tips

- Make sure locks are locked
- Never admit strangers inside
- Do not broadcast your travel plans
- Do not leave notes indicating your absence
- Do not keep valuables out in the open
- Join Operation Identification
- Join Neighborhood Watch

**Before Going on a Vacation or Week-end Trip . . .**

- ☑ PRE-VACATION HOME SECURITY
- ☐ Property has been marked under "OPERATION IDENTIFICATION"
- ☐ Neighbors have been instructed to watch my home
- ☐ Arrangements have been made to have my lawn mowed
- ☐ Deliveries have been stopped, or someone will pick up delivered items
- ☐ Automatic timers are in use for lights and radio
- ☐ Shades and blinds are in normal positions
- ☐ My home will have that "lived in" look
- ☐ Police have been notified to watch my home

*(Mecklenberg County Police Department)*

**Figure 15–3 Home security educational materials.**

and condominium complexes, with emphasis on limiting the access of nonresidents.

According to Green (1987, p. 29): "The future of security in high-rise apartment buildings and housing complexes offers great potential for the security professional because of the growing emphasis on the concept of total environmental protection." Access control measures include doorkeepers in vestibules; external door locks to interior hallways that tenants activate by remote control; and monitoring of entrances with CCTV, sometimes connected so that tenants can view visitors seeking admittance. Some newer high-income apartment and condominium complexes have installed extensive alarm, monitoring, and access control systems that are monitored around the clock by a central console operator.

Many public housing authorities are implementing the same protective measures used by private apartment buildings in their high-rise complexes, including CCTV monitoring and access control. Housing authorities in some large cities with many housing projects maintain armed proprietary or quasi-public security forces with limited or full police powers. Smaller housing authorities often organize tenant patrols or hire contract security firms to provide services. Although the inherent dangers in using tenant patrols must be acknowledged, they frequently do provide a good deal of security for residents in the building. Many public housing authorities have also established recreation programs and youth activities programs in an attempt to reduce the incidence of vandalism and crimes committed by juveniles.

As in business and industry, there is an architectural emphasis in designing neighborhoods and buildings that seeks to create safer environments that will minimize opportunities for the commission of crimes. Demonstration projects indicate that architectural features, lighting, building and neighborhood layout, and site design can reduce the incidence of crime.

## ☐ HOTEL/MOTEL SECURITY*

Crime in lodging establishments has climbed to dangerous heights, both in terms of the number of incidents and the severity of the incidents, as have lawsuits against hotels and motels. There has been an unprecedented increase in civil filings against these establishments, charging that security negligence resulted in harm to a guest, a tradesperson, or an employee. In many cases, a new innkeeper's case law is developing as the hotels appeal adverse court decisions.

Says Green (1987, p. 29): "The hotel and motel industry has been characterized in the past by serious neglect of many security responsibilities, an attitude that has only slowly been changing in spite of a number of very large awards by the courts in recent years against hotels or motels charged with negligent security, particularly in the area of protecting guests. However, this neglect, coupled with court-mandated responsibility, has created opportunity for security professionals."

---

*Hotel/Motel Security—See *Private Security,* pp. 49–50.

## Security Problems in Hotels/Motels

In its efforts to make hotels and motels more convenient for guests, management has increased the vulnerability to theft, vandalism, and assault. Elevators and parking garages provide outside thieves, employees, and guests with greater access to unprotected areas and less probability of detection while committing crimes.

---

➤ *Major security problems* of the hotel/motel industry include both internal and external theft, vandalism, vice, and fire.

➤ *Items most frequently stolen* from hotels and motels include money, credit cards, jewelry, linens, silver, food, liquor, and other easily concealed articles.

---

The most significant internal theft losses result from inadequate procedures for cash handling, housekeeping activities, receiving and storing supplies, laundry services, and restaurant/bar services. Many employees of hotels and motels must have master or submaster keys to perform their jobs. Therefore, they have access to secured hotel/motel property as well as to the personal property of guests.

Guests are vulnerable to theft not only by hotel/motel employees, but also by professional thieves and burglars who obtain master keys and loot rooms while the guests are away. Hotels and motels in resort areas encounter additional security problems because most guests are occupied with recreation or sightseeing and spend much time away from their rooms, often leaving large sums of cash, plane tickets, sporting equipment, cameras, credit cards, jewelry, and expensive clothing in their rooms. Likewise, hotels and motels hosting large conventions and conferences face special security problems as the guests' schedules are easily predetermined and the times when rooms will be empty anticipated.

Guests are not always the victims, however. Sometimes guests are the criminals, whether they consider their actions "criminal" or not. The American Hotel and Motel Association estimates that millions of dollars worth of property are lost each year because guests take items such as ashtrays and towels as souvenirs. Millions of dollars more are lost as the result of carelessness with hotel property and furnishings, as well as by intentional vandalism. Conventions pose an additional problem in that conventioneers can be extremely unruly. Further, some guests do not pay their bills, or they pay them with bad checks or invalid credit cards.

In addition to these losses, the hotel/motel industry must deal with problems such as prostitution and gambling, which frequently occur in semipublic establishments. The emphasis placed on this problem is determined by management.

One extremely important security hazard is fire. The National Fire Protection Association reported sixty-five hundred hotel fires in 1989. According to Thompson (1991, p. 86): "Fewer than half of all U.S. hotel rooms have fire sprinklers. Surprisingly, only five states—Connecticut, Florida, Hawaii, Massachusetts, and Nevada (and Puerto Rico)—require sprinklers in hotel rooms."

In the fall of 1990, however, the Hotel-Motel Fire Safety Act (HR94) was passed. This law, which will be phased in over six years, requires federal employees who stay or meet in hotels or motels of three stories or more to use facilities that have sprinkler systems.

Another safety hazard exists in facilities with indoor swimming pools: carbon monoxide poisoning. This deadly gas is given off by the pool's heater. Adequate ventilation is a necessity to prevent such hazards.

## Security Measures in Hotels/Motels

Providing free movement and open facilities to guests must be balanced with implementing procedures to minimize criminal opportunities. Sound security measures not only increase the guests' safety, but also raise the profitability of the establishment. With huge losses sustained from employee theft and the growing frequency of guestroom theft and attacks on guests, more and more hotel and motel operators are turning to private security to reduce their losses. The security practices of a particular hotel or motel are usually the responsibility of the individual owner or the franchise holder. Large, nationwide lodging chains often have corporate security staffs to provide support and guidance to the franchise owners. The corporate security staff conducts security surveys; investigates specific losses; establishes guidelines for security policies and staffing; makes recommendations on cash-handling procedures, preemployment screening, and emergency plans; and maintains liaison with local law enforcement agencies.

Security measures in hotels/motels include stringent key control and frequent rekeying, careful preemployment screening, monitoring systems, and use of unmarked towels and ashtrays.

At the heart of the hotel/motel security system is adequate key control, which is a difficult procedure given the large number of employees and guests having keys. Nonetheless, a procedure for ensuring that keys are not duplicated and that departing guests and terminated employees turn in their keys is required. Frequent rekeying is often part of the key control system. Many hotels now use plastic access control cards that contain no room number. Of course, guests must make a point of remembering that number.

The increase in the number of armed robberies at motels has prompted many to follow the lead of hotels and install CCTV monitoring systems in lobby and cashier areas. Increasingly, hotels and motels are using monitoring systems in parking areas, ancillary lobbies, and elevators. They have also begun to use central access-control systems for guestrooms.

Motels have generally avoided one problem that has traditionally plagued the hotel industry: "skips" or nonpaying guests. Most motels require guests to pay in advance or to establish valid credit. In most hotels, on the other hand, room charges and other costs incurred are accumulated and paid at checkout time. Guests may check out before all charges have been posted to the bill or, in some cases, not check out at all.

Although security usually requires the identification of items, an exception to this is the practice of identifying towels, ashtrays, and any other items which tempt guests to "take" them as souvenirs. Unmarked towels and ashtrays have little sentimental value to travelers.

The checklist in Figure 15–4 can be used to assess fire and pool safety in hotels and motels.

Thompson (1991, p. 897) stresses: "Having safety plans in writing is central to a strong legal position. This goes way beyond just keeping a file of checklists. It means documentation and contracts." This would include contracts and warranties with those supplying fire safety equipment as well as an accurate record of the dates on which smoke detectors, fire extinguishers, and sprinkler systems are checked. It would also include documentation of all training conducted for staff and guests. Educating guests is particularly important. Some facilities do more than simply post the location of fire exits. For example, the Red Lion Hotels and Inns has a "fire safety and survival guide" in every room, described by Thompson (p. 86):

---

### CHECKLIST FOR FIRE AND POOL SAFETY

Here is a checklist of basics for evaluating hotel safety. Each group is different. If you have elderly or handicapped attendees, be sure to consider their special safety needs.

**FIRE**

☐ Do all areas of the hotel have sprinklers and fire alarms?
☐ Are fire-alarm systems regularly tested?
☐ Does the hotel have a *written* emergency plan?
☐ Does the plan include meeting and dining areas?
☐ Has the hotel staff been trained in evacuation procedures?
☐ Are there alarm switches on each floor?
☐ Do fire alarms alert the fire department directly?
☐ Are all exits clearly marked and unobstructed?
☐ Do all exit doors open in the direction of travel?
☐ Are stairwells open to ground and roof?
☐ Do meeting rooms have at least two exits? (or more, if the room is large)?
☐ Does the hotel have emergency lighting?
☐ How far away is the fire department?
☐ When was the hotel last inspected by the fire department?
☐ What is the fire department's phone number?
☐ What is the hotel's security office phone number?
☐ Where are fire extinguishers located?
☐ Is the hotel in compliance with local fire codes?
☐ Are there any outstanding fire code violations?
☐ Are stairways and exits obstructed in any way?
☐ Are exits clearly marked with an exit sign?
☐ Are diagrams of emergency exits, stairways, and fire extinguisher locations posted in each room?

**POOLS**

☐ If pools are enclosed in hotel atriums, do rooms have a window that can be opened for ventilation?
☐ Are any of the rooms adjacent to the pool heating system?
☐ What codes or inspections apply to the pool heating system?
☐ Has the pool heating system been inspected and certified as safe?

---

**Figure 15–4 Checklist for fire and pool safety.**
*Reprinted with permission from SUCCESSFUL MEETINGS Magazine. Copyright ©
1991, Bill Communications, Inc.*

The one-page sheet, illustrated so that children can readily grasp the basics, counsels guests to find two exits; learn the layout of their room; keep a key nearby as they sleep; act, not investigate, if they hear a fire alarm; leave the room, if possible, but stay in if the door is hot; crawl low in smoke; and avoid elevators.

In addition to the preceding essential components of adequate protection against loss from fire, many motels and hotels have flashlights, first-aid kits, oxygen, and wheelchairs on each floor.

Hotel/motel executives and security directors generally agree that security should be given a greater emphasis in the training of managers, owners, and franchise holders. Specifically, degree programs in hotel and restaurant management should require courses in security, including civil liability issues.

## Court Cases

Court cases related to hotel/motel security include the following:

*Delema v. Waldorf Astoria,* 1984. A federal court held that a hotel *is* liable for the theft of a guest's property, provided it has first accepted responsibility for safeguarding a guest's property.

*Meyers v. Ramada Inn,* 1984. An Ohio court held that hotel owners *can* be held liable for any injuries a guest suffers as a result of a criminal assault. However, the court stated that the guest must first demonstrate that the defendant should have anticipated the assault.

*Pitlard v. Four Seasons Motor Inn,* 1984. A New Mexico court held that a hotel *can* be held liable if one of its employees assaults a guest, provided the injured party could demonstrate that the hotel had notice of similar past conduct by the employee in question.

Some cases deal not with liability, but rather with constitutional issues related to searches of hotel/motel guests' rooms.

*United States v. Lyons,* 1983. A U.S. Court of Appeals held that a guest in a hotel room *is* entitled to constitutional safeguards against unreasonable searches and seizures. However, the court did observe that the privacy to which hotel guests are entitled is not comparable to that of owners or tenants of a house.

*State v. Weiss,* 1984. A Florida court held that the search of a guest's suitcase by a hotel employee did *not* constitute an illegal search and seizure unless the employee was following police instructions.

## ☐ PUBLIC GATHERINGS*

Private security plays a significant role in maintaining order and controlling traffic at large public gatherings such as conventions, entertainment events, festivals, parades, political rallies, rock concerts, sporting events, and trade shows. Many cities have built large, multipurpose facilities which they lease to organizations such as a professional football or baseball franchise, on a long-term seasonal basis, or for events such as auto, boat, and home shows or concerts on a short-term basis.

---

*Special Events—See *Private Security,* p. 58.

Security problems at public gatherings include maintaining order, preventing admission of nonpaying people, preventing internal and external theft, providing first aid for injuries, and regulating pedestrian and vehicle traffic.

Most multipurpose facilities and stadiums maintain a small security force and then require the lessee or promoter of an event to provide additional security as the circumstances dictate. The number of patrons at a special event can vary considerably. For example, a stadium may host a football game attracting eighty thousand persons one night and a rock concert attracting only one thousand persons the next night. Security directors estimate the number of patrons by keeping a careful watch on advance ticket sales and then use those figures to determine the amount of security required.

Security personnel are the primary means of reducing problems at public gatherings.

Security personnel often work closely with local law enforcement agencies to control traffic and to reduce problems such as pickpocketing and disorderly or abusive behavior. Some cities require local law enforcement officers to be present at public gatherings. Other cities hire off-duty law enforcement officers to supplement security personnel, a highly controversial practice.

The specific problems to be anticipated depend partly on the type of function. For example, sports spectators tend to be unruly, and they often get caught up in the emotion, competition, and aggressiveness of the game. Spectators often try to bring alcoholic beverages into a stadium, and some stadiums sell beer. In either case, drunken sports fans may have to be ejected from the stadium. Spectators may also attempt to get onto the playing field or to get to players for autographs.

Rock concerts pose a different type of problem. The spectators for such events are often emotionally excited young people who may be on drugs. The concerts are often sold out in advance, and people without tickets often mill about outside, hoping to see the rock stars and causing disturbances. They may attempt to crash the gate en masse, a dangerous action—vividly evident at a Who rock concert when eight people were trampled to death.

The major problems at exhibitions and trade shows are protecting high-value merchandise and exhibits from theft and vandalism and maintaining access control. When exhibits are dismantled, special precautions must be taken to avoid theft by people posing as truckers or exhibitors.

Shirley (1987, pp. 251–52) cites several incidents that "illustrate the recent negative trends in crowd behavior":

➤ Eleven were killed in a panic at a rock concert.
➤ A security officer was thrown head first over the rail by football fans.
➤ A riot occurred in a stadium after a rock group failed to perform in the rain. Many police officers and spectators were injured.

Large public gatherings may require security.

➤ Fans stormed the stage at a concert causing injuries to police and security officers.

Shirley (p. 256) suggests that such incidents occur because "raw emotions surface in individuals during a crowded situation where one often feels a mask of anonymity is worn."

Large public gatherings usually pose security problems in four specific time frames and locations:

➤ *Parking lots*—before and after the event (with theft and vandalism a threat during the event).
➤ *Ticket windows*—before the event—sometimes hours or even days.
➤ *Gates and turnstiles into the facility*—primarily before the event.
➤ *Inside the facility itself*—during the event.

## Parking Lots

Shirley (1987, p. 253), although speaking of sporting events, offers suggestions that fit most large public gatherings. He notes that in parking areas, crimes on the rise are "auto thefts, rapes, robberies, ticket scalping, assaults, and even murder." He notes that: "Good parking lot security has a profound influence on the fans prior to entering" and that "diverse techniques are essential" with observation, lighting, and communication being major concerns. Included in the security might be helicopters, mounted horse patrols, and motorized golf carts, supplemented by stationary cameras and observation towers. Some facilities hosting large public gatherings are planning to have parking lots farther away and make use of rapid transit systems, including computerized trains and people movers.

Shirley suggests that parking lots may soon have "computerized machines [that] will receive the money and make the necessary change.

As the drivers proceed through the parking lot, computerized machinery will direct the driver to a designated space. Proper surveillance of such vast facilities can only be successfully achieved through the use of mounted cameras freely moving on cables stretched above all areas. In addition, the sophisticated 'eyes' will include night vision, zoom lenses, and a public announcement system.''

## Ticket Windows

Another security problem is ticket windows, especially if fans begin lining up hours before the windows open. Among the problems are ''sanitation, pickpockets, placement in line, and general panic'' (Shirley, 1987, p. 254). Crowd control can be maintained by creating a buffer zone between the ticket window and the fans. Shirley suggests creating a fifty to seventy-five foot buffer zone using crowd control stands or sawhorses. He suggests that soon ''computerized automation will be necessary to provide the most convenient means of ticket sales. As the fan approaches the ticket window, available seating will be listed on a computerized screen. After the customer has selected and paid for the requested seats, the computer will dispense the tickets.'' Security personnel will still be needed, however, to monitor the ticket window and ensure crowd control.

## Gate and Turnstile

To keep crowd control, the facility must have enough entrances to avoid pushing and shoving. Shirley (1987, p. 255) says: ''Efficient ticket tak-

Security personnel check a car entering Tampa Stadium before Super Bowl XXV, due to increased worries of a terrorist attack as a result of the Gulf War.

ers, uniformed security personnel, clearly stated policies on posted signs, and gates in good working order are all matters to be considered currently when handling gate security." He again suggests that in the future gates and turnstiles will be computerized and that "mechanically controlled gates will be encased with emergency lighting, panic bars, P.A. systems, cameras, and automatic locking devices."

## Inside the Facility

As with gate control, having a large, well-trained, uniformed security force, often supplemented by public police, can maintain crowd control. Shirley (1987, p. 256) stresses that: "Procedures incorporating video taping of unruly spectators, emergency lighting, and emergency evacuation should already be in practice. . . . Much emphasis should be placed on the public relations aspect as well. It is a proven fact that a well-trained, uniformed security person who is courteous and helpful will encourage fans to visit the facility again."

## ☐ RECREATIONAL PARKS

Large crowds are common at theme parks and recreational parks throughout the country: Disney Land, Marine Land, Knotts Berry Farm, and the like. Disney World offers one example of security at its finest. According to Shearing and Stenning (1987, p. 317): "[The Disney order] is a designed-in feature that provides—to the eye that is looking for it, but not to the casual visitor—an exemplar of modern private corporate policing. Along with the rest of the scenery of which it forms a discreet part, it too is recognizable as a design for the future." Shearing and Stenning (p. 319) say Disney World is able to have such order because: "Potential trouble is anticipated and prevented. Opportunities for disorder are minimized by constant instruction, by physical barriers which severely limit the choice of action available and by the surveillance of omnipresent employees who detect and rectify the slightest deviation. . . . Control strategies are embedded in both environmental features and structural relations. . . . Control is pervasive."

But most people never notice it. What visitors notice is the sense of security, the orderliness, the cleanliness, and the ever-present, helpful, smiling employees.

## ☐ RACETRACKS

Peter Ohlhausen (1986, pp. 51–55) suggests that "security at a racetrack is a microcosm of security in industry generally. . . . In particular, horses need to be protected from tampering by their owners or their opponents. Patrons need to be protected from con artists, pickpockets, and other, feistier patrons. Drivers need to be protected from patrons who bet on other drivers. Parking, gambling, drinking, large crowds, and the excitement of racing add up to a lot of fun for patrons, a lot of money for the track, and a lot of work for the security department."

> Security problems at a racetrack include access control, crowd control, parking security, vault security, alcohol control, and fraud detection.

The aim of racetrack security is to protect the patrons, horses, jockeys/drivers, owners, and grooms and to help the track meet the standards set forth by the various state racing commissions.

Some tracks use proprietary security guards in the backstretch area — the area where the horses, drivers, and grooms are quartered. This is the most problematic area of the racetrack, with drinking, fighting, and stealing being major security problems.

The public areas of the racetrack such as the grandstand are usually protected by contract security officers who play an important public relations role as well as handling brawls and drunken patrons, personal injuries, and protection of the big winners. They also frequently provide parking lot security.

Other services provided by security personnel include guarding the vault and the runners conveying cash to and from the betting area, providing travel information, paging, and handling lost and found articles.

An additional responsibility is determining who has a legitimate phone call to make within one hour of post time. All public pay phones at the track are disconnected an hour before post time by order of the racing commission (to discourage bookmaking). It is the responsibility of the security officer at security headquarters to determine if a patron's need to place an outside phone call is, indeed, urgent.

> Security problems at a racetrack can best be met by adequate access control and by the presence of well-qualified, well-trained security personnel.

As noted by Ohlhausen:

Racetracks throughout the country usually have minimum selection standards for security officers selected to work at the racetracks. These are usually set out by the racing commissions of the states affected and consist of:

➤ Applicant must be a citizen of the U.S.
➤ Complete a comprehensive written application
➤ Submit to a thorough background check
➤ Not have been convicted of a felony or a pari-mutuel horseracing or gambling crime
➤ Provide a set of fingerprints
➤ Undergo a thorough medical and psychological examination
➤ Pass an oral examination conducted by the appointing authority

Minnesota has what according to Ohlhausen "is believed to be the only comprehensive additional requirement to be eligible for a race track security officer's position": a forty-hour program developed jointly by Normandale Community College (the largest community college in Minnesota) in conjunction with the Canterbury Downs Race Track, which began operations in 1985, and approved by the Minnesota Racing Commission. That program consists of the following:

*Criminal Procedure* (14 hours). Selected Minnesota Statutes. Differentiation of the public peace officer's and private peace officer's applications of criminal procedure as they apply in the public and private sectors.

➤ Constitutional law
➤ Laws of arrest, search and seizure
➤ Use of excessive force; laws regarding force
➤ Civil liability
➤ Searching arrested persons

Other related operational procedures necessary for the officer to function in an effective and efficient manner.

*Report Writing* (12 hours). Report writing, of which two hours is devoted to evaluation of written reports in a simulated courtroom scene used in a civil or criminal case.

➤ Introduction to reports and report writing
➤ Characteristics of a well-written report
➤ Principles of clear writing
➤ Clear and understandable narrative reports
➤ Evaluating reports

*Human Relations* (8 hours).

➤ Handling stressful and emotional complaints
➤ Gathering information from people
➤ Crowd control
➤ The security officer and stress
➤ Behavior modification
➤ Crisis situations—personal power vs. position power

Other subjects related to human relations.

*Health* (4 hours). A modified first-aid course plus CPR to familiarize the security officer with the various types of calls for medical assistance he or she may be asked to respond to. Course covers recognition and symptoms of diabetes and asthma attacks, strokes, heart attacks, trauma, heat exhaustion, and other relevant medical problems.

*Defensive Tactics* (2 hours). A course designed to instruct security officers how to protect themselves without the use of a baton, club, nightstick, or gun.

On completing the forty-hour course, participants receive four continuing education credits and a certificate.

## ☐ AIRPORT AND AIRLINE SECURITY*

Skyjackings of commercial aircraft, bombings, bomb threats, and extortion attempts involving aircraft and hostages have made the need for

---

*Airport Security—See *Private Security*, pp. 41–43.

airport and airline security blatantly obvious. Terrorist groups have increasingly used such means to advance their causes, making some people afraid to travel by air because of these perceived dangers. Bomb threats can result in air traffic delays and in evacuation of entire sections of a terminal. Actual explosions result in serious injuries, deaths, and extensive property damage.

---

Security problems of airports and airlines include skyjackings; bombs and bomb threats; air cargo theft; theft of passenger baggage, airline tickets, credit cards, merchandise from airport retail shops, and items from vehicles in parking lots; crowd control; VIP escorts; traffic control; and the potential for large-scale disasters.

---

Although skyjackings and bombings receive the most publicity, other serious security problems exist in airports. Losses from air cargo theft are estimated to be in excess of $100 million annually and are especially serious at the airports infiltrated by organized crime. Air cargo is different from other types of cargo, because most is coordinated with passenger schedules. Also much air cargo is small and highly valuable, making it especially vulnerable to theft. In addition, because of the great number of people using airports, the maintenance of order and crowd control, VIP escorts, and traffic control must be provided by airline and airport security personnel.

A unique problem of airports and airlines is the potential for a large-scale disaster caused by a plane crash. Response to such a disaster requires close cooperation among fire, medical, law enforcement, private security, and airport personnel.

By 1972 the increasing frequency of skyjackings and bomb threats prompted the Federal Aviation Authority (FAA) to require certain security measures.

---

The FAA requires:

➤ Screening of all persons and carry-on baggage prior to entering an airport's departure area.
➤ The availability of a sworn law enforcement officer at the screening point within three to five minutes.
➤ Development by both scheduled airline carriers and airport managers of security programs for FAA approval.
➤ Development of an airport disaster plan.

---

The responsibility for screening passengers and baggage rests with the air carriers. In most major airports, this is done by a contract security firm with a sworn law enforcement officer within minutes of the screening point to apprehend anyone who makes threats or tries to carry a dangerous weapon into the departure area. Although employees of contract security firms usually conduct the passenger checks, they maintain close cooperation with law enforcement agencies and airline

Security check at San Francisco International Airport.

and airport security personnel. Overall airport security is usually provided by law enforcement officers.

Green (1987, p. 28) says of airport security:

> The field is relatively new, mushrooming especially since the hijacking scares which began in the late 1960s (and continue today, even with increased security standards). It seems clear that, with mandated security requirements including physical security and access controls, baggage screening, 100% screening of air passengers and carry-on luggage, cargo security, and other controls, the demand for personnel to fill these needs will continue to rise.

The Gulf War placed additional emphasis on airport security as the threat of terrorism became even greater. One of the first actions taken as the threat of war became a reality was to tighten airport security.

## ☐ MASS TRANSIT SECURITY*

Millions of Americans depend on public transit systems for transportation. Our public transit system developed at the beginning of the nineteenth century as the need for moving large numbers of people within congested major cities became apparent. The first mass transit systems were horse-drawn streetcars. They were eventually replaced by cable and electric cars, buses, and finally the rapid transit systems of today, including such systems as New York's subway, Chicago's El, and San Francisco's BART. The early transit systems were not immune from the crime problems of the congested urban environment in which they operated. By the early 1900s, thieves, vandals, roving gangs of youths, and pickpockets caused several states to authorize transit companies to

---

*Mass Transit Security—See *Private Security,* pp. 60–61.

establish security forces, some with full police authority. As crime increased nationally, it also increased at comparable levels in transit systems. As a result, most transit systems have established full-time security forces with full or limited police powers.

The major security problems faced by mass transit systems are robberies and assaults of operators, passengers, and fare collectors; rapes and murders; and theft of vehicles or their contents in park-and-ride areas.

Such crimes occur most often in the mass transit systems located in or near high-crime areas. People are most often victimized while waiting for transit vehicles, especially on platforms and in the rapid transit stations. Crime also occurs at station entrances and exits, stairwells, ramps, and tunnels, and on the vehicles themselves.

An additional problem making rapid transit transportation unattractive to riders is the antisocial behavior of some riders, for example, drunkenness, and the use of abusive conduct and language.

In the energy-conscious 1990s, a concerted national effort to promote use of rapid transit systems depends heavily on making such systems safe and attractive to the general public.

Security measures for rapid transit include security guards, CCTV in waiting areas and on vehicles, telephones and other emergency communications devices for riders, unbreakable glass as see-through barriers, and high-intensity lighting.

Installing such security equipment is expensive because of the large number of stations and vehicles in any given system, as well as the susceptibility of the equipment to vandalism. In addition, CCTV must be continuously monitored if it is to be effective, requiring more personnel than may be available.

## SUMMARY

Commercial enterprises that rely heavily on private security include financial institutions, office buildings, public and private housing, hotels and motels, facilities housing large public gatherings, racetracks, recreational parks, airports and airlines, and mass transit.

Financial institutions face unique security problems. The movement to make banking activities more accessible to citizens makes security more difficult. In addition, the large amounts of financial assets centralized in one location are extremely attractive to thieves. The most frequent losses in financial institutions involve theft of cash or stocks and bonds, check and credit card fraud, and embezzlement of funds.

The Bank Protection Act (1968) requires that all federally insured banks, savings and loan institutions, and credit unions designate a security officer; cooperate with and seek security advice from the FBI and other law enforcement agencies; develop comprehensive security programs and implement protective measures to meet or exceed federal standards; maintain "bait" money; periodically remove excess cash from tellers' windows and bank premises; and develop security-conscious opening and closing procedures and stringent security inspections. In addition, federally insured financial institutions must install and maintain vault area lighting systems, tamper-resistant exterior doors and window locks, cameras, and alarm systems.

Major security problems in office buildings include after-hours burglaries and theft; theft from a tenant by another tenant's employees; theft by service, maintenance, and custodial employees; assaults, rapes, and other crimes against persons; regulation and control of visitor traffic; bomb threats; protection of executive offices and personnel; and fire watch. The items most frequently stolen from office buildings include small office equipment such as typewriters, calculators, duplicating and photocopying machines, and computers and peripherals; office furnishings; securities and valuable documents; blank payroll checks; and check-writing machines. Primary security measures in office buildings are access control, proper authorization and documentation of the use of corporate assets by employees, and periodic fire inspections.

Security problems of residential units include theft, vandalism, and assaults, particularly muggings. Access control, patrol by security officers, and the provision of youth programs help to reduce these residential problems.

Major security problems of the hotel/motel industry include both internal and external theft, vandalism, vice, and fire. The items most frequently stolen from hotels and motels include money, credit cards, jewelry, linens, silver, food, liquor, and other easily concealed articles. Security measures include stringent key control and frequent rekeying, careful preemployment screening, monitoring systems, and use of unmarked towels and ashtrays.

Security problems at public gatherings include maintaining order, preventing admission of nonpaying people, preventing internal and external theft, providing first aid for injuries, and regulating pedestrian and vehicle traffic. Security personnel are the primary means of reducing these problems.

Security problems at a racetrack include access control, crowd control, parking security, vault security, alcohol control, and fraud detection. Such problems can best be met by adequate access control and by the presence of well-qualified, well-trained security personnel.

Security problems of airports and airlines include skyjackings; bombs and bomb threats; air cargo theft; theft of passenger baggage, airline tickets, credit cards, merchandise from airport retail shops, and items from vehicles in parking lots; crowd control; VIP escorts; traffic control; and the potential for large-scale disasters. The Federal Aviation Authority (FAA), which regulates airport and airline security, requires screening of all persons and carry-on baggage prior to entering an airport's departure area; the availability of a sworn law enforcement officer within three to five minutes of the screening point; development by both scheduled airline carriers and airport managers of security programs for FAA approval; and development of an airport disaster plan.

The major security problems faced by mass transit systems are robberies and assaults of operators, passengers, and fare collectors; rapes and murders; and theft of vehicles or their contents at park-and-ride areas. Security measures include security guards; CCTV in waiting areas and on vehicles; telephones and other emergency communications devices for riders; unbreakable glass as see-through barriers; and high-intensity lighting.

## APPLICATION

**1)** Develop a security checklist for three of the types of facilities discussed in this chapter.
**2)** Evaluate the burglary prevention materials shown in Chapter 4, Figures 4−5 and 4−6 in relation to commercial establishments.

## DISCUSSION QUESTIONS

**1)** Why is a properly trained security staff an asset to the hotel/motel business?
**2)** What are some legal requirements that security managers should inform hotel or motel guests of?
**3)** What areas of security does the Bank Protection Act ignore?
**4)** Which of the types of security discussed in this chapter seems most important to you? Why?
**5)** What types of public gatherings might pose a security problem in your area?

## REFERENCES

ASIS Standing Committee on Banking & Finance 1984−85. Keeping the lid on the cookie jar. *Security management,* September 1985, pp. 57−61.

Bureau of Justice Statistics. Electronic fund transfer fraud. March 1985.

Green, Gion. *Introduction to security,* 4th ed. Revised by Robert J. Fischer. Stoneham, MA: Butterworth Publishers, 1987.

Ohlhausen, P. Racetrack security. *Security management,* October 1986, pp. 51−55.

*Private security.* Report of the Task Force on Private Security, National Advisory Committee on Criminal Justice Standards and Goals. Washington, DC: U.S. Government Printing Office, 1976.

Shearing, Clifford D. and Stenning, Philip C. Say 'CHEESE!': The Disney order that is not so Mickey Mouse. In *Private policing,* by Clifford D. Shearing and Philip C. Stenning, eds. Beverly Hills, CA: Sage Publications, 1987.

Shirley, Joe. Sporting event security in the year 2000. In *Security in the year 2000 and beyond,* by Louis A. Tyska and Lawrence J. Fennelly, eds. Palm Springs, CA: ETC Publications, 1987.

Thompson, Richard. False security. *Successful meetings.* February 1991, pp. 82−87.

## ☐ INTRODUCTION

Like most commercial establishments, many of the institutions discussed in this chapter are considered "open to the public." Each has its own unique security problems and challenges.

---

Institutions that may require special security include hospitals and other health care facilities, educational institutions, libraries, museums and art galleries, and even religious facilities.

---

**DO YOU KNOW**

➤ What institutions may require special security?

➤ What security problems exist at health care facilities?

➤ Educational facilities?

➤ Libraries?

➤ Museums and art galleries?

➤ Religious facilities?

➤ What security measures can be taken to avoid or reduce these problems?

## ☐ HOSPITALS AND OTHER HEALTH CARE FACILITIES*

The United States has well over thirty thousand health care facilities, including publicly and privately owned hospitals, clinics, nursing homes, outpatient centers, and physicians' office complexes. In fact, health care is the fifth largest industry in the country. Of the health care facilities, hospitals have the most serious security problems. They must maintain a safe environment for patients, visitors, and employees, as well as protect physical assets such as medical equipment, supplies, buildings, and personal property.

Hospitals are big businesses, facing all the problems of restaurants, hotel/motels, offices, and retail stores. They are often spread over large areas, causing even greater security problems. One industry source estimates that theft losses amount to $1,000 per hospital bed annually. In addition, providing protection from violent crime to hospital users and employees is a major security problem. Little wonder that hospital security is one of the fastest growing fields in the industry.

Nonetheless, many hospital administrators are unaware of their security risks, or, if they are aware of such risks, think that they are of low priority. The risks should be very obvious, however. Hospitals have a stressful atmosphere for most patients, many staff members, and most visitors, and they have a reputation as being a "magnet" for criminals, drug addicts, and employee thieves.

Security officers who work in hospitals and health care facilities must be able to interact with the medical staff—physicians, nurses, therapists—the clerical staff, the administration, as well as patients and visitors—frequently under emergency conditions. Public relations skills are vital in this position.

---

*Health Care Facilities—See *Private Security,* pp. 48–49.

**403**

Most hospitals are very open, have few locked doors, and cover large areas. They often include coffee shops, gift shops, flower shops, laundries, pharmacies, and doctors' offices. The openness of most health care institutions makes access control more difficult. Any access controls must fit the institution's medical care objectives and its public relations program. Security restrictions that impede the primary goal of life preservation are unacceptable to administrative and medical staffs. For example, rigid procedures for checking out surgical equipment or supplies may hinder prompt medical treatment.

Security problems of hospitals include the heavy daily flow of people, including patients, visitors, medical personnel, other employees, and vehicle traffic; a substantial number of female employees; a high percentage of professional staff who often ignore security procedures; and large quantities of consumable items such as drugs, linens, food, medical supplies, and equipment, making property inventory and accountability extremely difficult.

Hospital emergency rooms, especially in county hospitals, pose a serious problem for security. Patients admitted to the emergency room are frequently drunk, disorderly, and very combative. Some are victims of gunshot or knife wounds or of muggings. At times both the victim and the assailant are brought to the emergency room, posing a great threat to the security of other patients and hospital personnel. Most county hospitals have a security officer on duty around the clock in the emergency room.

---

The major security problems of health care facilities are emergency room security, visitor control, internal and external theft, and the potential for fire.

---

Visitor control is a formidable security problem. Yet most hospitals encourage visitors because the patients usually benefit from such visits. This policy can also create problems, however, as often visitors are emotionally upset, do not know their way around the hospital, smoke in no-smoking areas, or steal. Most hospitals establish visiting hours in an attempt to control access during the hours when the hospital is not fully staffed and the corridors are not as well lit as usual. Some hospitals issue color-coded visitor passes that indicate the ward the wearer is authorized to visit. However, this system can cause lineups at the beginning of visiting hours and annoy visitors. To have to wait in line to visit someone who may be gravely ill could understandably cause anger and hostility.

A second major problem is internal theft. The items most frequently stolen are, in order, linens, patients' cash and personal effects, office supplies and equipment, food, radios and television sets, and drugs. To reduce such losses, inventory controls must be established so that administration can identify problems and determine the significance of each. Many hospitals also use an employee identification badge system, color coded to indicate the person's position, for example, nurse, volunteer, secretary. Employees and staff may be restricted to certain exits,

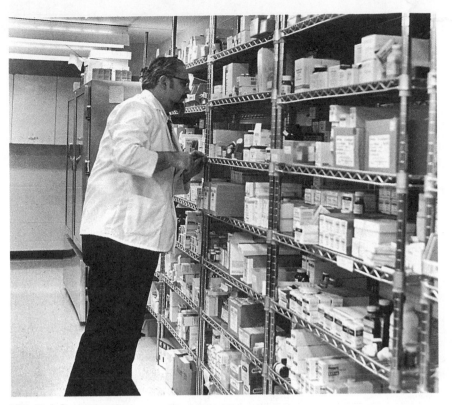

Hospital drug room.

and package inspections may be required. What can be locked should be
(see Figure 16–1).

Significant losses can result by not controlling services, cash, and
supplies. Services and supplies are especially difficult to monitor because
of the emergency nature of many situations. Medications and services
may be administered and never recorded or not charged to the appropriate patient. Not documenting medication given can also result in the loss
of accreditation by a hospital and endanger government funding as well
for failure to comply with regulations on certain listed drugs.

Theft from cars, especially physicians' cars, is another major problem.
Most hospitals encourage physicians to lock their medical bags in their
cars' trunks.

Crimes against persons, including simple assaults as well as violent
crimes such as rape and aggravated assaults on patients, nurses, and visitors, are also frequently committed in and around medical centers. Historically, hospitals have attracted peeping toms and sex criminals.
Therefore, many hospitals provide escort services for women.

An extremely important risk to guard against is the hazard of fire or
explosions. Hospitals have large quantities of flammable chemicals,
paper, and oxygen, making them fire-loaded. Patients, some under sedation, may smoke in bed or in chairs. In an actual fire, many patients
would not be ambulatory and would need to be evacuated on stretchers
or litters, and those patients who could walk might be under sedation.
Few patients or visitors know where the nearest stairs are because they

| Items with Locks | Number of Locks | Items with Locks | Number of Locks | Items with Locks | Number of Locks |
|---|---|---|---|---|---|
| Access Space | | Dispensers | | Mail Boxes | |
| Air Conditioning | | Sanitary Napkin | | Money Bags | |
| Alarms | | Soap | | | |
| Automotive | | Towel | | | |
| | | | | Penthouse | |
| | | Doors (Exterior) | | | |
| Book Cases | | Entrance | | | |
| Blood Bank | | Exit | | | |
| Bulletin Boards | | Doors (Interior) | | Refrigerators | |
| | | Closet | | | |
| | | Connecting | | | |
| | | Elevator | | Roof Vents | |
| Cabinets | | Entrance | | | |
| Electric | | Fire | | | |
| Filing | | Office | | Safe Compartments | |
| Instrument | | Storage Room | | Safe Deposit Boxes | |
| Key | | | | Screens | |
| Kitchen | | | | Slop Sink Closet | |
| Medicine | | | | Switch Key | |
| Narcotics | | | | | |
| Storage | | Drawers | | | |
| Supply | | Bench | | Tabernacle | |
| Suture | | Cash | | Tanks (Oil & Gas) | |
| Tool | | Lab. Table | | Thermostat | |
| Ward Room | | Safe | | Trap Doors | |
| | | Tool | | | |
| | | | | | |
| | | | | | |
| | | Gas Pump | | Valves | |
| Cash Boxes | | Gates | | Vaults | |
| Cash Register | | | | | |
| Chute Doors | | | | | |
| Clocks | | Lockers | | Watchman's Box | |
| | | Employee | | | |
| Dark Rooms | | Patients | | | |
| Desks | | Physicians | | X-Ray | |
| | | | | | |

**Figure 16–1 Key and lock survey for hospital administration.**
*Courtesy of TelKee Inc., Subsidiary of Sunroc Corp., Glen Riddle, PA 19037.*

customarily use the elevator. To lessen the risk of fire, smoking should be restricted to designated areas. All recommendations in Chapter 8 regarding preventing and extinguishing fires should be carefully adhered to. To avoid patient and visitor panic, a code word should be established to alert the staff to the existence of a fire if one occurs.

Hospital security problems can be reduced through recognition of the risks, careful inventory control, training in fire prevention and evacuation procedures, and surveillance.

Many hospitals have elaborate surveillance systems established to monitor patients from the nurses' stations. These same systems may also be used to increase security. In addition, security officers stationed in the main lobby area as well as security officers on patrol, equipped with radios, can do much to increase security.

Additional security problems are encountered when hospitals admit criminals or celebrities and must ensure their safety. For example, the security to protect the Shah of Iran when he was hospitalized in New York City Hospital was the maximum possible (Kmet, 1980, pp. 22–36). Security was made more difficult by the fact that New York City Hospital, the oldest in the city and one of the largest in the world, has 9,200 doors, 6 miles of corridors, and 20 miles of air ducts. It has 1,400 beds, 5,500 employees, and 80 clinics serving 10,000 patients a day, in addition to 2,500 employees at the adjoining Cornell Medical College and Hospital.

Security at the hospital is provided by a staff of one hundred security officers, with twenty-five to thirty officers on three shift patrols covering thirty different posts. Three of the officers are sergeant/investigators who have been granted special police powers and the power of arrest. This security team has at its disposal sophisticated security hardware, including thirty CCTV cameras which cover the main entrances, the cashiers' offices, and the tunnels. The CCTV also has videotape capability. The hospital requires all employees to be photographed and fingerprinted upon employment and to wear ID badges when working. It also requires passes for all packages that leave the building.

When the Shah was admitted, the security director chose to have his own security officers work overtime rather than hire outside officers. The one hundred officers of the hospital put in four thousand hours of overtime during the Shah's stay. All employees who had any contact with the Shah were cleared by the Secret Service. The security officers screened all mail, flowers, and gifts sent to the Shah. Although the Shah refused to allow CCTV in his room, the corridor was monitored. The officers who guarded the Shah's ward wore helmets, batons, and bulletproof vests. The most difficult aspect of security was providing protection when the Shah had to be moved for surgery and treatments. Routes were carefully secured prior to each move, were changed frequently, and were heavily guarded. A minimal number of people knew when or by what route the move would occur. The tight security provided the Shah ensured his safety while at the hospital.

## ☐ EDUCATIONAL INSTITUTIONS*

Educational institutions are responsible for providing a safe learning environment for staff and students, yet they are also subject to the same risks faced by business and industry. Employees and students from the elementary through the college level may be victims or perpetrators of crimes.

---

*Educational Institutions—See *Private Security,* pp. 44–46.

Security needs of schools vary tremendously, depending on the size of the school system and the location of the facilities. For example, the New York City Public School System has one thousand schools and four hundred auxiliary buildings which cover over one hundred million square feet. Problems faced by systems such as New York's will be more complex than those faced by small, rural schools. Nonetheless, crime in schools is not limited to the large school systems. It has increased substantially in both suburban and rural school systems. Some school administrators place the blame on the open school concept, which they contend encourages an influx of idlers and dropouts who disrupt academic functions.

Vandalism is a serious problem for the vast majority of schools, compounded by general public apathy. People who live close to a school may see vandalism occurring at night, on weekends, or during holidays, yet do nothing and notify no one. One solution to this problem has been to use the school for community functions after school hours. This not only decreases the opportunity for undetected vandalism, but also improves community interest in protecting its facilities.

Court-ordered desegregation of school systems has also created serious problems, including the constant threat of violence. Crimes of violence in general are a significant problem in schools.

Increased violence, along with increases in burglaries, arson, and vandalism coupled with the school's civil liability for its students' safety, has caused many school systems to develop a comprehensive security program, including intrusion-detection systems and nonbreakable windows. Some schools are even constructed without windows. The primary objectives of most school security programs are to protect staff and students and their personal property and to protect the school's facilities and equipment.

Two court cases of relevance to individuals involved with security in educational institutions are *In re T.L.O.* and *Kuehn v. Rento School District No. 403*. In *In re T.L.O. (1983)*, the Supreme Court of New Jersey held that school officials and teachers must have reasonable grounds before they can conduct a search. In *Kuehn v. Rento School District No. 403 (1985)*, the Supreme Court of Washington held that the search of a student's luggage by school officials *does* constitute a violation of the Fourth Amendment if school officials were acting under the authority or on the behalf of state authorities.

Access control, lighting, and security personnel are means to reduce risks at educational institutions.

School systems use varying combinations of contract and proprietary personnel to establish security programs. In some states county and local ordinances give police powers to school security personnel. Many of these personnel have primary jurisdiction over criminal incidents that

Tufts University Police takes information from a complainant.

occur in the schools. Alarm systems are commonly used. For example, 70 percent of New York's public schools have some sort of alarm system. Other schools require all students to carry ID cards so that if they are involved in an incident, they can be easily identified. Educational programs are a key component of most school security programs.

The security problems of colleges and universities are somewhat different from those of secondary school systems. A major difference is that some college and university facilities are used almost continuously (except at community colleges which typically close by midnight). The twenty-four-hour access to areas such as student unions that are heavily trafficked and usually have several entrances and exits is a major constraint in using electronic security. However, closed-circuit television and alarm systems are often installed in bursars' and cashiers' offices, and in the areas that serve as central collection points for all cash from campus facilities such as student unions and cafeterias.

The installation of electronic sensor detection devices in libraries has significantly reduced the number of stolen library books. Installation of photocopy equipment has likewise reduced the number of mutilated books and periodicals.

College campuses sustain significant losses from theft of college property. The items most frequently stolen are audiovisual and laboratory equipment, typewriters, calculators, computers, and educational materials such as books and art objects. Theft of examinations is also a major concern at colleges and universities, as is protecting the computer system, particularly against grade changing. Locks and effective key control can significantly reduce such losses. Figure 16–2 illustrates a checklist that could be used to enhance key and lock security.

The large numbers of residential housing units for students and staff create a densely populated community. Some campuses are larger than many towns. These campuses have the same problems as cities, particularly crime, including rapes, assaults, student robberies, muggings, and

| Items with Locks | Number of Locks | Items with Locks | Number of Locks | Items with Locks | Number of Locks |
|---|---|---|---|---|---|
| Access Space | | Dispensers | | Mail Boxes | |
| Air Conditioning | | Sanitary Napkin | | Money Bags | |
| Alarms | | Soap | | | |
| Athletic Supplies | | Towel | | | |
| Automotive | | | | Penthouse | |
| | | Doors (Exterior) | | Plan Case | |
| | | Entrance | | | |
| Book Cases | | Exit | | | |
| Bulletin Boards | | Doors (Interior) | | Refrigerators | |
| | | Cafeteria | | Rolling Grills | |
| | | Classroom | | Roof Vents | |
| Cabinets | | Closet | | | |
| Electric | | Connecting | | | |
| Filing | | Elevator | | Safe Compartments | |
| Instrument | | Fan Room | | Safe Deposit Boxes | |
| Key | | Fire | | Screens | |
| Medicine | | Garage | | Slop Sink Closet | |
| Storage | | Office | | Switch Key | |
| Supply | | | | | |
| Wardrobe | | | | | |
| | | Drawers | | Tabernacle | |
| | | Bench | | Tanks (Oil & Gas) | |
| | | Cash | | Thermostat | |
| | | Drafting Room | | Trailers | |
| | | Lab. Table | | Trap Doors | |
| Camera Cases | | Safe | | Trucks | |
| Cash Boxes | | Tool | | Trunks | |
| Cash Registers | | | | | |
| Chute Doors | | Gasoline Pump | | | |
| Clocks | | Gates | | Valves | |
| | | | | Vaults | |
| | | Lockers | | | |
| | | Gym | | | |
| Dark Rooms | | Paint | | Watchman's Box | |
| Desks | | Student | | | |
| Display Cases | | Teachers | | X-Ray | |
| | | | | | |

**Figure 16–2 Key and lock survey for education.**
*Courtesy of TelKee Inc., Subsidiary of Sunroc Corp., Glen Riddle, PA 19037.*

theft of college or university property, as well as the problem of nonpaying dormitory users.

Population density in high-rise dormitories makes it difficult to protect students and their personal property. The high concentration of students makes it impossible for them to know all the other residents of the dormitory; therefore, an intruder can easily pose as a student. Many colleges have installed extensive locking and access control systems to restrict access to student housing areas.

Besides dense population, the physical size of the campus may pose security problems. For example, the University of Houston campus covers 390 acres. Large campuses frequently provide motorcycle patrols and/or foot patrols equipped with portable radios and emergency call boxes along pedestrian walkways.

The need for organized, well-trained security personnel at colleges and universities was dramatically demonstrated in the late 1960s by campus demonstrations, student strikes, forceful occupation of school buildings by students, and violent riots. Local and/or state law enforcement agencies were frequently called in such situations, but their intervention was viewed negatively by many students, faculty members, and administrators. Increasingly, however, both students and staff are supporting comprehensive security programs.

A primary concern is safety of individuals. Armed robberies, assaults, muggings, and rapes at college campuses have increased dramatically throughout the country. On some campuses, students have organized rape-crisis centers to counsel and assist rape victims. On other campuses, male students have formed protective night escort services for female students.

Like secondary schools, higher education institutions use a combination of contractual and proprietary security personnel and security hardware to protect their campuses, students, and employees.

Green (1987, p. 29) suggests that: "Unlike many areas of modern security, campus security has generally been evolving from a low visibility operation in the direction of a highly visible, police-oriented image in response to rising crime problems of the 1980s."

As noted by Powell (1981, p. 3) a decade ago: "The growth and trend towards the professionalism of campus security has been the most rapid in the private security field in recent years." That trend has continued.

Powell traces the origins of campus security to Yale University and the late 1800s when a "Town-Gown ad hoc committee" was formed to address the problem of the bloody riots that often occurred between the townspeople and the students. Their solution was to assign two New Haven police officers to Yale University to "protect students, their property, and University property." In 1894 Yale hired the officers away from the city, establishing the Yale Campus Police. The campus police retained their full police authority, a situation that still exists today.

In 1958 the National Association of College and University Traffic and Security Directors was formed. This organization changed its name to the International Association of Campus Law Enforcement Administrators in 1967, during the period of student dissent which, according to Powell (p. 5) "provided campus security with its greatest impetus toward professionalism." Following this period (pp. 5–7):

Physical changes also took place. Campus security emerged from the basements and boiler houses where, for the most part, they had utilized office equipment and lockers discarded by other departments. They were relocated into attractive, well-equipped, businesslike office space with lockers and squad rooms for the officers. New, unmarked police vehicles were purchased for patrol purposes and equipped with two-way mobile radios. . . .

Truly professional departments emerged that could relate to all segments of the campus community. *Service* and *prevention* were the watchwords. . . .

The advent of the 1990s will present new challenges to campus security, such as escalating crime, threats to personal safety, and possible acts of terrorism. Campus administrators must more and more face up to the fact that a well-trained, professional campus security department is an absolute necessity in order to insure the safety and well-being of students, faculty, and staff.

The trend is to establish proprietary security forces and appoint directors of security for colleges and universities. Approximately forty states have legislation providing police authority for proprietary security personnel on campus. Most restrict such police powers to public institutions of higher education, but some states also make these powers available to private institutions.

At some larger institutions, security personnel are responsible for comprehensive law enforcement, traffic and fire safety, and loss prevention functions. For example, the University of Connecticut Public Safety Division not only serves a police function, but also maintains a fire department, a mounted patrol, locksmith and key controls, an ambulance service, and a campus transportation system.

Another trend in campus security is the active involvement of students in crime prevention. On some campuses, students informally assist in crowd control and traffic direction at large public events such as sporting events. Other campuses have a more formal organization of student patrol or student marshal programs. At Syracuse University, students equipped with two-way radios and identified by arm patches as "student security services" patrol parking areas and general residence halls. The University of Georgia campus security department consists entirely of students with undergraduate degrees who are taking graduate programs in police science or criminal justice. Other universities offer incentives such as free tuition or tuition assistance to campus security workers.

Among the crime prevention programs used in many colleges to reduce criminal activity are Operation Identification, Neighborhood Watch, security surveys, working with architects, rape awareness programs, office security, key control, escort services, and orientation programs. These programs and any other crime prevention strategies for college campuses should involve students, employees, and staff.

Improved lighting has also proved to be a sound security measure. Installing mercury vapor lamps, removing bushes and shrubs, and adding a number of direct-ring emergency phones along all major walkways provide "corridors of security." The improved lighting acts as a psychological deterrent, allows people to see farther and thus to avoid would-be attackers, allows campus police to see potential trouble, and, if a crime should occur, makes identification of the perpetrator easier. To meet energy conservation needs, after high-traffic periods are over, every other light is turned out for the remainder of the night.

## ☐ LIBRARIES*

The value of certain library holdings, such as special collections, rare books, and out-of-print or irreplaceable books, magazines, and manu-

---

*Libraries—See *Private Security,* p. 54.

scripts, cannot be estimated accurately. Usually valuable books and periodicals are kept in closed stacks, and their use is restricted and closely supervised. Libraries frequently use security personnel to deter disorderly behavior and vandalism during the hours they are open and to provide fire and security protection at night.

> ➤ The major losses in libraries result from theft of or damage to books.
> ➤ Library losses can be reduced by the electronic marking of books and by providing photocopy equipment.

Using electronic markings on books and detection sensors at main exits can significantly reduce book theft. Book mutilation can be minimized by providing photocopying machines so that material can be reproduced rather than torn from the books or periodicals. Some libraries have also instituted an annual or semiannual "amnesty" period during which time overdue books can be returned without a fine.

## ☐ MUSEUMS AND ART GALLERIES*

Criminal problems most frequently encountered by museums and art galleries are theft of collection pieces and the inadvertent purchase of works of art fraudulently presented as authentic or that have been stolen. Museums also experience order-maintenance and vandalism problems, but the trend toward charging admission fees has reduced these problems.

Major security problems of museums and art galleries include theft, fraud, vandalism, and arson.

Many objects in museums are priceless and irreplaceable. Most frequently stolen are small items that can be easily concealed and sold for cash. Such items are often stolen while the museum is open to the public, but more valuable items are generally stolen at night. Sometimes precious metals and gems are removed from artifacts, reset, and then sold. The primary areas of concern are vaults, reserve collections, study collections, and public exhibition sections.

Public exhibition sections are particularly vulnerable if a controversial exhibit is on display. For example, a Russian cultural or art exhibit on loan to U.S. museums or galleries could be threatened by activist groups.

The importance of protecting our country's museum treasures is apparent from the federal funds available for renovating, developing, and expanding protection programs. The following areas may qualify for federal support: organizing and using guard forces; physical security, including windows and doors, security hardware and locks, and storage facilities; fire safety plans; fire alarm systems; intrusion detection sys-

*Museums—See *Private Security,* pp. 53–54.

tems; surveillance, including lighting and CCTV; and communications. Loss prevention is vital because once an art treasure is stolen, chance of recovery is less than 5 percent.

---

# Museums and galleries can reduce losses by:

➤ Establishing a basic security system, including locks, alarms, and security officers at stations and on patrol.
➤ Maintaining detailed inventories.
➤ Having each object professionally appraised and authenticated.
➤ Positively identifying and registering each item.

---

Recall that alarm systems can provide three types of protection: (1) *perimetric,* to control access to the building, (2) *volumetric,* to detect motion and entry into a showcase or room, and (3) *fixed-point,* to protect individual pieces. Whether to use an alarm for an individual object depends on several factors, including its history of loss or damage, the alarm's compatibility with the overall system, exhibition procedures, and budget. Alarms on objects, however, are the last line of defense.

Several years ago the president of the International Association of Art Security, T. P. Kissane (1977), stressed the importance of identification: "Perhaps the most important defense against well-organized art theft is having a central recording location with a computerized record of the unique characteristics of all valuable works; and a reporting point of all art works stolen. . . . Lack of positive identification of most objects—documented visual evidence of the existence and condition of the work—is a critical factor in the soaring art theft statistics" (pp. 7−8).

Such a system, called ARTCENTRAL, has been developed in New York by the International Association of Art Security. This organization registers works of art using computer-oriented **photogrammetry,** a process comparable to fingerprinting. Photogrammetry provides a permanent, exact identification of works of art that is impossible to duplicate. It can identify two-dimensional works such as paintings, lithographs, wall hangings, and tapestries, as well as three-dimensional works such as artifacts, antiques, silverware, porcelains, and sculptures.

All identified works are visibly and invisibly labeled, indicating that they are on file with INTERPOL (International Criminal Police Organization). A central file is located in New York, another at INTERPOL, and a third at a secret, heavily guarded location. If a work registered with ARTCENTRAL is stolen, the theft is reported to INTERPOL, which in turn notifies state and local authorities as well as the FBI because it is assumed that interstate transportation of stolen goods will be involved.

This system is a deterrent to theft because the stolen objects are less marketable. It also greatly aids in recovery of stolen objects and their return to the rightful owner.

ARTCENTRAL is also available to individuals and to corporations. It is important for security directors of businesses and corporations to be aware of this, because many corporations are now acquiring art collections. Such security managers may need to become familiar with the procedures for safeguarding artwork, including access control, closed-circuit television, and security patrols.

## ☐ RELIGIOUS FACILITIES

Churches, synagogues, temples, and other places of worship are also in need of security. Fey (1986, p. 115) emphasizes this: "Both the news media and police officials report dramatic increases in crimes against religious property and personnel in recent years. . . . Burglary, robbery, assault, vandalism, and arson have shown the greatest increases in spite of the fact that, according to police, many of these crimes go unreported. The Metropolitan Police Department of Washington, DC, estimates only one-third of church, synagogue, and temple crime is reported."

Historically, the church was considered relatively immune from criminal actions because of its special status in the community. Such is no longer the case. To hard-core criminals and even to many juvenile delinquents, the church has no special status. In fact, as businesses and private homes tighten their security, churches are perceived as an easy mark.

In addition, according to Story (1987, p. 81): "Ritualistic crimes are occurring with greater frequency in America." Such crimes may involve religious articles stolen from churches. Further, hate groups such as the Skinheads may become involved in desecrating synagogues.

---

Security problems faced by religious institutions include the desire for easy accessibility at all times, their attractiveness to indigents and mental patients, and the individuals included in their social outreach programs.

---

Churches pride themselves on being there for people twenty-four hours a day, seven days a week, including all holidays. Many churches have valuable religious relics, statues, money boxes, and the like completely unprotected in their sanctuaries.

Fey points out a further complication (1986, pp. 115–20): "These institutions are opening their doors to a wider segment of the community than ever before. Even where the institutions themselves have not taken the initiative, many new clients in need have come calling. For example, one growing group seeking help from religious institutions is mental patients who are being discharged as soon as possible from institutions where the federal government is paying the bills. Homeless former patients come to houses of worship in search of shelter, food, and other help."

In addition to such individuals, numerous other individuals from the disadvantaged segments of society are attracted by the religious institutions' social outreach programs, for example, soup lines, shelters for the homeless, and food and clothing distribution outlets. Fey warns that "a small number of vocal and mentally unbalanced clients, some with violent tendencies, often appear for help. Over the long run one or more career criminals are likely to find their way into a program."

Another security problem presents itself when the religious institutions open their doors for use by outside groups, either free of charge or for a fee. A religious institution seldom has control over what these groups do within its facility.

Because religious institutions vary so greatly in size, basic philosophy regarding security measures, and actual vulnerability, no one security system is applicable to all. Nonetheless, most might benefit from certain commonsense procedures.

Security measures for religious institutions include perimeter protection, including lighting and fencing; safeguarding of valuables by such means as lighting, locks, and alarms; and contingency plans for handling disruptive individuals.

If cemeteries are being vandalized, security measures might include improved lighting and decorative fencing, particularly protecting any historically significant graves.

An additional area of concern is to take precautions when money is being collected at special events, concerts, fundraisers, and the like. Purse-snatchers and pickpockets may also be in attendance.

Fey also notes that "works of art and historically valuable objects in religious institutions require security techniques similar to those used by museums." Spot alarms might be used, such as a pressure-sensitive pad or a strip that is set under an object. If the object is lifted, an alarm sounds.

## SUMMARY

Institutions that may require special security include hospitals and other health care facilities, educational institutions, libraries, museums and art galleries, and even religious facilities.

The major security problems of health care facilities are emergency room security, visitor control, internal and external theft, and the potential for fire. These problems can be reduced through recognition of the risks, careful inventory control, training in fire prevention and evacuation procedures, and surveillance.

Major security problems of educational institutions are safety of students and staff, violence, vandalism, and theft, including burglary. Access control, lighting, and security personnel are means to reduce these risks.

The major losses in libraries result from theft of or damage to books. Such losses can be reduced by the electronic marking of books and by providing photocopy equipment.

The major security problems of museums and art galleries include theft, fraud, vandalism, and arson. These can be reduced by establishing a basic security system which includes locks, alarms, and security officers at stations and on patrol; maintaining detailed inventories; having each object professionally appraised and authenticated; and positively identifying and registering each item.

Security problems faced by religious institutions include the desire for easy accessibility at all times, their attractiveness to indigents and mental patients, and the individuals included in their social outreach programs. Security measures for religious institutions include perimeter protection, including lighting and fencing; safeguarding of valuables by such means as lighting, locks, and alarms; and contingency plans for handling disruptive individuals.

## APPLICATION

1) Develop a security checklist for three of the types of facilities discussed in this chapter.
2) Evaluate the burglary prevention materials in Figures 4–5 and 4–6 in relation to institutional security.

## DISCUSSION QUESTIONS

1) Which of the types of security discussed in this chapter seem most important to you? Why?
2) How can security directors enhance the public relations of a health care facility?
3) What kind of security is provided at your campus?
4) Do you have art galleries or museums in your community that might be at risk? If so, what kind of security do they have?
5) Have there been instances of crimes committed against any religious facilities in your community?

## REFERENCES

Fey, T. M. The holy war. *Security management,* October 1986, pp. 115–20.

Green, Gion. *Introduction to security.* 4th ed. Revised by Robert J. Fisher. Stoneham, MA: Butterworth Publishers, 1987.

Kissane, T. P. Protecting works of art from theft and fraud. *Security management,* May 1977, pp. 6–9.

Kmet, M. A. Handling a hot potato—the Shah in NYC. *Security management,* March 1980, pp. 22–36.

Powell, John W. *Campus security and law enforcement.* Woburn, MA: Butterworth Publishers, 1981.

*Private security.* Report of the Task Force on Private Security, National Advisory Committee on Criminal Justice Standards and Goals. Washington, DC: U.S. Government Printing Office, 1976.

Sabation, L. N. Security in the NYC public school system. *Security management,* March 1980, pp. 92–93.

Story, Donald W. Ritualistic crime: A new challenge to law enforcement. *Law and order,* September 1989, pp. 41–42.

# On Becoming a Security Professional

The future for private security professionals is bright, filled with opportunities for growth and advancement, along with increasing professional acceptance. However, Wainwright (1984, p. 295), cautions that this growth will involve many changes:

> The transition from smokestack industries to an information economy will require security practitioners to relate to a new kind of organization in the future. The information age, with its associated technologies, is causing the creation of more decentralized organizations with integrated networks. As a result, the security practitioner will need to understand the formal and informal movement of security programs through complex organizations. Training in intuitive management and a global view of the organization's environment will be necessary. Security practitioners will need to establish the link between the security function and various business and environmental issues that affect the organization. . . . The challenge is clear: we must measure the impact of technology and develop our own alternative security futures. Futuristics methodology is a good way to approach the complexity caused by technological and social change.

Knowledge and skills beyond those associated with the security field are clearly needed and involve communications, critical thinking and problem solving, and intuitive management. Security professionals who acquire such additional skills will find ample opportunities in this exciting field.

As noted by Green (1987, p. 24):

> Positive considerations for the future not only of jobs in security but also the potential for advancement or growth include the following:
>
> ➤ The increasing professionalism of security is reflected in higher standards of educational criteria and experience and correspondingly higher salaries, especially at the management level.
> ➤ The rapidity of the growth of the loss-preventive function has created a shortage of qualified personnel with management potential meaning less competition and greater opportunities for advancement for those who are qualified.
> ➤ The shift in emphasis to programs of prevention and service, rather than control or law enforcement, has broadened the security function within the typical organization.
> ➤ The acceleration of both two-year and four-year degree programs in criminal justice and/or security at the college level is creating at the corporate management level a new awareness of a rising generation of trained security personnel. Many companies, especially the larger corporations, are actively emphasizing the degree approach in hiring.

Appendix B contains a listing of college and university programs in security available in the United States.

According to Taitz (1990, p. 3), executive placement consultants say "the demand for security professionals is growing." To ensure upward mobility, Taitz suggests:

➤ Get a good criminal justice background—a baptism by fire—through working with an investigative agency, whether private or governmental.
➤ Educate yourself about as many aspects of the field as possible, and learn as much as you can about such subjects as access control, CCTV cameras, security surveys, and so on.
➤ Stay with your strengths. Skills may be transferable from one industry to another, but according to one management recruiter, corporations tend to prefer security executives who are knowledgeable and experienced in their particular industry.
➤ Be able to interface with all levels of management, including top management.
➤ Develop good rapport with the people who work in the field and those who would work for you.
➤ Strive to become the "ideal security management candidate," which another executive placement consultant defines as "a strong technical individual who, hopefully, has a college degree, has excellent communications skills, understands business principles, and is not rigid in approach."

The security field enters the 1990s as a challenging, high-tech profession aimed at preventing losses in every way possible.

## REFERENCES

Green, Gion. *Introduction to security,* 4th ed. Revised by Robert J. Fischer. Stoneham, MA: Butterworth Publishers, 1987.

Taitz, Sharyn, ed. *Getting a job, getting ahead, and staying ahead in security management.* Port Washington, NY: Rusting Publications, 1990.

Wainwright, O. O. Security management of the future. *Security management,* March 1984, pp. 47–51, 295.

# Appendixes

## Appendix A  State Statutes Regulating Security Guards*

| State | Statute | Registration | In-house Exclusion | Requirements | Liability Requirement | Remarks |
|---|---|---|---|---|---|---|
| Alabama | None | None | | | | Local licensing |
| Alaska | Article 4, AS 18.65.400 | Yes | | | Bond | $25.00 per guard |
| Arizona | ARS 32, Ch. 24 & 26 | Yes | | | $300,000.00 | Local licensing |
| Arkansas | ARK ST. 71-2122-71-2159 | Yes | Unarmed only | Exam | $100,000.00 | Exam administered by trainer. Exam & 2 yrs. experience required for trainer |
| California | PI/ADJ ACT Ch. 11 | Yes | Yes | Exam | Bond | Powers to arrest |
| Colorado | None | Yes | | | | Local licensing |
| Connecticut | Ch. 534 Sec. 29153–29161 | Yes | | | Bond | |
| Delaware | DEL. Code Title 24 Ch. 13 | Yes | | | $10,000 bond | |
| Florida | FLA. Statute Ch. 493 | Yes | | | $100,000 per person, $300,000 per occurrence | |
| Georgia | GA. Code Title 43 Ch. 38 | Yes | Pending | 8 hrs. classroom instruction | $25,000 bond | Can work 30 days before training |

*Compiled by Minot B. Dodson, CPP, Security Management, January 1984, pp. 45, 48.

**Appendix A** *(continued)*

| State | Statute | Registration | In-house Exclusion | Requirements | Liability Requirement | Remarks |
|---|---|---|---|---|---|---|
| Hawaii | Ha. Statute Ch. 463 | Yes | | | $5,000 bond | |
| Idaho | None | | | | | New reg. pending. House Bill 643 |
| Illinois | Ill. Statute Ch. 111–2601 thru 2639 | Yes | | | | |
| Indiana | IC25-30-1 | Yes | Yes | | | |
| Iowa | Ch. 80A–State Code | Yes | Yes | Local exam administered by law enforcement | $2,000 bond | |
| Kansas | None | | | | | Local requirements |
| Kentucky | None | None | | Local | None | House Bill 367—state requirements pending |
| Louisiana | None | | | Local | | |
| Maine | MRSA Title 32 Sec. 9412 | Company | | | Bond | |
| Maryland | MD Code Art. 56, Sec. 79–92 | State ID card | | | $5,000 bond | Company must be licensed as PI agency |
| Massachusetts | Gen. Law Ch. 147 Sec. 22–30 | | | | $5,000 bond | Company must maintain records subject to audit |

**Appendix A** (*continued*)

| State | Statute | Registration | In-house Exclusion | Requirements | Liability Requirement | Remarks |
|---|---|---|---|---|---|---|
| Michigan | MI Act 330 1968 | | | | $10,000 bond, L$25,000/ $100,000/ $20,000 | |
| Minnesota | Sec. 326.32–.339 | | Yes | | Bond | |
| Mississippi | | | | Local | | |
| Missouri | SEC. 84.340 Revised Statute of Missouri 1978 | Local | | Local 3 days training & exam | | |
| Montana | Mon. State Code Ch. 60 Title 37 | Yes | | | | New legislation pending |
| Nebraska | | Local | | | | |
| Nevada | Ch. 648.140 | Yes | | | $325,000L | |
| New Hampshire | Ch. 106F | Yes | Yes | | Bond | |
| New Jersey | N.J. Statute 4519–8 thru 27 | Yes | | | $5,000 bond | |
| New Mexico | Ch. 61–27(ff) | Yes | Yes | | Bond | |
| New York | Art. 7 Gen. Bus. Law Sec. 70–89a. | Company only | | | | |
| North Carolina | Ch. 74c, Private Protection Security Act | State ID Card | | $50,000/ $100,000/ $20,000 | | |

**Appendix A** (*continued*)

| State | Statute | Registration | In-house Exclusion | Requirements | Liability Requirement | Remarks |
|---|---|---|---|---|---|---|
| North Dakota | 43-30-01/16 | Yes | Yes | Training | Bond | New legislation took effect 1/1/84 |
| Ohio | Ch. 4749 | Yes | Yes | | $100/300,000 | |
| Oklahoma | | | | Local | | |
| Oregon | | | | Local | | |
| Pennsylvania | Private Detective Act 1953 | | | State police check | $10,000 bond | Company must be licensed as PI agency |
| Rhode Island | None | | | | | |
| South Carolina | Act 387 | Yes | | 4 hrs. training | $10,000 bond | |
| South Dakota | None | | | | | |
| Tennessee | | | | Local | | |
| Texas | Art. 4413 29(bb)VACS | Yes | Yes | | Bond | New legislation took effect 1/1/84 |
| Utah | Senate Bill #95, Security Licensing & Regulation Act, 1979 Gen. Section | Yes | | Training | $300,000L | Training administered by state qualified agent |
| Vermont | Title 26, Ch. 59 | Yes | | Exam | Bond | |
| Virginia | Code of VA. 54–729.27 | Yes | Yes | Training (12 hours) | $5M bond or L-100/300 M | 120 days to complete training |

**Appendix A** (*continued*)

| State | Statute | Registration | In-house Exclusion | Requirements | Liability Requirement | Remarks |
|---|---|---|---|---|---|---|
| Washington | | | | Local | | |
| West Virginia | Ch. 30–18 | Yes | Yes | Training | $2500 surety bond | Employer training requirements approved by state |
| Wisconsin | Sec. 440.6 | Yes | | | $10M-L | |
| Wyoming | | | | Local | | |

## Appendix B  Academic Programs in Security and Loss Prevention[1]

| State | Institution | City | Offerings |
|---|---|---|---|
| ALABAMA | Athens State College | Athens | Course(s) |
| | Auburn University | Auburn | BS/MS |
| | Chattahoochee Valley Community College | Phenix City | AAS |
| | Community College of the Air Force | Maxwell AFB, Montgomery | AA |
| | Jacksonville State University | Jacksonville | Course(s) |
| | Jefferson State Junior College | Birmingham | Course(s) |
| | Samford University | Birmingham | Course(s) |
| | Troy State University | Troy | Course(s) |
| | Troy State University—Dothan | Dothan | Course(s) |
| | University of Alabama | University | Course(s) |
| | University of Alabama at Birmingham | Birmingham | Course(s) |
| | University of Alabama in Huntsville | Huntsville | Course(s) |
| | University of Alabama | Mobile | Course(s) |
| | University of North Alabama | Florence | Course(s) |
| | University of South Alabama | Mobile | Course(s) |
| | Wallace State Community College | Hanceville | Course(s) |
| ALASKA | University of Alaska | Fairbanks | BS |
| ARIZONA | Cochise College | Douglas | Course(s) |
| | Maricopa Technical Community College | Phoenix | Course(s) |
| | Northern Arizona University | Flagstaff | BS/MS |
| | Phoenix College | Phoenix | Course(s) |
| | Scottsdale Community College | Scottsdale | Course(s) |
| ARKANSAS | Arkansas Technical University | Russellville | Course(s) |
| | University of Arkansas at Fayetteville | Fayetteville | Course(s) |
| | University of Arkansas at Pine Bluff | Pine Bluff | Course(s) |
| CALIFORNIA | Antelope Valley College | Lancaster | Course(s) |
| | Barstow College | Barstow | Cert. |
| | Cabrillo College | Aptos | Course(s) |
| | California State College | Bakersfield | Course(s) |
| | California State University, Fresno | Fresno | Course(s) |
| | California State University, Long Beach | Long Beach | BS/MS |
| | California State University, Los Angeles | Los Angeles | Course(s) |
| | California State University, Sacramento | Sacramento | Course(s) |
| | California State University, San Bernadino | San Bernadino | Course(s) |
| | Cerritos College | Norwalk | Cert./AA |
| | Chabot College | Hayward | Cert. |
| | Coleman College | La Mesa | Course(s) |
| | College of Marin | Kentfield | AS |
| | College of the Canyons | Valencia | Cert./AA |
| | College of the Sequoias | Visalia | Course(s) |
| | De Anza College | Cupertino | AA |

[1]This list of colleges and universities that offer academic programs undoubtedly contains errors and omissions. Please report any needed corrections to the authors. Those corrections will be incorporated into later editions of this text.
From Introduction to Private Security, by H. W. Timm and K. E. Christian. Copyright © 1991 by Wadsworth, Inc. Reprinted by permission of Brooks/Cole Publishing Company, Pacific Grove, CA 93950.

| State | Institution | City | Offerings |
|---|---|---|---|
| | East Los Angeles College | Monterey Park | Cert. |
| | El Camino College | Torrance | AA |
| | Fresno City College | Fresno | Course(s) |
| | Fullerton College | Fullerton | Course(s) |
| | Golden Gate University | San Francisco | BS |
| | Golden West College | Huntington Beach | Course(s) |
| | Grossmont College | El Cajon | Cert. |
| | Hartnell College | Salinas | AA |
| | Lake Tahoe Community College | South Lake Tahoe | Course(s) |
| | Lassen College | Susanville | Course(s) |
| | Long Beach City College | Long Beach | Course(s) |
| | Los Angeles Southwest College | Los Angeles | Course(s) |
| | Los Angeles Valley College | Van Nuys | Course(s) |
| | Merritt College | Oakland | Course(s) |
| | Monterey Peninsula College | Monterey | Cert./AA/AS |
| | Mount San Antonio College | Walnut | BS |
| | Napa Valley College | Napa | AA/AS |
| | Ohlone College | Freemont | Course(s) |
| | Palomar College | San Marcos | AA |
| | Rio Hondo College | Whittier | AA |
| | San Diego Miramar College | San Diego | AS |
| | San Joaquin Delta College | Stockton | Course(s) |
| | San Jose State University | San Jose | Course(s) |
| | Sierra College | Rocklin | Course(s) |
| | Sonoma State University | Rohnert Park | BS |
| | Ventura College | Ventura | AA/AS |
| COLORADO | Arapahoe Community College | Littleton | Cert. |
| | Colorado Mountain College | Breckenridge | Course(s) |
| | Community College of Denver | Denver | Course(s) |
| | Metropolitan State College | Denver | Course(s) |
| | Pikes Peak Community College | Colorado Springs | Cert./AS |
| | Red Community College | Golden | Cert. |
| | Trinidad State Junior College | Trinidad | Course(s) |
| CONNECTICUT | Eastern Connecticut State University | Willimantic | Course(s) |
| | Housatonic Regional Community College | Bridgeport | AA |
| | Mattatuck Community College | Waterbury | Course(s) |
| | Northwestern Connecticut Community College | Winsted | Course(s) |
| | Norwalk Community College | Norwalk | Course(s) |
| | Sacred Heart University | Bridgeport | BS |
| | Tunxis Community College | Farmington | Cert. |
| | University of New Haven | West Haven | BS/MS |
| | Western Connecticut State University | Danbury | Course(s) |
| DELAWARE | Delaware Technical and Community College | Newark | AS |
| DISTRICT OF COLUMBIA | George Washington University | Washington, DC | MA |
| | University of the District of Columbia | Washington, DC | Course(s) |

| State | Institution | City | Offerings |
|-------|-------------|------|-----------|
| FLORIDA | Broward Community College | Ft. Lauderdale | Course(s) |
| | Daytona Beach Community College | Daytona Beach | Course(s) |
| | Florida State University | Tallahassee | Course(s) |
| | Gulf Coast Community College | Panama City | Course(s) |
| | Lake–Sumter Community College | Leesburg | Course(s) |
| | Manatee Junior College | Bradenton | AS |
| | Miami–Dade Community College | Miami | AS |
| | Miami–Dade Community College—South | Miami | AA/AS |
| | Nova University | Ft. Lauderdale | MS |
| | St. Thomas University | Miami | Course(s) |
| | Tallahassee Community College | Tallahassee | Course(s) |
| | University of Central Florida | Orlando | Course(s) |
| | University of North Florida | Jacksonville | Course(s) |
| | University of South Florida—Bayboro | St. Petersburg | Course(s) |
| | University of South Florida—St. Petersburg | St. Petersburg | Course(s) |
| | Valencia Community College | Orlando | Cert./AA |
| GEORGIA | Albany State College | Albany | Course(s) |
| | Armstrong State College | Savannah | Course(s) |
| | Brenau Professional College | Gainesville | BA/BS |
| | Brunswick Junior College | Brunswick | Cert. |
| | Columbus College | Columbus | Course(s) |
| | Fort Valley State College | Fort Valley | Course(s) |
| | Georgia Southern College | Statesboro | Course(s) |
| | Valdosta State College | Valdosta | Course(s) |
| HAWAII | Hawaii Community College | Hilo | Course(s) |
| | Honolulu Community College | Honolulu | Course(s) |
| | Maui Community College | Kahului | Course(s) |
| IDAHO | Lewis–Clark State College | Lewiston | Course(s) |
| ILLINOIS | Belleville Area College | Belleville | Cert./AA |
| | Carl Sandburg College | Galesburg | Course(s) |
| | City Colleges of Chicago, Harry S Truman College | Chicago | Course(s) |
| | City Colleges of Chicago, Loop College | Chicago | Cert./AS |
| | College of DuPage | Glen Ellyn | Course(s) |
| | College of Lake County | Grayslake | Cert./AA |
| | Frontier Community College (EPE) | Fairfield | Course(s) |
| | Illinois Central College | East Peoria | AAS |
| | John A. Logan College | Carterville | Course(s) |
| | Joliet Junior College | Joliet | Cert./AS |
| | Kankakee Community College | Kankakee | Course(s) |
| | Lake Land College | Mattoon | Course(s) |
| | Lewis and Clark Community College | Godfrey | Cert./AAS |
| | Lincoln Land Community College | Springfield | Cert. |
| | McHenry County College | Crystal Lake | Course(s) |
| | McKendree College | Lebanon | Course(s) |
| | Moraine Valley Community College | Palos Hills | Cert./AAS |

| State | Institution | City | Offerings |
|---|---|---|---|
| | Oakton Community College | Des Plaines | Course(s) |
| | Parkland College | Champaign | Course(s) |
| | Rend Lake College | Ina | AAS |
| | Rock Valley College | Rockford | Cert./AA |
| | Saint Xavier College | Chicago | Course(s) |
| | Sangamon State University | Springfield | Course(s) |
| | Southeastern Illinois College | Harrisburg | Course(s) |
| | Southern Illinois University | Carbondale | BS/MS |
| | Spoon River College | Canton | Course(s) |
| | State Community College of East St. Louis | East St. Louis | AS |
| | Triton College | River Grove | Course(s) |
| | University of Illinois | Chicago | Course(s) |
| | Waubonsee Community College | Sugar Grove | Course(s) |
| | Western Illinois University | Macomb | BS |
| | William Rainey Harper College | Palatine | Cert. |
| INDIANA | Indiana Northern Graduate School of Professional Management | Marion | MPM |
| | Indiana State University | Terre Haute | BS/MS |
| | Indiana Vocational Technical College | Indianapolis | Cert./AS |
| | University of Evansville | Evansville | Course(s) |
| IOWA | Des Moines Area Community College | Ankeny | Course(s) |
| | Ellsworth Community College | Iowa Falls | AA |
| | Hawkeye Institute of Technology | Waterloo | AA |
| | Indian Hills Community College | Ottumwa | AAS |
| | Mount Mercy College | Cedar Rapids | Course(s) |
| | Saint Ambrose College | Davenport | BA |
| | Southeastern Community College | West Burlington | AA |
| | Wartburg College | Waverly | BA |
| KANSAS | Butler County Community College | El Dorado | Course(s) |
| | Garden City Community College | Garden City | AA/AA |
| | Johnson County Community College | Overland Park | Course(s) |
| | Washburn University | Topeka | Course(s) |
| | Wichita State University | Wichita | BS |
| KENTUCKY | Eastern Kentucky University | Richmond | AA/BS |
| | Franklin College | Paducah | Course(s) |
| | Kentucky State University | Frankfort | BS |
| | Murray State University | Murray | Course(s) |
| | Thomas More College | Crestview Hills | BA |
| | University of Louisville | Louisville | Course(s) |
| LOUISIANA | Grambling State University | Grambling | Course(s) |
| | Louisiana State University at Eunice | Eunice | AS |
| | Louisiana State University in Shreveport | Shreveport | Course(s) |
| | McNeese State University | Lake Charles | Course(s) |
| | Northeast Louisiana University | Monroe | Course(s) |

**430**

| State | Institution | City | Offerings |
|---|---|---|---|
| MAINE | Bangor Community College—Orono | Bangor | BA |
| | Southern Maine Vocational Technical Institute | South Portland | Course(s) |
| | University of Maine | Augusta | Course(s) |
| MARYLAND | Anne Arundel Community College | Arnold | Cert. |
| | Catonsville Community College | Catonsville | AA |
| | Chesapeake College | Wye Mills | Course(s) |
| | Community College of Baltimore— Harbor Campus | Baltimore | AA |
| | Coppin State College | Baltimore | BS |
| | Essex Community College | Baltimore | Cert. |
| | Hagerstown Junior College | Hagerstown | Course(s) |
| | Harford Community College | Bel Air | Course(s) |
| | Montgomery College | Rockville | AA |
| | Prince George's Community College | Largo | AA |
| | University of Maryland | College Park | BA |
| MASSACHUSETTS | American International College | Springfield | Course(s) |
| | Bristol Community College | Fall River | Cert. |
| | Bunker Hill Community College | Charlestown | Course(s) |
| | Cape Cod Community College | West Barnstable | Course(s) |
| | Dean Junior College | Franklin | Course(s) |
| | Greenfield Community College | Greenfield | Course(s) |
| | Holyoke Community College | Holyoke | Course(s) |
| | Middlesex Community College | Bedford | AA |
| | Mt. Wachusett Community College | Gardner | Course(s) |
| | Northeastern University | Boston | BS/MS |
| | Northern Essex Community College | Haverhill | Cert. |
| | Quinsigamond Community College | Worcester | Course(s) |
| | University of Lowell | Lowell | Course(s) |
| | Westfield State College | Westfield | Course(s) |
| MICHIGAN | Central Michigan University | Mount Pleasant | MS |
| | Delta College | University Center | AA |
| | Detroit College of Business Administration | Dearborn | Course(s) |
| | Ferris State College | Big Rapids | BS |
| | Grand Valley State University | Allendale | BS |
| | Henry Ford Community College | Dearborn | AA |
| | Jackson Community College | Jackson | Cert./AA |
| | Kalamazoo Valley Community College | Kalamazoo | AA |
| | Lake Superior State College | Sault Ste. Marie | BS |
| | Lansing Community College | Lansing | AA |
| | Macomb County Community College—Center Campus | Mt. Clemens | AA |
| | Madonna College | Livonia | AS/BS |
| | Mercy College of Detroit | Detroit | AA/BA |
| | Michigan State University | East Lansing | BS/MS |
| | Muskegon Community College | Muskegon | AA |

| State | Institution | City | Offerings |
|---|---|---|---|
| | Northern Michigan University | Marquette | BS |
| | Northwestern Michigan College | Traverse City | Course(s) |
| | Oakland Community College | Bloomfield Hills | Cert./AS |
| | Saginaw Valley State College | University Center | Course(s) |
| | St. Clair County Community College | Port Huron | Course(s) |
| | Schoolcraft College | Livonia | Cert./AS |
| | Suomi College | Hancock | Course(s) |
| | University of Detroit | Detroit | BS/MS |
| | Wayne State University | Detroit | Course(s) |
| MINNESOTA | Bemidji State University | Bemidji | Course(s) |
| | Inver Hills Community College | Inver Grove Heights | AA |
| | Metropolitan State University | St. Paul | Course(s) |
| | Normandale Community College | Bloomington | Cert. |
| | North Hennepin Community College | Minneapolis | Course(s) |
| | St. Cloud State University | St. Cloud | BA/MS |
| | University of Minnesota | Duluth | Course(s) |
| MISSISSIPPI | University of Southern Mississippi | Hattiesburg | Course(s) |
| MISSOURI | Central Missouri State University | Warrensburg | BS/MS |
| | Drury College | Springfield | AS |
| | Missouri Southern State College | Joplin | BS |
| | Penn Valley Community College | Kansas City | Course(s) |
| | St. Louis Community College at Florissant Valley | St. Louis | Course(s) |
| | St. Louis Community College at Forest Park | St. Louis | Course(s) |
| | St. Louis Community College at Meramec | St. Louis | Course(s) |
| | Tarkio College | Tarkio | BS |
| MONTANA | Dawson Community College | Glendive | Course(s) |
| NEBRASKA | Kearney State College | Kearney | BS |
| | Metropolitan Technical Community College | Omaha | AAS |
| | Northeast Technical Community College | Norfolk | AA |
| | Wayne State College | Wayne | BS |
| NEVADA | Clark County Community College | North Las Vegas | AAS |
| | Truckee Meadows Community College | Reno | AAS |
| | University of Nevada | Las Vegas | Course(s) |
| NEW HAMPSHIRE | Hesser College | Manchester | AA |
| | Keene State College (Safety Studies) | Keene | Course(s) |
| NEW JERSEY | Atlantic Community College | Mays Landing | Course(s) |
| | Bergen Community College | Paramus | Cert./AAS |
| | Brookdale Community College | Lincroft | Course(s) |
| | County College of Morris | Randolph | Course(s) |
| | Essex County College | Newark | AA |
| | Fairleigh Dickinson University | Rutherford | Course(s) |
| | Glassboro State College | Glassboro | Course(s) |
| | Gloucester County College | Sewell | Cert. |
| | Jersey City State College | Jersey City | BS/MS |

| State | Institution | City | Offerings |
|---|---|---|---|
| | Mercer County Community College | Trenton | Course(s) |
| | Monmouth College | West Long Branch | BS |
| | Passaic County Community College | Paterson | AA |
| | Rutgers University | Newark | Course(s) |
| | Rutgers University | New Brunswick | Course(s) |
| | Thomas A. Edison State College | Trenton | Course(s) |
| | Union College | Cranford | AA |
| | Upsala College—Wirths | Sussex | Course(s) |
| NEW MEXICO | Eastern New Mexico University | Clovis | Course(s) |
| | New Mexico State University | Las Cruces | BS |
| | Northern New Mexico Community College | Espanola | AAS |
| | Western New Mexico University | Silver City | Course(s) |
| NEW YORK | Adirondack Community College | Glens Falls | Course(s) |
| | Broome Community College | Binghamton | Course(s) |
| | Clinton Community College | Plattsburgh | Course(s) |
| | Columbia—Greene Community College | Hudson | Course(s) |
| | Erie Community College—City Campus | Buffalo | Course(s) |
| | Erie Community College | Williamsville | AA |
| | Erie Community College—North Campus | Amherst | Course(s) |
| | Herkimer County Community College | Herkimer | AA |
| | Hilbert College | Hamburg | AA |
| | Hudson Valley Community College | Troy | AA |
| | Iona College | New Rochelle | BS |
| | Jamestown Community College | Jamestown | Course(s) |
| | Jefferson Community College | Watertown | Course(s) |
| | John Jay College of Criminal Justice, CUNY | New York | AA/BS/MS |
| | Long Island University—Brooklyn | Brooklyn | BS/MS |
| | Long Island University—C. W. Post Center | Brookville | BS/MS |
| | Mercy College | Dobbs Ferry | AS/BS |
| | Monroe Community College | Rochester | AAS |
| | Nassau Community College | Garden City | AA |
| | New York Institute of Technology | Old Westbury | BS |
| | Niagara University | Niagara University | BS |
| | Onondaga Community College | Syracuse | Course(s) |
| | Orange County Community College | Middletown | Course(s) |
| | Rochester Institute of Technology | Rochester | BS |
| | Rockland Community College | Suffern | AAS |
| | Russell Sage College | Troy | Course(s) |
| | St. John's University, St. Vincent's College | Jamaica | BS |
| | St. John's University, St. Vincent's College | Staten Island | BS |
| | Schenectady County Community College | Schenectady | Course(s) |
| | State University of New York at Albany | Albany | Course(s) |
| | State University of New York College at Brockport | Brockport | BS |
| | SUNY | Farmingdale | Cert./AAS |
| | Westchester Community College | Valhalla | Course(s) |

**433**

| State | Institution | City | Offerings |
|---|---|---|---|
| NORTH CAROLINA | Alamance Community College | Haw River | AA |
| | Appalachian State University | Boone | Course(s) |
| | Bladen Technical College | Dublin | Course(s) |
| | Cape Fear Technical Institute | Wilmington | Course(s) |
| | Central Piedmont Community College | Charlotte | AAS |
| | Cleveland Technical College | Shelby | AAS |
| | East Carolina University | Greenville | Course(s) |
| | Edgecombe Technical College | Tarboro | AAS |
| | Fayetteville Technical Institute | Fayetteville | AA |
| | Gaston College | Dallas | Course(s) |
| | Haywood Technical College | Clyde | AA |
| | Martin Community College | Williamston | Course(s) |
| | Mayland Technical College | Spruce Pine | AAS |
| | Nash Technical Institute | Rocky Mount | AAS |
| | Pfeiffer College | Misenheimer | BA |
| | Piedmont Technical College | Roxboro | AAS |
| | Surry Community College | Dobson | AAS |
| | Western Carolina University | Cullowhee | Course(s) |
| | Western Piedmont Community College | Morganton | Course(s) |
| | Wilkes Community College | Wilkesboro | Course(s) |
| NORTH DAKOTA | Bismarck Junior College | Bismarck | AA |
| OHIO | Bowling Green State University | Bowling Green | BS |
| | Case Western Reserve University | Cleveland | Course(s) |
| | Cincinnati Technical College | Cincinnati | AA |
| | Columbus Technical Institute | Columbus | AAS |
| | Cuyahoga Community College | Cleveland | Course(s) |
| | Hocking Technical College | Nelsonville | Cert./AAS |
| | Jefferson Technical College | Steubenville | AAS |
| | Kent State University | Kent | Course(s) |
| | Kent State University | Tuscarawas | AA |
| | Lakeland Community College | Steubenville | AS |
| | Lorain County Community College | Elyria | AAS |
| | Michael J. Owens Technical College | Toledo | AAS |
| | North Central Technical College | Mansfield | Course(s) |
| | Ohio University | Chillicothe | AAS |
| | Sawyer College of Business | Cleveland | AA |
| | Sinclair Community College | Dayton | AAS |
| | University of Akron | Akron | Cert./AA |
| | University of Dayton | Dayton | Course(s) |
| | University of Toledo | Toledo | Course(s) |
| | Youngstown State University | Youngstown | BS/MS |
| OKLAHOMA | Cameron University | Lawton | Course(s) |
| | Connors State College | Warner | Course(s) |
| | Eastern Oklahoma State College | Wilburton | Course(s) |

**434**

| State | Institution | City | Offerings |
|---|---|---|---|
| | Oklahoma City Community College | Oklahoma City | AA |
| | Oklahoma City University | Oklahoma City | Course(s) |
| | Oklahoma State University | Stillwater | Course(s) |
| | South Oklahoma City Junior College | Oklahoma City | |
| OREGON | Lane Community College | Eugene | AS |
| | Portland Community College | Portland | Cert. |
| | Southern Oregon State College | Ashland | Course(s) |
| PENNSYLVANIA | Allentown College of St. Francis de Sales | Center Valley | Course(s) |
| | Alvernia | Reading | BA |
| | Bucks County Community College | Newton | Course(s) |
| | Community College of Allegheny County | Monroeville | AS |
| | East Stroudsburg University of Pennsylvania | East Stroudsburg | Course(s) |
| | Edinboro University of Pennsylvania | Edinboro | Course(s) |
| | Harrisburg Area Community College | Harrisburg | AA |
| | Indiana University of Pennsylvania | Indiana | Course(s) |
| | King's College | Wilkes-Barre | Course(s) |
| | Lehigh County Community College | Schnecksville | Cert./AA/AS |
| | Luzerne County Community College | Nanticoke | AAS |
| | Mansfield University of Pennsylvania | Mansfield | Course(s) |
| | Mercyhurst College | Erie | BS |
| | Mercyhurst College | Glenwood Hills | AS/BA |
| | Pennsylvania State University—Harrisburg Capital College | Middletown | Special BA |
| | Pennsylvania State University—University Park | University Park | Course(s) |
| | St. Joseph's University | Philadelphia | Course(s) |
| | Shippensburg University of Pennsylvania | Shippensburg | Course(s) |
| | Temple University | Philadelphia | Course(s) |
| | Triangle Tech | Pittsburgh | Cert. |
| | University of Pittsburgh | Pittsburgh | BA/MA |
| | Villanova University | Villanova | Special BA |
| | West Chester University | West Chester | Course(s) |
| | Westmoreland County Community College | Youngwood | Course(s) |
| | York College of Pennsylvania | York | Course(s) |
| RHODE ISLAND | Salve Regina—The Newport College | Newport | Course(s) |
| SOUTH CAROLINA | Beaufort Technical College | Beaufort | Course(s) |
| | Denmark Technical College | Denmark | Course(s) |
| | Florence—Darlington Technical College | Florence | Course(s) |
| | Horry—Georgetown Technical College | Conway | Cert. |
| | Midlands Technical College | Columbia | Course(s) |
| | Orangeburg—Calhoun Technical College | Orangeburg | Cert. |
| | Sumter Area Technical College | Sumter | Course(s) |
| | Tri-County Technical College | Pendleton | Course(s) |
| | University of South Carolina | Columbia | Course(s) |
| TENNESSEE | Aquinas Junior College | Nashville | Course(s) |
| | Cleveland State Community College | Cleveland | AS |

| State | Institution | City | Offerings |
|-------|-------------|------|-----------|
| | Dyersburg State Community College | Dyersburg | Course(s) |
| | East Tennessee State University | Johnson City | Course(s) |
| | Memphis State University | Memphis | Course(s) |
| | Middle Tennessee State University | Murfreesboro | BS |
| | Shelby State Community College | Memphis | Cert. |
| | University of Tennessee at Chattanooga | Chattanooga | Course(s) |
| | University of Tennessee at Martin | Martin | Course(s) |
| | Walters State Community College | Morristown | AS |
| TEXAS | American Technological University | Killeen | Course(s) |
| | College of the Mainland | Texas City | Cert. |
| | Dallas Baptist College | Dallas | Course(s) |
| | Houston Community College System | Houston | AA/AS |
| | Lee College | Baytown | AA |
| | McLennan Community College | Waco | AA |
| | Odessa College | Odessa | Cert. |
| | Pan American University | Edinburg | Course(s) |
| | Sam Houston State University | Huntsville | Course(s) |
| | San Jacinto College | Pasadena | AA/AS |
| | Southwest Texas State University | San Marcos | Course(s) |
| | Stephen F. Austin State University | Nacogdoches | BA |
| | Texarkana Community College | Texarkana | Course(s) |
| | University of Houston—Downtown | Houston | BS |
| | University of Texas at Arlington | Arlington | Course(s) |
| | University of Texas at San Antonio | San Antonio | BA |
| | Victoria College | Victoria | Course(s) |
| UTAH | Southern Utah State College | Cedar City | AAS |
| | Weber State College | Ogden | AA |
| VERMONT | Castleton State College | Castleton | Course(s) |
| | Southern Vermont College | Bennington | Course(s) |
| VIRGINIA | Blue Ridge Community College | Weyers Cave | Course(s) |
| | Central Virginia Community College | Lynchburg | AA |
| | Germanna Community College | Locust Grove | Course(s) |
| | J. Sargeant Reynolds Community College | Richmond | AA |
| | Liberty University | Lynchburg | Course(s) |
| | Northern Virginia Community College | Annandale | AA |
| | Northern Virginia Community College— Alexandria | Alexandria | AAS |
| | Northern Virginia Community College— Manassas | Manassas | AAS |
| | Northern Virginia Community College— Woodbridge | Woodbridge | AA |
| | Old Dominion University | Norfolk | Course(s) |
| | Paul D. Camp Community College | Franklin | Course(s) |
| | Piedmont Virginia Community College | Charlottesville | Course(s) |
| | Radford University | Radford | Course(s) |
| | Virginia Commonwealth University | Richmond | BS |
| | Virginia Western Community College | Roanoke | Course(s) |

| State | Institution | City | Offerings |
|-------|-------------|------|-----------|
| WASHINGTON | Clark College | Vancouver | Course(s) |
| | Eastern Washington University | Cheney | BS |
| | Everett Community College | Everett | AA/AS |
| | Fort Steilacoom Community College | Tacoma | Cert. |
| | Olympic College | Bremerton | Course(s) |
| | Shoreline Community College | Seattle | AA |
| WEST VIRGINIA | Fairmont State College | Fairmont | BS |
| | Marshall University | Huntington | Course(s) |
| | Parkersburg Community College | Parkersburg | Course(s) |
| | Salem College | Salem | BA |
| | West Virginia Northern Community College | Wheeling | AS |
| | West Virginia State College | Institute | Course(s) |
| WISCONSIN | District One Technical Institute | Eau Claire | Course(s) |
| | Fox Valley Technical Institute | Appleton | AA |
| | Gateway Technical Institute | Kenosha | Course(s) |
| | Milwaukee Area Technical College | Milwaukee | Course(s) |
| | Northeast Wisconsin Technical Institute | Green Bay | Course(s) |
| | University of Wisconsin—Platteville | Platteville | AA/BS |
| | University of Wisconsin—Whitewater (Safety Studies) | Whitewater | Course(s) |
| | Waukesha County Technical Institute | Pewaukee | Course(s) |
| WYOMING | Casper College | Casper | Course(s) |
| | Sheridan College | Sheridan | Course(s) |
| CANADA | Algonquin College | Ottawa, Ontario | BS |
| | College of Trades & Technology | St. Johns, Newfoundland | Cert. |
| | Concordia University | Montreal, Quebec | Cert. |
| | Fanshawe College | London, Ontario | Course(s) |
| | Humber College | Toronto, Ontario | AA |
| | Lethbridge Community College | Lethbridge, Alberta | Cert. |
| | Mohawk College | Hamilton, Ontario | Cert. |
| | Mount Royal College | Calgary, Alberta | AA |
| | Sheridan College | Brampton, Ontario | LSA |
| | Sir Stanford Fleming College | Petersborough, Ontario | Dip. |
| | University of Alberta | Calgary, Alberta | Cert. |
| ENGLAND | College of Technology | Letchworth, Herts | Course(s) |
| | Twickenham College of Technology | Middlesex | Course(s) |

| | |
|---|---|
| AD | Alzheimer's disease |
| ADT | American District Telegraph |
| AMC | American Motor Corporation |
| ASIS | American Society for Industrial Security |
| ATM | automatic teller machine |
| CAD | computer-assisted design |
| CAE | computer-aided engineering |
| CAM | computer-assisted manufacturing |
| CCTV | closed circuit television |
| CEO | chief executive officer |
| CIA | Central Intelligence Agency |
| CIM | computer-integrated manufacturing |
| CPP | certified protection professional |
| CPR | cardio-pulmonary resuscitation |
| CPTED | crime prevention through environmental design |
| CSR | community service representative |
| DOD | Department of Defense |
| DPMA | Data Processing Management Association |
| DTI | Drug-Testing Initiative |
| EDP | electronic data processing |
| EPPA | Employee Polygraph Protection Act |
| FAA | Federal Aviation Authority |
| FBI | Federal Bureau of Investigation |
| H/M | hazardous materials |
| IACP | International Association of Chiefs of Police |
| ICSC | International Council of Shopping Centers |
| LEIU | law enforcement intelligence unit |
| NBFAA | National Burglar and Fire Alarm Association |
| NCCCD | National Center for Computer Crime Data |
| NCPI | National Crime Prevention Institute |
| NIAA | National Institute of Alcohol Abuse and Alcoholism |
| NIDA | National Institute on Drug Abuse |
| NSA | no such account |
| NSF | Nonsufficient funds |
| OSHA | Occupational Safety and Health Administration |
| PA | public address |
| PC | personal computer |
| PI | private investigator |
| PIN | personal identification number |
| PSE | psychological stress evaluation |
| UAW | United Auto Workers |
| UCR | Uniform Crime Reports |
| UL | Underwriters Laboratory |
| VTR | videotape recording |

# Glossary†

**ADMINISTRATIVE REPORTS**
Reports that deal with the routine functioning of the business or agency.

**AFFIRMATIVE ACTION** Actions to eliminate current effects of past discrimination.

**AGENDA** Items to be accomplished, usually during a meeting.

**\*ALARM RESPONDENT** Person employed by an organization to answer an alarm condition at a client's protected site, to inspect the protected site to determine the nature of the alarm, to protect or secure the client's facility until alarm system integrity can be restored, and to assist law enforcement according to local arrangement. The alarm respondent may be armed and also may be a servicer.

**\*ALARM SYSTEMS** Devices that, on detection of an intrusion, transmit and articulate messages for help. An alarm system is composed of three fundamental parts: (1) *sensor*—detects or senses a condition that exists or changes, be it authorized or unauthorized; related directly to the senses of touch, hearing, sight, smell, and taste; (2) *control*—provides power, receives information from the sensors, evaluates the information, and transmits the required information to the annunciation function; (3) *annunciation*—alerts a human to initiate a response that will result in investigating the sensor environment. Could be a bell, buzzer, light flashing, etc.

---

†Items preceded by \* are adapted from the glossary of *Private Security,* Report of the Task Force on Private Security, National Advisory Committee on Criminal Justice Standards and Goals. Washington, DC: U.S. Government Printing Office, 1976.

**ALZHEIMER'S DISEASE** A condition affecting the elderly and causing such symptoms as gradual memory loss, impairment of judgment, disorientation, personality change, decline in ability to perform routine tasks, behavior change, difficulty in learning, loss of language skills, and a decline in intellectual function. Individuals with Alzheimer's disease may appear to be intoxicated.

**AREA ALARMS** Alarms that protect a portion of or the total interior of a room or building. Also called *space alarms*.

**\*ARMED COURIER SERVICES**
Companies that provide armed protection and transportation, from one place to another, of money, currency, coins, bullion, securities, bonds, jewelry, or other articles of value; transportation is provided by means other than specially constructed, bullet-resistant armored vehicles.

**\*ARMED PERSONNEL** Persons, uniformed or nonuniformed, who carry or use at any time any form of firearm.

**\*ARMORED CAR SERVICES**
Companies that provide protection, safekeeping, and secured transportation of money, currency, coins, bullion, securities, bonds, jewelry, or other items of value by means of

specially constructed, bullet-resistant armored vehicles and vaults under armed guard.

**ARREST**  Taking into custody, in a manner authorized by law, a person to be taken before a magistrate.

**ARSON**  The willful, malicious burning of a building or property.

**ARTCENTRAL**  An organization in New York that registers works of art using computer-oriented photogrammetry, comparable to fingerprinting.

**ASSAULT**  An attack on a person.

**ASSIZE OF ARMS**  A provision of the Statute of Westminster requiring every male between ages fifteen and sixty to keep a weapon in his home as a "harness to keep the peace."

**AUTHORITARIAN**  Manager who uses strong control over personnel. Also called *autocratic*.

**AUTHORITY**  Right to give orders.

**BACKSTRETCH AREA**  The area of a racetrack where the horses, drivers, and grooms are quartered.

**BAIT MONEY**  Money in a bank, placed in such a way that when it is picked up an alarm sounds.

**BATTERY**  The unconsented, offensive touching of another person, either directly or indirectly.

**BIOMETRIC SECURITY SYSTEM**  System which uses physical traits such as fingerprints, voices, and even eyeballs to identify individuals.

**BLIND RECEIVING**  Going by the packing slip rather than actually counting a received shipment.

**BOOSTER BOX**  A box whose top, bottom, or end is hinged so that articles can be placed inside without actually opening the box. Apparatus of a shoplifter.

**BOW STREET RUNNERS**  The first detective unit; established in London by Henry Fielding in 1750.

**BUREAUCRATIC**  Reliance on rules and regulations.

**BURGLARY**  Entering a structure (1) without the owner's consent (2) with the intent to commit a crime.

**\*CENTRAL STATION**  A control center to which alarm systems in subscribers' premises are connected, where circuits are supervised, and personnel are maintained continuously to record and investigate alarm or trouble signals. Facilities are provided for reporting alarms to police and fire departments or to other outside agencies.

**CENTRAL STATION ALARM**  A system in which the secured area is directly connected to an alarm panel in a centrally located alarm receiving station via a pair of leased telephone wires.

**CERTIFIED PROTECTION PROFESSIONAL (CPP)**  Program of the American Society of Industrial Security that provides certification for individuals who meet specific experience and educational requirements and pass a common knowledge examination as well as an examination in four speciality subjects.

**CHANGE KEY**  A key that opens only one specific door.

**CIVIL OFFENSES**  Actions prohibited by law, but not classified as crimes.

**COCAINE**  A white crystalline powder extracted from the South American coca plant; a narcotic.

**CODE OF ETHICS**  Self-enforcing moral and professional guidelines for behavior in a given field.

**COMMUNICATIONS PROCESS**
Involves a sender, a message, a channel, and a receiver. It may also include feedback.

**COMPUTER CRIME** Accessing a computer's database without authorization or exceeding authorization, for the purpose of sabotage or fraud. It includes theft or destruction of software and hardware as well.

**COMPUTER VIRUS** An unwanted software program that can cause serious memory problems, destroying files or even entire programs. It can spread undetected from one computer to another, thwarting the computer's normal functions and often garbling data.

**CONCERTINA** Rolls of barbed wire 50 feet long and 3 feet in diameter.

**CONTRACT SERVICES** Outside firms or individuals who provide security services for a fee.

**CORE CONCEPT** A style of building design in which all elevators, rest rooms, lobbies, and service facilities are located at the building's center, allowing more effective control of public areas while also permitting more flexible use of office space.

**\*COURIERS** Armed persons assisting in the secured transportation and protection of items of value.

**CRACK** Freebase cocaine processed to remove the hydrochloride. Like freebase, it is smoked in a pipe. Because it can be obtained for from five to ten dollars, it is often called "poor man's coke."

**CRASH BAR** An emergency exit locking device. The door can be opened only from the inside, and if it is, an alarm sounds. Also called a *panic bar.*

**CRIME** An action that is harmful to another person and/or to society and that is punishable by law.

**CRITICALITY** Level of importance or seriousness of consequences.

**CYLINDRICAL LOCK** A lock that uses disk tumblers or pin tumblers.

**DEAD BOLT** A non-spring-loaded metal bar manually inserted into or withdrawn from a strike.

**DEFAMATION** Injuring a person's reputation, such as by falsely inferring, by either words or conduct, in front of a third disinterested party, that a person committed a crime.

**\*DEFENSIBLE SPACE** The name of a hypothesis developed by Oscar Newman holding that building designs that hinder crime give occupants a sense of security, thus encouraging them to guard themselves and their property.

**DELEGATION** Assigning tasks to others.

**DEMOCRATIC** Manager who involves personnel in decision making.

**DICTATORIAL** Manager who is closed-minded and uses threats with personnel.

**DISCIPLINE** Actions taken to get personnel to follow rules and regulations.

**DYNAMIC RISK** Risk with the potential for both benefits and losses, e.g., extending credit or accepting checks.

**ECONOMIC CRIME** Crimes such as shoplifting, employee theft, pilferage, credit card fraud, and check fraud.

**EMBEZZLEMENT** Fraudulent appropriation of property by a person to whom it has been entrusted.

**\*EMPLOYMENT RECORD** Normal business information, including employment application, health records, job performance records, and other records maintained on an employee.

**ENCRYPTION**   The coding of a message. Used to thwart computer crime.

**ENVELOPE**   A building's exterior; the first line of defense.

**EPILEPSY**   A disorder of the central nervous system in which a person tends to have recurrent seizures. These seizures may look like street drugs or alcohol at work.

**EQUAL EMPLOYMENT OPPORTUNITY COMMISSION (EEOC)**   Commission set up to enforce laws against discrimination in the workplace.   -

**ESPIONAGE, INDUSTRIAL**   Theft of trade secrets or confidential information.

***FACSIMILE**   An exact copy or reproduction.

**FACT**   A statement that can be proven.

**FALSE IMPRISONMENT**   Unreasonably restraining another person using physical or psychological means to deny that person freedom of movement.

**FELONY**   A serious crime such as murder, robbery, or burglary that is punishable by death or by imprisonment in a state prison or penitentiary.

**FEUDALISM**   A form of government whereby peasants (serfs) labored for a nobleman who answered to the king.

***FIREARM**   A pistol, revolver, other handgun, rifle, shotgun, or other such weapon capable of firing a missile.

**FIRE-LOADING**   The amount of flammable materials within an area.

**FIRE TRIANGLE**   The three elements necessary for burning: heat, fuel, and oxygen.

**FLOOR RELEASE LIMIT**   A value limit that cannot be exceeded with a check or credit card unless the clerk clears it with the central office.

**FLOORWALKER**   An employee who poses as a customer and seeks to remain unnoticed so as to catch shoplifters "in the act."

**FOUR-SYSTEM APPROACH TO MANAGEMENT**   Likert's management theory going from System One which is a traditional, authoritarian style to System Four which is a participative management style.

**FRANKPLEDGE SYSTEM**   The Normans' modification of the Tithing system: the king demanded that all free Englishmen swear to maintain the peace.

**FRAUD**   Intentional deception to cause a person to give up property or some lawful right.

**FREEBASE**   A form of cocaine made by chemically converting the street drug into a basic form that can be smoked.

**GOAL**   End result desired.

**GRAND LARCENY**   Larceny that is classified as a felony, based on the value of the property stolen.

**GRAND MASTER KEY**   A key that opens all locks in two or more buildings.

**GRIEVANCE**   A complaint, usually written, made to one's supervisor.

***GUARD**   A person paid a fee, wage, or salary to perform one or more of the following functions: (a) prevent or detect intrusion, unauthorized entry or activity, vandalism, or trespass on private property; (b) prevent or detect theft, loss, embezzlement, misappropriation, or concealment of merchandise, money, bonds, stocks, notes, or other valuable documents or papers; (c) control, regulate, or direct the flow or movements of the public, whether by vehicle or otherwise, to ensure the protection of property; (d) protect individuals from bodily harm; and (e) enforce rules, regulations, and policies related to crime reduction.

**HACKER**   A computer enthusiast who engages in electronic snooping, software piracy, and other types of high-tech illegal activities.

**HEADER**   A barrier made of strands of barbed wire extending outward from the top of the fence at a 45-degree angle; also called a *top guard*.

**HIERARCHY**   Levels. Management hierarchy goes from on-line personnel (lowest level), to supervisors, to managers, to the chief executive officer (highest level).

**HIERARCHY OF NEEDS**   Human needs identified by psychologists, placed in order from lower level (food, shelter, etc.) to higher level (self-actualization); most well-known psychologist using this theory is Maslow.

**HONESTY SHOPPING**   A procedure in which an individual, often security personnel, is hired to shop in such a way that will test the honesty of sales personnel who handle cash. Also called a *shopping service*.

**HUE AND CRY**   The Anglo-Saxon practice whereby if anyone resisted the watchman's arrest, the watchman cried out and all citizens chased the fugitive and assisted in capturing him.

**IGNITER**   A device to start a fire; includes matches, candles, cigarettes, explosives, and the like.

**IGNITION TEMPERATURE**   The specific temperature at which a sub-

stance will ignite and burn as long as oxygen is present.

**INDUSTRIAL ESPIONAGE**   See *espionage*.

**INFERENCE**   A statement about the unknown based on the known; a deduction, using logic. Sometimes referred to as a *judgment*.

**INFRARED DETECTOR**   A fire detector that responds to flame.

**INTEGRITY INTERVIEW**   A face-to-face, nonaccusatory interview consisting of a series of questions addressing issues such as significant thefts from prior employers, use of illegal drugs during work hours, participation in criminal activities, falsification of the application form, and similar job-related concerns.

**INTENTIONAL INFLICTION OF EMOTIONAL DISTRESS**   Outrageous or grossly reckless conduct intended to and highly likely to cause a severe emotional reaction.

**INTERPOL**   International Criminal Police Organization.

**INTERROGATION**   A controlled conversation with persons suspected of direct or indirect involvement in a crime.

**INTERVIEW**   A controlled conversation with witnesses to or victims of a crime.

**IONIZATION DETECTOR**   A fire detector that responds to invisible particles of combustion.

**INVASION OF PRIVACY**   Unreasonable, unconsented intrusion into the personal affairs or property of a person.

**JOB DESCRIPTION**   Statement of duties and responsibilities for a specific position.

**KEYWAY** A passage containing obstacles through which a key must pass to unlock a lock.

**KLEPTOMANIAC** A compulsive thief.

**LARCENY/THEFT** The (1) unlawful taking (2) of the personal goods or property of another (3) valued above [grand larceny] or below [petty larceny] a specified amount, (4) with the intent to permanently deprive the owner of the property or goods.

**\*LICENSING** Permission from a competent authority to carry on the business of providing security services on a contractual basis.

**LOCAL ALARMS** Alarms that sound on the premises and require that someone hears them and calls the police.

**MAGNA CHARTA** A decisive document in the development of constitutional government in England that checked royal power (King John) and placed the king under the law. Similar to our Bill of Rights, it gave Englishmen "due process" of law (1215). Also known as *Magna Carta*.

**MANAGEMENT** The "bosses" in an organization.

**MANAGEMENT BY OBJECTIVES (M.B.O.)** Management and staff set goals and timelines within which to accomplish the goals.

**MANAGER** One who accomplishes things through others.

**MANAGERIAL GRID** Blake/Mouton's management theory that maps management styles based on their emphasis on people and production. The "ideal" management style has a balance between the two, emphasizing an energetic team approach.

**MARIJUANA** The most socially acceptable of the illegal drugs, made from the cannabis plant and usually smoked.

**MASTER KEY** A key that opens the locks in an entire building.

**MATURE EMPLOYEE THEORY** Argyris' management theory in which employees and their organization are seen as interdependent.

**MENTOR** Teacher, role model.

**MISDEMEANOR** A minor crime punishable by a fine and/or a relatively short jail sentence.

**MORALE** How a person feels; the general mood of an organization or company, e.g., morale is high/low.

**MOTIVATE** Encourage, inspire.

**NEGLIGENCE** Occurs when a person has a duty to act reasonably but fails to do so and, as a result, someone is injured.

**NEUTER HEAD BLANK** A key blank that has an unusual shape and contains no embossed stock numbers or coining marks, so that it cannot be identified using a catalog.

**NONDELEGABALE DUTY** One for which authority can be given to another person, but responsibility for it cannot. Civil liability remains with the person who has the legal duty to act.

**NONVERBAL COMMUNICATION** Includes the eyes, facial expressions, posture, gestures, clothing, tone of voice, proximity, and touch. In writing, it includes neatness, paper quality, copy quality, binding, and the like.

**OBJECTIVE** Neutral, unbiased, impartial.

**OCCUPATIONAL SAFETY AND HEALTH ACT OF 1970 (OSHA)** Makes employers responsible for providing a safe workplace.

**ON-LINE PERSONNEL** Those who do the work, e.g., security guards and patrols.

**OPERATIONAL REPORTS** Reports that deal with the activities taken by private security officers.

**OPINION** A statement of personal belief, e.g., chocolate is better than strawberry.

**OSHA** The Occupational Safety and Health Administration.

**PANIC BAR** An emergency exit locking device that can be opened only from the inside; if it is opened, an alarm sounds. Also called a *crash bar*.

**PARISH** A geographical area defined by the congregation of a particular church; the local unit of government in rural areas of England.

**PERFORMANCE APPRAISAL** Evaluation of an employee's work.

**PERIMETER ALARMS** Alarms that protect fences and gates, exterior doors, windows, and other openings.

**PERIMETER BARRIERS** Any obstacle defining the physical limits of a controlled area and impeding or restricting entry into that area.

**PERMISSIVE** Manager who has or exercises little control over personnel.

**PERPETUAL INVENTORY** A policy of keeping track of supplies/merchandise on hand almost daily; this is in contrast to an annual inventory, i.e., taking stock only once a year.

**PETTY (PETIT) LARCENY** Theft classified as a misdemeanor, based on the value of the property stolen.

**PHOTOELECTRIC DETECTOR** A fire detector that responds to smoke.

**PHOTOGRAMMETRY** A process comparable to fingerprinting; provides a permanent, exact identification of works of art which is impossible to duplicate.

**PILFERAGE** Internal theft, an important concern of private security.

**POINT ALARM** An alarm that protects specific items such as safes, cabinets, valuable articles, and small areas. Also called a *spot alarm*.

**POLICE CONNECTION SYSTEM** An electronic system that directs an alarm via telephone wires to the nearest police department.

**POLYGRAPH** A lie detector; scientifically measures respiration and depth of breathing, changes in the skin's electrical resistance, and blood pressure and pulse.

**PRIMA FACIE EVIDENCE** Evidence that establishes a fact if not contested, e.g., the specific blood alcohol level for intoxication is stated in state laws.

**PRIVATE SECURITY** A profit-oriented industry that provides personnel, equipment, and/or procedures to *prevent* losses caused by human error, emergencies, disasters, or criminal actions.

**PROBABILITY** The likelihood of something occurring.

**PROBABLE CAUSE** The situation in which individuals have facts and circumstances within their knowledge and of which they have reasonable trustworthy information that are sufficient in themselves to warrant a person of reasonable caution in the belief that the suspect has committed a crime (*Carroll v. United States*).

**PROGRESSIVE DISCIPLINE** Goes from the least severe reprimand, a warning, to the most severe, termination.

**PROPRIETARY ALARM** An alarm that uses a constantly monitored alarm panel that may receive visible and/or audible signals to indicate exactly where a security break has occurred.

**PROPRIETARY SERVICES** In-house security services, directly hired and controlled by the company or organization, usually for a salary rather than a fee.

**PUBLIC RELATIONS** A planned program of policies and conduct designed to build confidence in and increase the understanding of a business or organization; includes all activities undertaken to bolster image and create good will.

**PURE RISK** Risk with the potential for injury, damage, or loss with no possible benefits, e.g., crimes and natural disasters.

**PYROMANIAC** A pathological firesetter.

**RAZOR RIBBON** Barbed tape.

**\*REGISTRATION** Permission from a state authority before being employed as an investigator or detective, guard, courier, alarm system installer or repairer, or alarm respondent.

**REINFORCEMENT THEORY** Skinner's management theory suggesting that positive reinforcement increases a given behavior and that negative reinforcement decreases a given behavior.

**REPORT** A permanent written record that communicates important facts to be used in the future.

**RISK** A known threat that has effects that are not predictable in either their timing or their extent.

**RISK ACCEPTANCE** The recognition that some losses are likely to occur and that 100 percent security is virtually impossible.

**RISK ELIMINATION** Adopting a practice that does away with a risk, e.g., not accepting checks.

**RISK MANAGEMENT** Anticipating, recognizing, and appraising a risk and initiating some action to remove the risk or reduce the potential loss from it to an acceptable level (NCPI).

**RISK REDUCTION** Taking steps to minimize a risk, e.g., installing alarms.

**RISK SPREADING** Ensuring that potential loss in any single incident is minimized, e.g., placing expensive jewelry in separate display cases; closely related to *risk reduction.*

**RISK TRANSFER** Putting the risk elsewhere, e.g., taking out insurance or raising prices to cover losses.

**ROBBERY** (1) The unlawful taking of personal property (2) from a person or in the person's presence, (3) against the person's will by force or threat of force.

**SABOTAGE** The intentional destruction of machinery or goods, or the intentional obstruction of production.

**SAFE** A semiportable strongbox with combination lock.

**\*SECURITY SERVICES** Those means, including guards, detectives or investigators, couriers, and alarm system installers, repairers, or respondents, that are provided on a contractual basis to deter, detect, and prevent criminal activities.

**SECURITY SURVEY** An objective, critical, on-site examination and analysis of a business, industrial plant, public or private institution, or dwelling to determine its existing security, to identify deficiencies, to determine the protection needed, and to recommend improvements to enhance overall security.

**SHOPLIFTING** The theft of retail merchandise while lawfully on the premises. Concealment of merchandise is prima facie evidence of intent to shoplift. In many states, price changing is also considered shoplifting.

**SHOPPING SERVICE** See *honesty shopping*.

**SHRINKAGE** Loss of assets.

**SKIPS** Nonpaying hotel or motel guests.

**SLIDING** The practice in which a clerk sells articles to friends or relatives at lower cost.

**SLIPPING A LOCK** The insertion of a plastic credit card or thin screwdriver above the bolt of a lock, thereby forcing it downward and releasing the spring.

**SMART OBJECTIVES** Objectives that are *s*pecific, *m*easurable, *a*ttainable, *r*elevant, and *t*rackable.

**SPACE ALARM** An alarm that protects a portion of the total interior of a room or building. Also called an *area alarm*.

**SPAN OF MANAGEMENT** Number of people a manager is responsible for.

**SPOT ALARM** An alarm that protects specific items such as safes, cabinets, valuable articles, and small areas. Also called a *point alarm*.

**SPRING-LOADED BOLT** A bolt that automatically enters the strike when the door is closed. Also called a *latch*.

**STATUTE OF WESTMINSTER** A law issued by King Edward I that formalized England's system of criminal justice and apprehension. Established the *watch and ward, hue and cry,* and *assize of arms* (1285).

**STRIKE** The part of a locking system into which the bolt is extended.

**SUB-MASTER KEY** A key that opens all locks in a specific area.

**SUPERVISOR** Directly oversees the work of on-line personnel. Usually reports to a manager.

**TELEPHONE DIALER** An alarm system that automatically sends a recorded message or signal to a central station, the establishment's owner or manager, or the police station.

**THEFT** See *larceny/theft*.

**THEORY X/THEORY Y** McGregor's management theory in which Theory X sees employees as basically lazy and not liking to work. They need close supervision and should not participate in decisions. Theory Y sees employees as willing workers, motivated by growth and development opportunities. They should share in decisions.

**THERMAL DETECTOR** A fire detector that responds to heat, usually temperatures in excess of 135 degrees Fahrenheit.

**TITHING SYSTEM** In Anglo-Saxon England, a unit of civil administration consisting of ten families; established the principle of collective responsibility for maintaining law and order.

**TOP GUARD** A barrier made of strands of barbed wire extending outward from the top of a fence at a 45-degree angle; also called a *header*.

**TORT** A civil wrong for which the court seeks a remedy in the form of damages to be paid.

**TRAILER**   A path of paper or accelerant that spreads fire from one location to another.

**TRESPASSING**   The unlawful presence of a person on a property or inside the premises of someone else.

**TWENTY-FOUR HOUR CLOCK**
Begins at midnight and does *not* start over in numbering at noon; it adds 12 to each hour in the afternoon, for example, 1 pm is 1300 hours. Also called *military time*.

**TWO-FACTOR HYGIENE/MOTI-VATION THEORY**   Herzberg's management theory in which hygiene factors are tangible rewards that cause dissatisfaction if lacking. Motivation factors are intangible rewards that cause satisfaction. Hygiene factors must be provided; motivation factors are where managers should concentrate.

**UNIFORM CRIME REPORTS**   Statistics on crime, compiled annually by the FBI.

**UNITY OF COMMAND**   People have only one supervisor.

**UNLAWFUL TAKING**   A category of crime that includes *larceny/theft, burglary,* and *robbery.*

**VANDALISM**   The malicious or intentional damaging and/or destroying of public or private property. Also called *criminal damage to property* or *malicious destruction of property.*

**VAULT**   A completely fire-resistive enclosure used exclusively for storage.

**VIRUS**   See *computer virus.*

**VULNERABILITY**   An organization's susceptibility to risks.

**WARDED LOCKS**   Locks that have an open keyway; commonly used up to the 1940s.

**WATCH AND WARD**   A custom that provided town watchmen to patrol the city during the night and the ward to patrol the city during the day. (In Middle English, *Wardien* meant to keep watch.)

**WATCH CLOCK**   A seven-day timepiece. Keys are located at various stations in a facility; the security officer simply inserts the key into the watch clock at each station, and a record is automatically made of the time the location has been checked.

**WHITE-COLLAR CRIME**
Business-related crime, such as embezzlement, bribery, and receiving kickbacks.

# Index